Becoming Taiwanese

HARVARD EAST ASIAN MONOGRAPHS 420

Becoming Taiwanese

Ethnogenesis in a Colonial City, 1880s to 1950s

Evan N. Dawley

Published by the Harvard University Asia Center
Distributed by Harvard University Press
Cambridge (Massachusetts) and London 2019

Printed in the United States of America

The Harvard University Asia Center publishes a monograph series and, in coordination with the Fairbank Center for Chinese Studies, the Korea Institute, the Reischauer Institute of Japanese Studies, and other faculties and institutes, administers research projects designed to further scholarly understanding of China, Japan, Vietnam, Korea, and other Asian countries. The Center also sponsors projects addressing multidisciplinary and regional issues in Asia.

The Harvard University Asia Center gratefully acknowledges a generous grant in support of the publication of this work from the Chiang Ching-kuo Foundation for International Scholarly Exchange.

Library of Congress Cataloging-in-Publication Data

Names: Dawley, Evan N., author.
Title: Becoming Taiwanese : ethnogenesis in a colonial city, 1880s–1950s / Evan N. Dawley.
Other titles: Harvard East Asian monographs ; 420.
Description: Cambridge, Massachusetts : Published by the Harvard University Asia Center, 2019. | Series: Harvard East Asian monographs ; 420 |
Includes bibliographical references and index.
Identifiers: LCCN 2018034040 | ISBN 9780674237209 (hardcover : alk. paper)
Subjects: LCSH: Ethnicity—Taiwan—Keelung City—History—19th century. | Ethnicity—Taiwan—Keelung City—History—20th century. | Nationalism—Taiwan—History. | Keelung City (Taiwan)—Social conditions—19th century. | Keelung City (Taiwan)—Social conditions—20th century. | Japan—Colonies—Asia.
Classification: LCC DS799.9.K44 D39 2019 | DDC 951.249—dc23
LC record available at https://lccn.loc.gov/2018034040

Copy-editing by Julie Hagen
Index by Mary Mortensen
Printed on acid-free paper
Last figure below indicates year of this printing
26 25 24 23 22 21 20 19

For Alan, who did not get to see this,
and for Katy, who did

Contents

Figures, Tables, Maps

Figures

Tables

Maps

Acknowledgments

This book has been a very long time in the making. The first inklings came to me when I heard elderly locals on the streets of Taipei speaking Japanese, years before I even knew I would undertake studies to earn a PhD, and wondered why a formerly colonized populace would choose to speak the language of their colonizers. As a student at what was then the Inter-University Program (IUP) at National Taiwan University, I clearly had a lot to learn about Taiwan and its identities. I began to treat the project as a viable topic during my graduate studies at Harvard University, and it evolved during my sojourn at the U.S. Department of State's Office of the Historian, and my career in academia, as a professor at Goucher College and Reed College, with stints at George Washington University and Georgetown University. I conducted the vast majority of research for this book while affiliated with the Institute of Taiwan History at Academia Sinica on many different occasions. I gladly and deeply thank all of those institutions and their staffs for their support and assistance. In particular, my gratitude goes to the colleagues and students I interacted with, and the many friends I made at each place, for their intellectual and moral contributions to this project and to my survival over many years.

Turning from institutions to individuals, I want to begin by thanking William Kirby, under whose guidance I started this project. Without his insights, training, and inexhaustible willingness to provide advice and support, I would never have finished the dissertation, let alone the book. The other members of my dissertation committee, Akira Iriye and Andrew Gordon, made similar contributions along the way, for which I am grateful. From my time at Harvard, I also wish to acknowledge, first and foremost, the late Philip Kuhn, and to thank Hue-tam Ho Tai, Peter Bol, Henrietta Harrison, Michael Szonyi, Dani

Botsman, and Iain Johnston. For their earlier influence at Oberlin College, I thank Heather Hogan, David Kelley, Michael Fisher, and especially the late Ron DiCenzo.

In Taiwan, for their assistance with my research and their intellectual engagement, I extend my gratitude especially to Chang Lung-chih and Lin Man-houng, who supported this project every step of the way, and also to Lin Yu-ju, Shi-chi Mike Lan, Wu Rwei-ren, Wu Huey-fang, Chung Shu-ming, Michael Shi-yung Liu, the late Wang Shih-ch'ing, Tang Yu, Paul Katz, Wang Jianchuan, Chen Tsu-yu, Hsu Yu-liang, Chen Kai-wen, and Tzeng Shih-jung. In Japan, for similar reasons I thank Toshihiro Minohara, Masato Kimura, Torsten Weber, Christian Hess, Kawashima Shin, Shinohara Hatsue, and Yanai Shinichi. I would also like to thank a few residents of Jilong, past and present, who shared their memories and materials with me in the early stages of my research: Ts'ai Eing-ch'ing, Chen Ch'ing-song, Wang Jinyi, Hiroshige Kiyohiko, and Itō Keisuke. Since no work of this sort could have been even contemplated without extensive language training, I express my deepest appreciation for their expertise and patience to all of my Chinese and Japanese teachers at Oberlin, Beloit, IUP, Harvard, and the Hokkaido International Foundation.

I have amassed a great number of additional debts over the years owed to a long list of individuals. For their substantial input into the project in its many iterations, my thanks to: Micah Muscolino, Joe Wicentowski, Tom Gold, Miriam Kingsberg, Tobie Meyer-Fong, Ed McCord, Charlie Musgrove, Carol Benedict, Nianshen Song, Douglas Fix, Paul Barclay, Daniel Buck, Inhye Han, Megan Greene, Emma Teng, Steven Phillips, Meredith Oyen, William Rowe, James Lin, Erika Evasdottir, Georgia Mickey, Fann Meeiyuan, Jina Kim, Marjan Boogert, Sei Jeong Chin, Rustin Gates, Hoi-Eun Kim, Jungwon Kim, Yoichi Nakano, Jun Uchida, Emer O'Dwyer, Matthew Mosca, Loretta Kim, Lawrence Zhang, Pär Cassel, Rob Cliver, James Dator, Chelsea Schields, Matthew Hale, Julie Jeffrey, John Corcoran, Tina Sheller, and Robert Beachy. Three anonymous readers also provided extremely detailed and helpful feedback on drafts of the manuscript. At the Harvard Asia Center, my gratitude goes to Kristen Wanner and Bob Graham for leading me through this process so skillfully and patiently. All of these people are in some measure responsible for the good aspects of this book; none bears any blame for its flaws. I also owe my cohorts of Fulbright Fellows and Taiwan Fellows and the members of Taipei Disc a special debt for dragging me away from research throughout my time in Taiwan.

The staffs of the following institutions gave tremendous assistance in obtaining materials essential to this project. In Taiwan, I wish to thank the Taiwan Branch of the National Central Library (now the National Taiwan Library), the National Central Library, the National Taiwan University Library, Academia Historica, Taiwan Historica, the Guomindang Party Archives, the many libraries of Academia Sinica, and the Jilong Cultural Center. In Japan, I want to thank the Japanese National Archives; the Foreign Ministry Archives; the National Diet Library; the Taiwan Association; and the libraries at Tokyo, Kyoto, Waseda, Hitotsubashi, and Kobe Universities. In the United States, I am grateful to the Library of Congress, especially the Asian Studies and the Prints and Photographs Reading Rooms; the National Archives; the Hoover Institution; and the libraries of Harvard, Johns Hopkins, Goucher College, and George Washington University.

Financial support for this project has come from a variety of sources. I completed the final stages of research and writing in Taiwan, with the generous support of a Taiwan Fellowship from the Ministry of Foreign Affairs of the ROC. I was able to take advantage of that opportunity thanks to a timely and deeply appreciated pre-tenure leave from Goucher College. Prior work was done with funding from a Fulbright Program–Institute of International Education Multi-Country Dissertation Research Grant; the Edwin O. Reischauer Institute of Japanese Studies; the Harvard Graduate School of Arts and Sciences; the Fairbank Center for East Asian Research; the Harvard Graduate Student Council; the Chun and Jane Chiu Family Foundation's Scholarly Exchange Program; the AAS/China–Inner Asia Council; and Goucher College. I cannot overstate my gratitude for all of the support that I have been privileged to receive.

To return to the personal, my only real regret over the amount of time it took me to finish this project is that too many people did not live to see its completion: in particular, my grandparents, Bea and Lew Wechsler, and my father, Alan Dawley, who also happened to be the first great historian I ever met. Writing this book without him has not been easy, and he never got to see that I am a much slower writer than he was. Fortunately my mother, Katy Dawley, never stopped reviewing drafts when asked, and more important, never stopped prodding me to keep working on it. She made sure it would see the light of day. Finally, since I have been sustained—and often happily diverted—on this long journey by legions of family members and friends around the globe, I give to them my deepest thanks. You are all in here somewhere.

END
Baltimore, MD

Abbreviations

Archives

GSG   Guoshiguan (Academia Historica)

GSG-SD   Guoshiguan shuwei dang'an (Digitized archives of Academia Historica)

JACAR   Kokuritsu kōbun shokan Ajia rekishi shiryō sentā (Japan Center for Asian Historical Records, National Archives of Japan)

NKKS   Nihon kokuritsu kōbun shokan (National Archives of Japan)

TSS   Zhongyang yanjiuyuan Taishisuo dang'anguan (Archives of the Institute of Taiwan History, Academia Sinica)

TSTF   Taiwan sōtokufu kōbun ruisan (Documentary Records of the Taiwan Government-General)

TWG   Guoshiguan Taiwan wenxianguan (Taiwan Historica)

XZZG   Taiwan sheng xingzheng zhangguan gongshu dang'an (Documentary Archives of the Taiwan Province Civil Administration)

Newspapers and Journals

AS   *Asahi shimbun* 朝日新聞 (*Asahi News*), Osaka

DMB   *Damingbao* 大明報 (*Daming News*), Quzhou

GSB   *Guoshengbao* 國聲報 (*Nation's Voice News*), Gaoxiong

LHB   *Lianhebao* 聯合報 (*United Daily News*), Taipei

MB   *Minbao* 民報 (*The People's Press*), Taipei

NS	*Niitaka shinpō* 新高新報 (*Niitaka News*), Jilong
SJT	*Shakai jigyō no tomo* 社會事業の友 (*The Social Work Companion*), Taipei
TKKH	*Taiwan kyōkai kaihō* 台灣協會會報 (*Taiwan Association Journal*), Tokyo
TMB	*Taiwan minbao* 台灣民報 (*Taiwan People's News*), Tokyo, Taipei
TNS	*Taiwan nichinichi shinpō* 台灣日日新報 (*Taiwan Daily News*), Taipei
ZRB	*Zhongyang ribao* 中央日報 (*Central Daily News*), Taipei

Organizations and Institutions

CAA	Jilong Customs Assimilation Association (Jilong tongfenghui)
CICU	Jilong Commercial and Industrial Credit Union (Jilong shanggong xinyong zuhe)
CZB	Ministry of Finance (Caizhengbu)
JCU	Jilong Credit Union (Kiirun shinyō kumiai)
JFA	Jilong Fraternity Association (Jilong haku'aikai)
JFG	Jilong Fraternity Group (Jilong bo'aituan)
JJB	Ministry of Economic Affairs (Jingjibu)
JTB	Ministry of Transportation (Jiaotongbu)
NRC	National Resources Commission (Guojia ziyuan weiyuanhui)
NZB	Ministry of the Interior (Neizhengbu)
PCU	Jilong People's Credit Union (Kiirun shomin shinyō kumiai)
PWS	Jilong Public Welfare Society (Kiirun kōekisha)
SCU	Jilong Social Civilization Union (Kiirun shakai kyōka rengōkai)

SWA	Social Work Association (Shakai jigyō kyōkai)
SWC	Social Work Conference (Shakai jigyō taikai)
TCA	Taiwan Cultural Association (Jp., Taiwan bunka kyōkai; Ch., Taiwan wenhua xiehui)
TPP	Taiwan People's Party (Jp., Taiwan minshūtō; Ch., Taiwan minzhongdang)
XZY	Executive Yuan (Xingzhengyuan)

Note to the Reader

A note on Romanization is necessary, as multiple systems have been used—and are in use—in Taiwan, and I transliterate both Chinese and Japanese. For Chinese, for the sake of simplicity I mostly use Hanyu pinyin, which has long been the standard Romanization of Mandarin names and terms, except in a few cases where an alternate is so well known as to cause confusion among nonspecialists (for example: Taipei, Sun Yat-sen, Chiang Kai-shek, Manchuria), and for the names of authors and artists who have published in English. For Japanese, I also use the standard system, known as modified Hepburn.

I applied the following guidelines in determining when to use Chinese or Japanese pronunciations of the same characters: proper names are always transliterated according to their native written system; city names follow the same rules, except when quoting directly from a source or in publication titles, in which case the language of the source prevails; areas within cities, as well as other terms, are primarily transliterated according to the language of the ruling state at a given moment in time, and therefore Chinese pronunciations are followed up to 1895 and after 1945, and Japanese in between. Some terms are common in both Chinese and Japanese sources; therefore at times I include both pronunciations, separated by a slash. In chapters 1–5 the Japanese comes first, while in chapters 6 and 7 Chinese comes first, to reflect the prevailing language in the sources of the time.

In creating abbreviations, I have followed different patterns in the text and in the notes. For names of organizations and institutions referred to in the text, I use acronyms based on their English names in most cases, since I use the translations throughout the book; for names of publications (newspapers and journals) and archives cited in the notes, I use acronyms based on the original language, as these are necessary for referencing sources.

I use characters, with a few essential exceptions, only in the abbreviations list, footnotes, glossary, bibliography, and index.

Introduction

The Chinese town of Kelung is without a doubt the filthiest
abode of human beings in the whole island.
   —John Dodd, British merchant, *Journal of a Blockaded
      Resident*, 1888

The people of Taiwan, with Jilong as its entryway, can go
out to the Pacific, north to the home islands of Japan,
south to the islands of the southern seas, east to the Amer-
icas, and west to China and Europe. Like nearby Xiamen
and Hong Kong, it is truly an important harbor on world
shipping routes, and a marketplace of commerce.
   —Jian Wanhuo, Taiwanese journalist, *Jilong Gazetteer*,
      1931

The light of hope shines brightly on Asahigaoka, and the
light of our hopes shines on. We have harmony on our
shoulders. If we each strive daily in our work, here will be
the foundation of our self-governance, and it will prosper
forever, our Kiirun City.
   —Katō Haruki, Japanese settler, Jilong's city song, 1933

Jilong is Taiwan's most important port.
   —Taiwan Province News Bureau, *Taiwan Guidebook*,
      1948

"We poor Taiwanese. Once we were under the Japanese, now we are
under the Chinese." Thus laments a main character in Hou Hsiao-
hsien's cinematic masterpiece, *A City of Sadness* (*Beiqing chengshi*). This
film's release in 1989 marked a watershed moment in the reexamination

of Taiwan's past and the public expression of a Taiwanese national identity. Most scholars agree that Taiwanese consciousness underwent a dramatic transformation during the end of martial law and the political liberalization of the 1980s and 1990s. For some, the period's volatility enhanced, or even produced, a Taiwanese nationalism that opposed the hegemony of Chinese nationalism and advanced Taiwan's drive to be an independent nation-state.[1] For others, Taiwanese national identity represented the long-delayed inclusion of Taiwan's indigenous peoples in the Taiwanese collectivity.[2] Hou's film channeled some of these trends through the experiences of one family that we meet in the opening scene, set in their house on August 15, 1945, at the end of World War II. Emperor Hirohito is proclaiming Japan's surrender on the radio, but the main character and his family are much more concerned with bringing a new member, the man's son, into the world. The end of the Pacific War heralds the birth of a new era and appears to be a moment of liberation for the Taiwanese, a chance to be free from the repressive policies of Japanese colonial rule. Tragically, relations with Taiwan's new Chinese rulers turn sour by early 1947, as represented in a series of events that devastate the family. The new father is killed, one of his brothers is debilitated, and a third brother is arrested.[3] Nonetheless, the protagonist's declaration of adherence to his Taiwanese identity crystallized a view that prevailed in the late 1980s and after, of the Taiwanese as members of a timeless national community, forged in the distant past and subject to the repression of Japanese and Chinese colonial regimes.

We must recognize, however, that like all dramatic depictions of historical events, the film is a memory of the past, shaped by the confluence of the events it depicts and references, subsequent history, and the prevailing concerns of its era. Each layer of experience and meaning contributes to determining the chronological moorings of that particular Taiwanese consciousness, and thus we should not accept that

1. Hsiau, *Contemporary Taiwanese Cultural Nationalism*, 11–19.

2. Brown, *Is Taiwan Chinese?*, chaps. 2–3.

3. *Beiqing Chengshi* (*A City of Sadness*) (1989), directed by Hou Hsiao-hsien; my translation. June Yip argues that the film was "a milestone in [the] process of decolonization" in the late 1980s and early 1990s, when Taiwanese people began to openly reexamine their colonial and postcolonial past. See Yip, *Envisioning Taiwan*.

nationalism is or was the only form of Taiwanese identity. Pierre Nora, who pioneered the study of history and memory, describes the antagonistic relationship between them, through which history—"how modern societies organize a past they are condemned to forget because they are driven by change"—effectively destroys real memory. The remnants of this destruction, and the products of modern historians, are *lieux de mémoire*, realms or sites of memory that include museums, monuments, archives, history books, geographies, festivals, and treaties.[4] Nora's formulation is excessively oppositional in that it ignores the possibility of a more dynamic, mutually constitutive connection between history and memory. Yet the attention he and others have drawn to the distinction between them highlights a disjuncture between the past as it is remembered and the past as it unfolded. To the extent that the latter can be reconstructed, rather than seeking only the origins of the present we should pursue the answers to more open-ended questions: Who were the Taiwanese? When, by whom, and how was Taiwanese identity constructed? Was it only a national identity or were there other formulations, such as ethnic, cultural, regional, or linguistic?

If *A City of Sadness* is an example of history as memory or myth, then this book is, in contrast, history as event, to borrow two of Paul Cohen's three historical "keys."[5] This study examines a history and a historical process—Taiwanese ethnogenesis—that, for reasons that I discuss at greater length in the epilogue, have largely been forgotten. In contrast to the contentions of backward-looking, present-focused memories, identities are not constant across eras but, rather, are historically contingent and constructed by processes that move through time along partially open trajectories. In the following pages, I conduct a detailed historical investigation of the people who forged identities in Taiwan, the tools and materials that they used, and principally the ethnic and urban identities that they produced, from the late nineteenth century to the middle of the twentieth. The specific location for this study coincides with the setting of Hou's film: the northern port city of

4. Nora and Kritzman, *Realms of Memory*, quotation on 2 and realms of memory listed on 6–7, 14–19.
5. Cohen, *History in Three Keys*.

Jilong (Keelung) and its environs, for Jilong stood in the vanguard of Taiwan's historical transformations throughout this period.

Although the new father's statement in Hou's film referenced only one result of those dramatic changes and not the processes, it nonetheless points us toward answers to the questions of when and who. Successive rule by the Qing, Japanese, and Chinese governments, each with its own vision for modernizing and civilizing the island and its residents, fundamentally influenced the formation of Taiwanese consciousness from the 1880s through the 1950s. The era of Japanese rule (1895–1945) was of paramount importance because it inserted the people who became Taiwanese into new ideological and cultural contexts, provided them with a new, contrasting "other" to define themselves against, and exposed them to the full power of the nation-state, a combination of factors that sparked a largely defensive process of identity formation. However, none of those regimes sought to create a Taiwanese identity; rather, each attempted to instill in Taiwan's inhabitants a distinctive state-centric and culturally based consciousness. Therefore, it was the people, specifically the subsection who had some ancestral roots in China, who came to define themselves as Taiwanese through their interactions with the successive groups of rulers and settlers.

What did it mean to become and be Taiwanese in these contexts? Within a substantial body of scholarship on Taiwanese identity, much of it highly admirable for both empirical depth and interpretive insight, the search has almost invariably been for the origins and early florescence of Taiwanese nationalism or ethnonationalism.[6] Scholars such as Wakabayashi Masahiro, Leo Ching, Ming-cheng Lo, and Wu Rwei-ren, among others, have convincingly demonstrated that intellectuals, professionals, and other members of Taiwan's society, both elites and nonelites, constructed a national or combined ethnonational identity, both before and after 1945.[7] More recently, Andrew Morris has shown how Taiwanese made baseball, with its origins as a multicultural pastime under Japanese rule, central to their vision of the Taiwanese

6. I explore much of this scholarship at greater length in Dawley, "The Question of Identity."

7. Wakabayashi, *Taiwan kangRi yundong*; Ching, *Becoming "Japanese"*; Lo, *Doctors within Borders*; Rwei-ren Wu, "The Formosan Ideology."

nation as a multiethnic space, and Ann Heylen has proven that linguistic movements of the 1920s and 1930s advanced a Taiwanese identity.[8] However, other work offers reason to question the urgency of a formally independent national identity in Taiwan. Arguments by Wu Rwei-ren on "pragmatic nationalism," Shelley Rigger on the status-quo orientation of most Taiwanese, and Christopher Hughes on the postnationalist trajectory of Taiwanese identity all indicate that the island's peoples have at least a cautious attitude toward the nation-state.[9]

Scholars have not ignored the subject of ethnicity in Taiwan. Those who have explored it, such as Zhang Maogui, Wu Naide, and Wang Fu-ch'ang, have concentrated on the era after 1945. Wang, in particular, explores the development of multiple ethnicities following the events of 1947, delineating the existence of four main ethnic groups during the 1980s and 1990s: Hoklo (Minnanese/Fujianese), Hakka, indigenous, and mainlanders.[10] During the post–martial law era, in particular, language became a central, politically charged feature dividing these groups. John Shepherd has argued that postwar disputes among them have their roots in Qing- and Japanese-era patterns of settlement and competition between Hoklo and Hakka people.[11] Nevertheless, in spite of the extensive existing scholarship, the precise relationship between national and ethnic identities, particularly before 1945, and the process of identity formation through the everyday lived experiences of Taiwan's residents, have been underexamined. In this book, I attempt to avoid the pitfalls of presentist, nation-centered history and pursue a forgotten, or ignored, construction of Taiwanese consciousness.

The first group of people identified, and identifiable, as Taiwanese came to Taiwan from China's southeastern coast. They became

8. Morris, *Colonial Project*; Heylen, *Japanese Models*.

9. Rwei-ren Wu, "Toward a Pragmatic Nationalism: Democratization and Taiwan's Passive Revolution," in Corcuff, *Memories of the Future*, 196–218; Rigger, *Taiwan's Rising Rationalism*; Hughes, "Post-Nationalist Taiwan," 215–33.

10. Wang Fu-ch'ang, *Dangdai Taiwan shehui*; Zhang Maogui, "'Gongtongti' de zhuixun yu zuqun wenti: xulun," and Wu Naide, "Shengji yishi, zhengzhi zhichi he guojia rentong: Taiwan zuqun zhengzhi lilun de chutan," both in Zhang Maogui, *Zuqun guanxi*, 1–26 and 27–52.

11. John Shepherd, "Ethnicity, Mortality, and the Shinchiku (Xinzhu) Advantage in Colonial Taiwan," in Morris, *Japanese Taiwan*, 93–111.

Taiwanese through a multistage historical process that involved self-definition in contrast to, and interaction with, the island's indigenous populations, as well as gradual identification with their sites of settlement. Their relations with indigenous populations included trade, open conflict, intermarriage, and coerced assimilation. Under Japanese colonial rule these people were classified as islanders (*hontōjin*), but over the course of several decades they became Taiwanese through relationships with Japanese settlers and officials that altered their sense of group membership.[12] They drew borders around a defined, relatively cohesive population and a set of elements from their cultural heritage, as well as between themselves and both the Japanese, who were deeply engaged in these acts of border definition, and those who lived in their ancestral homeland, who moved along a divergent trajectory. They constructed urban, ethnic, and national identities, all of which were deeply imbued with characteristics of the modern world. Generally, though not exclusively, "modern" included industrial capitalism, mass culture, steam and electric-powered transportation and communications infrastructure, and the nation-state, with its characteristic mass involvement in politics.[13] Of these identities, ethnic identity assumed particular strength, forged as it was as an imagined alternative to the Japanese and Chinese national identities.

During the early twentieth century, the "age of the city," urbanization went hand in hand with modernization, and modernization fostered rapid identity change.[14] Therefore it was in Taiwan's cities that the Chinese on the island became "islanders," and islanders became Taiwanese.[15] My urban focus coincides with the work of Emer O'Dwyer and Todd Henry, who have identified cities as crucial locations for defining and implementing Japanese colonization in Manchuria and

---

12. The Japanese colonial government created the category of "islanders" and included within it both people from southeastern China and Taiwan's indigenous people, but the term became firmly linked only with the former.

13. Louise Young provides a useful summary of these criteria in Young, *Beyond the Metropolis*, 3–6.

14. The phrase "age of the city" comes from ibid., 5.

15. E. Patricia Tsurumi argued long ago that a new Taiwanese consciousness emerged in urban settings, but she did not develop that point. See Tsurumi, *Japanese Colonial Education*, 217.

Korea.[16] It also reflects Louise Young's emphasis on the city as a place where a set of institutions combined with the "social imaginary"—ideas of the urban and what it meant to belong to an urban community—to stimulate a radical transformation among the inhabitants and the social orders they created.[17] The extensive literatures on Shanghai, less-studied Chinese cities such as Chengdu or Hankou, and other colonial cities all attest to the centrality of urban environments as crucibles of change.[18] In Taiwan, as elsewhere, the specific circumstances of place and space mediated individual and group experiences with the colonizing state and its agents, and thus cities linked local developments to broader trends. The particular features of urban identity, therefore, facilitated and reinforced changes to geographically broader categories of consciousness.

The present inquiry into these processes is rooted in the social history of Jilong, a place uniquely situated to provide insight into the origins of Taiwanese ethnicity. Hou's film drew me to the city during the early stages of my research, and I quickly discovered that it had been the site of significant historical changes. While the judgment of John Dodd, the British merchant quoted in the first of the four epigraphs to this introduction, may have held some validity in its moment, the next three evaluations accurately reflect the subsequent physical and mental transformation of Taiwan and its residents. As this project evolved, I uncovered evidence of remarkable urbanization, as the small treaty port of Jilong, with its tenuous links to regional and global commerce networks, became the island's third largest city and largest port. Along the way, three regimes—the Sino-Manchu, imperial Japanese, and Nationalist Chinese—prioritized the development of Jilong before all cities save Taipei, and it became home to some of the largest concentrations of Japanese people in Taiwan before 1945, and mainland

16. O'Dwyer, *Significant Soil*; Henry, *Assimilating Seoul*.

17. Young, *Beyond the Metropolis*, 11–12.

18. For Shanghai, see, for example Henriot, *Shanghai, 1927–1937*; Yeh, *Shanghai Splendor*; Goodman, *Native Place*; and Lee, *Shanghai Modern*. For Chengdu, see Stapleton, *Civilizing Chengdu*; Hankou, see Rowe, both *Hankow: Commerce and Society* and *Hankow: Conflict and Community*; Hong Kong, see Carroll, *Edge of Empires*; Hanoi and Saigon, see Cooper, *France in Indochina*; and for colonial cities in general, see King, *Colonial Urban Development*.

Chinese after. These realities promoted the social, economic, and political interactions conducive to identity construction and ethnic formation. From at least the 1860s through its decades as the primary point of entry to Taiwan under Japanese and early Nationalist Chinese rule, Jilong was, like many port cities, a "nodal point of change," a location for exchanges that fostered social, economic, and cultural transformation in the city and its hinterland.[19] Other places, like Gaoxiong (Kaohsiung) and Taizhong (Taichung), shared Jilong's experience of swift urban development; Taipei held pride of place as the administrative center; and Tainan had a much longer history of settlement and as a cultural hub, and all could serve as subjects for study. In this era, however, both Taiwan's governments and its residents consciously built up Jilong as a model for the rest of Taiwan, and what happened there reflected and influenced broader islandwide developments. Gaoxiong may have surpassed it as a trading port decades ago, and in the early twenty-first century it has slipped in Taiwan's urban rankings.[20] Yet from the 1880s to the 1950s, Jilong was the main city in which local actors created Taiwanese ethnic identity.

Theorizing Ethnicity through Taiwan's Colonial Pasts

The making of the modern world has largely been told as the history of the nation-state, a sociopolitical destination toward which all peoples have been seen to move, and national identities have been deemed the most important during the nineteenth and twentieth centuries. Existing counternarratives of transnationalism or the deterritorialized nation have certainly helped us decenter the nation-state.[21] Two decades ago Prasenjit Duara called on us to examine the nation-state as a contested space, and Antoinette Burton and other practitioners of

19. Andrew McPherson, "Port Cities as Nodal Points of Change: The Indian Ocean, 1890s–1920s," in Fawaz, Bayly, and Ilbert, *Modernity and Culture*, 75–95.

20. According to recent official statistics, in 2017 Jilong was the eighth most populous municipality. See Neizhengbu huzhengsi, "Renkou tongji ziliao."

21. See Duara, "Transnationalism and the Predicament of Sovereignty."

"the new imperial history" have destabilized the precedence of the nation.[22] Yet it continues to dominate our historiographies. Historians explore other stories as well—histories of the environment, migration, gender, commerce, slavery, world regions—but many of these, too, are tied to the sovereign nation-state. Moreover, it shows no sign of vanishing from human society, even as nonnational actors have played important and disruptive roles in the twenty-first century. As a representation of these historic and historiographical realities, scholars have expended considerable effort on theorizing about the nation-state regarding both its origins and its penetration into and control over the lives, minds, and bodies of its citizens.[23] Scholars of nation-state formation have paid particular attention to the concept of territoriality, or sovereignty over bounded space, and to the centrality of exclusionary boundaries for the creation of seemingly unbreakable bonds between people, state, and space.[24]

These scholars have also addressed the connections between nations and nationalism, on the one hand, and ethnicity, on the other hand. One school of interpretation frames the latter as a building block

22. Duara outlined an ambitious agenda for "rescuing history from the nation" that called our attention to "the nation as the site of contested meanings." See Duara, *Rescuing History*. Nevertheless, most recent studies of nineteenth- and twentieth-century China, Japan, and Taiwan have remained within the confines of national history, as scholars have continued to write the histories of nations whose existence they have shown to be contingent. Antoinette Burton, "Introduction: On the Inadequacy and Indispensability of the Nation," in Burton, *After the Imperial Turn*, 1–23.

23. On the origins of the nation-state, see Anderson, *Imagined Communities*; Chatterjee, *The Nation and Its Fragments*; Greenfeld, *Nationalism*; Gellner, *Nations and Nationalism*; and Anthony Smith, *The Nation in History*. Regarding its penetration into the lives of citizens, I reference a large body of scholarship that drew inspiration from the work of Michel Foucault on the prison as an example of the disciplinary power of the modern nation-state. See Foucault, *Discipline and Punish*. A few works on Japanese and Chinese history that draw on Foucault's insights in illuminating ways include: Botsman, *Punishment and Power*; Dikötter, *Crime, Punishment*; Janet Chen, *Guilty of Indigence*.

24. On territoriality as the defining characteristic of the "long twentieth century," see Maier, "Consigning the Twentieth Century." For the long-term process of border definition, Sahlins, *Boundaries*, and Thongchai, *Siam Mapped*. On boundary-definition and the creation of modern Japan and China see, respectively, Iriye, "Japan's Drive to Great-Power Status," and Zhao, "Reinventing China."

for the former, whereas a second view posits ethnicity as an obstacle that gets overrun and erased in the drive to modern nationhood.[25] In both cases, nationalism is accepted as a modern construct, but ethnic identity is associated with a premodern age as something that is either wholly antimodern or gains a modern quality only when it is fused with a national consciousness.[26] In contrast, Max Weber long ago suggested that ethnicity had modern origins, Clifford Geertz argued that ethnic structures offer specific evidence of modern processes, and Immanuel Wallerstein linked ethnic construction to the establishment of modern colonial empires, a point that is particularly useful for the present study.[27] Nevertheless, in the literature on the nation-state, ethnic identities are seen as nonmodern or acquiring modernity only in the form of ethnonationalism.[28]

This tendency to consign ethnic consciousness to a purportedly backward stage in the evolution of human society obscures the tremendous similarities between ethnic and national groups. Ethnicity can be defined as a type of regional identity—that is, one that is shared across spaces that are too large to allow consistent, direct contact between members of the identity group, whatever its character—in which the adherents share similar cultural, genealogical, and geographic traits as well as past experiences.[29] As Weber argues, ethnic groups are historical and political creations—that is, not natural or primordial—but, as

25. Anderson, *Imagined Communities*; Anthony Smith, *Ethnic Origins of Nations* and *Ethnicity and Nationalism*; Gellner, *Nations and Nationalism*.

26. There is a counternarrative that posits the antiquity of nations and nationalism, a particularly fine example of which is the work of Aviel Roshwald, who argues that modern nationalism is based on ancient roots and models. See Roshwald, *The Endurance of Nationalism*. I do not envision a stark break between tradition and modernity, nor do I privilege the latter era over the former. Nevertheless, the broad social, political, and territorial unity of the nation-state has no complete manifestation prior to the nineteenth century.

27. Weber, *Economy and Society*, chap. 5; Clifford Geertz, "The Integrative Revolution: Primordial Sentiments and Civil Politics in the New States," in Geertz, *The Interpretation of Cultures*, 308. Immanuel Wallerstein, "The Two Modes of Ethnic Consciousness: Soviet Central Asia in Transition," in Wallerstein, *The Capitalist World-Economy*. See also Royce, *Ethnic Identity*, chap. 3.

28. For an earlier formulation of this point, see Royce, *Ethnic Identity*, chap. 4.

29. This range of factors distinguishes ethnicity from the more narrowly defined cultural nationalism.

Anthony Smith emphasizes, they do not require the presence of political rights or responsibilities, or of a governing structure.[30] Moreover, scholars have long emphasized that a sense of territorial boundedness is essential to the process of ethnogenesis. In Fredrik Barth's classic formulation of the transactional nature of ethnic formation, an ethnic identity takes on particular significance only when boundaries are drawn around it and subsequently monitored to maintain a sense of separation between in-group and out-group members. For Barth, these boundaries function largely as zones of interaction, because it is only through interchange that the divisions become clearly delineated and preserved.[31] Recent work on the histories of China and Japan has demonstrated the dynamic construction of ethnicity both internally by members of the ethnic group-in-formation, and externally by state policies that seek to define national (or imperial) ethnicities.[32] There is also evidence of transition from one ethnicity to another.[33] In light of the foregoing, ethnic and national identities share several features in common: both are highly contingent regional identities, and both require the strict definition of physical or imagined geography, or

30. Weber, *Economy and Society*, 389; Anthony Smith, *The Nation in History*, 65. Smith defines the nation as "a named human population occupying a historic territory or homeland and sharing common myths and memories; a mass, public culture; a single economy; and common rights and duties for all members" (3), and the ethnic group, or *ethnie*, as "a named human population with myths of common ancestry, shared historical memories, one or more elements of shared culture, a link with a homeland, and a measure of solidarity, at least among the elites."

31. Barth, *Ethnic Groups and Boundaries*, 9–38. Barth's conceptualization has been challenged by primordialist and instrumentalist visions, which argue either for biological and cultural essentialism, or fabrication by political interest and status groups, respectively. Hutchinson and Smith, *Ethnicity*, 8–10.

32. Most relevant to the present work are David Howell's examination of the interlinked construction of Japanese and Ainu ethnicities during the Meiji period; Dru Gladney's and Thomas Mullaney's studies of the creation of ethnic groups in the People's Republic of China; and especially Sow-Theng Leong's finding that the Hakka truly became Hakka only in response to the process of Chinese nation-building. Howell, *Geographies of Identity*; Gladney, *Muslim Chinese*; Mullaney, *Coming to Terms*; and Leong, *Migration and Ethnicity*. Also useful for establishing the dynamism of ethnic construction is Elliott, *The Manchu Way*.

33. Brown, *Is Taiwan Chinese?*

both, to coalesce.[34] Given these many similarities, it is unsurprising
that the two are so often linked in both scholarly interpretation and
the popular imagination.

These theories conceive of ethnicity as a constructed and modern
sociopolitical category, but more relevant is the fact that Japanese and
Chinese scholars and ideologues simultaneously formulated definitions for concepts of nation, ethnicity, and race in the late nineteenth
and the mid-twentieth centuries. One word, 民族 (Jp., *minzoku*; Ch.,
minzu), sat at the center of their debates, because at different moments
and in different parts of East Asia it served as the translation for all
three of these imported ideas.[35] In Japan, where the acquisition of Taiwan sparked debates over the meaning of *minzoku*, this early fluidity
stabilized during the late 1920s and 1930s: the term *jinshu* (人種; Ch.,
renzhong) came to be used for "race," a concept tied to biology, whereas
minzoku became a conflation of ethnicity and nation.[36] The differentiation between "race" and "ethnicity/nation" resulted partly from Yanagita Kunio's formulation of ethnography (Jp., *minzokugaku*; Ch.,
minsuxue; 民俗學 rather than 民族學) as the study of popular customs, the goal of which was to comprehend a Japanese essence. Borrowing from Western field-study techniques and ideas that he learned
while in Switzerland with the League of Nations, Yanagita modified
his early interests in folklore and folk religion to frame the study of
Japan's peripheral regions—Hokkaido and Okinawa—as storehouses
for an authentic Japanese culture rather than as autonomous local
cultures. In other words, "Yanagita ethnography" connected these
minzoku as customs to *minzoku* as ethnonation because the objects

34. Edward Said's concept of imaginative geography, expressed in the sense of
the Orient as a territory constructed and imbued with a range of immutable
characteristics in the minds of Europeans, has had some influence on my sense of
imagined geography. See Said, *Orientalism*. However, I use the term in a more flexible
sense, in which people draw boundaries between different social groups in their
minds, without necessarily fixing them in physical space or associating them with
unchanging features.

35. Dikötter, *The Construction of Racial Identities*.

36. Doak, *A History of Nationalism in Modern Japan*, chap. 6, esp. 222–25; Morris-
Suzuki, *Re-Inventing Japan*, 32, 98–99.

under study were, ultimately, Japanese.[37] In colonial Taiwan, prevailing views differentiated ethnicity as something separate from and, for some, inferior to nationality. For example, *Taiwan Ethnology* (民俗 台灣; *Minzoku Taiwan*) was an important journal of the 1940s, staffed by both Japanese and Taiwanese, that cataloged and analyzed the social practices of the islanders at a time when those traditions came under strong attack.[38] In this context, the objects of study were the same, but for the Japanese who studied them they had to be eradicated to nationalize the Taiwanese as Japanese, whereas Taiwanese contributors likely saw the customs as important things to be preserved as the basis for an autonomous ethnicity.

In China, early revolutionaries like Zhang Binglin and Sun Yat-sen (Sun Zhongshan) initially combined race, ethnicity, and nation in their concept of *minzu*, but over time they distinguished among these categories. At first they used *minzu* to justify their anti-Manchu revolutionary activities in the name of returning the Han Chinese (Hanzu) to their rightful status as China's rulers. Soon, however, Zhang differentiated between the narrow category of Han people and the larger entity of the Chinese nation-state (*Zhonghua minzu*), which could encompass multiple descent-based groups (*zu*).[39] Sun's initial formulation of his Three People's Principles (*Sanmin zhuyi*) in 1905 blurred the distinction between nation and ethnicity, but his final presentation of these terms made it clear that the first, *minzu*, referred to a national entity that fully combined a people, state, and territory. Under the leadership of Chiang Kai-shek (Jiang Jieshi) the Guomindang (GMD) rigidly held to this notion of *minzu*-as-nation, in part to oppose the Communist Party, which defined it as ethnicity to gain local support from non-Han groups.[40] When the Nationalists arrived in Taiwan in

37. See Kawada, *The Origin of Ethnography in Japan*; Morris-Suzuki, *Re-Inventing Japan*, esp. chaps. 2, 4, 5.

38. Wu Micha, "The Nature of *Minzoku Taiwan* and the Context in Which It Was Published," in Liao and Wang, *Taiwan under Japanese*, 358–87.

39. Kai-wing Chow, "Imagining Boundaries of Blood: Zhang Binglin and the Invention of the Han 'Race' in Modern China," in Dikötter, *The Construction of Racial Identities*, 34–52.

40. Mullaney, *Coming to Terms*, chap. 1. In some instances, *minzu* continued to blur ethnicity and nationality in Republican China, a fact that I could not miss when

1945, their vision of *minzu*-as-nation clashed with the Taiwanese, who saw themselves as an ethnic group worth preserving, but it facilitated the reproduction of earlier efforts to nationalize the Taiwanese.

I have dwelt on these multiple meanings of *minzoku/minzu* to emphasize that the structural context of colonial rule forced Taiwan's islanders to distinguish between ethnic and national identities. In both Japan and China, as in the nationalizing world more broadly, a modern national identity was inextricable from a state-building project. Yet Taiwan's historical experience of colonization by three successive regimes left its residents consistently outside of the government.[41] Access to state power remained highly restricted in each instance, fundamentally preventing the correlation between people and government that is characteristic of at least the rhetoric of the nation-state. As colonized subjects, Taiwan's residents were excluded from the Japanese and Chinese state-building projects and discouraged from developing an independent national identity. Moreover they were treated as ethnic groups, defined by successive states on the basis of language, blood, and customs as expressly nonnational entities. Therefore, the overlap of intensifying discussions of ethnicity and radical national assimilation policies during the 1930s and 1940s solidified an autonomous ethnic identity as a real, if threatened, option for Taiwan's islanders.[42] I argue that the main objective of an ethnic identity is the social survival of the ethnic group, and when that collectivity came under attack by Japanese and Chinese colonial regimes, its defense within the prevailing systems, rather than the formation of a new independent

---

researching and writing this book at Academia Sinica in Taiwan, where Minzuxue yanjiusuo is translated as the Institute of Ethnology. It originated as the Ethnic Research Group (Minzuxue zu) within the Institute of Sociology, in 1928.

41. Six colonizing regimes, if one includes the Dutch, Spanish, and Zheng regimes that preceded Qing colonization. See, for example, Jacobs, *Democratizing Taiwan*, chap. 2.

42. Chen Chung-min, Chuang Ying-chang, and Huang Shu-min made a similar claim in 1994, when they argued that "a new ethnic category, the so-called 'Taiwanese,' then emerged; this new label carried important sociopolitical meanings that appeared to surpass previous categorizations." See Chen, Chuang, and Huang, *Ethnicity in Taiwan*, 17. In spite of this statement, their edited volume overlooks ethnic formation in the crucial era of Japanese rule.

nation, became the primary goal.[43] Taiwan's history was particular, but research on the Soviet Union and colonial Africa suggests that it was far from unique in its production of nonnational options for identity-formation.[44]

Besides my emphasis on avoiding the nation-state as the primary unit of analysis, I also explore issues of territorialization and de- or reterritorialization—that is, processes of imparting sociopolitical meanings to space and place—as they relate to national and nonnational identities. I use these concepts in a manner that is similar to the way John Tomlinson discusses them in his summary of how globalization dissolves "the connection between everyday lived culture and territorial location." However, although Tomlinson sees de- or reterritorialization as an unintentional but inevitable outgrowth of globalization, in Taiwan these concepts were the mostly intentional projects of colonizing regimes and local residents.[45] Settlers or descendants of settlers from southeastern China, principally the coastal regions of Fujian and Guangdong Provinces, created Taiwanese ethnicity out of their interactions with Sino-Manchu, Japanese, and Chinese states, and with Taiwan's indigenous peoples as well as Japanese and postwar Chinese migrants. Moreover, the people who shaped Taiwanese ethnic consciousness out of elements of both their historic background and their contemporary context were self-consciously modern. Although the Japanese and Chinese who attempted to impose their own national identities attacked the residents of Taiwan for being backward and uncivilized, those who became Taiwanese embraced much of what they then considered modern—urbanization, hygiene, scientific methods and rationality, and the ideal of mass participation in politics—but did

43. This point is consistent with the work of Anthony Smith but the idea is my own. See Smith, *The Nation in History*.

44. See Martin, *The Affirmative Action Empire*, and Cooper, *Africa in the World*, 67–68. Cooper's work is particularly useful because he argues that, from the 1940s until at least 1960, leaders within French Africa envisioned federation or confederation as alternatives to both empire and the nation-state. "Rather than see real independence as the attainment of the bounded nation-state," writes Cooper, "they argued for a more layered approach to sovereignty, balancing territorial autonomy with inclusion in a larger entity."

45. See Tomlinson, *Globalization and Culture*, chap. 4, quotation on 128.

not necessarily absorb an external nationalism or construct a hegemonic one from within.

Social History, Performative Identity, and the Gatekeepers of Taiwanese Ethnicity

Capturing the identities that formed and reformed in Jilong can be
accomplished only through a careful analysis of the historical processes
and factors that shaped local society—that is, through social history.
The colonial states, with their mechanisms of control and power, loom
behind and frequently enter the narrative. Nonetheless, I am more concerned with the lived experiences of Jilong's residents, with particular
attention to the members of the elite stratum who created and supported key institutions, molded the social structure, and served as
essential intermediaries between the state and the majority of the
population. The divisions and interactions between islanders and Japanese, Taiwanese and Chinese, and subjects/citizens and state institutions necessitate a transactional approach like Barth's that calls
attention to the people who demarcated and protected ethnic boundaries as well as the contents of various identities. As they defined the
border between Taiwanese ethnicity and Japanese or Chinese nationalism, they served as gatekeepers for identity formation. This approach
does not rely on the social history of the politics of social movements,
but rather on an examination of key figures and their webs of connections across society, the effects of a modernizing economy on an
expanding population, the popular institutions that sustained social
cohesion, and the relationship between government programs and the
semi-state actors and non-state actors who managed and utilized those
initiatives.[46]

In exploring the subject of Taiwanese identity, I adopt a performative approach that departs from the textual studies that have dominated
the field. Examining the performance of identity, or the connections

---

46. Perhaps the definitive work of Taiwanese social history is Wakabayashi
Masahiro's magisterial study of anti-Japanese social movements. See Wakabayashi,
Taiwan kangRi yundong.

between what people do and how they see themselves or are seen by others, provides certain advantages. It connects the elite actors who are the center of this study to a range of constituencies for whom they enacted their identities, including the colonial government that affirmed their status, other elites who enhanced their influence, and the broader populations that could accept or reject their leadership.[47] Moreover, the ways that people organize and operate in particular social contexts can be indicative of their identities even in the absence of declarative statements. Not all individual or group activities represent identity, and not all people who participate in particular behaviors share the same sense of self. Nevertheless, people manifest their identity through their actions when they act in ways that contrast with or oppose prescribed behavior, maintain particular behaviors outside of their initial historical context, or modify specific activities to accord with new circumstances without abandoning them in favor of newly invented traditions.[48] In these and other cases, an act is not simply an act, but rather it is representative of the collective sense of what makes a specific group unique. Indeed, my performative approach offers a means of studying group identities in any context that lacks internally produced sources, because it reveals voices and ideas that might otherwise remain hidden, and allows historians to probe beyond imposed categories.

47. Shih-jung Tzeng has studied the identity transformations of elite islanders from the 1920s through the 1950s. Through a close reading of two diaries, he provides a provocatively fluid picture of identity shifts from Chinese nationalism to Japanese nationalism and back, with a Taiwanese national consciousness emerging during the 1920s and remaining a contrasting, but not exclusive, identity thereafter. Tzeng, *From Hōnto Jin*. Tzeng confirms the existence of Taiwanese nationalism, but he conflates ethnicity with it. More significantly, he relies on private writings that were not meant to be shared, and it is difficult to accept these diaries as evidence of a collective, broadly shared identity.

48. Judith Butler's work illuminates some of my view of performative identity, although I derived my ideas independently. In particular, in her analysis of hate speech, Butler distinguishes between failed and felicitous performance: "A felicitous performative is one in which I not only perform the act, but some set of effects follows from the fact that I perform it." See Butler, *Excitable Speech*, 17. To put it in the terms of this volume, the "felicitous performative" can be seen as an act that appeals to one constituency or another and achieves the goal of defining or protecting borders.

Linking elites to nonelites through the analysis of shared activities
highlights how islander-Taiwanese elites shaped an ethnic community.
Status and economic distinctions within Taiwan's society created internal heterogeneity, and the stratification of islander society produced
significant variations in interactions with Japanese or Chinese officials
and nonofficials. Islander-Taiwanese elites most frequently and directly
engaged with foreign regimes and settlers, and therefore they occupied
a liminal place in the colonial setting. Their elite status was shaped in
large part by their willingness to accommodate the dictates of the colonial state and mimic the sociocultural norms of colonial settlers, but
they were not fully assimilated into the dominant culture nor were they
completely separated from their roots.[49] Officially sanctioned status
and persistent exclusion from the politically dominant identity group
held these elites in the zone of interaction, in which they articulated
Taiwanese identities through their efforts to define and defend them.

Their in-between position meant that they had to perform their
identities for multiple audiences in order to attain and maintain their
status. Given their historical and cultural affinities with the islander
community, and the fact that their access to that community was a key
reason why the Government-General affirmed their elite status, the
islander elites had to present an identity that resonated with other islanders without threatening the power of the Japanese. In keeping with
the transactional model of ethnic formation, the interactions between
islander-Taiwanese elites and their Japanese or Chinese counterparts
defined and ultimately reinforced the borders of Taiwanese ethnicity.
Jun Uchida, in her pathbreaking study of settler colonialism in Korea,
referred to Japanese settler elites in Korea as "brokers of empire," because they made possible the imposition of Japanese rule, even when
they struggled with the colonial government for autonomy and influence.[50] For my purposes, it is more useful to understand both colonized

49. Homi Bhabha's work on mimicry is relevant because it highlights how people
across Taiwan's society—southeastern Chinese and aborigine, elite and nonelite—
increasingly spoke and wrote in Japanese, studied in the colonial education system,
attended Shinto shrines, and worked for the colonial state, but were never accepted
as Japanese. See Bhabha, "Of Mimicry and Man: The Ambivalence of Colonial
Discourse," in Bhabha, The Location of Culture.

50. Uchida, Brokers of Empire.

and colonizing elites as the gatekeepers who controlled access to their respective identity groups, shaping and reshaping the nature of those identities in the process. They also, not coincidentally, preserved their social status by playing this role.

Becoming Taiwanese in Colonial Jilong

What *is* in a name? From the four epigraphs to this introduction it should be apparent that the name of the city, written with two different pairs of ideographs (雞籠 before 1885, 基隆 after; their pronunciations are the same, but the first means "chicken cage" and the second means "base of prosperity"), has been rendered in multiple ways.[51] To Westerners like John Dodd, the city was known as Keelung or Kelung.[52] To Japanese like Katō Haruki, who wrote the lyrics to the city song, it was Kiirun.[53] To Taiwanese, such as the local chronicler Jian Wanhuo, and Chinese, like the authors of an early postwar guidebook, it was either Gelang (the Minnan/Hokkien pronunciation) or Jilong (Mandarin pronunciation).[54] These varied renditions suggest that the place held different meanings for the people who lived there and helped transform it from what some saw as a wretched village into a bustling, vibrant port of which its residents were justifiably proud. That is, the names express the identities that Taiwanese, Japanese, and Chinese—though not Westerners—imported and constructed even as they built the city itself. Therefore, what we call the city does matter. Although Japanese was the official language for most of the years under study, the emergence of a Taiwanese consciousness is at the heart of our

51. I take up the origins of this name in chapter 1.

52. Dodd, *Journal of a Blockaded Resident*, epigraph quotation is on 179.

53. Sources disagree over authorship of this song. The official version, issued in the name of Jilong's mayor in 1933, Kuhara Masao, credited an Ichijō Shinzaburō; see Kuhara, *Kiirun no uta*. However, another source likely more accurately states that Ichijō wrote the melody and Katō wrote the words; see Mitsubashi, *Wa ga Kiirun*, epigraph on 1. The lines quoted in the epigraph are from the third and final verse. Asahigaoka was the Japanese name for a hillside near the mouth of the harbor that in the early 1930s was voted one of the most scenic spots in Taiwan.

54. Jian Wanhuo, *Jilong zhi*, introduction, epigraph on 6; *Taiwan zhinan* (*Taiwan Guidebook*), in Yang and Chen, *Minjian sizang, chanye pian yi*, 293.

story, and thus Kiirun is inappropriate. For the same reason, Keelung, the most common Romanization since the late nineteenth century, is also out of place. Most residents are, and have long been, speakers of Minnan/Hokkien, and the city has been most frequently referred to as Gelang. However, this rendition is unknown outside of that linguistic community, so it cannot be used for ease of communication. In contrast, all of the elite gatekeepers—islander-Taiwanese, Japanese, and Chinese—were well versed in written Chinese, and many spoke it as well. For these reasons, I will refer to the city as Jilong.

A Taiwanese ethnic consciousness emerged in Jilong during the period of Japanese rule and its immediate aftermath. Indeed, it was only in such a local context that the relationships among residents, and interactions between residents and government policies, occurred to produce ethnicity. When Japan gained sovereignty over Taiwan from the Qing dynasty in 1895, most of Jilong's residents could be (and were) considered Chinese, and they identified most closely with their homelands in the southeastern part of Qing territory, although they constituted an internally diverse and at times violently divided group. Following Madeleine Yue Dong's work on Republican Beijing, this Chinese cultural background would be recycled to shape their future consciousness.[55] Changes in rulership and sovereignty established political barriers between the island and the mainland, and the Japanese colonial government enforced or reinforced new boundaries between Chinese-descended islanders (*hontōjin*), aborigines (*banjin*), Japanese (*naichijin*), and Chinese subjects or citizens (Shinkokujin; after 1911, Shinajin). Although the early policies of the Japanese Government-General created social categories, those policies did not make the islanders Taiwanese any more than the later programs of assimilation made the Taiwanese Japanese. Rather, state actions applied common policies to a defined population over a fixed terrain, encompassing—but not eliminating—prior divisions of native place, Hoklo or Han, and Hakka. From the 1890s through the 1930s, externally and geographically defined islanders transformed themselves into socially and culturally defined ethnic Taiwanese, a new consciousness that overlapped or nested with other identities. Colonial policies and the islanders held the indigenous

55. Dong, *Republican Beijing*.

peoples as external to this social group, as the islander-Taiwanese firmly rooted their identity in a set of behaviors, practices, institutions, and historical contexts. Once established, Taiwanese ethnicity was strong enough to withstand external assaults by both Japanese and Chinese rulers from the 1930s onward. The genius of this expressly nonnational identity lay in the fact that it was constructed without existential connection to any nation-state, real or imagined, and thus could survive regardless of which national government ruled the territory in which the Taiwanese lived.

Taiwanese forged their ethnic consciousness in contradistinction to two nationalisms, Japanese and Chinese, both of which were imposed on Taiwan in the guise of intentional projects to modernize, civilize, and deterritorialize or reterritorialize the place and its people. In both cases, limited state capacities and complex negotiations within Taiwan prevented the fulfillment of these efforts, but that incompleteness did not diminish the attempt.[56] Japanese officials and settlers arrived in Taiwan with a well-defined though by no means fixed sense of who they were as subjects or citizens of a modern nation-state, one that had developed out of state building, territorial expansion, and relations with China and Korea during the early Meiji period.[57] As the Japanese empire grew in the twentieth century, the Japanese increasingly saw themselves as the bearers of civilization to the backward peoples of Asia, as Stefan Tanaka has demonstrated.[58] However, in light of what Takashi Fujitani describes as "Japan's ambition for a postcolonial, multiethnic nation-state and empire," they also allowed for, and even approved, the construction of Taiwanese ethnicity.[59] Over time, owing partly to domestic and international developments as well as to the failure of moderate assimilationist policies in Taiwan during the 1920s, Japanese nationalist consciousness became more rigid, aggressive, and intolerant, an evolution that manifested in Taiwan in an effort to wipe

56. There is a parallel here to Charles Musgrove's point about the ongoing conflict between the state and city residents in Nanjing as the former pursued a tentative legitimacy in the face of shifting loyalties. Musgrove, *China's Contested Capital*, chap. 6.

57. Iriye, "Japan's Drive to Great-Power Status"; Howell, *Geographies of Identity*.

58. Tanaka, *Japan's Orient*.

59. Fujitani, *Race for Empire*, 12; Lie, *Multiethnic Japan*.

out the new Taiwanese consciousness even before the intense Japanization of the Pacific War era. A strong discourse of fundamental
racial commonality underlay this assimilationist agenda.[60] Under these
conditions, the Taiwanese people could not feasibly pursue a separate
national identity, but they did maintain their ethnicity.[61] Following that
war, the Republic of China (ROC) gained Taiwan from the fragmentation of Japan's empire, just as the republic entered a new phase of civil
war between Nationalists and Communists. The Nationalist regime
and its citizens, motivated by their own intense national consciousness,
pressed their identity onto Taiwan.[62] After five decades of divergent
identity construction, Chinese and Taiwanese viewed each other from
across a considerable gulf that the new colonial rulers sought to bridge
with a re-Sinicization project, which they couched in the language of
modernization and supported with a willingness to destroy overt resistance. Perhaps because of their common cultural background, the
Nationalist Chinese were more open to accepting Taiwanese people
into their national community than the Japanese had been, but they
were no less brutal in their efforts to enforce membership. Even though
Nationalist assimilation policies treated Taiwanese and indigenous as
essentially the same in their non-Chineseness, these communities did
not make common cause.

Three main groups—islander-Taiwanese, Japanese, and Chinese—
interacted within the city of Jilong and further constructed a new Jilong
identity, embodied in a sense of civic pride and a desire to improve the
city and the lives of its residents. This sense of being *Jilongese*, which
in fact preceded Taiwanese ethnicity before evolving in concert with

60. Fujitani, *Race for Empire*, 12, 23–26.
61. Wu Rwei-ren offered a similar view on the disappearance of Taiwanese
nationalism during the late 1930s in an unpublished conference paper, Wu, "Monument of the Vanishing?" Ming-cheng Lo argues that, during these years, Taiwanese
doctors became "medical modernizers" and deemphasized their own ethnic
distinctiveness; see Lo, *Doctors within Borders*, 6. Lo tends to conflate ethnicity and
nationality, which might account for our disagreement on the wartime salience of
Taiwanese ethnicity.
62. I will address this complex process in chapter 6. For the moment, it is worth
citing two comprehensive surveys, Zarrow, *China in War*, and Zhao, *A Nation-State
by Construction*.

it, allowed at least some of those residents to carve out a shared imaginary space and cooperate on a number of different urban and social development projects. The efforts of Japanese settlers to assert their autonomous interests against the colonial regime, a move that was common to Korea and Manchuria as well, at times facilitated such alliances within local society.[63] During the first decades of Japanese rule the gatekeepers loosely patrolled the borders, allowing for a relatively free interchange at the elite levels of society. As a result, the local Jilong identity developed and flourished, especially from the late 1910s into the early 1930s. However, these moments of urban solidarity and shared civic boosterism ultimately contributed to the sharp divisions between Taiwanese and Japanese, and later Taiwanese and Chinese, because the different groups had contrasting views of what it meant to be Jilongese. For the Japanese and Nationalist Chinese, Jilong was a place that they created or re-created to fulfill their dreams of modernization, civilization, and nationalization. Although islander-Taiwanese shared certain modernizing goals, for them Jilong was the site of their most important religious, social welfare, and economic activities. The disparity in understandings of local identity ultimately served to intensify the separation between ethnic and national groups.

This book traces a chronological arc defined by fluctuations in the intensity of policies of cultural and political assimilation. The period covered begins with the late Qing policy to "open the mountains and pacify the savages" (*kaishan fufan*) and thus Sinicize the indigenous people and incorporate the entire island into Chinese territory; runs through the moderate, relatively tolerant policies of Japanese colonial rule that prevailed into the 1930s; and ends with the successive waves of intense Japanization and re-Sinicization. Within this temporal framework, the first two chapters explore the construction of Jilong during the Qing and Japanese eras. Since the city was a crucial site for urban and ethnic identity construction, I open the book by establishing that location and its internal context. Chapter 1 provides the social and political backdrop against which identity formation took place in both Jilong and around the island, situated within the context of imperial expansion, territorial transfers, and colonial settlement. It

---

63. Uchida, *Brokers of Empire*; O'Dwyer, *Significant Soil*.

also introduces the key social and business elites who led Jilong's development during the period of Japanese rule, a group of half a dozen islanders and Japanese who founded or managed all of Jilong's most important social, economic, and religious institutions. In the process, it lays out the different social and official constituencies for whom these elites performed their identities, and how they did so. The central figures were all men, which suggests that, even though these identities were conceived and presented as comprehensive, they nonetheless were gendered, and potentially exclusionary, in their formulation. Chapter 2 builds on this historical and human foundation to explain how residents of the growing city developed and expressed their Jilong identity, and describes some of the fissures that ultimately fragmented this contested imaginary space. It examines social construction, local political activities, a local history movement, and gendered manifestations of identity.

The next three chapters detail the key elements that enabled islanders to forge and defend a Taiwanese ethnic identity in Jilong up through 1945: the organizations established by local leaders to structure and transform the expanding and urbanizing society; the city's religious institutions and festivals; and the provision of social welfare in the form of social work. Each of these factors contributed to identity construction in distinctive though interconnected ways. Chapter 3 examines the core individuals of the Japanese era in their dual roles as the creators of a temporarily inclusive Jilong-centered urban identity, and as gatekeepers for Taiwanese and Japanese identities, through a study of some of the organizations they established and the contributions they made to building the city. This chapter also addresses the ways in which the islander-Taiwanese elites, in particular, negotiated their position by appealing to other islander-Taiwanese, to Japanese settlers, and to the colonial state. Chapter 4 picks up the subject of religion, a facet of life that both Taiwanese and Japanese residents made a central component of their respective identities. They used it to bind their in-group members together on both local and regional levels, and also fought over it when Japanese settlers and the colonial state attempted to transform and civilize the Taiwanese by eradicating their religious traditions. The centrality of religion in Taiwanese ethnogenesis helps to explain why popular religion remains so prominent in Taiwan today.

In fact, until very recently, that religiosity was a key marker of distinction between the societies of Taiwan and the People's Republic of China (PRC).[64] Social work, the subject of chapter 5, also promoted a sense of group cohesion, both within Jilong and across the island, which proved to be essential for the expression and maintenance of Taiwanese ethnic identity. As a self-consciously modern form of social welfare, it also imparted a sense of being modern to Taiwanese consciousness. In these sections of the book, I trace multiple layers of identity performance, with islander-Taiwanese and Japanese in Taiwan shaping their identities through engagement with multiple audiences. During the war years, 1937–45, national and global events overwhelmed the local as a site of activity and identification, and thus Jilong faded into the historical background after it played its crucial role in forming Taiwanese ethnicity.

The last two chapters examine the early years of ROC rule, 1945–55, and frame the reassertion of both urban identity and Taiwanese ethnic consciousness within the Nationalist Chinese project of rebuilding, re-Sinicizing, and modernizing Taiwan. Here I explore the urban construction plans of the developmentalist state and the joint Taiwanese and Chinese effort to use rebuilding Jilong as a unifying goal, both before and after the explosive uprising of February 1947.[65] Finally, I examine how the Taiwanese defended their ethnic group against a new nationalizing project through the local municipal council, social welfare efforts, and especially temples and religious festivals. Throughout the book I draw from a variety of sources—government documents, newspapers, journals, organization reports, local histories, city gazetteers, and other archival and published materials—to piece together the actions of city residents and state agents. The breadth and depth of these resources make it possible for me to tell a new history of Taiwanese identity formation, and to break through the teleology of both Chinese and Japanese national histories. Far from inevitably ending in a seamless nation-state, these nation-building projects sometimes failed entirely to incorporate their objects.

64. For the resurgence of popular religion in the PRC since the reform era, see Johnson, *The Souls of China*.
65. Greene, *Origins of the Developmental State*.

Jilong stood at the forefront of Taiwan's modern transformations. As part of a physical and imagined frontier that changed sovereign territorial designations from the Great Qing to the Empire of Japan to the Republic of China, it occupied a crucial space in the borderland between Chinese and Japanese cultural spheres, empires, and nation-states. These circumstances, along with the inequities and power differentials inherent in multiple waves of colonization, promoted more rapid shifts in identification in that swiftly expanding city than occurred in most other parts of the island. Jilong's residents played a vanguard role in the historic process of becoming Taiwanese, and thus a careful examination of their experiences and activities is crucial to a complete understanding of modern Taiwanese identities. From the 1880s to the 1950s, Jilong was a city of bounded possibilities, a place where negotiations in the spaces between social groups, and with state actors, allowed unexpected identities and meanings to be constructed. This book recounts the history of how, through these complex, contingent relationships, a Taiwanese ethnicity was born.

CHAPTER ONE

Building and Populating
a Vanguard City

One of the earliest visual sources from the era of Japanese rule over Jilong, a woodblock print from 1896 held in the collection of Japan's National Diet Library, presents an ambivalent picture of the small harbor that the new colonial regime received as part of its territorial acquisition from Qing China (figs. 1.1 and 1.2). Across its three panels, two of which are reproduced here, the print depicts a section of the eastern side of the harbor as a place ringed by jumbled and treacherous rocks, with vaguely defined hills in the background. Although a few buildings, such as the treaty port–era customshouse with its tall flagpole and what were likely warehouses, stand as bright spots of clarity and order, the overall impression is one of a wasteland of mostly uncontrolled and unused space. Two figures dressed in clothes apparently made of woven grasses, one carrying a bamboo fishing pole, the other a basket, walk on the rocks in the foreground and highlight the wildness of the place. The small, formerly Qing town on the southern edge of the harbor is beyond the frame and thus absent, and the overall effect created by streaks of gray ink that represent Jilong's characteristic rain—one of the city's monikers is "Rainy Port" (Yugang)—is one of gloom and desolation.[1] To the extent that this image conveyed a typical contemporary view of Jilong and Japan's first colony, it

1. Kiyochika, *Taiwan san kei.*

suggests that the Japanese in Taiwan felt that they faced an enormous task in building a model colony here, but also a nearly empty canvas on which they could draw themselves and their nation.[2] The print thus conveys a few important points: at the historical moment of its transfer from Qing to Japanese sovereignty, Jilong had a numerically small human presence and a limited territorial footprint, it had recently been incorporated into broad networks of global commerce and colonial acquisition, and it was a site for colonial territorialization.

These points evoke the realities of Jilong's condition at the end of the nineteenth century and hint at the transformation that it would undergo as it rapidly grew into an international port of no small significance, and a site of identity construction. Although Jilong had been a port of call for merchants and fishers since at least the sixteenth century, a destination for Qing official missions since the late seventeenth century, and a focus of Western merchants and navies and Qing officials since the 1860s, it would require significant inputs in terms of population and capital to meet the needs of an expansionist imperial state like Meiji Japan. The Japanese colonial officials and settlers, given their ambitious agendas for developing their first formal colony and making it Japanese, would thus play a significant role in shaping both the physical and social terrain of Jilong over the next five decades and beyond.[3] Moreover, multiple generations of the island's non-Japanese residents would bear the stamp of Japanese influence, although the effects were not uniform across time, as a result of the shifting character of Japanese imperialism and the varied positions of age, status, gender, and social grouping from which the islanders met the Japanese. None of these developments was foreordained; rather, they were the contingent products of the everyday lived experiences within this and other locations.

2. The artist was not alone in this view of Taiwan: the Japanese government considered selling Taiwan to another colonial power soon after assuming control of the island.

3. As the work of David Howell on Hokkaido and Alan Christy on Okinawa suggest, the Meiji government enacted similar projects in those peripheral regions from the 1870s onward; thus Taiwan may not have been Japan's first colonial endeavor. See Howell, *Geographies of Identity*; Christy, "Making of Imperial Subjects."

In fact, the contributions made by the islanders to building Jilong and shaping their own identities cannot be underestimated, nor should the islanders be viewed as passive recipients of Japanese punishment or largesse, or blank slates onto which Japanese inscribed their vision. The colonial regime had numerous and varied mechanisms of observation and control that enabled it to reach much further into the lives of its subjects than had the Qing state before it, but its power was never absolute, for reasons of limited resources, the need to use islander elites to gain access to the broader islander population, and the undeniable agency asserted by Taiwan's residents. Similarly, although Japanese settlers held clear advantages in terms of economic opportunity, legal standing, and access to state power, they needed to gain the compliance or cooperation of islanders to achieve their goals. In practice, islanders rose to heights of social and economic status that matched and in many cases outstripped those of the supposed power-holding group, and most Japanese settlers had exactly the same political rights as the islanders—that is to say, neither group could vote in national elections, and local elections rarely took place. The attainment of roughly equivalent levels of economic wealth and the imposition of almost complete political disenfranchisement meant that a simple colonizer-colonized dichotomy did not automatically define the most salient lines of separation. Instead, residents of Taiwan drew imaginary borders as they decided which people, and which sets of institutions and cultural characteristics, were part of their in-group and were most important to defend against imposed transformation. In the process, a handful of islanders and Japanese residents achieved paramount status at the advent of Japanese rule and defined both the local Jilong identity and the contours of Taiwanese ethnicity. Although later generations of elites challenged the status of the first, and interacted across the Taiwanese-Japanese divide in different ways, their actions were largely interpolations on the framework established by their predecessors. After outlining the contexts in which Jilong was built and inhabited, I will also present the collective biography of its leading residents, along with an explanation of how they gained their status and the constituencies for which they performed their identities.

FIGURES 1.1 AND 1.2. Center (fig. 1.2, right) and left (fig. 1.1, above) panels of the triptych *Three Views of Taiwan: The Rain of Kiirun (Taiwan san kei no nai: Kiirun no ame)*, a woodblock print by Kiyochika (1896). Images obtained from the online collection of the National Diet Library, Tokyo.

Qing Taiwan and the Origins of Jilong

The northern and eastern coasts of the place that Portuguese mariners named the Beautiful Island (Ihla Formosa), which by the seventeenth century the Chinese were calling Taiwan and the Japanese, Takasago, are mountainous regions with few natural harbors.[4] The western coast has a thin band of fertile lowlands that widens in the southern half of the island, but even there a person is never far removed from the hills and peaks that dominate the terrain. Along the western shore are a number of bays and coves that face the turbulent waters that separate island from mainland and that served as small ports as legal and illegal trade developed between Taiwan and neighboring territories. In the north, one of the two largest harbors, that of Danshui (Tamsui), faces northwest toward what has long been China's Fujian Province, and another, that of Jilong, points northeast, toward what is now Okinawa in Japan (see map 1.1). The orientations of these two harbors hint that the two most important external sources of influence on Taiwan's history came from the societies, states, and cultures of China and Japan. Taiwan's history from the seventeenth to the twentieth century can be seen as an extended process of colonial territorialization, of attempting to make the island Chinese, then Japanese, then Chinese again.

In human terms, however, both the Chinese and the Japanese were latecomers. Although the precise origins of Taiwan's first inhabitants are not definitively known, nor are the pathways that brought them to the island certain, they fall under the broad rubric of the Austronesian linguistic group, whose members are spread throughout the Pacific

---

4. The definition of "Chinese" changed over time, with substantive shifts occurring in the Qing era and then again from 1895 to 1945. I use it as an aggregate term that, during the Qing period, contained divergent groups that engaged in frequent disputes with each other and may not have recognized themselves as part of a common category. Nevertheless, the term is useful for two purposes: one, to emphasize the identity shift of the group that became Taiwanese; and two, to highlight the connection between the people living in Qing territory and the Chinese of the modern nation-state that emerged in the twentieth century. For the pre-1945 period, I use "Han Chinese," "Han," and "Chinese" interchangeably, although sometimes I distinguish between "Hoklo/Minnanese" and "Hakka" to clarify tensions and complexities in Taiwan's society. For the post-1945 years, "Chinese" refers to the Nationalist regime and its adherents, and I interchange it with "mainlanders."

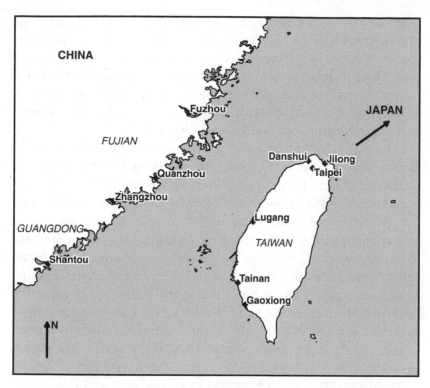

MAP 1.1. Taiwan and the southeast coast of China. Map made with shapefiles from naturalearthdata.com.

zone and most probably trace their origins to Taiwan. Living in villages that were differentiated by both language and custom, and that reportedly engaged in frequent violent conflict with one another, Taiwan's aborigines did not constitute a unified political, social, or identity community. The first humans recorded as inhabiting Jilong's vicinity belonged to a prominent group called the Ketagalan. Little is known about their settlement of the harbor area, or what they called it, but they may have indirectly given it its current name. The earliest visitors from the Chinese mainland spoke a dialect particular to the region of Fujian from whence they came, a spoken language commonly referred to as Hokkien, Hoklo, Minnan (after the name of the region), or more recently as "Taiwanese." These Fujianese visited the harbor to engage in initially unsanctioned trade for local products, chiefly sulfur and gold. Traders from China came so frequently, in fact, that after the Ming dynasty began to regulate the cross-strait trade, half of the official licenses it issued in 1593 were for trade with Jilong.[5] According to one story, these merchants took the last part of the indigenous residents' name, "-galan," and adapted the sound to their Fujianese dialect as "Gelang," which, when written in Chinese characters and given a Mandarin Chinese pronunciation, became "Jilong."[6]

During the seventeenth century, Europeans and Chinese set in motion Taiwan's prolonged history of colonization. The first colonies on the island were European, as the rivalry between the Dutch East India Company (Vereenigde Oost-Indische Compagnie, or VOC) and the Spanish crown brought the former to the area near present-day Tainan and the latter to Jilong during the 1620s. The Spanish presence was a chronological blip of less than twenty years, owing to the limited enthusiasm of Spanish colonial officials in Manila and an attack on the Spanish outpost by Dutch forces in 1642. For a brief period, however, the Spanish had a fort named San Salvador on the islet at the mouth of the harbor and a small settlement called Santisima Trinidad on the main island, and they engaged in extensive Catholic proselytizing among the aborigines in the area. A Dominican missionary named Jacinto Esquivel converted the inhabitants of two villages and established churches there.[7] The Dutch colony lasted for almost forty years and was most significant for the system of alliances that the VOC eventually forged with indigenous groups and the practice of "co-colonization," to borrow Tonio Andrade's term, through which they recruited Chinese from Fujian with promises of security, land rights, and licenses to trade with aborigines for deer products and other commodities.[8] A third wave of colonizers came in the form of the maritime trading empire of Zheng Chenggong, or Koxinga, who resisted the Manchu

5. Andrade, *How Taiwan Became Chinese*, 82. Ming officials issued ten licenses in all, five for Jilong and five for Danshui.

6. Kita and Kiirun shi kyōikukai, *Kiirun shi*, 1.

7. Andrade, *How Taiwan Became Chinese*, 87–92. See also Borao Mateo, *The Spanish Experience*, chap. 6, for a longer discussion of Spanish missionary efforts.

8. Andrade, *How Taiwan Became Chinese*. See also Wills, "Maritime Asia, 1500–1800."

conquest of Ming China and the powerful Qing armies longer than most of the Chinese opposition. Unable to hold out on the mainland any longer, he abandoned his base near Xiamen in Fujian, sailed across the Taiwan Strait, and drove the Dutch, his long-time trading partners, from southern Taiwan in 1662. The Dutch held onto Jilong until 1668, when Zheng's successors dealt them a final defeat.[9]

Despite the extensive maritime network that it controlled, the Zheng regime ultimately cracked in the face of concerted Qing military and economic pressure and surrendered, after about twenty years of prolonged conflict. Zheng Chenggong's grandson accepted an official title and left the island in the hands of Shi Lang, the former Zheng admiral who led the Qing attack. Emperor Kangxi and most of his court initially favored a plan to remove all Chinese settlers from Taiwan and return the island to Dutch control. Kangxi himself described Taiwan as a "ball of mud" and saw little benefit in establishing rule over it. However, Shi Lang fiercely advocated for retention, citing the potential danger of allowing foreigners or rebels to make use of the island as the Zhengs had, and insisting that Taiwan could serve as a defensive shield for the southeastern provinces.[10] Shi Lang's strategic reasoning convinced Kangxi; thus, in 1684 the Great Qing Empire officially incorporated Taiwan into its territory as a prefecture of Fujian Province. For the first time, Taiwan became a part of a continent-based state and its indigenous residents faced the possibility of becoming Chinese.

Over the next two centuries, the so-called island frontier was gradually transformed from an unknown region into a regular part of the Sinicized empire.[11] The three emperors who sat on the throne at the apogee of Qing power—Kangxi (r. 1661–1722), Yongzheng (r. 1723–35), and Qianlong (r. 1736–96)—devoted the bulk of imperial resources to

9. Cao and Blussé, *Around and about Formosa.*

10. Shi Lang referred to Taiwan as a protective "bamboo fence" (*fanli*), and argued that the aborigines could pose a threat if the dynasty did not pacify them. See Shepherd, *Statecraft and Political Economy,* 106–7.

11. The phrase "island frontier" is borrowed from the title of Knapp, *China's Island Frontier.*

the massive project of expansion into Central Asia, a series of conquests that fundamentally redefined China and created the territorial and conceptual basis of the multiethnic modern Chinese nation-state.[12] With most of its resources directed inland, the Qing court sought to contain the cost of managing its coastal defensive shield by minimizing potentially expensive conflicts between Chinese settlers and the indigenous people. It restricted the pace of Han settlement; dispatched troops and officials to control the settlers; drew boundaries between Chinese and indigenous zones to protect the latter from encroachment by the former; and upheld the land ownership rights of some indigenous peoples by forcing the Chinese to pay land-use rents. These policies did not prevent the eruption of violence between Chinese and indigenous groups, and proved even less effective in controlling conflicts among the Chinese settlers and forestalling antistate violence. However, they mostly contained settled Chinese society within a strip of territory running from Taiwan's lowlands in the south and southwest, along the western coast, and up to the northeastern tip of the island.[13]

These administrative efforts, along with practices of mapping and ethnological description, enhanced both the imagined boundaries between Chinese and indigenous inhabitants and the "Chineseness" of the coastal zone.[14] The Qing state clearly demarcated a boundary on its maps, which it expressed in physical space with stone markers placed amid the foothills, to indicate the limits of both Han settlement and effective Qing rule.[15] Jilong sat on the Chinese side of that line. Until the latter half of the nineteenth century, some Qing maps of Taiwan were drawn from a sea-level view and captured the western coast in impressive detail, whereas others offered only the vaguest sense of what

12. Perdue, *China Marches West*. For the long-term impact of the conquests, see especially chap. 14.

13. For the history of Qing administration of Taiwan, see Shepherd, *Statecraft and Political Economy*.

14. Laura Hostetler makes a similar argument regarding Qing continental territory, emphasizing that such trends were part of a temporal shift toward the early-modern era rather than a geographic shift toward Westernization. See Hostetler, *Qing Colonial Enterprise*.

15. Chang, "From Island Frontier."

lay beyond the Chinese-indigenous boundary.[16] During Kangxi's reign, Chinese literati created new categories of indigenous islanders—the plains and mountain aborigines—and expressed the distinction between them with the metaphor of "cooked" (*shufan*) versus "raw" (*shengfan*).[17] The educated Chinese who visited or resided in Taiwan used a range of cultural markers, including dress, language, and marital practices, to indicate the outward emanation of Chinese civilization into Taiwan. In their view, the "cooked" plains aborigines had absorbed some elements of Chinese culture and were partially civilized, whereas the "raw" mountain aborigines remained pure savages. The former lived within the frontier of Chinese territory, the latter beyond it.

As the physical boundary moved inland from the sea, so, too, were the imagined divisions between plains and mountain aborigines, or between Chinese and indigenous people, redrawn to demarcate new human and geographic terrain. The indigenous could become Han through intermarriage, usually between an indigenous woman and a Chinese man, or through the performance of cultural practices associated with Han society.[18] Chinese literati set the criteria according to which both people and territory became Sinicized. The travel writings and ethnographic imagery produced by Chinese elites redefined some indigenous people as primitive rather than savage, and thus made them civilizable. Elite Chinese discourses also made Taiwan more familiar and facilitated its full incorporation as Chinese territory. As both human and geographic terrain, Taiwan was transformed from a land beyond the seas (*haiwai*) into a part of the core (*neidi*) of China's "imagined geography." The culmination of this process came in 1875 with a new policy to "open the mountains, pacify the aborigines" (*kaishan fufan*), which aimed at the final Sinicization of all indigenous people

16. See the Qing dynasty maps contained in Teng, *Taiwan's Imagined Geography*, especially 91–92, 142, 146–47, and color plates 3 and 5.

17. Ibid., 125–27.

18. Shepherd, *Statecraft and Political Economy*, 386–88. Melissa Brown disputes Shepherd's statistics on intermarriage during the seventeenth century in highlighting what she refers to as the "short route to Han identity," through which supposedly large numbers of aborigines became Han in that period. Brown, *Is Taiwan Chinese?*, 144–149. Chinese men sometimes married into indigenous families, but that seems to have occurred more rarely.

save those few who were, allegedly, irreparably savage and had to be eradicated.[19] Post-1895 events indicated that this project did not achieve its stated goal, but the plan nevertheless represented a radical effort to territorialize all of Taiwan as Chinese.

During the two-hundred-plus years of Qing rule, the Sinicization of Jilong occurred very slowly through settlement, literary description, and trade. The demographics will be discussed later, but Yu Yonghe, the first Qing chronicler of Taiwan, introduced Jilong into literati discourse when he described the place and the origins of its name in his account of his 1697 journey across Taiwan in search of sulfur for the imperial armory.[20] The eighteenth-century Zhuluo County gazetteer noted Jilong's position on regional trade routes that extended as far as Japan, and it also repeated old rumors about what was called the "Jilong snowpack" (jixue), an unlikely feature given the climate at that near-tropical latitude.[21] A late-Qing gazetteer indicated that Jilong had "entered the map" (ru bantu) of China's imagined geography when it listed eight scenic spots (bajing) around the harbor.[22] Jilong's gradual rise in significance within the island's trade networks accompanied this growing familiarization. During the first two phases of Taiwan's Qing-era trade, expansion (1683–1780) and stabilization (1780–1860), Jilong served as the northern terminus of two trade networks: first, the central route (zhu xitong), focused on Luermen (near present-day Tainan), and then a north-central network based at the mouth of the Danshui River. Jilong acquired its own secondary trade network that extended around the northeastern tip of Taiwan, and before it became a treaty port it encompassed around seven hundred families.[23]

---

19. Teng, *Taiwan's Imagined Geography*, chaps. 4–6, 9.

20. Yu, *Small Sea Travel Diaries*, 94–95. Yu only sailed past the harbor and linked the name to the chicken cage–like shape of the hills.

21. Zhou and Chen, *Zhuluo xian zhi*, 18, 123. This gazetteer was written in 1717 and was one of the first published about Taiwan. The author retained some skepticism about the snowpack, which probably referred to volcanic ash or sulfur residue on Mount Jilong.

22. Chen Peigui, *Danshui tingzhi*, 2–4, 41.

23. For Jilong's place in the periodization of Taiwan's trade, see Lin Yuru, *Qingdai Taiwan*, 319–23, 181, 232–35, and 250–52. See also Dai, *Jindai Taiwan haiyun*.

The expansion of intra-Asian and global commerce from the mid-nineteenth century onward linked Jilong to international markets.[24] Commodore Matthew Perry recommended that the United States establish a settlement in Jilong, which he had learned was near rich deposits of coal, a prelude to colonizing Taiwan that led nowhere.[25] But the worldwide demand for camphor and tea from northern Taiwan brought increasing numbers of ships and merchants, principally British and Chinese, to Jilong and Danshui.[26] The global desire for Taiwan's products pushed these two ports to the core of a new central network for Taiwanese trade that extended from Lugang (Lukang) to the northeastern tip of the island.[27] The search for those commodities also led to further encroachment on indigenous territories, although the maps produced by Perry's mission showed that indigenous villages remained near Jilong at least into the 1850s.[28] Historical patterns of settlement and economic development differentiated northern from southern Taiwan in ways that made Chinese society in the north smaller and slightly weaker than in the south, but the north was still part of the cultural sphere of Southeast China.

Jilong's new status brought it some unwelcome attention that, in turn, linked it more closely to late-nineteenth-century modernization. In the midst of the Sino-French conflict over influence in Vietnam, French forces bombarded and then occupied Jilong for six months in 1884 and 1885 in an effort to force the Qing court to surrender.[29] This

24. Chinese merchants were central actors in the expansion of these networks. Hamashita, "Tribute and Treaties."

25. Perry sent two ships to Jilong after completing his mission to Japan in 1854 and recommended that the United States turn Jilong into "a port of general resort for vessels of all nations." Perry, Lilly, and Jones, *Narrative of the Expedition*, 173–82; quotation on 178.

26. Lin Man-houng, *Cha, tang, zhangnao*.

27. Lin Yuru, *Qingdai Taiwan*, 295–303.

28. Perry, Lilly, and Jones, *Narrative of the Expedition*. A report from Commander Jones contains a detailed map of Jilong that shows about six villages scattered around the harbor, some of which bear names—Perreang, Sendong, Sowwan—that are more likely aborigine than Chinese.

29. See Garnot, *L'expédition française de Formose*; Dodd, *Journal of a Blockaded Resident*; and Liu Mingchuan, *Liu Zhuangsu gong zouyi*, 168–69, 173–75. The French forces established a cemetery in Jilong that exists to this day.

threat to its southeastern perimeter prompted the Qing government to remove the island from Fujian's jurisdiction and establish it as a province in its own right, an act that took effect in 1887. The first governor, Liu Mingchuan, advocated for self-strengthening reforms and took office with a bold vision for making Taiwan a model of modernization. Aware of Jilong's sheltered harbor and proximity to valuable exports, he proposed the construction of modern port facilities, a telegraph system, and a rail line from the harbor to the new provincial capital of Taipei (Taibei) and then to the rest of the island. He also made a semantic change, using different characters for "Jilong" that were more appropriate to his vision of a modern port.[30] His plans brought an unexpected economic benefit when workers building the railroad discovered gold in the Jilong River just south of town, sparking a brief gold rush in the early 1890s.[31]

However, Liu's ambitions ultimately had a very limited impact on Jilong. The railway reached Taipei and trade expanded, but his successors did not share his vision or pursue the funds to complete his initiatives. Owing to environmental factors that limited the size of ships that could enter the harbor and prevented easy access to the camphor- and tea-producing regions, neither trade nor settlement expanded dramatically.[32] By the early 1890s foreign observers were very pessimistic about the productivity of the state-run and privately owned coal mines in the area.[33] Of the port on the eve of the Japanese takeover, an American observer proclaimed, "Kelung was dead! It might have dropped off the island completely without causing the least inconvenience to any one save the pitiably poverty-stricken natives who lived in their squalid huts in the tumble down village."[34] This extreme statement reflected, more than anything, the general Western opinion of Taiwan.[35] That view,

30. Speidel, "Administrative and Fiscal Reforms." Liu selected parts of a four-character phrase, *jidi longsheng*, that roughly translates as "basis of great flourishing."

31. Davidson, *The Island of Formosa*, 464–65.

32. Lin Yuru, *Qingdai Taiwan*, 298–99.

33. Inspector General of Customs, *Decennial Reports*, 440.

34. Davidson, *The Island of Formosa*, 251.

35. For example, W. A. Pickering, consul in Anping (Tainan) and later "protector" of Singapore, described his post as "filthy and loathsome." Quoted in Weng, *Gucheng, xindu*, 94.

however was not entirely off the mark for Jilong. Two centuries of Qing rule and Han settlement had made Jilong a Chinese place with at most a small remnant of its indigenous population, but it remained one of limited significance.

Building a Modern Colony and the Physical Construction of Jilong

Commodore Perry had failed to convince his government to colonize Taiwan, but Japan, the country that he is wrongly credited with opening, took that step four decades later. It was, of course, a very different Japan than the one with which Perry had signed a treaty in 1854 in the menacing presence of his so-called Black Ships. No longer a decentralized political order under the leadership of a military regime, with a rigidly hierarchical social system, Japan after the Meiji Restoration of 1867 had become a nominally social-egalitarian and centralized nation-state, established in the name of the Meiji emperor (1868–1912) but run by a coterie of oligarchs who worried over Japan's survival in a world of contending empires. Japan's national construction involved territorial expansion, and it moved north to incorporate all of Hokkaido and its Ainu residents, looked westward in the "invade-Korea debate" (*seiKan-ron*) of 1871 and the 1876 Treaty of Kanghwa, and turned south to the Ryukyu Kingdom, over which Satsuma domain had avowed suzerainty since 1609.[36] Taiwan proved instrumental to Japanese sovereignty over Ryukyu because, acting on the advice of Charles Le Gendre, the former U.S. consul general at Xiamen, in 1874 Japan launched an invasion of southeastern Taiwan on the pretext that indigenous people there had murdered Ryukyuan fishermen three years earlier. In a move that Robert Eskildsen has termed "mimetic imperialism," Japan justified its actions by arguing that if the Qing government would not directly control

---

36. This very brief account of the process through which Japan became a modern nation-state is based largely on Iriye, "Japan's Drive to Great-Power Status." It is informed by the extensive literature on the end of the Tokugawa order and the Meiji Restoration, including: Craig, *Chōshū in the Meiji Restoration*; Thomas Smith, *Native Sources*; Fujitani, *Splendid Monarchy*; Gluck, *Japan's Modern Myths*.

and civilize the aborigines, then Japan would bring them into the modern world.[37] Japan gained Qing acquiescence to its sovereign claims over Ryukyu—soon thereafter incorporated as Okinawa Prefecture—in exchange for what proved to be a temporary withdrawal from Taiwan. Two decades later, the escalating rivalry between China and Japan over influence in Korea, and East Asia more broadly, led to war in and around the Korean Peninsula. Japan's victories both on the battlefield and at the negotiating table produced the Treaty of Shimonoseki in April 1895, under the terms of which Japan gained Taiwan and the Penghu Islands as its first formal colony.[38]

Although the acquisition of these territories by treaty seemed straightforward, Japan's ascent into the ranks of the colonial powers required more than just the stroke of the brush. The islands joined the list of demands in part because the Japanese Navy, with an eye toward future expansion in the Southern Ocean (Nanyō, maritime Southeast Asia), attacked Penghu while negotiations at Shimonoseki were underway. Thereafter, claiming this prize required the application of considerable military force. In preparation for the official handover that occurred on June 2, on a ship offshore from Jilong, Japanese forces landed on the northeastern coast at Aodi at the end of May. Under the command of Prince Kitashirakawa no Miya Yoshihisa, they fought their way into Jilong against stiff resistance, subduing a much larger Chinese garrison to claim control of the town on June 3.[39] Two days later, Governor-General Kabayama Sukenori and Prince Kitashirakawa established the provisional office of the Taiwan Government-General

37. Eskildsen, "Of Civilization and Savages." For a complete record of Le Gendre's activities in Taiwan, with encyclopedic notes, see Le Gendre, *Notes of Travel in Formosa*.

38. One of Japan's negotiators, Foreign Minister Mutsu Munemitsu, left a revelatory record of Japan's diplomatic triumphs over the Qing envoys. See Mutsu, *Kenkenroku*.

39. The Japanese seizure of Jilong is recounted in Davidson, *The Island of Formosa*, 291–99; Kita and Kiirun shi kyōikukai, *Kiirun shi*, 13. Shortly before the handover, a group of former officials, military officers, and elites established the Republic of Taiwan under the leadership of Taiwan's last governor and first president, Tang Jingsong. This was a last ditch effort to gain foreign support to keep Taiwan out of Japan's hands, rather than any sort of proto-Taiwanese nationalism, and it failed after a little more than a week. See Lamley, "The 1895 Taiwan Republic."

(Taiwan sōtokufu) in what just days before had been the Chinese imperial customshouse. Jilong thus became Japanese territory.

However, as the prolonged processes of Qing incorporation and transformation had shown, conquering Taiwan, ruling it, and fundamentally making it part of the empire—that is, reterritorializing it as Japanese—were very different tasks, and Japan's empire builders approached them with some ambivalence. The Japanese regime asserted its possession and rule of Taiwan largely through the development of the colonial economy. From the outset, Japan aimed to make Taiwan financially self-sustaining so that it could provide the metropolitan economy with needed agricultural and mineral products without being a drain on the national treasury. The initial costs of suppressing resistance and building infrastructure were enormous, representing 7 percent of all national expenditures from 1895 through 1902 and leading to a public outcry to sell the island to another power or even back to China. However, the fourth governor-general, Kodama Gentarō, and his civil administrator, Gotō Shinpei, used a combination of aggressive land-tax reform, Government-General monopolies on a number of key commodities (opium, tobacco, alcohol, camphor, and salt), and a bond issue that gave metropolitan Japanese citizens a stake in the colony's success, to liberate the national treasury from financing Taiwan by 1905. Taking advantage of reforms that established private land ownership among the islanders, Japanese capital transformed Taiwan's sugar production into a major source of tax revenue and the dominant supplier for the Japanese market.[40] Moreover, although islanders did not benefit as much as did Japanese from these changes in Taiwan's economy, a local capitalist class emerged through the alliances land owners and entrepreneurs forged with the colonial state and Japanese settlers.[41]

Japanese officials and settlers were enthusiastic about profiting from the colony, but they were hesitant about making it more fundamentally Japanese. Meiji leaders carefully studied the British and

40. Ka, *Japanese Colonialism in Taiwan*, 50–57.

41. Gold, "Colonial Origins," 101–17; and Samuel Pao-san Ho, "Colonialism and Development: Korea, Taiwan, and Kwantung," in Myers and Peattie, *Japanese Colonial Empire*, 347–98.

French imperial models and implemented what they saw as an improved version of the French civilizing mission (*mission civilisatrice*), through which the non-Japanese peoples of the colonized lands would eventually become Japanese.[42] This vision framed Japan not as a colonial power but as a nation engaged in a process of national extension (*naichi enchō*) to new lands with which Japan shared certain cultural and even racial affinities. In contrast to this assimilationist objective, however, state policies set obstacles to the thorough Japanization of Taiwan.[43] Law 63, passed by the Japanese Diet in 1896 and in effect for most of the next forty-nine years, granted the governor-general authority to institute laws and regulations particular to Taiwan, which kept Taiwan at least partially outside of the legal structures of metropolitan Japan. Although much of Japanese law eventually arrived, it did so via a gradual process that accentuated the distance between metropole and colony.[44] Moreover, the Government-General did not establish local elected assemblies until the 1930s, well after they had become the norm in Japan, and no residents of Taiwan—whether Japanese, islander, or indigenous—had the right to vote in national elections or serve in the National Diet until 1945. These legal measures indicated that, although Taiwan occupied a position within Japan's physical territory, it did not become fully Japanese in administrative terms.

Nevertheless, the Government-General consciously aimed to make Taiwan a modern colony, with the same sorts of technologies, state practices, and internal linkages found in Japan and other imperial cores, a determination that facilitated processes of identity transformation. In particular, it emphasized a rigorous system for disciplining the islanders, developing islandwide transportation and communication networks, and applying the modern tools of census taking and mapmaking to classify the population and fix it in space. To establish

42. Takekoshi, *Japanese Rule in Formosa*, 25–34. For the French in West Africa, where reality only rarely lived up to the promise, see Conklin, *A Mission to Civilize*.

43. Robert Tierney also emphasizes the tensions between ideas of sameness and distinctions between civilized and savage within Japanese colonialism. See Tierney, *Tropics of Savagery*, 28–35.

44. Tay-sheng Wang, *Legal Reform in Taiwan*; Edward I-te Chen, "The Attempt to Integrate the Empire: Legal Perspectives," in Myers and Peattie, *Japanese Colonial Empire*, 240–74.

and maintain order—primary functions of all modern states—the Government-General installed a modern police force and military police (*kenpeitai*) to keep a close watch on the populace, and built new prisons for punishing bandits and criminals.[45] It also adapted a much older institution, the *hokō* or *baojia* mutual-responsibility system, to enlist the islanders in self-policing and facilitate mass mobilization.[46] The Government-General embarked on a major program of road and railroad building to improve intra-island communications. The center-piece of this project fulfilled Liu Mingchuan's vision of a trans-island railway from Jilong to Gaoxiong (or Dagou, as it was known until around 1915; in Japanese, it was always Takao) and opened for use in 1908 (fig. 1.3).[47] Whereas roads and railways improved mechanisms of transit and communication around the island, the establishment of numerous local newspapers, the islandwide *Taiwan Daily News* (*Taiwan nichinichi shinpō*), and a multitude of professional and literary journals facilitated the growth of discursive networks that linked people across Taiwan in ways that had not previously existed. As Benedict Anderson suggests in his work, the *Taiwan Daily*, topographic surveys that produced detailed maps of the island, and the censuses that categorized and counted the population collectively made possible the formulation of a modern Taiwanese consciousness that transcended local and clan identities.[48] Context did not create identities, but these new features of rule and methods for transmitting ideas facilitated the process of identity construction without predetermining its direction.

Jilong stood at the forefront of Japan's colonial modernization project. The first governor-general, Admiral Kabayama, stressed Jilong's centrality when he compared Taiwan's harbors to the human throat as the body's entrance and said, "The construction of this port, with dredging and building a breakwater, is something that must not be

45. Ching-chih Chen, "Police and Community Control Systems in the Empire," in Myers and Peattie, *Japanese Colonial Empire*, 213–19; Wicentowski, "Policing Health"; Botsman, *Punishment and Power*, 206–20.

46. Ts'ai, *Taiwan in Japan's Empire-Building*.

47. Cai Longbao, *Tuidong shidai de julun*.

48. Anderson, *Imagined Communities*, chaps. 2, 3, 10.

昭和十一年三月廿三日基隆要塞司令部御許可済   （臺灣基隆）基 隆 停 車 場

FIGURE 1.3. The Jilong train station in 1936. Image courtesy of the National Central Library, Taipei.

halted, for the sake of administering Taiwan."[49] To complete the pacification of anti-Japanese resistance and create the infrastructure for Taiwan's economic exploitation, the new rulers needed a point of entry into the island. Its geographic orientation toward Japan, proximity to the colonial capital of Taipei, and sheltered harbor, and the unsuitability of other locations, made Jilong the best choice.[50] Following a two-year survey, the Jilong port authority embarked on multiple phases of port construction that lasted into the 1940s; by the early 1930s, the project had given the harbor the precise, rectangular form that it has today. Two small islands were removed from the center of the harbor, and the whole area was dredged to an even depth to accommodate 10,000-ton ships; marshy areas were filled in and made suitable for habitation; and a canal running to the east, away from the bottom of the harbor, was widened and extended toward the coal and gold mines

49. This is from a lengthier statement made by Kabayama in 1896 that is replicated in Ishizaka, *Kiirun kō*, 83–85, quotation on 84.

50. The accumulation of silt deposits made the other likely port, Danshui, less suitable.

in the hinterland.[51] The original plan proposed by the Government-General's survey committee called for an investment of some ten million yen, but the Diet initially approved only about one-quarter of that amount and intermittently designated additional sums thereafter. External events created other priorities that consistently took precedence over full funding for the Jilong project, including the Russo-Japanese War, annexation of Korea, the need to develop Gaoxiong to support Japan's push into maritime Southeast Asia, and the Great Kantō Earthquake of 1923. Nevertheless, the physical contours of the harbor remain among the most lasting legacies of Japanese colonial rule (for a comparison, see maps 1.2 and 1.3).

Japan's empire building transformed Jilong from a subsidiary port in the Danshui-Jilong intra-island network into one of the largest and most vibrant cities in Taiwan. Within five years of the handover Jilong was handling the largest volume of trade, as Taiwan's commercial orientation shifted from the west (China) to the northeast (Japan), a position that Jilong held into the 1950s (fig. 1.4). Although it never became a global center of commerce on the order of Kobe, Shanghai, or Hong Kong, Jilong nevertheless became a frequent stop for ships on trade routes to and from the Japanese home islands, the Chinese mainland, Southeast Asia, and even North America and Europe. The number of vessels entering Jilong harbor rose from 318 in 1899 to 1,943 in 1931, and the total tonnage increased more than fortyfold, from 148,496 to 6,604,176.[52] The majority of this trade was between colony and metropole, but even so Jilong had substantive commercial ties to other parts of the world (fig. 1.5). The most important commodities sent out of the port were rice, sugar, and tea, whereas coal, bananas, camphor, and fishery products also made up a significant portion of its exports. The intra-imperial focus of Jilong trade, combined with some topographical limitations and its all-too-frequent rain, prevented Jilong from becoming a world-class port, but as a centerpiece of Japan's colonial project Jilong became a flagship in Taiwan's transformation.

51. Chen Yanru, "Zhongyuan pudu yu zhengshang," 30–36. See also Ishizaka, *Kiirun kō*, 85–87; Ōmi, *Kiirun kō annai* (1930), 7–10.
52. Fushiki, *Gureito Kiirun*, 44.

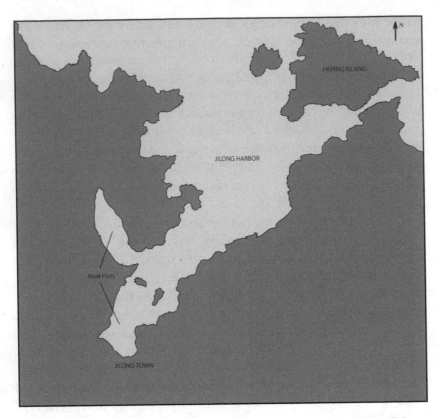

MAP 1.2. Jilong harbor, circa 1860. Map based on Admiralty Chart No. 2618, "China, North Coast of Formosa, Ke-lung Harbor, 1858," obtained from the digitized collection Formosa: Nineteenth Century Images, Reed College, https://rdc.reed.edu/c /formosa/home/.

Japanese planners worked on more than just the harbor in Jilong. Much like administrators in other colonies around the globe, Japanese colonial officials in Taiwan instituted major urban development programs to ensure Jilong would reflect their vision of a modern, civilized city.[53] Their designs for building Jilong paralleled the renovation of

53. For a comparison, see Mitchell, *Colonising Egypt*, which discusses the influence of French and British urban development plans on transforming Egypt; King, *Colonial Urban Development*, which explores the rise of colonial cities as bifurcated sites containing both an old indigenous city and a new city created by the colonizers; and Cooper, *France in Indochina*.

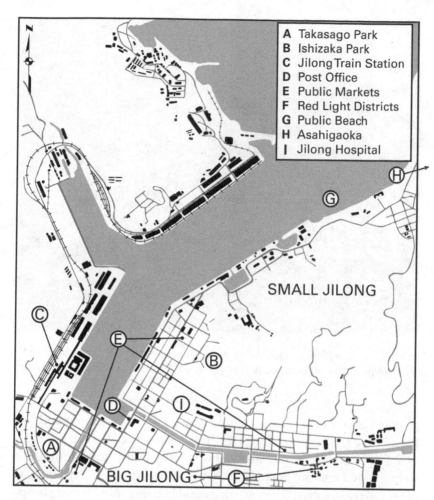

A Takasago Park
B Ishizaka Park
C Jilong Train Station
D Post Office
E Public Markets
F Red Light Districts
G Public Beach
H Asahigaoka
I Jilong Hospital

SMALL JILONG

BIG JILONG

MAP 1.3. Prewar Jilong. Map created by Scott Walker, based on a map designed by the U.S. Army Map Service, AMS L991, 1945, held in the Geography and Map Reading Room at the Library of Congress, Washington, DC.

metropolitan cities like Tokyo and Osaka, where central and local authorities negotiated a mixture of physical reconstruction and social reform as they created new urban environments.[54] In fact, the creation of urban spaces constituted both a central aspect and a long-standing

54. Hanes, *The City as Subject*; Sorensen, *The Making of Urban Japan*.

The Keelung Branch Office of the Osaka Shōsen Kaisha.   大阪商船會社基隆支店

FIGURE 1.4. The Jilong branch of the Osaka Shipping Company, a centerpiece of the city's port construction. Image courtesy of the National Taiwan Library, Taipei.

physical legacy of Japanese rule in Taiwan. Both Gaoxiong and Taizhong, like Jilong, were almost entirely creations of the Japanese era, and Taipei experienced consolidation as three distinct communities were merged into one metropolis.[55] Creating a modern city out of an older village involved building roads and housing; establishing hospitals and schools; installing plumbing and electrical systems; improving transportation and waterways; and building structures to house people, businesses, and official and private offices.[56] City planners also considered the livability of the built environment and designed several

55. For Gaoxiong, see Lin Shuguang, *Dagou suo tan*; Taylor, "History and the Built Environment." For Taizhong, see Chen Jingkuan, *Cong shengcheng dao Taizhong shi*. For Taipei, see Su, *Kanbujian yu kandejian de Taibei*; Allen, *Taipei*.

56. A brief summary of this urban development is found in Taihoku chō, *Taihoku chō shi* 2, 499–501; Chen Yanru, "Zhongyuan pudu yu zhengshang," 35.

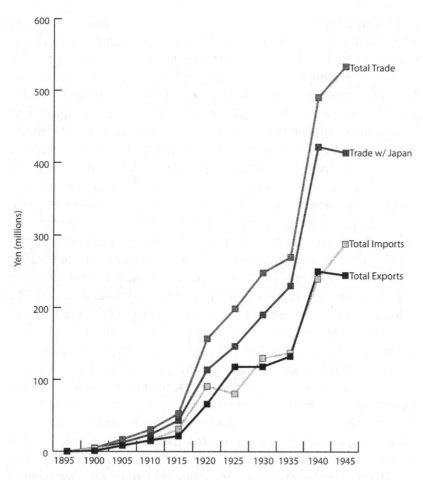

FIGURE 1.5. Jilong's import and export trade, 1897–1944. Data from Jilong shi wenxian weiyuanhui, *Shangye pian*, 86–90.

parks, including two in the hills overlooking the harbor from the east, and one on the south end of town called Takasago Park (Takasago kōen), which opened in 1900 to honor the marriage of the future Taishō emperor (r. 1912–26).[57] Green spaces, modern infrastructure, and medical and educational facilities were part of the urban design and

57. Ishizaka, *Kiirun kō*, 28. For the garden city movement in Japan, see Townsend, "Great War and Urban Crisis."

construction going on across Taiwan, and Jilong was on the leading edge.[58] All of these projects echoed the urbanization in Japan's other colonial cities, such as Seoul and Dalian.[59]

Incorporating Taiwan into the administrative structures of the Japanese empire required new, or at least renovated, systems of local governance that enlisted islander and settler elites in managing their communities. In 1896 the Government-General decreed that it would select one islander from each of the predominantly islander-inhabited city or town blocks to serve as the headman on a town council. The head of this council, also an islander, was placed at the intersection between the colonial state and islander society.[60] Establishing this intermediary set the stage for the systematic inclusion of islanders in a general framework for security and social control. Built out of a preexisting Chinese mechanism for taxation and security, the redesigned *hokō* system clustered islanders together in a multilayered hierarchy that the state used for both policing and policy implementation. The colonial regime also established ward committees (*chōnaikai*) and ward commissioners (*machiiin*) to organize and monitor the Japanese settler communities. The Government-General depended greatly on the cooperation of local residents, and particularly the elites who served as headmen and commissioners, for maintaining order and extracting profit from the colony. Ironically, the decision by the colonial government to rule Taiwan on the cheap helped establish local leaders as gatekeepers, a position that could be used both for and against state policies.

The regular bureaucracy and state power remained overwhelmingly in Japanese hands, especially at the upper levels. The hierarchical system, with the governor-general and head of the civil administration at the apex, spread downward through layers of diminishing power to the prefecture (*chō* or *shū*), subprefecture (*shichō*), county (*gun*), and

58. For schools in Gaoxiong, see Lin Shuguang, *Dagou suo tan*, 111–15; for general infrastructure and parks in Taizhong, see Chen Jingkuan, *Cong shengcheng dao Taizhongshi*, chap. 6; for the transformation of Tainan's existing roads and buildings, see Weng, *Gucheng, xindu*, 67–83; and for an excellent survey of Taipei's changing urban design, see Allen, *Taipei*, chap. 1.

59. Henry, *Assimilating Seoul*; O'Dwyer, *Significant Soil*.

60. TSTF, 23.4, Aug. 3, 1896.

city, town, or village (*shigaison*) levels.[61] Until around 1935 the governor-general appointed all state officials from a pool that included civil servants from the home islands and, increasingly, Japanese within Taiwan. After a major redistricting in 1920 to bring the administration of the colony more in line with that of the metropole, prefectural officials assumed some of the powers of general administration and, later, appointment.[62] Owing to repeated administrative reforms and urban growth, Jilong went through multiple classifications and resided within several jurisdictions. Originally a town (*gai*), as it grew it became a city (*shi*) in 1924 and was, successively, part of Jilong County, Jilong Prefecture, and Taibei Prefecture. Jilong's physical growth was substantial, but only in a relative sense, as it expanded from a tiny one-half square kilometer to about three square kilometers.[63] Through these types of structural changes, emerging colonial cities like Jilong, Gaoxiong, and Taizhong increasingly resembled Japanese cities, although they always stood at least slightly apart from the administrative institutions of the home islands, much as Taiwan itself was not fully incorporated as regular sovereign Japanese territory.

This tension between inclusion and exclusion in physical and administrative terms draws attention to the ambivalence of the urban development under Japanese colonial rule. In many ways, the narrative thus far foregrounds an apparent success story for the transformative objectives of Japanese colonialism, but it should not be taken as celebratory. Although the policies of the Government-General greatly resembled those outlined by Liu Mingchuan, the Japanese Empire after 1895 had much greater transformational capacity than the late Qing, in part because it had fewer constraints on its territorial sovereignty and economy. Thus it was the Japanese government, not the Sino-Manchu state, that created a port city with modern harbor facilities, railway connections, water treatment and electric power plants, and a number of buildings that, except for a few characteristic design elements, would have fit into any urban landscape of the early twentieth

61. The fact that Taiwan's prefectures had different names (*chō* or *shū*) than those on the home islands (*ken*) accentuated the separation between metropole and colony.
62. Huang Zhaotang, *Taiwan zongdufu*, chap. 5.
63. Chen Yanru, "Zhongyuan pudu yu zhengshang," 34.

century. However, that evident achievement concealed the limited extent of official Japanese influence. Although colonial planners designed
the physical milieu, islander-Taiwanese and Japanese residents of Jilong
created the everyday lived environment. Without their efforts and activities, Jilong could not have been built, nor its spaces used in identity
construction. Furthermore, the partial exclusion of Taiwan from the
legal and administrative structures of the Japanese nation-state complicated the process of imposing a Japanese national identity on the
islanders. By providing the institutional and intellectual contexts that
are known to produce nationalism, Japanese colonization created a
situation in which new identity formation was likely to occur. By deny-
ing the islanders full membership in the Japanese national community,
however, the Government-General left open the question of what sort
of identity, or identities, would emerge.[64] The answer(s) depended on
how islander and Japanese residents negotiated their positions in
Jilong's society, and its everyday environment, in relationship to each
other and the colonial state.

The People of Jilong

The history of how islanders became Taiwanese and remained so in the
face of an intense, albeit ambivalent, Japanization program revolves
around the people who shaped and defended that identity. Jilong's
population was less than 9,500 at the end of the nineteenth century,
although it went through a phase of considerable growth during the
treaty-port era, perhaps even tripling after 1850.[65] The Chinese town

64. What I describe here is essentially the condition of colonial modernity, in
which a colonized population actively participates in its own modernization but is
blocked by colonial power structures from the political participation that is inherent
to the ideal of modern nationalism. For an extended discussion of colonial
modernity in Japan's other main colony, Korea, see Robinson and Shin, *Colonial
Modernity in Korea.*

65. Jilong contained around 700 families in 1860, a figure that is roughly consistent
with the estimate of 3,000 inhabitants given by Commodore Perry's crew in 1854. See
George Jones, "Reports Made to Commodore Perry of a Visit to the Coal Regions of
the Island of Formosa," in Perry, Lilly, and Jones, *Narrative of the Expedition.*
Estimates for the population in 1895 run from a low of around 7,000 to a high of

consisted predominantly of migrants from the Zhangzhou region of Fujian Province, a feature that differentiated Jilong from many of Taiwan's Quanzhou-dominated settlements (see map 1.1). This distribution of native-place origins, which Jilong shared with nearby Yilan (Ilan), was characteristic of late-settled areas in northern Taiwan.[66] Indigenous groups lived around the harbor until the middle of the 1800s, but those sites are not evident on maps of the 1880s or 1890s.[67] Pre-1895 maps and written sources tell us very little about what happened to the inhabitants of those villages, but Japanese-era gazetteers report a small number of "cooked aborigines" in Jilong's hinterland as late as 1915, and a 1920 survey found 171 people of mixed indigenous and Han Chinese parentage.[68] The point is that the people who came under Japanese rule in 1895 either predominantly or entirely had lineage ties to southeastern China and, in many cases, relatively short histories in Taiwan. It was, therefore, a relatively young society.

Following the advent of Japanese rule, the economic opportunities promised by port construction brought a rapid influx of both Japanese and islanders to Jilong. The population expanded at a tremendous rate over the next fifty years, with particularly large growth in the first decades and then in a couple of bursts during the 1930s (fig. 1.6). There were about 15,000 residents in 1905, more than 50,000 in 1921, more than 70,000 in 1930, and the population had reached 100,000 by 1940.

---

around 9,500, and the local census of 1898 counted 8,360 people within Jilong's jurisdiction. See Jilong shi wenxian weiyuanhui, *Yange pian*; Jilong shi zhengfu minzhengju, *Hukou pian*, 89, 98.

66. Li Shinn-cherng, "Qingdai Yilan," 67.

67. Digitized French and British maps held in the collection Formosa: Nineteenth Century Images at Reed College do not indicate any indigenous settlements. See Formosa: Nineteenth Century Images, Reed Digital Collections, http://cdm.reed.edu /cdm4/formosa/, accessed June 28, 2015.

68. Taihoku chō, *Taihoku chō shi 2*, 114–15. The gazetteer notes ninety males and sixty-eight females in Jilong *bao*, an area that covered most of northeastern Taiwan. The 1915 census counted seventeen indigenous residents in the Jilong municipality, twelve male and five female; see Dainiji rinji Taiwan kokō chōsa (Second Special Taiwan Population Survey), in Renwen shehui kexue yanjiu zhongxin, "Ri zhi shiqi hukou diaocha ziliao ku." On the aboriginal population, see Chen, Ye, and Li, *Chongsu Taiwan Pingpuzu tuxiang*, 48. This information is from a report published by Kawai Takatoshi in *Taiwan Ethnology*, Mar. 1944.

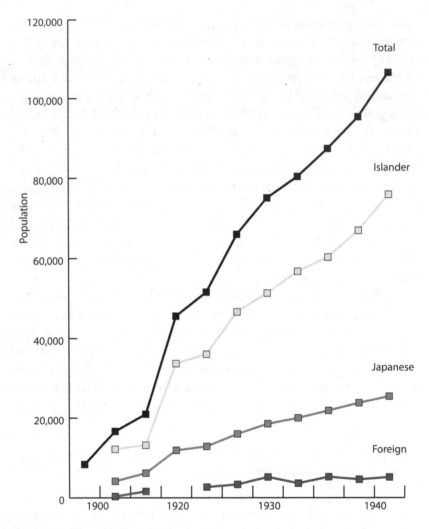

FIGURE 1.6. Population of Jilong, by origin, 1898–1941. Data sources: for 1898, Jilong shi zhengfu minzhengju, *Hukou pian*, 98; 1905–7, Kiirun chō, *Kiirun chō dai ichi*; 1905–31, Taiwan sōtokufu kanbō tōkei ka, *Taiwan genjū kokō*; 1932–41, Taihoku shū chiji kanbō bunsho ka, *Taihoku shū tōkei sho*, and Taihoku shū sōmu bu sōmu ka, *Taihoku shū tōkei sho*. The category of "Foreign" includes both Chinese and Koreans, with the latter never accounting for more than a few hundred people in any given year.

A huge increase between 1920 and 1921 resulted from urban redistricting that expanded the city and incorporated significant numbers of
new residents from the hinterland. Islanders were the dominant group
throughout these years, but Japanese represented 25 to 30 percent of
the total population, and Chinese (mostly) and Koreans made up a
small percentage (fig. 1.7). Males held a slight majority in comparison
to females in any given year, a sex division more characteristic of a
settled society than a migrant one. The proportion of men to women
was almost exactly the same among the islanders, whereas among the
Japanese in Jilong, males constituted a large majority at first, until an
influx of Japanese women after 1905 brought near equalization within
about a decade.[69] The categories that the colonial government used to
classify and track the population established the basic divisions for the
main social groups in Jilong and set the stage for future patterns of identity formation. Whereas indigenous groups had served as the "other"
for Chinese settlers in the Qing period, after 1895 Japanese colonials
became their new foil.

Jilong became one of the most populous cities in Taiwan, and it
had the second highest concentration of Japanese residents. Among the
five largest cities, Jilong ranked third by 1921, behind Taipei and Tainan,
the current and former capitals of the island, although it fell to fourth
in 1940, eclipsed by Gaoxiong's meteoric rise as the key port for Japan's
wartime southern advance.[70] Only Taipei had a consistently larger Japanese population, and as a fraction of the total urban population, Jilong
had a higher percentage in some years. Taizhong and Gaoxiong, both
of which shared Jilong's rapid expansion from small village to major
urban center, had demographic compositions similar to Jilong, although in Gaoxiong an influx of islanders during the war years swung

69. In most years, the aggregate percentage was 53:47 or 52:48, males to females.
Among islanders, except for the first two years of redistricting, neither sex amounted
to more than 51 percent of the population. Only the foreign population, mostly
mainland Chinese and Koreans, was vastly skewed towards males, who never made
up less than two-thirds of that group. Statistics taken from Taiwan sōtokufu kanbō
tōkei ka, *Taiwan genjū kokō*.

70. Barclay, *Colonial Development*, 116.

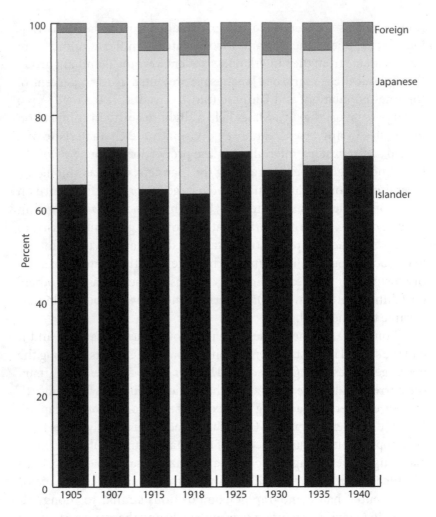

FIGURE 1.7. Composition of Jilong population, by origin, 1905–41. Data sources: for 1898, Jilong shi zhengfu minzhengju, *Hukou pian*, 98; 1905–7, Kiirun chō, *Kiirun chō dai ichi*; 1905–31, Taiwan sōtokufu kanbō tōkei ka, *Taiwan genjū kokō*; 1932–41, Taihoku shū chiji kanbō bunsho ka, *Taihoku shū tōkei sho*, and Taihoku shū sōmu bu sōmu ka, *Taihoku shū tōkei sho*. The "Foreign" category includes both Chinese and Koreans, with the latter never accounting for more than a few hundred people in any given year.

the balance more toward that side.[71] Alone among the major cities, Tainan had a very small Japanese population, a characteristic that it shared with most of the island, since Japanese settlers congregated in the larger cities.[72]

All of the five largest cities experienced substantial growth, with each one at least doubling in population between 1920 and 1940, even though the urbanized population did not grow as dramatically in Taiwan overall, rising from 12.69 percent to 17.25 percent of the total.[73] Thus, even though Taiwan retained a significant urban-rural divide in raw numbers, roughly one-sixth of the islander population experienced a common process of state-driven urbanization, especially during the 1920s and 1930s. More significantly, they encountered the colonial techniques of categorization and control, as well as the tensions between assimilation and exclusion, in analogous ways; thus we cannot take Jilong's experience as unique. The higher percentages of Japanese residents in Jilong, Taipei, and Gaoxiong meant that Japanese settlers were a more regular presence for islanders living in those cities than in Tainan, Taizhong, and nonurban environments. That was especially true of compact Jilong, which by 1930 had only one-tenth the area of Gaoxiong, encompassing both its urban core and some thinly populated suburbs.[74] Both urbanization and population growth supported

71. For a more detailed discussion of Gaoxiong's population, see Wen, "Gaoxiong diqu renkou."

72. Figure 1.7 shows that Japanese residents in Jilong peaked at 31.5 percent of the population in 1920 and remained at roughly 25 percent thereafter. In Taipei they consistently represented 28 to 29 percent of the population from 1915 onward; Taizhong and Gaoxiong matched Jilong in percentage if not numbers through at least 1930, although the Japanese population in both cities declined to below 20 percent in the following decade. See Barclay, Colonial Development, 119; Taihoku chō shomu ka, Taihoku chō daisan; Taihoku shū chiji kanbō bunsho ka, Taihoku shū tōkei sho.

73. In 1920, 463,758 people out of a total population of 3,655,308 lived in the nine largest cities (Taipei, Tainan, Jilong, Gaoxiong, Taizhong, Jiayi [Chia-i], Zhanghua [Chang-hua], Xinzhu [Hsin-chu], and Pingdong), and in 1940 those numbers had risen to 1,013,258 out of 5,872,084. See Barclay, Colonial Development, tables 2, 24.

74. Wu Wen-hsing, "Gaoxiong diqu shehui," 134. After incorporating new areas in 1924, Gaoxiong covered thirty-three square kilometers, in comparison to Jilong's three.

Japanese efforts to reterritorialize Taiwan, in turn making the cities prime locations for identity change.

The variations that existed in wages and types of employment during the Japanese period make it difficult to use categories of labor as clear markers for social groups or foundations for identity formation. Among skilled and unskilled workers in Taipei and Taizhong, both male and female Japanese workers consistently earned two to three times as much as their islander counterparts, with the gap narrowing for all types of labor only during the Pacific War.[75] Jilong had a similar wage gap early in the Japanese period, and Japanese settlers there occupied the vast majority of civil service positions and were overrepresented in both industry and fishing.[76] However, some sectors of the economy were relatively well integrated. For example, islanders worked in commerce and transportation at a level equivalent to their share of the population, and by the mid-1930s they held a similar proportion of positions in the medical, teaching, and business professions.[77] Wage differentials meant that, at an aggregate level, Japanese simply had more money than islanders, a fact that accentuated differences by linking wealth to national and ethnic categories. However, the nuances of

75. See Taiwan sheng xingzheng zhangguan gongshu, *Taiwan sheng wushiyi nian*, tables 301 and 302. These ratios are composites, based on the wages for a number of different types of labor, compiled in a major postwar statistical survey of the colonial period. The relative wages fluctuated depending on the year and field of work. The categories of workers included tailors, metalsmiths, dyers, carpenters and other types of construction workers, typesetters, day laborers, and domestic servants. Most laborers were paid relatively low wages for a day's work, ranging from .6 and .33 yuan a day in Taipei in 1905 for Japanese and islander day laborers, respectively, to 4.5 and 3.5 yuan a day, respectively, for masons in 1940. Only domestic servants (male: *nanpu*; female: *nübi*) made more substantial amounts, reaching a peacetime high daily wage of 20 and 16 yuan, for male Japanese and islanders, respectively, and 18 and 6 yuan, for females. For nondomestic labor, the statistical charts do not differentiate by sex.

76. "Kiirun rōdōsha no jōkyō," in *TKKH*, no. 32, May 1901. This is the only year for which I could find figures for Jilong, but the ratios match those for Taipei and Taizhong.

77. Taken from Taiwan sōtokufu kanbō rinji kokusei chōsa bu, *Dai ikkai Taiwan kokusei*; Taihoku shū chiji kanbō bunsho ka, *Taihoku shū tōkei sho*. These charts make it clear that far fewer women than men held any sort of employment.

economic activity show that some islanders had financial opportunities that matched or even outstripped those of Japanese settlers. Furthermore, because of the integration of certain professions, class cannot be directly tied to nationality or ethnicity, so we must look elsewhere for a more complex understanding of Taiwanese identities.

Patterns of residence in Jilong reflected both the fundamental separation on the basis of place of origin and greater integration in some occupations. The islanders congregated mostly in the southern and western parts of the city, around the older Chinese settlement, in an area that maps and written sources referred to as Big Jilong (Da Jilong). In contrast, Japanese settlers concentrated most heavily in districts east of the harbor and north of the canal, in what was called Small Jilong (Xiao Jilong). The spatial arrangement of the most important religious, commercial, and social institutions of the Japanese era roughly mirrored the distribution of settlement. This division concretized the representation of Jilong in the 1896 woodblock triptych *The Rain of Kiirun* (see figs. 1.1 and 1.2), which shows a relatively open space that might have been more easily Japanized even as it ignores the longer-established areas less receptive to Japanese penetration. However, these patterns were not thoroughly exclusionary for most of the downtown area, where either islanders or Japanese constituted more than 80 percent of the population in only a couple of neighborhoods.[78] In fact, partially integrated habitation, along with Jilong's confined geography, forced islanders and Japanese to interact with, or at least be aware of, each other on a daily basis. Overall, the city's residents mapped Taiwanese and Japanese identities onto physical spaces that were roughly contiguous with the districts of Big and Small Jilong (figs. 1.8 and 1.9). However, the bridges that spanned the canal separating those two areas also served as physical metaphors for the elites who defined and monitored the borders of multiple identities.

The imposition of Japanese rule in Jilong and other cities stimulated the creation of an elite social stratum that included new arrivals

78. Cheng-siang Chen, *Port City of Keelung*, 20–21. The maps here show population distribution in 1940, but the patterns were likely similar, or even more segregated, in earlier times.

（新原雜誌店發行）　　基　隆　新　店　街　（基隆要塞司令部許可濟）
SHINTANAGAI STREET, KIIRUN.

FIGURE 1.8. Shintanagai (Ch., Xindian) Street in the islander district of Big Jilong, between 1907 and 1918. Image courtesy of Special Collections and College Archives, Skillman Library, Lafayette College, and the East Asia Image Collection, http://dig ital.lafayette.edu/collections/eastasia/.

from Japan, members of the Qing-era literati class, and islanders who rose to prominence through channels opened by the colonial context.[79] This elite group defies easy characterization because its members engaged in a wide range of activities and performed a tremendous array of functions. Although many members had strong ties to the colonial regime that to an extent created their class, they also held prominence because of their business enterprises, leadership of religious institutions, or engagement in social welfare enterprises. Thus they cannot be described as simply a political elite, a business elite, or a religious elite. Instead, they functioned primarily as a positional elite, a group distinguished by the roles its members played in mediating between colonial regime and colonial subjects, and between different social groups. To

79. Several works have looked at the transformation of islander elites in Taiwan during the colonial period, including: Wu Wen-hsing, *Ri zhi shiqi*; Lo, *Doctors within Borders*; Lamley, "The Taiwan Literati and Early Japanese Rule."

FIGURE 1.9. Gijū (Ch., Yizhong) Street in the heart of the Japanese district of Small Jilong, undated. Image courtesy of the National Central Library, Taipei.

maintain their status and assert influence in multiple directions, they had to appeal to varied constituencies, including the Government-General and its agents, other members of elite society, and the larger groups of islanders or Japanese. The individuals who sat at the center and top of Jilong society included, among islanders, the brothers Yan Yunnian (1874–1923; fig. 1.10) and Yan Guonian (1886–1937; fig. 1.11), leaders of the mining industry, business sector, and a number of social welfare projects; and Xu Zisang (1874–1945; fig. 1.12), an important figure in local governance, religion, and business. On the Japanese side, the three most notable figures were the multitalented Ishizaka Sōsaku (1870–1940; fig. 1.13), the mining and construction magnate Kimura Kutarō (1867–1936; fig. 1.14), and a businessman named Ōmi Tokigorō (1871–?; fig. 1.15). No other individuals were as central to Jilong's twentieth-century history as these six men, and their collective biography in many ways provided the basis for the physical and imagined construction of Jilong and the emergence of Taiwanese consciousness.

像肖人主園附

FIGURE 1.10. Yan Yunnian. Image courtesy of the National Taiwan Library, Taipei.

許梓桑君

FIGURE 1.12. Xu Zisang. Image courtesy of the National Taiwan Library, Taipei.

顏國年君

FIGURE 1.11. Yan Guonian. Image courtesy of the National Taiwan Library, Taipei.

FIGURE 1.14. Kimura Kutarō. Image courtesy of the National Taiwan Library, Taipei.

FIGURE 1.13. Ishizaka Sōsaku. Image courtesy of National Taiwan University Library, Taipei.

FIGURE 1.15. Ōmi Tokigorō. Image courtesy of the National Taiwan Library, Taipei.

As men who belonged to the first generation of Taiwan's modern colonial elite, they embodied particular experiences and perspectives that had a discernible impact on the identities that they helped create. Common experiences shape a historical generation, but only if the moments of change are disruptive enough to create substantially new contexts, and if the people who confront those ruptures are both old enough and malleable enough to notice and adapt to them. Chou Wan-yao, in an assessment of Taiwan at the end of the Japanese era, cites three generations of intellectuals: the "grandparents," who were already established in the Qing system before 1895; the post–Sino-Japanese War generation, which was fundamentally shaped by the transfer of sovereignty and the early decades of Japanese rule; and the wartime generation that came of age in the 1930s and '40s but was deprived of a role in the postwar period.[80] Although these six men varied somewhat in age and experience in 1895, they all fit into the middle generation because they were not dependent on the power structures of Qing Taiwan and thus could take advantage of the spaces created in the new order. Their adaptability in the face of dramatic change promoted the formation of new identities that had a degree of flexibility when confronted with subsequent contextual shifts. The absence of a significant disjuncture during the 1910s and 1920s meant that even as new individuals rose to prominence in Jilong during the 1930s, they remained part of a chronologically expansive middle generation in their outlook. Moreover, historic similarities between the post-1895 and post-1945 periods facilitated the inheritance—contextually rather than genetically—by the wartime generation of key features of middle-generation identity. Therefore, the actions of these men, and the larger elite stratum that they represented, had a long-term impact on identity formation in Taiwan.

Their individual biographies up to 1895 reflect trends and fluctuations in nineteenth-century China and Japan, as well as the different rates of change in the two countries. Xu Zisang, the only one who lived in Jilong at the time of the Japanese takeover, came from a family that had moved there several generations earlier as the Chinese settlers

80. Chou, *Hai hang xi de niandai*, 1–11.

spread into the north.[81] The Yan brothers were in the first generation of their family born in Taiwan and grew up to the east of Jilong where their grandfather and father had settled in the 1860s, drawn by the opportunities for mining and selling coal that resulted from Jilong's opening as a treaty port.[82] All three received a classical Chinese education at family schools and private academies (*shufang*)—Xu and Yan Yunnian were classmates at one of the latter—and Yunnian failed the official examinations in Fujian in 1894.[83] Ishizaka Sōsaku grew up north of Tokyo, where he was educated in the Chinese classics, engineering, and English. He then joined the Imperial Guard (Konoe hei) on its missions to Korea and Manchuria during the war with China.[84] Kimura Kutarō hoped to join Japan's modern army or navy, but when he did not meet the entrance requirements he went abroad on a foreign merchant ship before returning to Osaka, where he worked with a land development company engaged in that city's massive urbanization project.[85] Ōmi Tokigorō received a middle school education and spent a few years as an elementary school teacher.[86] He left teaching for mining and soon took charge of mines in his native Akita Prefecture, in the north, and Shimane Prefecture, in the south, before moving to Osaka to work for the mining division of an industrial conglomerate, the Fujita Group (Fujita gumi).[87] In short, the new alternatives in education, overseas

81. "Jilong Ke Xu liangjia fenjiu zhi zhenxiang," *NS*, July 15, 1932, 17. Xu Zisang was adopted into his immediate family shortly after his birth, likely an example of the common practice among Chinese families in which older or better-off members of an extended family network adopted the sons of younger or poorer members.

82. Sima, *Taiwan wuda jiazu*, 16.

83. For Xu, see TSTF, 6887.3, Jan. 1, 1920. For Yunnian, see Tang, *Jilong Yanjia*, 127, 335. For Guonian, see NKKS, 1-2A-017-00 jo-01368-100, 1937.

84. Hara machi shi hensan iinkai, *Hara machi shi*.

85. Ōzono, *Taiwan jinbutsu shi*, 200–201. Another source mentions that he was deemed too short for the navy; see Nomura, *Kimura Kutarō ō*, 8.

86. Tokyo denpō tsūshinsha, *Senji taisei shita*, 272. I viewed this source in August 2005 through a database of digitized biographies, the *Taiwan renwu zhi ziliaoku* 臺灣人物誌資料庫 or *Taiwan Who's Who Database*, tww.ith.sinica.edu.tw/login _whoswho.htm, compiled by researchers at Academia Sinica, Taipei, Taiwan, from Japanese-era biographical compendia. The database is accessible only from within Academia Sinica.

87. Taiwan shinminpōsha chōsa bu, *Taiwan jinshi kan*, 70; Niitaka shinpō sha, *Taiwan shinshi*, 91.

experience, and occupation that characterized late-nineteenth-century East Asia established a more cosmopolitan context that placed identities in flux for islanders and Japanese prior to 1895.

Similarly, the colonial setting determined their presence or prominence in Jilong after the cession to Japan. Ishizaka followed the imperial forces to Taiwan to help suppress resistance in the south and then stayed on when he obtained a position as a reporter with the *Taiwan Daily News* in Jilong. Soon thereafter, the Government-General made him the local agent for the state's monopolies on sales of tobacco, nonmilitary explosives, and surveying equipment, and in 1904 it tapped him to assist with the land tax survey.[88] Xu Zisang also benefited from the early attention of the colonial government, which built ties with islander elites by awarding the status of "Taiwan gentry" (*Taiwan shinshi*) to individuals who had a classical education. In 1903, the Government-General bestowed this status on Xu and appointed him the Jilong district chief (*kuchō*), a position he held for the next thirty years.[89] Kimura and Ōmi both left Japan to take advantage of the opportunities for mining in Jilong's hinterland, arriving in 1896 just before the state began issuing new licenses for opening mines.[90] After working with the colonial police force in his hometown, Yan Yunnian moved to Jilong, where he soon got involved in the mining industry as well.[91] His younger brother joined him in Jilong, and in business, not long after, and the Yan brothers became the most famous individuals ever to call the port city home.[92] Over the next few decades, these four men expanded their mining operations across Taiwan, founding numerous companies in cooperation with each other and with many other

---

88. Hara machi shi hensan iinkai, *Hara machi shi*.

89. Taiwan sōtokufu, *Taiwan lieshen zhuan*, introduction, 2–3. Xu's entry, on 26–27, indicates that he was the youngest person in Jilong to receive this honor.

90. For Kimura, see Maeno, *Yonjūnen no Taiwan*, 155–57. Kimura first came to Taiwan with his elder brother, a friend, and a number of Japanese laborers, but dysentery killed his brother and most of the other workers, and he returned to Japan after three months. His second trip to Taiwan, in 1897, proved much more successful.

91. "Gan shi no meiyo," *TNS*, Feb. 10, 1923, 121–23.

92. A number of books have already been written about the Yan family, including Tang, *Jilong Yanjia*; Tang, *Luguo Jilong*; Chen Tsu-yu, *Taiwan kuangye shi*; Sima, *Taiwan wuda jiazu*. Yan Yunnian is profiled in Gold, "Colonial Origins," 111–12.

坑 二 第 鑛 炭 港 蓼 田

FIGURE 1.16. One of the coal mines owned by Kimura Kutarō, in the Denryōkō area east of Jilong. Image courtesy of the National Taiwan Library, Taipei.

Japanese and islanders (figs. 1.16, 1.17). As a result at least two of them gained considerable notoriety: Kimura became known as the Mine King (Kōyama ō) and Yunnian as the Coal King (Tankō ō) of Taiwan.[93] Furthermore, to facilitate their operations and to promote transportation in the northeast of Taiwan, Kimura and the Yan brothers founded

93. For Kimura's extensive mining operations and some of Ōmi's activities, see Irie, *Kiirun fūdo*, 130–32; Ōzono, *Taiwan jinbutsu*, 201. Kimura used his profits from Taiwan to start mining operations in the Japanese home islands and in Korea, and to found a regional enterprise called the Pacific Coal Mining Company (Taiheiyō tankō kabushiki kaisha). See Nomura, *Kimura Kutarō ō*, 13–15. This company continues to operate today; for its genealogy, see Taiheiyō kōhatsu, 太平洋興発 (Pacific Corporation), www.taiheiyo.net/guide/index.html, accessed Mar. 4, 2012. For Yan Yunnian, see "Kōtei no matsuei? Gan Unnen," *NS*, Mar. 24, 1932, 3; and Irie, *Kiirun fūdo*, 124–29; for Guonian, see NKKS, 1-2A-017-00 *jo*-01368-100. After his older brother's death, Guonian established two entirely islander-owned companies, Taiwan Sun Mining (Tai yang kuangye zhushi huishe) and the Jilong Coal Mining Corporations (Jilong tankuang zhushi huishe).

坑 一 第 礦 炭 年 久

FIGURE 1.17. One of Yan Yunnian's coal mines, probably jointly owned with Kimura Kutarō as the original caption calls it the Ku-Nian Mine. Image courtesy of the National Taiwan Library, Taipei.

the Jilong Light Rail Corporation (Jilong qingtie zhushi huishe), for which Ōmi was a member of the board.[94] Through direct connections to the colonial state and their early leadership in economic activities highly valued by Japanese authorities, they established themselves in the top tier of Jilong's society.

The Government-General was not the sole arbiter of elite status, for islanders like the Yan brothers also built and enhanced their status themselves by extending business networks among Taiwan's emergent capitalists.[95] In the economic arena, they had particularly strong

94. Niitaka shinpō sha, *Taiwan shinshi*, 91; NKKS, 1-2A-017-00 *jo*-01368-100; Yan Chuangyin, *Sōgyō nijūnen shi*.

95. Thomas Gold has done substantial research on the growth of capitalism in Japanese-era Taiwan, some of which has appeared in his published work, including his essay "Colonial Origins," and in Gold, *State and Society*. I am grateful to him for sharing his extensive unpublished notes on islander businessmen and their numerous companies.

connections in northern Taiwan, home of the majority of the large coal-mining companies.[96] Yunnian and Guonian held prominent positions in the Taiwan Mining Association (Taiwan kōgyōkai), a network of islander and Japanese leaders in the industry, founded during the 1910s.[97] Islanders from all over Taiwan sat on the boards of their mining companies, and Guonian also served as a board member for numerous companies that operated outside of Jilong, including companies in the sugar and banking sectors.[98] The Yan brothers further strengthened their business relationships through dense networks of marriage, by marrying their sons and daughters to the children of other prominent islander capitalists.[99] Jilong's prominent islanders also placed themselves firmly within a larger community through frequent contacts with their peers in other cities, highlighting the fact that, even when they pursued their own interests and promoted their city, they were connected to a broader web of like-minded individuals.

However, these men were not simply business elites, for their status in Jilong society and with the colonial government also depended on the time and resources that they devoted to social construction. All six men made significant financial contributions to building or renovating important temples and shrines. Xu Zisang became manager of the Qing'an Temple (Qing'an gong), one of the most important religious sites for Jilong's islanders, in 1903, and Ishizaka Sōsaku served for a decade as the head of the Jilong Shrine Parishioners Representatives (Kiirun jinja ujiko sōdai). They all also supported educational opportunities in Jilong. Yan Guonian made numerous donations for building

---

96. Chen Tsu-yu, *Taiwan kuangye shi*, 56–57. Of the seventeen companies capitalized at more than one million yen, only one was located south of Xinzhu (Hsin-chu), in Taizhong.

97. For more on the Taiwan Mining Association, see Tang and Taiwan kuangye-hui zhi xiuzhi weiyuanhui, *Taiwan kuangyehui*. Tang edited this compilation of the association's original journal in conjunction with the Taiwan Mining Association Gazette Revision Committee (Taiwan kuangyehui zhi xiuzhi weiyuanhui). He kindly shared some of his research materials on the Yan family with me at an early stage in this project.

98. See NKKS, 1-2A-017-00 jo-01368-100; and Taiwan shinminpōsha chōsa bu, *Taiwan jinshi kan*, 31.

99. Chen Tsu-yu, "Ri zhi shiqi Yanjia de chanye" and "Hunyin yu jiazu shili."

or renovating schools.[100] Ishizaka founded two of the most well
known private institutions in Japanese-era Taiwan, the Jilong Night
School (Shiritsu Kiirun yagakkō), in 1903, and the Ishizaka Library
(Ishizaka bunko), in 1909.[101] Both the school and the library went
through several name and administrative changes, but they endured
in some form throughout Japanese rule and beyond.[102] For these and
other projects, city residents and officials named one of the city's parks
in Ishizaka's honor.

Finally, these six men also developed lateral ties with other members of Taiwan's elite and vertical ties with both the government and
the larger islander community by joining public assemblies and providing for social welfare. When the Government-General established
municipal, prefectural, and islandwide consultative councils during
the 1920s and 1930s, several of them served as delegates. Similarly, when
the colonial state introduced to Taiwan a system of local welfare commissioners (hōmen iin) in the early 1920s as part of an empirewide
expansion of social support and control, it appointed Yan Guonian, Xu
Zisang, and Ishizaka Sōsaku to lead the way in Jilong.[103] Even before
that, in the wake of a destructive typhoon in 1919 Yan Yunnian joined
with his business associates from the Taipei region, Gu Xianrong and
Lin Taizheng, to found an organization called the Jilong Fraternity
Group (Jilong bo'aituan), which became one of the most well-known
welfare institutions in Taiwan after it built a large settlement house
south of downtown Jilong.[104] These examples, which do not constitute
an exhaustive list, illustrate the fact that Jilong's elite residents, much
like elites in other parts of Taiwan, maintained their positions—and
their interests—by serving both the colonial state and society at large.

100. NKKS, 1-2A-017-00 jo-01368-100. According to this source, Yan made fifty-
five large and small donations between 1923 and 1937.

101. On the Jilong Night School, see TSTF, 5393.31, June 1, 1911. 1. See also Ujigo,
Ishizaka Sōsaku to "Kiirun yagakkō." On the Ishizaka Library, see Ōzono, Taiwan
jinbutsu, 27–29. See also Chen Qingsong, "Ri zhi shiqi de wenshi guibao."

102. The Jilong Night School was still open under a different name in 1945, at which
time the principal was Yan Qinxian, eldest son of Yan Yunnian.

103. The translation of the term hōmen iin is borrowed from Ambaras, "Social
Knowledge."

104. Irie, Kiirun fūdo, 180–86. See also Nagahama, Gan Kokunen kun, 47.

The Yan brothers, Xu, Ishizaka, Kimura, and Ōmi promoted and underwrote much of the city's development, and their multifarious activities received notice across the island. The *Taiwan Daily* frequently chronicled their commercial enterprises, welfare projects, and religious activities, ensuring that events in Jilong and the acts of its leading residents became interwoven with similar projects and developments in other cities and towns, in the minds of the Japanese and islanders who read the paper. Their deaths, too, became events of considerable note. Yan Yunnian departed the scene first, when he died of a sudden illness in February 1923. In recognition of his stature, he received nearly one hundred notes of commemoration from such eminent individuals as Gotō Shinpei and the first civilian governor-general, Den Kenjirō.[105] Kimura Kutarō passed away in 1936, and even though he had divided his time between Jilong and Tokyo since 1917 and had sold his Jilong estate to Yan Guonian to raise capital for new enterprises in Korea and Manchuria, local residents held a large memorial service in his honor.[106] Yan Guonian died in the spring of 1937 and, according to the report in the *Taiwan Daily News*, some 2,500 guests attended his memorial service, including five members of the Government-General. Jilong's business elites selected Ōmi Tokigorō to pay their respects.[107] Ishizaka Sōsaku died early in 1940, and even though it was wartime, he received a prominent obituary in the newspaper for which he had once worked, and tombs in his honor were built in both Jilong and his hometown in Gunma Prefecture.[108] In death as well as in life, these core elites served as focal points for Jilong's evolving society and economy, and as acknowledged leaders in the construction of Taiwan.

In a colonial context, native elites who have such wide and deep connections to the colonizing regime and its settlers can be easily dismissed as collaborators who sell out their own people for personal gain.

---

105. Tomoseikai, *Gan Unnen ō*. See the section on eulogies, beginning at 143.

106. "Kiirun kensetsu no dai onjin Kimura Kutarō shi haru chōshiki," *NS*, Oct. 31, 1936, 4.

107. "Ko Gan Kokunen no ogosoka na kokubetsushiki," *TNS*, May 10, 1937, 7. The article described the service as the grandest event in the city's history.

108. "Ishizaka Sōsaku shi seikyo," *TNS*, Jan. 20, 1940, 2. I have not seen these tombs but have spoken with someone who has, Ujigo Tsuyoshi, who is the author of two works on Ishizaka cited herein that he kindly shared with me.

Some of the Japanese-era islander elites were indeed criticized for their close ties with the colonial regime, both at the time and subsequently by the Nationalists in their campaign against *Hanjian* (Chinese traitors). However, the concept of collaboration is highly complicated by the realities of living under occupation, as scholars such as Rana Mitter and Timothy Brook have already demonstrated, respectively, for Manchuria between 1931 and 1937 and the Yangzi delta in 1937–38.[109] The intensity of Chinese nationalism varied widely according to place and class in these settings, as did the spectrum of interactions ranging between resistance and collaboration. Similarly, the vast majority of the population that remained in Taiwan after 1895 subsequently worked within the legal parameters set by the colonial regime and with that Japanese state and its agents. In a milieu of overwhelming cooperation, how is a historian to parse collaborator from noncollaborator? A second issue is the concept of one's "own people," a category that presumes the preexistence of a strong group consciousness. Although there was strong evidence of the localization of southeastern Chinese in Taiwan by 1895, and of an elite stratum that identified with China in the form of the Qing state, proof of universal identification with China or of unity within Taiwan's Qing society does not exist. As I will demonstrate, an identity with the force of "our people" came into existence only in the decades after 1895, and it was not primarily rejectionist vis-à-vis Japan. Finally, the term "collaboration" has become so heavily laden with the ex post facto assessments of particular historical contexts—Wang Jingwei's Nanjing regime or Nazi-occupied France, for example—that it lacks utility for assessing the complexity of relationships within Japanese-era Taiwan.[110]

Instead of viewing these elite islanders as one-dimensional puppets of the Japanese, they can be more fruitfully viewed as complex individuals who, like thousands of others similar to them around Taiwan, navigated the imagined terrain between the colonial regime that affirmed their status and the social groups from which they emerged,

109. Mitter, *The Manchurian Myth*; Brook, *Collaboration*.

110. Both Mitter and Brook retain the term "collaboration," as does Keith Schoppa in his excellent, succinct discussion of the complexities of collaboration in wartime China; see Schoppa, "Patterns and Dynamics."

unable or unwilling to alienate themselves from either side. In their interactions with elite Japanese and the Government-General, they performed functions that made their presence essential to both: mediating between mining companies and miners, obtaining local knowledge necessary to open new fields of business, gaining access to commercial networks across East Asia, occupying positions of local governance and control, and providing welfare when the economizing state required it.[111] The elite stratum in Gaoxiong, made up of both islanders and Japanese, was almost identical to the one in Jilong in terms of how its members gained and maintained their positions.[112] The islander community, divided though it was between elites and non-elites, and subdivided again within each category, represented an important constituency to which both the colonial regime and local elites sought access. Men like Xu and the Yan brothers bound themselves to other islanders by establishing companies and banks with broad-based management, by renovating temples and underwriting annual festivals, and by aiding those in need. Included as members of the colonial elite but excluded from ever being Japanese, these individuals played the most significant roles in delineating one identity group from another.

Conclusion

The expansion of empires, and the arrival of subsequent waves of colonizing settlers, fundamentally shaped the history of Taiwan and defined Jilong's place within, and contribution to, that larger narrative. Before this time, indigenous communities dotted the island with a wide range of linguistic and cultural variety, and a reportedly high frequency of conflict. The Dutch and the Spanish colonial outposts, and the Chinese who settled alongside and then replaced them, set in

111. On trade networks in particular, see Lin Man-houng, "Taiwanese Merchants."
112. Wu Wen-hsing, "Ri ju shiqi Gaoxiong." In Gaoxiong, there was a greater overlap between Qing elites and colonial elites, and in both places pre-1895 elite status was closely connected to the commercial opportunities of the treaty-port era. In both ports, those who became elites at the outset, both islanders and Japanese, retained their status and influence through most of the Japanese era, in some cases through a second generation of offspring.

motion a centuries-long process of foreign settlement and destruction of indigenous societies, for which there has been, as yet, no reckoning. The Chinese, through extended processes of territorial expansion and description by officials and literati, gradually incorporated all of Taiwan within Qing sovereignty and included Jilong in the creation of a Chinese Taiwan. The incremental northward shift of Taiwan's political and economic centers of gravity made Jilong an increasingly significant port, and Governor Liu Mingchuan gave it a key role in his plans for self-strengthening and modernization, yet the settlement remained small and the harbor was usable only by junks and other small vessels. With the shift in sovereignty in 1895, Chinese territorialization gave way to Japanese reterritorialization, a project pursued through the creation of new administrative, educational, and economic structures, as well as through interactions between settlers and islanders. Rule by a modern nation-state, with all of its mechanisms of control and classification, brought a combination of urbanization, capitalist economic accumulation, and social categorization that redesigned Taiwan's physical and imagined topography. The Japanese Government-General made Jilong a centerpiece of its modernizing, civilizing colonial project. Port construction transformed the harbor and its surroundings into a booming hub for trade. A concurrent population explosion created a mostly bicultural society, and brought groups of people from different cultural backgrounds into close proximity and contact with one another.

Within this zone of interaction, in Jilong and urban centers across Taiwan, an elite stratum emerged out of the mandates and opportunities provided by the colonial regime, and owing to their own initiative and ability to appeal to islander and Japanese social groups. Islanders and Japanese at this level developed close business and organizational ties as they established the financial and institutional bases for social construction within the instability of rapidly expanding cities. To be sure, divisions within the elite class reflected the realities of colonial policies that divided islander from Japanese. Just as Taiwan remained outside of the legal and institutional systems of Japan's home islands, and official censuses separated islanders from Japanese as categories of demographic analysis, Japanese settlers did not admit islanders into their identity group. Nevertheless, whether local elites called the city Jilong, Gelang, or Kiirun, they collectively provided the foundation for the local society. Over five decades, their activities shaped the everyday environment within which the islander-Taiwanese and Japanese, officials and nonofficials, mediated their relationships with each other. In stark contrast to the gloomy, almost desolate image of Jilong provided by a Japanese woodblock artist in 1896, elite islanders and Japanese residents took evident pride in their home as they built it into a vibrant city where they formed their new identities.

CHAPTER TWO

"Love of City and Love of Self"
Constructing Identities in the Crucible of Jilong

In March 1931 a curious event took place in Taipei and Jilong, peculiar for a colony in which imperial subjects held no electoral power in national politics. Karazawa Shinobu, the Japanese head of the Jilong newspaper, organized mock national assemblies, or model Diets, to seize on and further develop political awareness among the people in Taiwan.[1] Karazawa staged a form of political theater in which prominent locals played the roles of a dozen cabinet ministers and vice ministers. At the assembly in Jilong, fifty-six mock delegates confirmed Ōmi Tokigorō as the prime minister and Ishizaka Sōsaku as the minister of culture; clearly, their generation still held sway. The men and women playing the delegates came from five political parties that Karazawa created for the occasion: the "ruling" Conservative Party (Hoshutō), the "opposition" Progressive Party (Shinpotō), the Labor Party (Rōdōtō), Constitutional Youth Party (Rikken seinentō), and Neutral Club (Kōsei kurabu). These mock assemblies mirrored the form of actual national gatherings in Tokyo, and the Japanese and islander delegates taking part aired both national and local concerns. In Jilong, they discussed how to improve their city in the third phase

---

1. A similar event took place in Dalian in 1928, when the Manchuria Youth Congress launched a campaign for mock parliamentary elections. See O'Dwyer, *Significant Soil*, 220–21. A key difference was that Japanese residents in Manchuria could vote in national elections and serve in the National Diet.

of port construction, city management of taxis and buses, welfare for children and the unemployed, *hokō* system reforms, and further urbanization.

However, the mock assemblies also revealed ethnic distinctions among local residents. In both cities, Japanese citizens were assigned all but one of the ministerial posts—in Taipei, the lone islander served as the minister of labor, and in Jilong an islander was the minister of colonies—and in Jilong the majority of party delegates were Japanese, especially within the ruling party. At a preparatory meeting, an islander delegate of the Labor Party went so far as to call for the removal of Prime Minister Ōmi. Fierce debate erupted when a Japanese woman raised the issue of marriage between Japanese and islanders, as well as of reforming the islanders' practice of paying a bride price.[2] Everyone present shared an interest in developing Jilong, but beyond that, separate identities divided them along the lines of Japanese nationalism, on the one hand, and Taiwanese consciousness, on the other.

The model Diets were singular events, never held again, but they provide a window onto the shaping of identity in Japanese colonial Taiwan. In Jilong, as elsewhere, the historical processes of settlement and urban development created an environment conducive to the formation of new identities. The local setting mattered because that was the context within which the populace encountered the colonial policies that linked Jilong to the rest of Taiwan. There, through the actions and interactions of islanders and Japanese, specific identity groups took shape and the borders between them became clearly defined. As they built the city and reterritorialized the space into which it grew, both islanders and Japanese created a new, collective sense of being Jilongese. The islanders' prior attachment to localities in Taiwan,

2. Both the preparations for the Jilong assembly and the event itself were heavily covered in the local press, in both Japanese and Chinese. See the following articles in *NS*: "Mogi gikai no mae keiki," Mar. 12, 1931, 3; "Zenshōsen: Kiirun mogi gikai seiken happyō ensetsu," Mar. 19, 1931, 2; "Jilong moni yihui zhi zhengjian fabiao li hui yanshuo hui," Mar. 19, 1931, 11; "Kiirun mogi gikai: dai ichi hō," Mar. 26, 1931, 2. Karazawa published an extensive study of the Taipei mock assembly, together with press coverage from four papers across the island; see Karazawa, *Mogi gikai*. The Taipei assembly only had four parties; Jilong's Progressive and Labor Parties were apparently combined into one Socialist People's Party (Shakai minshutō).

combined with the Japanese settlers' willingness to advance their own interests against colonial and national governments, facilitated that process.[3] Meanwhile, their engagement with a range of islandwide political movements, social reforms, and cultural assimilation policies defined the boundaries between Japanese and islanders during the 1920s and 1930s, and sparked conflicts over imagined space that contributed to the creation of a Taiwanese ethnicity.

Early Residents and Their Identities

To understand how Taiwanese ethnic identity took shape between 1895 and 1945, we must first establish a baseline against which change can be evaluated. When they fell under Japanese rule, most of the people categorized as islanders by the colonial census held a range of identifications in terms of the Qing Empire, their native places and families, and their locations in Taiwan. The complexity of this mental tapestry resulted from a process of migration and settlement that shared many features with internal migration and social mobility within Qing China, as well as with Chinese communities around the globe. Across time and space, Chinese migrants of heterogeneous origins engaged in varied relations with indigenous communities and adopted a range of methods of social organization, some of which accentuated and replicated identities of origination, whereas others facilitated either closer ties with the Chinese imperial state or localization in their new homelands. Chinese sojourners in domestic urban centers like Shanghai and Hankou, and in port cities and other locations abroad, built coherence and structure for their communities through ties of compatriotism, kinship, corituality, and brotherhood.[4] These lines of connection linked

---

3. In this regard, settlers in Taiwan had much in common with Japanese settlers in Korea and Manchuria. See Uchida, *Brokers of Empire*; O'Dwyer, *Significant Soil*.

4. Philip Kuhn, in his magisterial survey of overseas Chinese, identifies these four types of affinity. See Kuhn, *Chinese among Others*, chap. 4. An extensive literature on internal migration highlights the significance of native-place ties. For example, Skinner, "Urban Social Structure," 521–53; and Wakeman and Yeh, *Shanghai Sojourners*, especially the introduction by Wakeman and Yeh, and the chapters by Bryna Goodman, "New Culture, Old Habits: Native-Place Organization and the May

migrants back to their homelands and reinforced the perhaps hypo-
thetical intention of returning there one day.[5] Internal migrants engaged in a long-standing practice of wealth acquisition in order to
finance their sons' preparations for the civil service examinations, a
process that promoted both social mobility and greater identification
with the Qing state. External migrants, by contrast, were more suscep-
tible to a gradual localization that overlapped or even superseded their
bonds to native place and Qing Empire and rooted them within their
host communities.

As pioneers, sojourners, and settlers in Taiwan, those who colonized it from China both subjected the island to Sinicization (*neidihua*)
and went through a process of localization or indigenization (*tuzhuhua*
or *bentuhua*) themselves. Since the 1970s there has been considerable
debate among scholars on both sides of the Taiwan Strait as to which
of those trajectories prevailed.[6] On the Sinicization side, in addition to
the literati practices detailed by Emma Teng, Hokkien speakers from
Fujian, primarily Quanzhou or Zhangzhou, and Hakka who came
mostly from Guangdong, sustained strong loyalties to their communities.[7] They engaged in social construction on the basis of common
language, origin, kinship, and ritual ties, a web of links that sometimes
violently fractured local society along multiple lines of division. Chinese settlers mobilized for repeated incidents of violence that reached

---

Fourth Movement," 76–107, and Emily Honig, "Migrant Culture in Shanghai: In
Search of a Subei Identity," 239–65; Goodman, *Native Place*; Rowe, *Hankow: Commerce
and Society*, chaps. 7–10.

5. For sojourning among overseas Chinese, see Reid, Alilunas-Rodgers, and
Cushman, *Sojourners and Settlers*, especially the chapters by Wang Gungwu,
"Sojourning: The Chinese Experience in Southeast Asia," 1–14, and G. William
Skinner, "Creolized Chinese Societies in Southeast Asia," 51–93. Wang further
explores the issue of sojourning in Wang Gungwu, *The Chinese Overseas*, in which
he discusses intermarriage with local women and the process of re-Sinicization by
later infusions of sojourners from China.

6. Taiwan-based anthropologist Chen Qi'nan fired the first shot, as it were, when
he published his indigenization thesis in 1976. Mainland scholar Chen Kongli
summarized the debate in a 1988 essay in which he clearly came down on the
Sinicization side, and a Taiwan-based scholar, Chen Xinzhi, responded to Kongli's
essay in 1990, favoring the indigenization position. See Chen Kongli, "Qingdai Taiwan
shehui"; and Chen Xinzhi, "'Tuzhuhua' yu 'neidihua.'"

7. See chapter 1.

a high point during the decades of expanded migration from the late eighteenth to the mid-nineteenth century.[8] Between 1768 and 1860, almost sixty major armed clashes occurred across Taiwan, with the majority sparked by feuds over resources between groups from Quanzhou and Zhangzhou.[9] In addition to having their native-place identities, as migrants remained in Taiwan for several generations they used their accrued wealth to pursue lifestyles typical of the scholar-gentry elite class, an empirewide stratum that largely depended on the state for its privileges and status.[10] Some of Taiwan's new elites, like the prominent landholding Lin family of Wufeng, manifested their growing identification with the Qing by organizing militia to suppress acts of mass violence and fulfill other tasks that the state could not.[11] Others sought entry to the bureaucracy, either by passing an examination or purchasing a degree.[12] Between 1882 and 1891, eight residents of Taiwan obtained the highest *jinshi* degree and achieved the qualification necessary to hold high office, and 128 out of roughly seven hundred examination candidates obtained lower-level degrees.[13]

In contrast, however, Chinese who migrated to Taiwan, both elites and commoners, took root in the island as their immigrant society (*yimin shehui*) became a settled society (*tuzhu shehui*).[14] The destruction

8. John R. Shepherd, "The Island Frontier of the Ch'ing, 1684–1780," in Rubinstein, *Taiwan*, 128–29. Shepherd, citing the work of Harry Lamley, dates the peak of violence to between 1782 and 1862.

9. Chen Chiukun, "From Landlords to Local Strongmen: The Transformation of Local Elites in Mid-Ch'ing Taiwan, 1780–1862," in Rubinstein, *Taiwan*, 136–37. Lin Weisheng, *Luohan Jiao*, 46–58, notes around sixty incidents of factional strife between 1721 and 1894, over half of which arose from Zhangzhou-Quanzhou or Fujian-Guangdong disputes.

10. Robert Gardella, "From Treaty Ports to Provincial Status, 1860–1894," in Rubinstein, *Taiwan*, 165.

11. Chen, "From Landlords," in Rubinstein, *Taiwan*, 137–58; Meskill, *A Chinese Pioneer Family*, chaps. 6, 7, 12. Landholding elites sometimes provoked the unrest, as seen in the major revolts led by Lin Shuangwen and Dai Chaochun in 1786 and 1862, respectively.

12. Meskill, *A Chinese Pioneer Family*, especially chap. 15.

13. Inspector General of Customs, *Decennial Reports*, 6:455–56.

14. This transition is at the heart of Chen Qi'nan's thesis, of which he provides a later elaboration in Chen Qi'nan, *Chuantong zhidu*, chap. 9. Similar processes occurred among Chinese overseas and internal migrants. See Wang Gungwu, "Sojourning,"

and absorption of segments of Taiwan's indigenous Austronesian population was a part of that process, but the main points of contrast were indigenous people as a collective other and their homeland societies.[15] Thus, variations in certain structures of Chinese society became markers of localization. For example, the clans that evolved in Taiwan were based on shared surnames rather than true kinship ties, and migrants gradually built ancestral halls and based their ancestor worship on those who first landed in Taiwan, rather than on progenitors in the home villages.[16] Moreover, the accumulation of land and wealth helped to bind the Chinese population to Taiwan. From the mid-eighteenth century onward, Taiwan's multilayered land-use system tied three categories of migrants—the proprietors who owned the deed to the land, the farm managers who held permanent tenancy and became functional landlords, and the tenants who farmed it—to their respective investments on the island.[17] Especially after the advent of the treaty-port era, commercial opportunities in the north allowed merchants to sink financial roots and join landlords among the island's elites.[18] According to Lin Man-houng, the expansion of the tea, sugar, and camphor trades brought economic benefits to all groups and closed the gaps between the early-arriving Quanzhou natives and the later arrivals from Zhangzhou and Guangdong.[19] Improved financial circumstances somewhat ameliorated, though did not completely erase, divisions based on native place and language.[20] Owing to these factors, as Chen Qi'nan argues, those who migrated to Taiwan from China developed a consciousness that connected specifically to their locales on the island rather than their ancestral homes.[21]

in Reid, Alilunas-Rodgers, and Cushman, *Sojourners and Settlers*, especially 3; and Wakeman and Yeh, *Shanghai Sojourners*, especially 11–15 and 264.

15. Brown, *Is Taiwan Chinese?*
16. Li Shinn-cherng, "Qingdai Yilan" 108–9; Chen Qi'nan, *Chuantong zhidu*, 174–75.
17. Chen, "From Landlords," in Rubinstein, *Taiwan*.
18. Lin Man-houng, *Cha, tang, zhangnao*, 174–76.
19. Ibid., 176–80.
20. Gardella, "From Treaty Ports," in Rubinstein, *Taiwan*, 179.
21. Chen Qi'nan, *Chuantong zhidu*, 173. See also Rwei-ren Wu, "Zhong ceng tuzhuhua," 137.

Residents of Jilong enacted this mixture of native-place, China-centric, and localized identities. An outbreak of native-place rivalries in northern Taiwan during the 1850s swept through Jilong, where the majority Zhangzhou-origin residents resisted encroachment by people from Quanzhou. Although parochial identities remained strong into the middle of the nineteenth century, an exam-based literati culture emerged in Jilong at the very end of the Qing period.[22] As commerce and the plans of Liu Mingchuan brought more wealth and people to the Jilong-Danshui region, thirty local residents passed the county exams for the lowest degree (*xiucai*) or the provincial exams for the middle degree (*juren*).[23] Overall, the economic opportunities in and around Jilong had a substantive impact on the Chinese who settled there and gave the town a distinctive character. Involvement in the tea, camphor, and coal trades not only financially rooted Chinese migrants in northern Taiwan but also made them particularly open to mingling with people from other parts of the world in the pursuit of mutual financial benefit.[24]

The transfer of sovereignty in the spring of 1895 initiated intensive and multifaceted engagement between this identificationally complex Chinese population and a Japanese regime that was motivated by a strong sense of nationalism and purported colonial benevolence. Meiji-era Japanese viewed the frontiers of their empire as backward areas in need of their civilizing influence; thus they brought an assimilationist agenda to their first colonial territories, Hokkaido and Okinawa, that they later extended as Japan gained sovereign control over Taiwan, then Korea and parts of Manchuria during the early twentieth century.[25] Japanese confidence in their civilizing mission was particularly high as a result of a series of events that occurred between 1894 and 1905: treaty revision with Britain, followed quickly by victory over the Qing in 1894–1895; the Anglo-Japanese alliance of 1902; and a military defeat of Russia that enabled Japan to establish a protectorate over

22. Cheng, "Jindai Jilong de shehui," 92.
23. Inspector General of Customs, *Decennial Reports*, 6:455–56.
24. Such is the estimation of Jilong's Qing-era society provided by Cheng Chunpin, largely on the basis of reports from Westerners who visited Jilong from the 1840s onward. See Cheng, "Jindai Jilong de shehui," 89–93.
25. Morris-Suzuki, *Re-Inventing Japan*, 29.

Korea in 1905. Following the Russo-Japanese War, a Japanese sense of regional superiority was increasingly manifested in efforts to Japanize peripheral subjects and territories. In practice, as Tessa Morris-Suzuki points out, the pursuit of assimilation in these frontier zones forced the Japanese to clarify and affirm their definitions of, and boundaries around, Japaneseness.[26] Concern with the dangers that assimilation posed for Japanese settlers in the colonies moderated the application of transformative policies, but as Todd Henry reveals in his study of colonial Seoul, such policies operated across the public spaces of Japan's colonial cities.[27]

The triumphant, territorializing side of Japanese nationalism dominated among those who surveyed the colonial project in Taiwan. For example, Takekoshi Yosaburō, a member of the Diet who visited the colony twice during the early twentieth century, wrote an account of conditions in Taiwan based on his observations and research. His description of the effects of Japanese influence clearly displayed the modernizing biases that prevailed among the officials and settlers who were his main interlocutors: "Peace has been restored, order prevails, the productive power of the island has increased, the Government is respected and trusted, and on every hand are seen evidences of life and prosperity. In short, Japan can point to her successes thus far in Formosa as a proof of her worthiness to be admitted into the community of the world's great colonial powers."[28] If the last sentence betrayed hints of anxiety over Japan's position vis-à-vis Western nations, the overall tone celebrated Japan's superiority over its neighbors and its successful transformation of backward Chinese. Takekoshi even suggested that Japan had achieved more than the Europeans had in their colonies when he commented that "an entirely new Formosa has arisen unknown in past history."[29] The motivation he expressed, to build a new Taiwan as an example of Japan's imperial achievements, reflected

26. Ibid., 10. She concentrated on Okinawa and Hokkaido, but the point holds for Taiwan.

27. Henry, *Assimilating Seoul*, 3–5.

28. Takekoshi, *Japanese Rule in Formosa*, 2.

29. Ibid., 11, and see especially chaps. 18–19, on sanitation, education, religion, and philanthropy, for clear expressions of Japan's civilizing, modernizing mission.

part of the rationale behind the major projects of port construction and urban development that the Government-General carried out in Jilong. In fact, Takekoshi considered the improvement of Jilong's harbor and the installation of modern port facilities such as piers and loading equipment to be among the clearest signs of Japan's success as a colonial power.[30]

The Japanese performance of a modern, civilizing national identity involved defining and policing boundaries between themselves and the islanders, especially in the realms of sanitation and medicine. Enforcing a regime of "hygienic modernity" or "policing hygiene" meant that colonial officials such as Gotō Shinpei and Takagi Tomoe designed policies intended to domesticate Taiwan by installing the plumbing and sewer systems, water treatment plants, hospitals, and clinics that municipal governments of the home islands provided along with their Meiji-era urbanization projects.[31] Colonial medicine was a tool the Japanese used to sanitize Taiwan's disease-ridden terrain, assimilate islanders to Japanese and Western norms, and hold indigenous doctors perpetually in the status of students.[32] However, until Taiwan attained a sufficient level of hygiene, Japanese and islanders had to be separated from each other as much as possible.[33] Thus, a prescribed hygienic standard became a marker of group membership. In 1897 construction began in Jilong on a plumbing system to provide fresh water and improve sanitation in the town. The Japanese faced a substantial task, but just a year later, the Taiwan Association, a key organization for encouraging settlement in the colony, reported that Jilong's water quality matched that of home island ports such as Kobe and Osaka.[34] Officials

30. Ibid., 261–63. He compared it in importance to the British development of Cape Town and Dutch port construction in Java.

31. Rogaski, *Hygienic Modernity*; Wicentowski, "Policing Health"; Michael Shiyung Liu, *Prescribing Colonization*, especially chaps. 1 and 2.

32. Michael Shiyung Liu, *Prescribing Colonization*, 165–72.

33. Rogaski notes that, for Japanese in China, "*eisei/hygiene* meant isolating bacteria, but at the same time it meant guarding the boundaries between the pure and the impure, the Japanese and the native of the Qing empire." See Rogaski, *Hygienic Modernity*, 182.

34. "Kiirun shōsoku," in *TKKH*, no. 3, Dec. 1898; and "Kiirun no suidō kōji," *TKKH*, no. 31, Apr. 1901. For the waterworks themselves, located in Nuannuan, see Taiwan sōtokufu kanbō bunsho ka, *Taiwan shashin jō*, 22.

created state-regulated markets, supposedly to ensure that produce would be stored in hygienic conditions and that consumers would be charged fair prices. The Jilong municipal government used its sanitation funds to establish its first market in 1908, located at the southern edge of the core area of islander settlement. It later set up additional markets east of the harbor, in a predominantly islander neighborhood, and at the northern edge of the main Japanese district (see map 1.3).[35] The first market, which prioritized reforming the purportedly unsanitary conditions in the islander neighborhood, highlighted how hygiene policies enforced the islander-Japanese division. Moreover, local authorities used the medical system to define boundaries when they set up separate quarantine hospitals for islander and Japanese patients, although Japanese doctors were expected to treat all patients at both locations.[36]

The existence of a sort of cordon sanitaire within the Japanese civilizing mission also played out in relations between men and women in their daily lives. The official statistics on intermarriage between islanders and Japanese indicate that it occurred only very rarely. No mixed marriages were recorded in all of Taiwan in 1910, only two were recorded in 1925, seven in 1930, and the official population data for 1940 indicated five unions between Japanese men and islander women, and thirty-one between Japanese women and islander men.[37] These figures suggest that as islanders, and primarily islander men, became purportedly more civilized, or purified, by Japanese influence, they also became more acceptable to Japanese settlers as marital partners. Nonetheless, the standards of marital hygiene remained very high, and very few islanders ever crossed that particular boundary. In the realm of commercialized sex, separation between islanders and Japanese became stricter over time. In Jilong's pleasure quarter in the Denryōkō district, along the canal toward the east edge of town, Japanese and

35. Katō, *Kiirun Shi*, 21–22; "Kiirun suizokukan ato e shin kaigyō no fūki ichiba oo uridashi," *TNS*, Jan. 13, 1922, 7.

36. "Kiirun hibyōin no shinsetsu," *TNS*, Feb. 3, 1906, page number illegible.

37. Taiwan sōtokufu kanbō tōkei ka, *Taiwan jinkō dōtai tōkei*. In contrast to the rarity of islander-Japanese unions, into the 1910s the colonial regime used intermarriage as a strategy to gain greater control over certain indigenous groups. See Barclay, "Cultural Brokerage," 323.

PROTITUTE OF DENRYOKO, KIIRUN.   廓 遊 港 澡 田 隆 基 (唐可許都合司寫要隆基)

FIGURE 2.1. The red-light district exclusively for Japanese prostitutes in the Denryōkō district of Jilong. Image courtesy of the National Central Library, Taipei.

islander prostitutes worked in separate licensed brothels (fig. 2.1). By the 1930s officials had established a new red-light district that employed only islander women, in the Yutian district southeast of the harbor (see map 1.3).[38] The policies regarding the sex trade governed only the women, not their patrons, and the sources do not indicate who went to which brothels, but even so, the local authorities enforced segregation to limit the purported pollution of Japanese patrons by islanders.

Underlying the concern with medical, marital, and sexual hygiene was the tension between inclusionary and exclusionary impulses in Japanese empire building. This bimodal colonization was evident in the

38. "Hontōjin no shōrō," *TNS*, Apr. 27, 1922, 7; and "Kiirun kōshinkyoku: shinai angya," *NS*, Jan. 8, 1931, 4. The pleasure quarter (*karyūkai*) in Denryōkō grew along with the town itself in the first decade of colonial rule. By the end of 1905, there were 31 restaurants and 13 brothels there, employing 29 geisha, 117 prostitutes, 62 barmaids, and 10 waitresses; collectively, they constituted the vast majority of employed females in Jilong, where only 277 women were recorded as having jobs in that year. See Kiirun chō, *Kiirun chō dai ichi.*

education system as well.[39] On the one hand, Japanese officials maintained that all subjects of the emperor could become Japanese by adopting a range of cultural and behavioral traits that included speaking the Japanese language, displaying loyalty to Japan's emperor, and visiting Shinto shrines. In one key example, Governor-General Akashi Motojirō showed his support for assimilation in his 1919 Education Rescript, which stated: "The basic principle of education is to cultivate loyal citizens, on the foundation of the intention of the Imperial Rescript on Education. . . . The purpose of general education is to attend to improving the bodies and developing the morals of children, to promote the character of citizens by endowing them with the common knowledge and skills necessary to life, and to spread the national language."[40] Akashi's successor, Den Kenjirō, issued a new edict in 1922 that opened formerly Japanese-only primary schools (*shōgakkō*) and some institutions of higher learning to islanders who had sufficient language proficiency.[41] On the other hand, colonial officials and settlers held to ideas of Japanese uniqueness and superiority that were a part of their national identity and that emerged with differing levels of intensity at different moments in time. This tendency, too, appeared in the official proclamations, both of which supported the retention of common schools (*kōgakkō*) as places to educate only islander children who needed to learn Japanese language, history, and manners.[42] Similarly, the inclusionary strain was seen during the 1910s in Japanese support for the Assimilation Society (Dōkakai) and its agenda of rapid assimilation for the islanders, but the exclusionary side revealed itself when the Government-General shut the movement down.[43] Even during the

39. The best study of Taiwan's education system under Japanese rule, its transformational functions, and its ambivalence, is Tsurumi, *Japanese Colonial Education*, particularly chaps. 2–5.

40. "Taiwan kyōiku rei," Articles 2 and 5, Dec. 23, 1918, JACAR, www.jacar.go.jp/, accessed Dec. 16, 2016. This document contains Akashi's original text with additions from Japan's Privy Council that were incorporated when it was issued in January 1919.

41. Tsurumi, *Japanese Colonial Education*, 216.

42. "Taiwan kyōiku rei," JACAR; and Tsurumi, *Japanese Colonial Education*, 99–100.

43. On the Assimilation Society and its Japanese backers in Taiwan and the home islands, including the well-known political reformer Itagaki Taisuke, see Lamley, "The Taiwan Literati and Early Japanese Rule," 447–57.

thoroughgoing rapid assimilation program in the 1930s, which reached
its peak with the Kōminka movement, both colonial officials and settlers sustained the tension between inclusion and exclusion.

Creating Jilong Identity

Both islanders and Japanese came to identify themselves with the city
of Jilong, and they did so within the context of its rapid physical and
economic development. The middle decades of Japanese rule, roughly
1905 to 1935, encompassed the crucial years of urbanization for Jilong.
During this period, Jilong's population and geographic limits expanded
dramatically, it received the administrative designation of "city," and
it became a flourishing center of economic and cultural production.
Colonial officials mandated construction of a municipal swimming
pool, public beaches, an aquarium, over half a dozen elementary
schools, and two high schools, in addition to road-building and sanitation projects (fig. 2.2). Local residents opened theaters and cinemas,
established restaurants and shops, and ran a newspaper that catered
primarily to the city's business community, with articles in both Japanese and Chinese, just like the main islandwide paper. One of the four
longest-running local papers in Taiwan, it went through several name
changes, from *Takasago Puck* when it was first introduced as a monthly
in 1916, to the *Taisei News (Taisei shinpō)* in 1922, to the *Niitaka News
(Niitaka shinpō)* in 1924, which became a weekly paper in 1930.[44] Taizhong, Tainan, and Hualian all had longer-running papers than did
Jilong, but Gaoxiong did not get a local paper until 1935; local media
thus seems to have played a varied role in urban societies across Taiwan.[45] Additionally, during the 1910s, Yan Yunnian and Kimura Kutarō

44. Liao Ping-hui, "Print Culture and the Emergent Public Sphere in Colonial
Taiwan, 1895–1945," in Liao and Wang, *Taiwan under Japanese*, 85. By the 1930s, the
government classified the paper as "yellow" for its reportage on murders, rapes, and
other forms of violence, which might explain its closure in 1938. The first thirteen
years of the paper's run have not been preserved, but it serves as a key source of
information thereafter, from 1929 to its end.

45. On the first three locales, see ibid., 85. On Gaoxiong, see Lin Shuguang, *Dagou
suo tan*, 116–17.

基
隆
水
族
館
（基隆要塞司令部
許可第一四九號）

FIGURE 2.2. The Jilong Aquarium, depicted in a commemorative volume of the 1935 Taiwan Exhibition. Image courtesy of the National Taiwan Library, Taipei.

filled a gap in the officially sponsored railway network and built a light rail system that enhanced both the freight and transit connections between Jilong and its hinterland.[46] These developments created a framework on which residents could build a Jilong identity.

The chief business of Jilong's residents, to appropriate U.S. president Calvin Coolidge's phrase, was business. According to data published by Ishizaka Sōsaku in 1917, at that time Jilong had two banks, one credit union, twenty-five companies, and more than three hundred owners of small businesses in a population of around five thousand households. Of the larger enterprises, the financial institutions and some of the companies, more than 60 percent were branches of corporations not based in Jilong, suggesting that a local economic foundation had not yet developed, even though Yan Yunnian, Kimura, and Ōmi

46. The Yan family retained primary control of the rail company for as long as it operated. Its history and operations are described in Yan Chuangyin, *Sōgyō nijūnen shi.* The author was the brother of Yunnian and Guonian, and manager of the company.

already had substantial operations under way.[47] In 1931, when Ishizaka issued a new report on local economic activity, he counted four banks, six credit unions, and thirty corporations, and a population of around eighteen thousand households. Although all of the banks were branches of larger entities, all but one of the credit unions and sixteen of the corporations had their main offices in Jilong, and the overall capital valuation had increased dramatically. For example, in 1917 the largest of the locally based companies was capitalized at 1.5 million yen, whereas in 1931 one was capitalized at ten million and two at five million. Yan Guonian was whole or part owner of the four largest companies.[48] Those companies engaged in coal and gold mining, shipping, transportation, fisheries, fertilizer manufacturing, and other activities that linked Jilong to its immediate hinterland, the southern half of the island, and international trade networks. The shift to local ownership and the expansion in the scale of businesses from the late 1910s to the early 1930s indicate that locally based capital became both more substantial and more significant in those years, qualities that Jilong shared with Gaoxiong, at least, and probably other cities as well.[49] Although the growth of Jilong-based enterprises did not, in and of itself, mean that the businessmen came to think of themselves as Jilongese, there was nonetheless a strong parallel between these developments and the process of localization through economic activity that occurred in the last decades of the Qing period.

As Jilong's society and economy grew, the same citizens who buttressed the economic infrastructure also took an active interest in how to further advance and promote their city. At the end of World War I, which had given the Japanese Empire opportunities to expand its territorial reach and economic strength, twenty-two of Jilong's leading figures published a short book in which they described their views on

---

47. Ishizaka, *Kiirun kō*, 205–33 and 42. The source indicates that 215 islanders and 105 Japanese individuals owned 358 small businesses, each of which paid at least twenty yen a year in taxes.

48. Ishizaka, *Ora ga Kiirun*, 70–73, 13. In this volume, Ishizaka used a much higher tax threshold for including small businesses, 200 yen per year, as a result of which his list included only ninety-one businesses, a figure that far understated the quantity of small-scale economic activity in the city.

49. For Gaoxiong, see Wu Wen-hsing, "Ri ju shiqi Gaoxiong," 144–46.

developing the city, written for an audience that included both other elites and government officials. The editor of this 1918 volume, Ishizaka Sōsaku, provided the lead entry. He recommended enlarging the harbor by leveling some of the surrounding hills, to accommodate more and bigger trading ships, and advocated the construction of houses, parks, and hotels to make the place better for residents and more attractive to visitors. Yan Yunnian said that new factories and improved rail and shipping links were crucial for producing and exporting manufactured goods, activities that would enable Jilong to compete in the world market. Xu Zisang added that import tariffs should be lowered to reinvigorate a declining trade with China, and Ōmi Tokigorō criticized the narrow vision of the Government-General's plans for port construction and called for more to be done to expand the harbor and its connections to the hinterland.[50] To be sure, each of these men would have derived personal financial benefit from the implementation of their proposals, but their language consistently expressed a larger concern with the entire city, and in some cases, with Taiwan and East Asia beyond that, sometimes in ways that diverged from existing policies. Xu framed his vision of Jilong much as Governor-General Kabayama Sukenori had, stating that "Kiirun harbor is the entryway to the entire island."[51] Ishizaka linked Jilong to the advancement of South China and Southeast Asia, closing his entry with these words:

> If we foresee a position of great importance for our Kiirun harbor as if it were like the sun rising in the east, then the citizens who reside here must all work together in collaboration to promote the city's well-being, must devote themselves to planning parks and places of amusement, and must complete the installation of theaters, hotels, and pleasure quarters. In this way, if we are able to push the advancement of Kiirun by one stage, then soon we will be able to see the city's brilliance at its zenith.[52]

50. Ishizaka, *Kiirun hanjō*. Ishizaka's essay is on pp. 1–3, Yan's on 5–7, Xu's on 7–9, and Ōmi's on 16.

51. Ibid., 7. Xu, like all the contributors except Yan Yunnian, wrote his entry in Japanese.

52. Ibid., 3.

These proposals for improving Jilong, far more than the men's business
activities, show that after roughly two decades of urban development,
the city's elites had collectively made Jilong their city and shared a local
identity, expressed as a common interest in local improvement.

Jilong's elites, the Japanese in particular, expressed their civic pride
by documenting the city's former and current conditions through a
substantial collection of local gazetteers, historical works, travel guides,
compendia of trade statistics, and other materials. Their writings were
in keeping with a broad local-history movement in the Japanese home
islands that linked past events with present contexts, as well as with
efforts to use local education to promote nationalism and patriotism.[53]
Government institutions in Taiwan played a significant role in shaping
this trend by producing large numbers of city, county, and prefecture
gazetteers, but private citizens, especially in the 1930s, became prominent advocates of their locales.[54] Ishizaka produced the first text about
Jilong during the 1910s, a comprehensive volume that covers the city's
history since its settlement by aborigines; its topography and climate;
economic production; population; social institutions; religion and
customs; police and military matters; and governance. According to
an introduction written by the civil administrator of the Government-
General, Shimomura Hiroshi, Ishizaka wrote the book "to give the
citizens a complete knowledge of Kiirun's value."[55] A few publications
followed during the 1920s, and in the next decade the wave of interest
in studying and writing about Jilong reached its crest. Ishizaka, Ōmi
Tokigorō, and a protégé of Xu Zisang named Jian Wanhuo joined several other residents to publish approximately ten books about the city
between 1930 and 1934.[56] Japanese residents of other cities also became

53. On the local-history movement, see Young, *Beyond the Metropolis*, 141–64; on
education, Chou, *Hai hang xi de niandai*, chap. 7.

54. This point is based on my survey of the Japanese-era gazetteers and other
materials reproduced by the Chengwen Publishing Company, in several hundred
volumes, as part of a larger project of publishing local gazetteers.

55. Ishizaka, *Kiirun kō*, 2. Ishizaka produced several editions of this book of which
the third, from 1917, is the only one extant.

56. This list includes, but is not limited to, Katō, *Kiirun shi*; Ōmi, *Kiirun kō annai*,
1930; Ōmi, *Kiirun kō annai*, 1933; Nakajima, *Kiirun shi annai*; Jian Wanhuo, *Jilong*

practitioners of local history, such as in Gaoxiong where residents published six books about the city around 1930.[57] Subsequent publications on Jilong largely followed Ishizaka's original format, and they provided a historical foundation and teleological narrative that highlighted the great achievements of the colonial regime, city government, and local residents.[58] The publications varied in length, breadth, and depth of coverage, but collectively they demonstrated that considerable attention was being paid to the city in which the authors lived. Two Japanese residents displayed that sense of pride in being Jilongese when they composed a city song in 1933, the opening verse of which proclaims:

A good harbor, made by nature,
    and improved by the work of people,
It is the entry gate to Takasago Island,
    and its name is well-known. From morning to night
A thousand ships, a hundred ships,
    enter and assemble there.
Its blessings are numerous, our Kiirun City.[59]

As a group, these works gave voice to a sense of being Jilongese that locals developed during the early decades of the twentieth century. Moreover, although the authors of these materials sought to enhance Jilong's significance within the Japanese Empire, a project that had direct parallels among settlers in Dalian, they established a narrative that both emphasized the importance of Japan's colonization and,

zhi; Ishizaka, *Ora ga Kiirun*; Irie, *Kiirun fūdo*; Fushiki, *Gureito Kiirun*; Kuhara, *Kiirun kō to sono sangyō*; and Mitsubashi, *Wa ga Kiirun*. The last title was published for use by students in Jilong, to teach them more about their city.

57. Lin Shuguang, *Dagou suo tan*, preface.

58. The narrative of success in these local histories reflected both Takekoshi Yosaburō's approach to Taiwan and the historical documentation project initiated by Den Kenjirō in 1921 and completed in 1930. Hiyama, "Riben zhi Tai shiqi dui Tai renshi."

59. Kuhara, *Kiirun no uta*. The Gaoxiong city song, which also had a Japanese author, evokes similar themes of maritime significance and urban pride. See "Takao shimin uta," in Nakayama and Katayama, *Yakushin Takao*, 89–90.

contradictorily, created a storehouse of historical and contemporary information that undergirded a separate Taiwanese consciousness.[60] Whereas the texts presented a uniform history of progress, reaching a seemingly inevitable endpoint in colonial modernization, their attention to both macro-level events and everyday lived experiences highlighted the contingency of Jilong's historic evolution.

For islanders and for Japanese settlers, the 1920s and early 1930s were a period of social and political mobilization, conditions that prevailed both throughout the empire and across the Taiwan Strait. In the home islands, imperial subjects engaged in mass labor and agrarian movements, agitated for expanded suffrage, and worked within the boundaries of party politics during the Taishō democracy.[61] In Korea, under the relaxed restrictions of that era's "cultural rule" (*bunka seiji*), Japanese settlers and Koreans, acting sometimes together and sometimes separately, pushed for greater autonomy and at least limited suffrage, whereas in Manchuria settlers embraced mass politics, through a range of institutions, to advance their own interests.[62] Over in China, the student activism of the May Fourth era faded into a range of political movements supporting various forms of national unification and greater involvement in mass politics. In Taiwan, where civilians held the position of governor-general from 1919 to 1932, politically minded people formed popular movements and devoted their energies to the pursuit of greater autonomy, for example by launching a partially successful push for popularly elected councils at each level of the colonial bureaucracy. Their shared focus on greater political participation suggests that the most important objective of activists and nonactivists alike was to break the monopoly on political power held by the Government-General.[63]

60. Emer O'Dwyer demonstrates the significance of space and place for Japanese settlers in the Kwantung Leasehold, Japan's first territorial acquisition in Manchuria, who consistently promoted their city and region as central nodes for Japan's empire. See O'Dwyer, *Significant Soil*, 19 and chap. 3.

61. Gordon, *Labor and Imperial Democracy*; Garon, *State and Labor*.

62. Uchida, *Brokers of Empire*, chap. 6; O'Dwyer, *Significant Soil*, chaps. 3–6.

63. Huang Zhaotang argues that the Government-General's powers were, in fact, heavily circumscribed by both the strong military presence in Taiwan and the fact

Members of both Japanese and islander communities in Jilong attempted to assert themselves in local and islandwide politics during the 1920s and 1930s. The administrative reforms of 1920 established consultative councils (*hyōgikai*) and assemblies (*kyōgikai*) at the municipal, prefecture, and islandwide levels, which provided new channels for private citizens to contribute their voices to official matters. These assemblies existed across the island, providing similar experiences with civic engagement for local elites in other cities, but Jilong's may have been particularly useful for solidifying and expressing a local identity.[64] At first the government controlled access to these committees by appointing their members, and in Jilong it turned to prominent residents with which it already had significant connections, selecting established elites like Ishizaka, Ōmi, Xu, and Yan Guonian to sit on one or more of the advisory bodies. The new councils and assemblies had little real influence over the decisions of local or islandwide officials, but the appointees seemed to take their roles seriously. For example, the Japanese-dominated Jilong town assembly held two days of public meetings in 1922 during which its delegates discussed plans to manage the sale of drinking water to ships that entered the harbor, funding for a newly constructed common school, and the need to install plumbing throughout the city.[65] In the beginning, primarily Japanese settlers used the assemblies to promote a range of interests—including expanding trade, modernizing Taiwan, and transforming the islanders—and to pressure the colonial government to meet their concerns.

Over the next decade, islanders joined settlers on the Jilong municipal assembly to influence local conditions. Late in the 1920s, the city government conducted a land survey and evaluated economic and social conditions in Jilong in preparation for a new round of urban

---

that some of the powers of appointment devolved to the prefecture magistrates. See Huang Zhaotang, *Taiwan zongdufu*, 207, 216.

64. Chen Jingkuan looks at these assemblies in Taizhong, mostly through their membership, which was predominantly Japanese but saw increasing numbers of islanders in the 1930s and in elections for some seats in 1935. Overall, Chen sees the Taizhong assemblies as tools of official control rather than arenas for the assertion of nonnational identities. See Chen Jingkuan, *Cong shengcheng dao Taizhong shi*, 68–75.

65. "Kiirun gai kyōgikai," *TNS*, Jan. 31, 1922, 2.

reforms. Following the completion of this study, the mixed group of about ten council delegates discussed a number of proposals for projects that the government should undertake. The committee made a series of general recommendations for developing the city's outlying districts, and gave specific attention to the need for new construction in densely inhabited, islander-packed Big Jilong.[66] The following year, this same group emphasized that the city government should listen more closely to public opinion as it shaped municipal policies. It then issued specific calls for increasing support for industry and social welfare; expanding trade, especially with China; and providing more electricity to the city by tapping into a major hydroelectric project at Sun-Moon Lake in central Taiwan, which was soon to be completed.[67] In making these sorts of recommendations, local elites sought to advance their own economic interests, to be sure, but they also reached out to broader constituencies of city residents to make demands on the colonial state.

Although both islanders and Japanese saw the municipal assembly as an important institution, they became frustrated with its restrictions on membership and limited influence over policies, so they called for its reform in the late 1920s. Writing a lead article in the local newspaper under the heading, "Love of City and Love of Self" (*Aishi to aishi*), one Japanese resident complained that the assembly had become dominated by people prone to grandstanding, who were more interested in using it as a stage on which to draw attention to themselves than as a vehicle for local reform.[68] Similar concerns emerged when it came time for the prefectural magistrate to appoint new city councilors in late 1932, drawing from among a pool of candidates that indicated some generational change. Among islanders, the old leaders stepped aside in favor of second-tier elites who had close ties to either Xu Zisang or Yan Guonian, and some Japanese called for more recent arrivals from the home islands to replace Ōmi Tokigorō and Ishizaka Sōsaku. One account suggested strong factional differences between purported Xu and Yan camps, but even if that were the case, ultimately the selections

66. "Kiirun shi kyōgikai angai hei'on ni ryō," *NS*, Feb. 5, 1930, 5.
67. "Shin shi kyōgiin no nentō kan," *NS*, Jan. 8, 1931, 4.
68. "Aishi to aishi: kyōgi kaiin ka kyōgi kaiin ka," *NS*, May 25, 1929, 1.

came from both sides, and the first-generation elites remained influential in local society and politics.[69] The intense interest in the 1932
delegates displayed a widespread ambition to transform the assemblies
into a foundation for true self-government on both local and islandwide levels. Jilong's islanders urged that the functionally useless assemblies be replaced with a system in which all residents of Taiwan could
vote for representatives. Some called for Japanese leadership and training in the practice of self-government, because the settlers had experience with voting and political participation in the home islands that
could provide useful guidance for those in Taiwan.[70] Similarly minded
Japanese called for legislation to guarantee popular voting rights and
did not disagree with the idea that they should play a leading role in
implementing self-rule.[71]

However, government officials met the drive for autonomy and
political participation with skepticism and firm, if measured, rejection.
In late 1929, when more and more people were joining the movement
for self-government, Jilong's mayor, Katō Morimichi, issued his negative response. Katō acknowledged in principle that government needed
to be responsive to public opinion and that popular involvement was
a desirable state of affairs. He argued that Taiwan lagged behind the
home islands because the great majority of residents lacked the civic
knowledge and skills (*minchi minryoku*) necessary to run an effective
system of local self-government, and thus introducing one at that point
would only damage the public good. Only after islanders and Japanese
developed three "spirits"—public spirit (*kōkyō no seishin*), a collaborative spirit (*kyōdō no seishin*), and a spirit of self-sufficiency (*jisoku no*

69. Articles on replacing the councilors appeared over three successive weeks in
the local newspaper, including "Shi kyōgiin kaisen yosō," *NS*, Nov. 18, 1932, 10; "Kiirun
shi kyōgiin kaisen o mae ni shite Nakase shū chiji no mosei o unagasu," *NS*, Nov. 25,
1932, 3; and "Kiirun shi kyōgiin kaisen o mae ni shite hontōjin ma no an tō o ima-
shimu," *NS*, Dec. 2, 1932, 4. Given that Xu and Yan had very close relations, it is
likely that reports of a "secret feud" exaggerated but did not wholly fabricate the
situation.
70. "Jidai wa ugoku kanzen naru jichi sei e," *NS*, June 17, 1929, 3; and "Shi xiyihui
piping yanshuo," *TMB*, Feb. 5, 1928, 6. One of those critical of the assembly was Yang
Yuanding, a man who would take on a much larger role in the immediate postwar
period.
71. "Kiirun shi kyōgiin kaisen o mae," *NS*, Nov. 25, 1932, 3.

seishin)—he said, could genuine discussions of local autonomy begin.[72] Katō's response revealed a lack of awareness of the activities of the city's elites, and the colonial and metropolitan governments withheld the right of direct political participation well into the 1930s, in spite of the long-standing collaborative efforts, public-mindedness, and growing self-reliance of local leaders.

Even without legislative input, Jilong's civic leaders came together out of a devotion to both the city and their own economic fortunes. They expressed their Jilong identity with equal strength through a major effort to garner more funds for port construction in the late 1920s. Faced with the beginnings of economic contraction within the empire, the Diet removed the Jilong port construction fee from the annual budget for Taiwan in 1929. Japanese and islanders swiftly responded to this blow to their local pride and prospects by mobilizing to implement several strategies to have the funds reinstated. Joining with city officials, some members of the group contacted several former governors-general and other officials to plead their case, and others journeyed to Tokyo to petition the prime minister and other cabinet officials. Two settlers took charge of efforts in the capital: Kimura Kutarō, who by this point spent most of his time in the metropole, and Ōmi Tokigorō, who maintained a residence there.[73] Although their lobbying efforts did not meet with immediate success, they eventually achieved their objective because the Diet later budgeted more than ten million yen for harbor expansion between 1929 and 1932, and a slightly smaller amount for the next three years.[74] Regardless of the outcome, elites' mobilization to safeguard the ongoing development of the city's most important resource, its harbor, galvanized the collective aspects of Jilong identity.

Residents and the colonial state came together to celebrate Jilong in 1932, when the city completed a new municipal government building in the heart of the primarily Japanese district of Small Jilong and

72. "Chihō jichi no risō e," *NS*, Sept. 25, 1929, no page number.

73. This effort is detailed in two articles, "Totsujo wakideta: Kiirun chikkō jigyō hi no sakujo," *NS*, July 25, 1929, 8, and "Kiirun chikkō mondai," *NS*, Aug. 5, 1929, no page number.

74. Ōmi, *Kiirun kō annai*, 1933, 5.

FIGURE 2.3. The flag-raising ceremony at the new Jilong city government building in 1932, from a commemorative volume produced by the city government. Image courtesy of the National Taiwan Library, Taipei.

moved its offices from its old home at the southwest corner of the harbor, on the edge of islander-dominated Big Jilong (map 2.1). Local citizens joined officials to produce a major festival to mark the occasion (fig. 2.3). The new building housed exhibits showcasing the city's importance as a center of trade, its local products, and its achievements in engineering, construction, and education. Large crowds of islanders and Japanese residents, men and women, adults and children, turned out to see these displays and to participate in the public performances that celebrated Jilong's status as an important regional hub within the Japanese Empire.[75] The following year the city government published a several-hundred-page volume to commemorate its new home, filled with descriptions of how it was built and who had been involved in the dedication festivities, as well as pictures of the exhibits and the parades,

75. "Kiirun shin shi tei sha rakusei kinen tenrankai," *NS*, Mar. 31, 1932, 10.

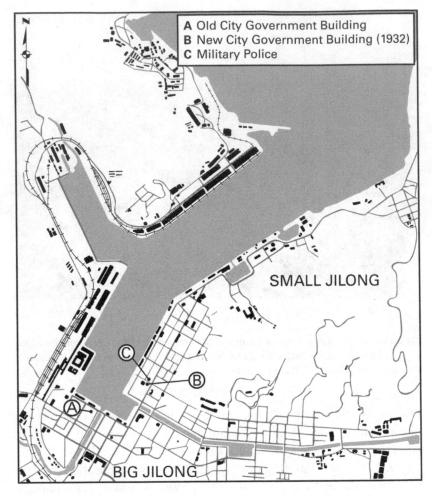

MAP 2.1. State institutions in Jilong. Map created by Scott Walker, based on a map designed by the U.S. Army Map Service, AMS L991, 1945, held in the Geography and Map Reading Room at the Library of Congress, Washington, DC.

sumo wrestling exhibitions, dramatic productions, and other events that had taken place.[76] This outpouring of civic pride displayed and solidified a shared identification with the city that cut across ethnic and national boundaries, although the shift in the local government's

76. Kuhara, *Kiirun shi tei sha.*

location hinted at a more divisive struggle under way. As powerful as the broad, inclusive Jilong identity was in the early 1930s, it did not remain a unifying force for long.

Border Construction and the Roots of Taiwanese Ethnicity

The sense of being Jilongese was not the only group identification that coalesced during the 1920s and 1930s; tensions that emerged in the local context aided the concurrent construction of a broader Taiwanese consciousness. Japanese identity shifted gradually toward a more intolerant and expansive nationalism, a result of both the greater self-confidence of Japanese citizens who had come of age in the context of empire and the rising tensions between Japan and China, as well as between Japan and Western states. Meanwhile, Taiwanese identities emerged in Jilong and elsewhere, binding islanders together throughout Taiwan. As particular varieties of ethnic and national consciousness took shape, social identity groups in the city built rigid barriers between them that shattered the inclusivity of being Jilongese. In the cultural realm and in debates over assimilation, as well as in the quest for a political voice, islanders and Japanese drew clear and distinct borders around Taiwanese ethnicity.

The islander community pulled from multiple sources as it drew sharper boundaries between islanders and the Japanese settlers. Central to their process of identity formation were the mass movements of the 1920s, of which Wakabayashi Masahiro has identified four main types: the new culture (*xin wenhua*), petition (*yihui shezhi qingyuan*), farmers' (*nongmin*), and labor (*laodong*) movements, all of which shared a fundamental anti-Japanese standpoint that overrode any larger political or ideological program.[77] To be sure, islanders looked across the strait to China as they drew inspiration for their activism from the nationalistic May Fourth and May Thirtieth movements, as well as the Northern Expedition, as seen in occasional public celebrations in Jilong of Double Ten Day (October 10) to mark the uprising

77. Wakabayashi, *Taiwan kangRi yundong*, 8, 171–72.

that brought an end to the Qing dynasty.[78] The salience of China for islanders was also evident in the Jilong history written by Jian Wanhuo, who included the China Guild (Zhonghua huiguan), founded in 1926 by Chinese workers in the city, among his list of important institutions and people.[79] However, the ongoing chaos among Chinese warlords and the weakness of the Chinese governments also had a contrary effect on islander consciousness, which might explain why Jian highlighted the guild's externality by expressing the year of its founding in terms of the Republic of China, as "ROC (*Minguo*) 15," instead of with the Japanese system that he used in most of the text.[80] Islanders held ambivalent views of China and, because many of those who led the mass movements in Taiwan had studied in metropolitan Japan, they had absorbed the social and political discourses prevalent there. Chief among them were a near obsession with the idea of culture and an associated quest to elevate the cultural level of everyday life to achieve "a dream of cosmopolitan modernity," in Jordan Sand's phrase.[81]

The metropolitan fascination with culture spilled over into the groups that led Taiwan's popular movements in the 1920s, the Taiwan Cultural Association (Taiwan bunka kyōkai/wenhua xiehui; TCA) and the left-leaning Taiwan People's Party (Taiwan minshūtō/minzhongdang; TPP). Often interpreted as the points of genesis for Taiwanese ethnonationalism, these groups placed tremendous emphasis on cultural persistence and reform.[82] Driven by the activism of Jiang Weishui and Lin Xiantang, two of the most prominent advocates for the islander community, Taipei and Taizhong became the epicenters of the activity

78. See, for example, "Difang tongxin, Jilong: Shuangshi jie jinian jiangyan," *TMB*, Oct. 6, 1927, page number illegible.

79. Jian Wanhuo, *Jilong zhi*, Appendix, 64–66.

80. Wakabayashi, *Taiwan kangRi yundong*, 13; Jian Wanhuo, *Jilong zhi*, Appendix, 64.

81. Sand, *House and Home*, especially 194–98 and 201–6. On the origins of the idea of culture in East Asia, see Lydia Liu, *Translingual Practice*, 312.

82. See Lo, *Doctors within Borders*, 64–70; Ching, *Becoming "Japanese*," 53; Wakabayashi, *Taiwan kangRi yundong*, 8–10; Taiwan sōtokufu, *Taiwan shehui yundong shi*, 9–13. Wang Shilang, in his introduction to his translation of the last source, a study published in 1939 by the Police Bureau of the Taiwan Government-General, does not specifically discuss Taiwanese identity, but his analysis of the text is consistent with the conclusions of the other authors.

guided by these institutions and the growth of an independence-oriented Taiwanese national identity.[83] The TCA sponsored a number of activities, none more significant than the numerous culture lectures (*wenhua jiangyan*) that began in the early 1920s and contributed to multiple identities. In Jilong and elsewhere, the lectures covered topics including education, women's liberation, social diseases, raising youth consciousness, social and political reform, and transforming local customs, such as funerals and religious festivals. The speakers included local residents, students returned from abroad, and the occasional Japanese visitor, and according to reports in the unofficial press, hundreds of people attended each of the talks. At one event on the subject of cultural change versus preservation, a speaker argued that not all old and long-established customs (*gulai guyou de fengsu*) were bad and not all new foreign customs (*jinri wailai de fengsu*) were good, but that standards of humanitarianism and progress should be used to determine which customs to abandon and which to adopt.[84] As this 1923 talk demonstrated, the islanders who spoke, and presumably at least some of the attendees, negotiated between the pressure from Japanese officials and settlers to change their culture to be more like that of Japan, and a desire to retain certain traits that they had inherited from the past and thus from China.

The colonial authorities responded to this sort of public discourse in much the same way their metropolitan counterparts did: they viewed any and all public gatherings with suspicion and anxiety, they dispatched police officers to observe as many speeches as possible, and they shut down any that posed too great a challenge to the imposed order.[85] Late one night in 1924, police visited the home of the leader of a major islander temple in Jilong, who had agreed to host a culture lecture at the temple, and warned him that the talk had to have beneficial

83. Chen Jingkuan, *Cong shengcheng dao Taizhong shi*, 241–52, 268.
84. "Shanliang fengsu de yiyi," *TMB*, Dec. 21, 1923, 3.
85. For responses in the home islands, see Gordon, *Labor and Imperial Democracy*, 160, and illustrations 6 and 7 following 109. The images show police gathered around a speaker at a public demonstration for May Day in 1926 and leading a participant away. The text describes how speakers and attendees at public gatherings expected the police to be present, and that "unless a few speeches were halted, the crowd left unhappy."

content and must not cause any disruption. The event proceeded as planned, but both police officers and local officials joined the audience to make sure that nothing objectionable took place.[86] Apparently colonial authorities found much to object to in these public gatherings, because as the decade went on, reports on culture lectures and other events invariably noted the presence of police officers who sometimes halted speakers midspeech or dispersed entire meetings.[87] The pattern of police supervision and detention in Taiwan matched the actions of Japanese authorities in Korea and the metropole, indicating an increasingly high degree of anxiety over challenges to the official state definitions of public order and public discussion of what it meant to be a Japanese subject.

The assertion of state control over the culture lectures had a subtext in Taiwan that gave it a particularly harsh bite. The vast majority of public events took place at temples, which served as important centers for social and economic activity in addition to fulfilling a spiritual function. Large-scale gatherings at temples made colonial authorities particularly nervous, because the last major uprising of islanders against colonial rule, in 1915, had originated in a religious institution in southern Taiwan.[88] In 1924 the mayor of Jilong attempted to limit the use of temples for large gatherings by appealing to islanders' spiritual sensibility, arguing that holding culture lectures or other public events at temples would defile their sacred ground. He also added a clear warning that continuing to do so could provoke the municipal government to take over the management of the temples.[89] Although local authorities did not immediately take such drastic action, later in the decade the temple where the vast majority of these events took place

86. "Jilong wenhua jiangyan huiji," *TMB*, Sept. 11, 1924, 12.

87. It is not possible to cite all accounts, but a quick survey of the *Taiwan People's News* reveals ten events between 1924 and 1930, roughly half of those reported on in Jilong, at which individual speakers were prevented from continuing or the meeting was stopped.

88. See Katz, *When Valleys Turned Blood Red*.

89. "Jilong wenhua jiangyan huiji," *TMB*, Sept. 11, 1924, 12. Jilong's mayor pointed out that such a takeover had already occurred in Yilan, so it was not an idle threat.

closed its doors, at least temporarily, to large public meetings.[90] The crackdown on nonreligious gatherings and the replacement of temple markets with public markets constituted two parts of a larger effort to reduce the power of religious institutions in the lives of islanders.

Language became one of the key cultural markers at which borders were drawn, largely because the colonial regime placed tremendous emphasis on teaching Japanese as a tool of assimilation.[91] Teaching Japanese to young islanders was one of the two main objectives of the common-school system, and in Jilong numerous opportunities existed for children to study Japanese outside of the regular schools, and for adults to learn it as well. So intent were the colonial authorities on pushing the acquisition of Japanese language that even when they allowed someone like Cai Qingyun, a shop owner and leading social worker in Jilong, to run a private academy, they required that the teachers give instruction in both Japanese and Chinese, and that the school use standard Japanese textbooks to prepare the children to enter the public school system.[92] However, a survey of Jilong's islander population in 1935 revealed that more than three decades of promoting Japanese had not succeeded: only 26 percent of islanders could understand it, let alone speak or write it (table 2.1). A gender-based breakdown for 1934 suggests that language instruction had almost completely failed to reach women and girls, a mere 14 percent of whom could speak Japanese in comparison to roughly 30 percent of male islanders.[93] These low rates were partly owing to the slow flow of people into Jilong from the countryside, where the public school system was not as well developed, but even so, in theory every single child raised in the city should have been taught Japanese at school, and that group would have been

90. "Difang tongxin, Jilong: guan xian yu guanliren jie tuo jinchi gongmiao wei jiangyanchang," *TMB*, Apr. 22, 1928, 6.
91. Tsurumi, *Japanese Colonial Education*, chap. 6; Ching, *Becoming "Japanese"*; and Heylen, *Japanese Models*.
92. "Jilong duanxun: shufang zhaosheng," *NS*, Mar. 5, 1930, 15. Historically, a *shufang* was a private academy where a small number of young students learned classical Chinese and studied the classical texts.
93. Kiirun shi yakusho, *Kiirun shi shakai kyōiku*, 7.

Table 2.1. Japanese language comprehension among Taiwanese in Jilong, 1932–35

Year	Number who comprehend Japanese	Percent of Taiwanese population
1932	11,454	20.12
1933	12,795	22.36
1934	14,545	23.26
1935	17,095	26.20

SOURCE: Kiirun shi kyōka rengōkai, *Kiirun shi shakai kyōiku kyōka*, 16–17.

larger than the 11,500 Japanese speakers counted in 1932.[94] As a group, the islanders in Jilong evidently did not swiftly embrace Japanese, and even those who learned it resisted assimilation, as they became at least bilingual rather than abandon their linguistic roots. Their spoken and written heritage were essential elements of their separate Taiwanese consciousness.[95] In fact, Ann Heylen's work on language reform movements suggests that the slow adoption of Japanese was, in part, the result of official accommodations to islanders' demands for the institutionalization of Chinese-language instruction in schools.[96] Much as Vicente Rafael has shown for the Spanish Philippines and Christopher Goscha for French Vietnam, Xu Zisang, Yan Guonian, and many others like them learned Japanese because it was a useful tool for their business activities and it helped to reinforce their elite status, not because they sought assimilation into the colonizing group.[97]

Although islanders used language and the culture lectures to define some of the core content of their identities, their political activities more sharply advanced the interests of members of the demographic category to which colonial policies had assigned them. In 1931 islanders led a movement for a Taiwan-wide mock election of representatives to

94. Roughly 23,000 islander children were born in Jilong between 1905 and 1931; see Taiwan sōtokufu kanbō tōkei ka, *Taiwan genjū kokō*. Even though not all of those children survived to school age, and many had not yet gone to school when the statistics were compiled, the number of children who should have received Japanese training at school was almost surely more than the number of Japanese speakers listed, a figure that included adults.

95. For a similar argument, see Tsurumi, *Japanese Colonial Education*, 218.

96. Heylen, *Japanese Models*, 195.

97. Rafael, *Contracting Colonialism*; Goscha, "'The Modern Barbarian.'"

local, prefecture, and colonial assemblies, in which islander candidates met with overwhelming success. At the prefecture level, islanders won all seats, but voters elected Japanese candidates to municipal councils in some locations. In Jilong, where a leading businessman with close ties to the Yan family, Pan Rongchun, received the most votes, Ishizaka Sōsaku was the only Japanese who gained a seat on the council; three Japanese candidates won in both Gaoxiong and Tainan, two in Taipei, and one in Tainan. A handful of women were elected to the local councils.[98] Islander residents of Jilong also called for equivalent, though not proportional, representation within the municipal government to expand their influence over what happened in their home city.[99] In these mock elections, and in the mock national assembly, islanders displayed their desire for a greater voice within the governing system, rather than rejecting Japanese rule in favor of an independent nation-state. Thus they built an emerging political consciousness in a way that was expressly separate from a national identity. The overwhelming victory of islander candidates made a strong statement in support of the interests of that social group, whereas the selection of a few Japanese at the local level only highlighted the fact that, by the early 1930s, clear lines had been drawn.

Islanders defined their side of the border during the first four decades of Japanese rule by resisting assimilation through the preservation of aspects of their Chinese cultural heritage. During the 1920s some islanders opposed the government's polices of ethnic fusion (*minzoku yūgō/minzu ronghe*) because they feared that the state's actions promoted the subjugation of one culture by another, rather than an actual merger that would preserve elements of both cultural traditions.[100] Others criticized Japanese settlers for creating inequities in the colony that derived from their biased patriotism (*pianxia de*

98. The local paper ran a series of articles on the mock election (*mogi senkyo*): NS, Dec. 13, 1930, 18–19; Dec. 20, 1930, 18–19; Jan. 1, 1931, 14–15; and Jan. 17, 1931, 17–18. Pan had initially trailed a social reformer named Cai Binghuang but overcame a large deficit in the last two weeks.

99. "Shisei kaikaku o shimin ni kiku," NS, July 25, 1931, 12. Here the islanders are referred to as *Taiwanjin shimin*, or Taiwanese townspeople. At the time, 106 people worked for the city government; all but 14 were Japanese.

100. "Minzu ronghe de yao di," TMB, Aug. 21, 1927, 2.

aiguoxin) and their superiority complex (*youyuegan*). More radical groups argued that equal citizenship would solve the problems of inequality, but they did so based on place of birth, quoting a dictum attributed to Napoleon, that "anyone born in France is French," rather than on a transformation of cultural characteristics.[101] The issues that islanders raised for defense, the manner in which they and their elite gatekeepers advocated on behalf of their assigned group, and the absence of an independent statist agenda together suggest that islanders had engaged in a process of ethnic formation from the 1910s into the 1930s.

When faced with the anti-Japanese aspects of the expanding political, social, and cultural movements, Japanese settlers and officials refined and strengthened their own imagined borders. Their reemphasizing of Japanese nationalism took many forms, one of the most intriguing of which occurred in Jilong during the early 1930s when the local newspaper sponsored a contest to select the most popular café waitress (*jokyū*) in the city, in the summer of 1933.[102] The competitors included 107 women, all but a very few of them Japanese, representing twenty-four cafés throughout the city. When the ballots were counted, the *Niitaka News* printed pictures of the top 10 contestants. The woman crowned "the queen of the glorious café world of all Kiirun," with more than 18,000 votes, was named Emiko, and she worked at a café in the core of Small Jilong. Based on her picture, she embodied the global phenomenon of the modern girl, with a bobbed, flapper-style haircut and what appeared to be a long, fitted dress or perhaps a V-neck blouse and a skirt.[103] The runner-up, some 4,000 votes back, was a woman named Yaeko, who worked at a café in the heart of Big Jilong and wore a full kimono, complete with a wide obi sash wrapped around her waist.[104] Although both women were individuals in their own

101. "Zai Taiwan Ribenren de wuguoxin," *TMB*, June 27, 1926, 1.

102. This was not a singular event; the contest was also held in 1931, and perhaps in other years. See "Tatakai no baku wa tojita ryūryō taru gaisen rappa: Kiirun jokyū tōhyō daidan'en," *NS*, Oct. 8, 1931, 17–18.

103. See Weinbaum and Modern Girl around the World Research Group, *Modern Girl around the World*.

104. "Tatakai no baku wa tojita ryūryō taru gaisen rappa: Kiirun jokyū tōhyō daidan'en," *NS*, Aug. 11, 1933, 19–21. The source pictures are a bit unclear, but there is no mistaking the contrast between Emiko's Western-influenced attire and

right, they also represented two of the most popular icons of Japanese womanhood, and the Japanese national self-image, of the early twentieth century.

The modern girl—*modan gaaru/moga*—became a crucial emblem of the times in the early 1920s, especially in the period after the Great Kantō Earthquake of 1923. Urban, cosmopolitan, and independent, she dressed in the latest fashions inspired by her counterparts in the West, and was most often found working or relaxing in the cafés and restaurants of major Japanese cities. She defined the cutting edge of modern Japanese fashion, social roles, and mores, a figure who showed that Japan was at least equal to the Western nations, and superior to the other countries of Asia. She was not, however, an uncomplicated or uncontested icon, and more conservative groups launched a backlash against what they saw as her libertine, promiscuous, and socially and politically disruptive ways.[105] In contrast to the modern girl was the purportedly more traditional figure from the Japanese pleasure quarters, the kimono-clad geisha who, in the colonial setting, with its separate red-light districts, represented a purely Japanese national essence. To be clear, all of the women who took part in this competition were modern archetypes, in the sense that they worked in new cafés;

Yaeko's kimono. My conclusion about the origins of the participants is based on an examination of their given names. Almost all of their names ended in -*ko*, and two others had names written in katakana, Midori and Naomi, which strongly suggests that all of these contestants were Japanese. Of the remaining three contestants, two others were likely Japanese—眸, Hitomi; and 薫, Kaori or Kaoru—and the last could have been Japanese, Korean, or Taiwanese (阿英, pronounced either Ae in Japanese, Ah Young in Korean, or Aying in Mandarin Chinese). I thank Sue Jean Cho for her help in figuring out which candidate might have been Korean.

105. Many authors have examined the modern girl in Japan, but the conception of her as a symbol of Japan's equality with the West and superiority within Asia is my own. For a good, brief explication of the complex condition of the modern girl, see Silverberg, "Modern Girl as Militant," which emphasizes that the modern girl was a political and cultural transgressor, who, though Japanese, represented un-Japanese (that is, primarily Western) influences in the 1920s. See also Sato, *The New Japanese Woman*, especially chap. 2. On the connections between the modern girl and the café waitress, see especially Silverberg, "Café Waitress"; and Tipton, "The Café." For the backlash against the modern girl, and the return of the Meiji-era "good wife and wise mother" (*ryōsai kenbo*) in the 1920s and 1930s, see Sato, "An Alternate Informant"; Shizuko, "'Good Wife and Wise Mother'"; and Miyake, "Doubling Expectations," 267–95.

the actual geisha in Jilong did not participate. Nevertheless, Yaeko's kimono held tremendous significance because she worked in the islander part of town. To defend herself from the dangerous influences she faced there and to exert a transformative influence on the islanders around her, she had to appear purely Japanese. Viewed through these iconic figures, the café waitress competition represented a strong reassertion of the Japanese national self-image as a modernizing, civilizing, and purifying influence in Taiwan.

Advancing Japanese identity through gendered symbols, although significant, received less official attention than the reinforcement of existing language policies, as officials in Jilong and around Taiwan displayed a near obsession with language instruction from the mid-1930s onward. Beginning in 1934, municipal authorities established more Japanese language training centers outside of the regular education system. They planned for ten new regular language schools, in addition to the eight that already existed, as well as two new basic training centers, bringing that total to three. More significantly, new regulations called for replacing the islanders who ran many of the existing institutions with Japanese administrators, in the hope of tripling the Japanese proficiency rate among islanders to around 70 percent of the Taiwanese population within seven years.[106] In light of the previous four decades of perceived failure, this expectation appeared to be a pipe dream, but the Government-General itself evidently shared the vision. It intensified language policies across the island under the intense Japanization of the Kōminka movement, outlawing Chinese-language newspapers and rewarding children who belonged to "national-language households" (*kokugo katei*), where Japanese was spoken at home, with easier entry to the better schools.

Settlers in Jilong, much like those in Dalian, reasserted their Japanese nationalism and showed a decreasing tolerance for alternative identities in the context of local politics.[107] When the islanders launched

---

106. Kiirun shi kyōka rengōkai, *Kiirun shi shakai kyōiku kyōka*. This source projected expectations for the rate of Japanese comprehension of 40 percent in 1938, more than 50 percent in 1940, and 70 percent in 1942.

107. On Dalian, see O'Dwyer, *Significant Soil*, 212.

their drive for mock elections and greater participation, the Japanese responded with dismissive and essentialist arguments about the nature of the indigenous residents, expressing serious doubts that they were ready to participate in self-government and noting, "On the surface they are like sages, but in their hearts and minds they are demon-like children."[108] The language used in this case and elsewhere in the early 1930s was much harsher and more derogatory than anything seen in articles discussing the islander residents during the 1920s. This denigrating paternalism, combining as it did references to children, subhumans, and duplicity in its assessment of the islanders, had been seen early in the years of Japanese rule, particularly in regard to islanders' customs and religious practices. Its resurgence at this time, however, had as much to do with the social movements that threatened the position of settlers in Taiwan as it did with international developments that increased Japanese anxiety in general over their national survival. The ongoing effects on Japan's economy of the Great Depression destabilized the entire empire, and the overwhelmingly negative worldwide reaction to Japan's military takeover of Manchuria in 1931 left the Japanese in both the metropole and the colonies with a greater sense of insecurity vis-à-vis other imperial powers than they had experienced in decades. Settlers in Taiwan reacted in this instance by trying to exclude islanders from the municipal assembly, thus asserting monopoly control over Jilong's limited political space.

It was, in fact, amid the intensifying contestation over who would define Jilong and what it meant to be Jilongese, and who would direct the city's reterritorialization, that settlers asserted the outward expansion of their national identity most forcefully. Fourteen years after Jilong's elites had collectively expressed their views on how to best develop and promote their city, the *Niitaka News* published a series of seven articles under the headline, "Citizens' Voice: Jilong Development Plan" that replicated the objective of the earlier volume. The new proposals included inward-looking ideas such as ensuring that items produced

---

108. "Kiirun shi kyōgiin kaisen o mae ni shite hontōjin," *NS*, Dec. 2, 1932, 4. The article uses *yasha*, which I translate as demon. The term is complex and does not necessarily connote evil, but in this context that rendering made the most sense.

in Jilong be sold in Jilong rather than down the rail lines in Taipei, and that Jilong's businesses be Jilongese-owned; outward-looking plans, such as following the models of Mojikō, a port in Kyushu, Japan, and San Francisco, both of which held large harbor festivals to promote tourism and city spirit; an effort to expand commerce by improving the group consciousness of merchants; and a general sense that all city residents had to pull together and work harder to improve economic conditions.[109] The specifics of the proposals in 1932 did not differ markedly from the earlier set, but there had been a significant change in contributors: only Ishizaka Sōsaku appeared in both sets, and in 1932 all the contributors were Japanese. Islander elites were no less prominent in 1932 than they had been in 1918; if anything, they held a higher profile in business and political activities and various social circles. Thus the exclusion of islanders here suggests that the settlers were aware of the shift in consciousness among them, felt threatened by that change, and responded by asserting sole ownership over Jilong as a Japanese space.[110]

Local officials joined this effort to reconstruct Jilongese identity as coterminous with Japanese nationalism, and they linked it with expansionist impulses. In a New Year's address at the outset of 1934, the mayor of Jilong, a career bureaucrat named Kuhara Masao, listed the many challenges that Japan faced in the world at the end of 1933: the collapse of the London Economic Conference, Japan's withdrawal from the League of Nations, and efforts by the Chinese in Fujian Province to separate it from the Republic of China.[111] However, he was bullish on Jilong's future as a centerpiece and bulwark of Japan's imperial policies, which he hoped would further the development of his city and promote the greater prosperity of the Japanese Empire. He exhorted the Jilongese, writing, "We residents of this strategic location for the motherland's

109. The recommendations cited here were published, in order, in *NS*, under the headline "Shimin no sei: Kiirun hatten saku," June 17, 1932, 21; July 1, 1932, 4; July 15, 1932, 3; and July 22, 1932, 3.

110. All talked to some extent about enhancing collective efforts, which may have indicated outreach to the islanders, but the Japanese set the terms of such cooperation to a much greater degree than they did in 1918.

111. Anti-Guomindang separatists in Fujian set up an autonomous regime there for a few years in the early 1930s, which caused concern for the Japanese in Taiwan because any instability across the strait could threaten the colony.

southern policies must increase our efforts to plan the expansion of this city's own productivity. We must be prepared to tide ourselves over in these difficult times."[112] Kuhara linked the fate of Jilong directly to the fate of the Japanese nation-state, and he did so in a spirit of self-sufficiency that echoed the national self-reliance campaigns underway in the home islands and later implemented in Manchuria.[113]

Later in 1934 settlers reiterated the connection between Jilong and national survival in a new, broader initiative for the expansion and development of Jilong's harbor. When the Diet granted only part of the amount requested by the colonial office for a new ten-year harbor development plan, local Japanese insisted that the project was crucial to Jilong, and thus to all of Japan. They argued that Taiwan's prosperity depended on enhancing Jilong as a regional nexus for trade, and that the island itself was the empire's southern lifeline (*teikoku nanpō no seimeisen*). If the colony could not defend itself from foreign enemies, then the imperial homeland (*teikoku hondo*) would be in danger.[114] To protect the city from external threats, they established the East Asia Co-Prosperity Association (Tōa kyōei kyōkai) with the aim of making Jilong a bastion of regional development. Thus, six years before Japan proclaimed the establishment of the Greater East Asia Co-Prosperity Sphere (Dai Tōa kyōeiken), colonists in Taiwan promoted a similar idea.[115] The founders had three main goals for their association: to thoroughly spread the spirit of the Imperial Way (*kōdō seishin no fukyū tettei*); to rouse the soul of the Japanese (*Yamato tamashii no hatsuyō*); and to accelerate the completion of assimilation (*dōka no jisseki no sokushin*). In Jilong, settlers hoped to achieve so-called Japanese-Taiwanese fusion (*naiTai yūgō*) by instilling in islanders the core elements of Japanese national identity and

112. "Hijō toki ni saishi bokoku nanpō seisaku no kakuritsu ni zenshosen," *NS*, Jan. 1, 1934, 15.

113. The officially promoted rural revitalization campaign of the 1930s emphasized that farmers had to rely heavily on their own initiative and actions to improve productivity. See Kerry Smith, *A Time of Crisis*, especially chap. 6; Young, *Japan's Total Empire*, 341–47.

114. "Taiwan no mamoru: Kiirun naikō kakuchō undo," *NS*, May 18, 1934, 2.

115. The actions of settlers in Jilong also predated by ten years a map of the Greater East Asia Co-Prosperity Sphere, with Taiwan at the center, that appeared in *Asahi News* in 1944. See Lin Man-houng, "The Ryukyus and Taiwan."

completing a sort of spiritual unification.[116] By advancing the goal of assimilation in the context of Jilong's harbor construction as a key aspect of imperial expansion and regional prosperity, Jilong's settler elites claimed the formerly shared spaces of Jilong as the proprietary domain of Japanese nationalism alone.

Nevertheless, even as Japan's assimilation policies reached a fervent peak in the second half of the 1930s, settlers retreated from their advocacy of fusion and reinforced their long-standing unwillingness to accept the transformation of islanders into full Japanese citizens. According to an article in the Jilong paper from early 1937, some islander government clerks had managed to gain full Japanese nationality owing to a legal loophole that said only Japanese nationals could be paid as clerks. The author of the article criticized the impure motives (*bujun na dōki*) of these people, saying they sought Japanese citizenship solely to gain economic benefits, and insisted that only those who had fully joined the Japanese family system (*kazoku seido*) could receive Japanese nationality, provided that they came from the educated classes and were only minimally influenced by old native customs.[117] By linking Japanese citizenship to the family system that fundamentally underlay the modern Japanese nation-state, and to a near absence of non-Japanese cultural characteristics, settlers built exceptionally high walls around their identity. Even during the peak of expansive Japanese nationalism and the rising crescendo of assimilationism in the latter half of the 1930s, Japanese kept islanders outside the borders of their group.

Conclusion

In the context of rapid urbanization, massive expansion of both population and trade, colonial policies of control and assimilation, and the mass movements of the 1920s and 1930s, Jilong became a crucible for

---

116. "Tōa kōei kyōkai minkan zadankai o kiku," *NS*, June 17, 1934, 3. The assimilation-as-fusion promoted by settlers in Taiwan was more aggressive than the Japanese-Korean harmony (*naiSen yūwa*) of interwar Korea, but it lacked the wartime mobilization aspects of the Japanese-Korean unity (*naiSen ittai*) of the Kōminka movement. See Uchida, *Brokers of Empire*, 144–48, 355–57.

117. "Hontōjin no naichi seki shutoku," *NS*, Feb. 20, 1937, 2.

the formation and reformation of identities, a quality it shared with Taiwan's other cities. The ever-growing numbers of urban residents were not blank slates but actively shaped and embraced a range of identifications that evolved and transformed in the context of everyday interactions. Japanese officials and settlers arrived with the goal of creating a modern city, and also with a sense of superiority over the existing inhabitants that fueled their mission to civilize and assimilate the islanders to Japanese cultural and social norms. Islanders initially identified with their clans, linguistic groups, native places, and the Qing Empire, as well as their current places of residence. However, the condition of being colonial subjects instead of colonizers, as they had been before 1895, created a new context that led to a greater focus on their lives as residents of Jilong and Taiwan. The intersection of existing identities, colonial policies, personal interests, and historic events determined how the imagined borders formed and shifted during the fifty years of Japanese rule.

The requirements of negotiating status and lifestyle, along with the project of creating the new urban spaces of Jilong, enabled islanders and settlers to produce an entirely new consciousness as both groups became Jilongese. This shared sense of self manifested most clearly in a civic pride, as elites transcended demographic categories to advocate collectively for improvements of the harbor on which their livelihoods depended, to found and maintain civic institutions, and to campaign for true self-government on municipal, prefectural, and islandwide levels. They also produced a wealth of information about the city's past and present, creating a collection of unofficial local histories and related materials intended at least in part to promote Jilong's reputation and ensure its status as a regional hub. For islanders, being Jilongese represented a major advance in terms of their sense of belonging to the island rather than to home villages on the continent. For the Japanese, it was a manifestation of their transformational, civilizing ethos and should be viewed as a new extension of their Japanese nationalism.

This expansion of Japanese nationalism clashed with the reformulation of islander consciousness during the 1920s and 1930s, producing a measure of conflict over Jilongese identity. Islanders in Jilong and across Taiwan engaged in a series of social and political movements through which they explored the cultural contours of their group

identity, resisted the assimilation policies promoted by Japanese officials and settlers, and looked to Japan for sociopolitical models even as
they retained much of their cultural heritage. Although the factors
discussed thus far were not in and of themselves sufficient to constitute a Taiwanese ethnicity, they outlined a community in Jilong that
rejected Japanization, and they linked that group to an islandwide
constituency through elite and mass activities, and through the local
experience of hierarchically nested colonial institutions. Anti-Japanese
and pro-islander sentiments reached a peak of sorts with the mock
elections of 1931, in which Japanese settlers won only a handful of seats
and only at the urban level, where local ties allowed a few individuals
to prevail. Faced with this evidence of islanders' resistance to both the
policies of the colonial state and the superiority of the Japanese community, settlers responded by strengthening the borders around their
own in-group. They attempted to reterritorialize Jilong as an exclusively Japanese place—unsuccessfully, as we shall see—by making the
city coterminous with expansive Japanese nationalism and diminishing
the contributions of non-Japanese to the ongoing urban construction.
The emergence of an islandwide context and the competing efforts to
gain a greater voice in local affairs through enhanced political participation were both crucial to the construction of Taiwanese ethnicity.

CHAPTER THREE

"Civilization Enters Here"
Local Elites, Social Organizations,
and the Reterritorialization of Jilong

Late in the fall of 1927, the Jilong Customs Assimilation Association (Jilong tongfenghui, or CAA) held a culture lecture to promote the reform of islanders' funerary practices. The crowd soon became restless and began to heckle the man running this public gathering, Xu Zisang, founder and chairman of the local CAA, which was part of an island-wide network. One person shouted, "Of all of the social organizations in Taiwan, the customs assimilation associations receive the most official credit!" An agitated youth picked up on this theme and reportedly called out, "The Jilong Customs Assimilation Association is the running dog of officialdom! If not in contributing to the regime by exploiting the blood of the people, then where else do its talents lie?" After attempting to complete his talk Xu eventually gave up and remained silent.[1] This exchange illuminates the process, more than the results, of identity formation in Japanese-ruled Taiwan. At its center: a member of the local elite, attempting to act as broker between the demands of the state that enshrined his status and an islander community that could reject or affirm his influence, and a debate over how to reform and retain elements of islander culture. The criticisms leveled at Xu and

---

1. "Sangji gailiang yanjianghui," *TMB*, Nov. 20, 1927, 6. It is not clear if the first heckler was referring to the islandwide associations or specifically to Xu's group.

his organization spoke to the multiple trajectories along which Taiwanese consciousness took shape, with the hecklers suggesting an anti-Japanese nationalism that contrasted with Xu's nonstatist ethnicity, but the significance of this episode lay in the process and the elements that defined it. Islanders engaged with the pressures and restrictions asserted by the Japanese colonial state and its settlers, and drew on their cultural background and contemporary politicization to create their identities.

This event contained one further piece of the puzzle of Taiwanese identity construction, a social organization that, along with other associations like credit unions and civic-minded societies, provided institutional mechanisms that facilitated group cohesion and demarcation.[2] Prominent local citizens established the largest and most important of Jilong's social and economic organizations, through which they supported and structured the growing city and its burgeoning population in ways that at times reinforced, and at times transcended, the demographic divisions imposed by the colonial regime. As overtly local institutions, they also strengthened connections between people and place and thus contributed to the multifaceted reterritorialization of Jilong. That is, by building social identities and defining and defending cultural content, they imparted meaning to the imagined urban terrain. Moreover, much like the movements for participation in local governance, these organizations were manifestations of an emerging public sphere and, established as they were with links to the Government-General and the settler and islander populations, they could facilitate both the government's control over settlers and islanders and the demands of those groups on the government. As such, they augmented the ability of the elites who created and ran them to serve as gatekeepers, interacting within and patrolling the borderland between islanders and Japanese, and protecting and in some cases advancing the developing identities of their respective in-groups. This chapter examines

2. Local associations issued the urban reform recommendations discussed in chapter 2. The Jilong Commercial and Industrial Association (Kiirun shōkōkai), a proto–chamber of commerce with a solely Japanese membership, solicited the 1918 set of reforms, and contributors to the 1932 reforms came from prominent Japanese-member organizations like the Jilong Harbor Association (Kiirun kōwankai).

in detail a handful of the most important local groups to see how they shaped the local Jilong consciousness and delineated the borders between islander-Taiwanese and Japanese.

Organizations and the Division of Jilong Society

Social organizations were formal groups that individuals established through their own initiative, either in conjunction with state representatives or with the approval of state institutions, or both. In most cases these semiprivate institutions had their own bylaws and governing bodies, which together expressed and controlled each group's activities, funding, and structure. Although there are times when I differentiate between types of organizations as social or economic to indicate the main operational focus of particular groups, in general I use the term "social organization" to encompass those institutions that dealt with various aspects of daily life as well as those that concentrated on labor, business, or financial issues. The "social" part of this broad category indicates that the various groups were formed and functioned primarily within society, as opposed to being simple extensions of state power. Even though these groups were never fully autonomous and thus should not be thought of as providing the basis for a true civil society, they were not simply tools through which the colonial government engineered society.[3] Instead, they constituted one part of a public sphere in which private citizens could organize themselves, develop ideas and plans for social and urban development, and express their ideas and expectations to the Taiwan Government-General as well as the home government in Tokyo. That discursive space was important for the Japanese settlers, whose interests and goals were not always contiguous with state objectives, and for islanders, who, although they often cooperated with colonial policies, sometimes operated in ways that opposed official plans.

Jilong's residents, drawing on preexisting patterns of social activity in Taiwan and Japan, imbued the city with a strong organizational

3. Ts'ai, *Taiwan in Japan's Empire-Building*, especially part 2 on colonial engineering.

culture. According to a list compiled by Ishizaka Sōsaku, in 1917 there were nineteen associations (*kai/hui*), seventeen unions (*kumiai/zuhe*), and one society (*sha/she*).[4] The distinctions among these three types revolved around the purpose of each organization: associations generally engaged in public activities, ranging from religious observances to sporting events; unions concentrated on economic behavior; and the society did both. Roughly fifteen years later, Jilong was home to twenty-eight associations, thirty-seven unions, and still the lone society. Total recorded membership ballooned from around two thousand to more than seventeen thousand people, almost 25 percent of the entire population at the time, though as we shall see, not all members joined voluntarily. Some groups had a mix of Japanese and islanders in leadership positions but most lacked diversity at the top level, and likely among the rank and file as well. An absolute majority of those who belonged to organizations were islanders. With very few exceptions, the elites who led these organizations were men, as were most of the members.[5] Individuals frequently belonged to multiple organizations, so the different groups constituted a predominantly male sphere and a densely interconnected social framework into which new arrivals could be incorporated, and which provided stability in times of duress.

The organizational culture found in Jilong and the rest of northern Taiwan, perhaps to a higher degree than in other parts of the island, had both Chinese and Japanese foundations.[6] A substantial body of scholarship on nineteenth-century China demonstrates that elites mobilized populations on the local and provincial levels to accomplish a range of tasks that the declining Qing state could not carry out, from

4. Ishizaka, *Kiirun kō*, 203–9.

5. Ishizaka, *Ora ga Kiirun*, 70–78. Ishizaka listed only a handful of islander groups, but given that islander-Taiwanese participated in many of the other groups he included, they likely founded more than he noted.

6. I base this comparison on my survey of a handful of Japanese-era official and popular gazetteers for comparable cities, like Gaoxiong and Taizhong. These materials did not contain lists of the sort provided by Ishizaka, possibly indicating that such groups were less prominent in those other cities, but in any event they seem to have had fewer organizations than Jilong.

the suppression of rebellions to the provision of welfare.[7] Elite activism reached a high point in the last decades of the nineteenth century, just when Jilong and other northern locales absorbed a new wave of settlers, who may have brought with them that late-Qing localism. To the extent that elites in Taiwan resembled their counterparts on the mainland, they shared this tradition of activism to resolve local or regional problems.[8] People like Xu Zisang, the Yan brothers, and numerous others whose training in the literati tradition was part of the reason for their prominence under Japanese rule had evidently absorbed this ethos of local engagement.[9] On the Japanese side, Meiji and Taishō elites embraced a strong associational culture with roots in the late Tokugawa activism that had brought down the samurai order as well as post-1868 patterns of local institution building.[10] The relatively high concentrations of these settlers in Jilong and Taipei meant they had a profound impact on their new home environments. Both islanders and Japanese settlers approached their goals—accumulating personal wealth, building social structure, and establishing space for their assigned demographic categories within a rapidly expanding city—with a predilection for leading or joining collective efforts, creating a confluence of historical streams that strengthened the social position of elite-led organizations.

The groups that settlers and islanders established addressed a wide range of concerns and interests, and thus linked elites to a number of constituencies. Residents created Buddhist and Christian associations, a tremendous array of professional and commercial organizations, numerous youth groups, and clubs for baseball and tennis. There is no

7. These works include Phillip Kuhn's classic book on the militarization of elites to defeat the nineteenth-century rebellions, Mary Backus Rankin's research on "elite bureaucratic management" and the "extrabureaucratic activities" performed by Jiangnan elites during the late nineteenth century, and Susan Naquin's exhaustive study of late-imperial Beijing, in which she found that elites filled some of the gaps left by receding state and religious institutions. See Kuhn, *Rebellion and Its Enemies*; Rankin, *Elite Activism*; Naquin, *Peking*.

8. Meskill's description of the Wufeng Lin family fits this pattern. See Meskill, *A Chinese Pioneer Family*, especially chap. 12.

9. On localism in late-imperial China, see Bol, *Neo-Confucianism in History*.

10. Garon, *Molding Japanese Minds*.

record that islanders set up native-place societies or guilds, the hallmark institutions of Chinese migrants, but the Japanese in Taiwan
established a range of associations that imported metropolitan village,
city, and prefecture affiliations into the colonial setting. They also set
up branches of empirewide groups, such as the Patriotic Ladies' Association (Aikoku fujinkai) and Imperial Veterans' Association (Teikoku
zaigō gunjinkai), that were intimately connected to Japan's imperial
expansion.[11] The most important organizations that residents established for economic support, urban development, and social and cultural reform were credit unions, the Jilong Public Welfare Society, and
the Jilong Customs Assimilation Association. These key organizations
flourished under, and contributed to, the general mood of tolerance
that prevailed through the 1920s, as a result of which they built strong
bonds with communities both within and outside of the city.

    Such dual connections help to explain how social organizations in
Jilong supported the construction of a broader Taiwanese identity. As
groups made up almost entirely of Jilong residents, often with explicit
agendas for urban development and social assistance as well as institutional connections to state bureaucracies, they were integral to
what Hui-yu Caroline Ts'ai terms "the creation of 'the local.'" These
groups facilitated the substantive contributions of colonial subjects.[12]
However, because some of the most important organizations consisted
either primarily or solely of Japanese or islanders and operated among
only one demographic category, they promoted a bifurcated reterritorialization of the city. The connections that some groups had to other
parts of the island, along both administrative and private pathways,
tended to replicate this divide. Over time, the groups helped to destroy
the shared space of Jilong identity and draw the borders between the
islander-Taiwanese and Japanese segments of society.

    11. For the connections between the Patriotic Ladies' Association and the Japanese
Empire, see Dawley, "Women on the Move." Unfortunately, documentation on the
Jilong branch was not sufficient to allow a deeper study of this group.
    12. Ts'ai, *Taiwan in Japan's Empire-Building*, 120, 146–54. Ts'ai argues that
islanders played a very limited role in creating the local, through the local self-
government movement (151).

Giving Meaning to Imagined Space

Credit Unions

Credit unions—small, member-owned financial institutions whose members determine how available funds should be lent to other members—played a significant role in supporting the economic activities that rooted people in Jilong and Taiwan. Financial institutions are not the most obvious agents of identity construction, but during the twentieth century they served as venues for creating and promoting nationalism. Georgia Mickey, in her exploration of the establishment of the Bank of China in 1912, has argued that its founders, cloaking their self-interest in the discourse of nationalism, convinced both Sun Yat-sen and Yuan Shikai of "the vital role of finance in nation building."[13] In his examination of the same bank's Tianjin branch, Brett Sheehan has emphasized that banks were key institutions for building both personal trust (kinship, interpersonal networks) and impersonal trust (localism, nationalism, faith in modern institutions) during the Republican era.[14] If distant, centrally mandated institutions could serve these functions, then member-dependent credit unions were likely more influential in building a sense of shared purpose and common experience that could advance new group identities.

During the first decades following the advent of Japanese rule, local leaders and the owners of the small businesses that constituted the bulk of daily economic life in Jilong faced a shortage of capital. Late in 1911 a group of Japanese businessmen, organized around a small core that included Ōmi Tokigorō and another early settler named Akabi Sanehira, formed the Jilong Credit Union (Kiirun shinyō kumiai; JCU) under the auspices of the preexisting Jilong Industrial Union (Kiirun sangyō kumiai), an organization that was somewhat out of place given that Jilong had no industry. The newer organization absorbed its progenitor when an 1899 law governing the formation of credit unions in Japan was extended to Taiwan in 1913. Its leaders reclassified it as a limited liability (yūgen sekinin) organization and received a charter for ten

---

13. Mickey, "'Safeguarding National Credibility,'" 140.
14. Sheehan, *Trust in Troubled Times.*

years of operation, which was extended to thirty years in 1926.[15] The
JCU was the first of at least half a dozen such groups that Jilong residents
established to give themselves easier access to funds to sustain their
economic activities. The Jilongese were not alone, for residents of Taipei
had formed roughly thirty credit cooperatives by 1933, by which time
Taibei Prefecture held around seventy industrial unions, fifteen of
which sent delegates to a prefectural branch of the Taiwan Industrial
Unions Association.[16] Gaoxiong residents established four credit unions
among a total of fifteen industrial unions; the three largest were started
during the 1910s.[17] Pooling resources in these collective finance organizations bound local residents to each other through monetary links, and
to people in other locations through institutional hierarchies.

Taiwan's credit unions came out of both long-term historical developments and more recent Japanese institutional borrowing from
Germany. In pre-Meiji Japan, rural commoners formed mutual aid
organizations (*kō*) to ensure their survival through famines and other
times of need, a pattern of association that became firmly entrenched
by the end of the Tokugawa era, thanks in large part to the self-help
ideology of the social reformer Ninomiya Sontoku. More recently, Japanese agrarian reformers observed two types of credit unions on their
trips to Germany during the 1870s, one that functioned regionally on
capitalist, profit-making principles, and another that was more locally
based, ad hoc, and philanthropic. They drew on these models when
they drafted legislation for a credit and loan system in the 1890s, a
plan based on humanitarian, communitarian, and capitalist principles that underlay the small lending institutions that the Meiji government ultimately established throughout Japan.[18] By the early twentieth

---

15. Ishizaka, *Kiirun shinyō kumiai*; TSTF, 5781.4, Jan. 7, 1914.

16. Taiwan sangyō kumiai kyōkai Taihoku shi shūkai, *Taihoku shū shita sangyō*.
The figures come from a count of the industrial unions listed in the source's table of
contents, where credit unions represent about 70 percent of the unions listed. The rest
were a mixture of usage, purchasing, and selling cooperatives.

17. Nakayama and Katayama, *Yakushin Takao*, 227–37. In addition to the credit
unions, the other eleven unions were more enterprise-based.

18. Najita, *Ordinary Economies in Japan*. To be clear, Najita does not argue that
the mutual aid societies evolved into the commercial unions, or that the latter were
explicitly built on the former; the *kō* he studied continued to exist well into the

century, the urban bourgeoisie who settled in colonial spaces like Jilong had embraced these state-sponsored commercial and credit unions, and imported them into the colony for both profit-making and social welfare purposes, where they became ubiquitous features of Taiwan's economic life.

During its first two decades, the JCU came to occupy a prominent position in Jilong. Credit union members contributed to the organization's funds by purchasing shares, which allowed them to then take out loans at favorable terms of interest and repayment. As a key alternative to the local branch of the Bank of Taiwan, which reserved most of its funds for port construction, the JCU's membership expanded remarkably, from twenty-one people in 1911 to more than twelve hundred by the mid-1930s, most of them small-scale capitalists.[19] In his history of the organization, Ishizaka Sōsaku discussed the purpose of cooperatives in general:

> In looking at contemporary economic conditions, capital has the greatest power as a means for participating in any sort of enterprise, and the small and medium producers are overwhelmed by the big capitalists and the large businessmen. . . . The rich become richer, and the poor become poorer, such that the gap between rich and poor becomes excessive, revealing a tendency for the middle class to decline and collapse in the face of the big capitalists. . . . The collapse of the middle class can in fact be said to endanger the integrity of national strength. . . . As for the credit unions, it can be said that they are a resource for the advancement of each economic level as a finance institution of the common people . . . and that they are based on the far-reaching ambition to advance national strength.[20]

Written in 1926, Ishizaka's account reflected both a nationalist agenda and the anxiety circulating within the establishments of Japan, much of

---

twentieth century. However, his analysis makes it clear that the preexistence of mutual aid traditions facilitated the growth and popularity of the new institutions. For the German origins of cooperative credit, see Moody and Fite, *The Credit Union Movement*.

19. Ishizaka, *Kiirun shinyō kumiai*, 3.

20. Ibid., 26–27.

Europe, and the United States over the spread of Marxist ideologies in the years following the Bolshevik triumph in Russia and the establishment of the Chinese Communist Party. Taiwan was not a hotbed for communist activism—the Taiwanese Communist Party was not founded until 1928 and it was based in Shanghai because the Government-General effectively prohibited its transfer to the island—nonetheless, many in Taiwan were concerned about the effects of severe economic inequality. Those fears intensified in the face of Taiwan's social movements and the financial constraints of the Great Depression, at which point the JCU enacted austerity measures by calling in its debts and curtailing new loans. Although membership remained relatively constant at this time, the total number of shares declined as individual members cashed in some of their holdings to weather their own difficulties.[21] As a bulwark for the middle classes, the JCU both sustained many livelihoods and facilitated the social stability sought by the state.

However, the JCU was only one of several credit unions, and as residents formed more, the unions highlighted the fissures between evolving identity groups. The JCU primarily served the interests of the settlers and promoted their economic advancement. It maintained offices in the northern part of Japanese-dominated Small Jilong, and islander shareholders never exceeded the prewar peak of about 12 percent in 1936. Women made up an even smaller percentage of the membership.[22] To rectify this disparity and extend the benefits of belonging to a credit union to a greater number of islanders, in 1922 Yan Yunnian and Xu Zisang joined with many other islander businessmen to establish the Jilong Commercial and Industrial Credit Union (Jilong shanggong xinyong zuhe; CICU). The CICU functioned in the same manner as the JCU, and the composition of its shareholders mirrored that of its counterpart. However, whereas the JCU primarily served the economic interests of middle- and upper-class settlers, the CICU consisted of mostly islanders and a minority of Japanese. According to one account,

21. Kiirun shinyō kumiai, *Kiirun shinyō kumiai jigyō*, reports for 1931, 1933, 1934.

22. The rate of 12 percent was an increase over the 9 percent of membership in 1931. Ishizaka, *Kiirun shinyō kumiai*; Kiirun shinyō kumiai, *Kiirun shinyō kumiai jigyō*, reports for 1931, 1936.

because the JCU's officers were all Japanese, islanders faced difficulties in obtaining loans; therefore it was necessary to form an additional credit union to serve the islander community in Jilong.[23] The CICU ultimately matched its predecessor in number of members, if not in overall assets, and joined it in the Taibei Prefecture umbrella union, becoming a key part of the city's socioeconomic fabric.[24] It did not always ensure islander unity, for the local paper reported a Xu-Yan factional split that emerged in 1933 over a substantial amount of money that Xu, the vice chairperson, owed the credit union and that Yan Guonian, the chair, had recently pushed to collect.[25] Nevertheless, even that article confirmed that the CICU was an islander organization, just as the JCU worked mostly with settlers; thus together the two credit unions institutionally solidified the division between the two communities.

However, a third credit union complicated the picture because it did not fit into this bifurcated, or rather yin-yang, membership model, although it did reveal fissures in Jilong society. Several years into the Depression, a large group of islanders and Japanese residents, in roughly equivalent numbers, joined together to form the fully integrated Jilong People's Credit Union (Kiirun shomin shinyō kumiai; PCU). The founders did not pursue integration as a social or cultural goal but hoped to establish an alternative to the existing credit associations, both of which counted big capitalists and other top elites—including such individuals as Yan Guonian, Ōmi Tokigorō, and Ishizaka Sōsaku, as well as several corporations—among their investors.[26] In that motivation, the PCU revealed a clear division between old established

23. Ishizaka, *Kiirun shinyō kumiai*, 19–20.

24. In 1931 the JCU had roughly twice the assets of the CICU, 26,000 yen compared to 14,000 yen; see Ishizaka, *Ora ga Kiirun*, 71. According to a 1933 list, the two organizations had roughly equivalent numbers of officers; see Taiwan sangyō kumiai kyōkai Taihoku shi shūkai, *Taihoku shū shita sangyō*, 36–39. Postwar reports (addressed in chapter 7) show that the two groups had similar-size memberships at the end of the Japanese era.

25. "Kiirun shōkō shinyō kumiai o meguri Wan shin ryō ha no tairitsu gekka? Ko Shisō no fuseii ni Gan ha sude ni tatsu sanman'en no shakuyō shin no seiri iyoiyo dankō?," *NS*, Sept. 22, 1933, 3.

26. A 1933 article in the *Taiwan Daily News* and a 1934 article in the *Niitaka News* reported on the PCU's founding meeting. See "Kiirun shomingumi sōritsu sōkai,"

elites and a new generation, which tried to assert itself within the existing socioeconomic hierarchy much as it had in its drive for local autonomy and in the mock elections.

Each of these three credit unions reflected its moment of creation and represented a different form of territorialization and a different trajectory of identity formation. The Japanese settlers who founded the JCU in 1911 manifested the late-Meiji priorities of colonial benevolence and Japanese advancement over other Asians; thus they formed a credit union that reinforced their role in developing Jilong, and Taiwan, for the common good. When islanders formed the CICU in 1922, they did so in a conscious defense of the economic interests of their demographic category and a perhaps unconscious display of their evolving group identity, but in adopting a Japanese model they expressed a willingness to accommodate and adapt to the colonial context. The creators of the PCU belonged to a generation that had come of age under the influence of the shared Jilong identity and now faced both a surge in population and prolonged economic contraction. In founding the new credit union they were less concerned with cultural divisions or demographic categories than with financial survival in the first half of the 1930s, but they also showed the continued strength of an inclusive Jilong consciousness.[27] These three organizations mapped onto the real and imagined terrain of Jilong in different ways, dividing or uniting the city, and the identities of its residents, in the process.

The Public Welfare Society

The history of the Jilong Public Welfare Society Foundation (Zaidan hōjin Kiirun kōekisha; PWS) highlights the increasingly sharp divisions within Jilong and Taiwan. Its roots go back to 1910, when seventeen Japanese businessmen met under the leadership of the Jilong

---

TNS, Sept. 27, 1933, 4; and "Kiirun ni shinyō kumiai shinsetsu undo: nai Tai jin o ichigan toshite keikaku," *NS*, Sept. 15, 1934, 2.

27. The main credit unions in Gaoxiong had the same demographic distribution, with one created and run by and for Japanese, one led by and for islanders, and one of mixed membership, although Gaoxiong's did not develop along the same timeline as Jilong's. Nakayama and Katayama, *Yakushin Takao*, 229–37.

subprefecture magistrate to discuss ways that they could influence the future development of Jilong. With the completion of the trans-island railway in 1908 and the recent progress in port construction, the city's prospects looked bright. They wanted to ensure that its promise would be realized, and that they would benefit from it.[28] All of the founding members were Japanese, and Kimura Kutarō served for five years as director before turning the post over to Ishizaka Sōsaku.[29] Although it always remained predominantly Japanese and entirely male, a few eminent islanders joined the organization. By 1922, fourteen of the society's eighty-two members were islanders, including Xu Zisang and both Yan brothers.[30] Similar organizations existed in Dalian, such as the Hongji Shantang, which grafted an opium farm sanctioned by the Japanese colonial government onto a long-standing Chinese "benevolence hall" (shantang) or charitable organization, and a number of pre-existing public service associations (gongyihui) that received official recognition.[31] However, as a Japanese-initiated, mixed-membership association devoted to urban socioeconomic development, the PWS seems to have had no exact cognate in either Taiwan or other Japanese colonies. It embodied an inclusionary vision of Jilong, which it fostered through a sense of collective responsibility for the city, but its links to colonial administrative hierarchies left it at the mercy of more exclusionary forces in the 1930s.

The founders of the PWS took the entire current and future area of Jilong as their purview, and they aimed to improve the physical, social, and economic environment for all residents. They stated these goals when they applied to the Government-General for formal incorporation: "We form the Jilong Public Welfare Society with the objectives of constructing a public hall and public beaches, and for public welfare and charitable activities, on behalf of the residents of Jilong

28. Tsubamoto, Kiirun kō daikan, 65.
29. The list of founding members is in TSTF, 2120.8, Sept. 1, 1913, 7–9. The transfer of chairmanship to Ishizaka is recorded in Tsubamoto, Kiirun kō daikan.
30. Tsubamoto, Kiirun kō daikan, 70–74. Xu Zisang and another islander joined the board within months of its founding. See TSTF, 5604.18, Oct. 1, 1913.
31. Kingsberg, Moral Nation, 103–6; O'Dwyer, Significant Soil, 91.

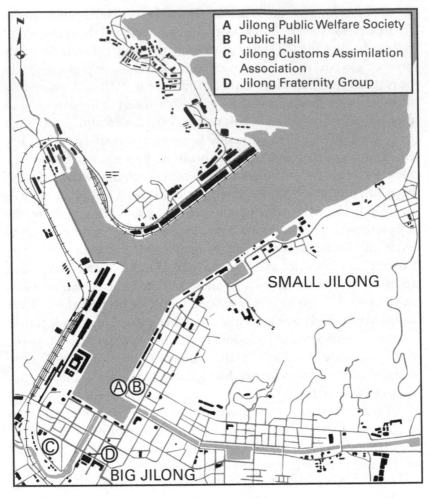

MAP 3.1. Social organizations in Jilong. Map created by Scott Walker, based on a map designed by the U.S. Army Map Service, AMS L991, 1945, held in the Geography and Map Reading Room at the Library of Congress, Washington, DC.

and its environs."[32] In 1914 the PWS sought the rights to a piece of land, to be used rent free, on which to build the Public Hall (Kōkaidō), which would serve as its institutional home and as a means of commemorating the Taishō emperor's accession to the throne, the anniversary of

32. TSTF, 2120.8, Sept. 1, 1913, 3.

FIGURE 3.1. The former post office building in Jilong, 1915. Image courtesy of Special Collections and College Archives, Skillman Library, Lafayette College, and the East Asia Image Collection, http://digital.lafayette.edu/collections/eastasia/.

his wedding, and twenty years of Japanese rule of Taiwan. The location its members selected was rich in symbolism because it was near the southern edge of Small Jilong, on the site of the Qing dynasty fort commander's office (*yaosai silingguan*), near recently reclaimed land at the southeastern corner of the harbor, and just steps from a bridge that crossed the canal into Big Jilong (see map 3.1). This space, where "every day hundreds of people pass by," was perfectly suited for a public venue where people from near and far could gather to see "the good fortune of the local residents and the development of this place."[33] In short, the PWS planned to use its location, in the heart of the city and at an intersection between the islander and Japanese communities, to erase vestiges of the former Qing regime and display the achievements of the

33. Ibid., 2372.3, May 1, 1915, 4.

colonial period. The Government-General approved the proposal in May 1915 and over time the city government offices, the military police, the Jilong branch of the Bank of Taiwan, the post office, and Ishizaka Sōsaku's shop would all be located within a block of the Public Hall (fig. 3.1).

Structurally, the organization was a mini bureaucracy that reflected Japanese priorities for colonial development. It had a director (shachō) who ran the day-to-day business and also represented it to both the government and Jilong society. The board of directors (rijikai) selected the chief officer, and the board was drawn from a larger body of appointed consultative members (hyōgiin), who each served six-year terms. A consultative committee (hyōgikai) proposed and determined most of the important business.[34] Although the society consisted primarily of settler and islander elites, it was not entirely private, as sometimes both the mayor and the official in charge of defense (gunshu) for Jilong County were members of the PWS, and any substantive changes to its articles of incorporation required official approval.[35] The Government-General enforced its oversight authority when it approved a 1918 request to increase the membership and ensure that Japanese members retained their dominance on the consultative committee.[36] This stipulation indicated tension between an inclusive desire to develop Jilong for the benefit of all residents and an exclusive concern for ensuring the predominance of a Japanese vision and identity for the city, which would bedevil the organization throughout its existence. The extent to which the group shifted to one side or the other, in conjunction with the prevailing tenor of official policies and state ideology, affected the society's survival.

The ability of the PWS to operate on behalf of the general public was enhanced by its various sources of funding. Rents on nearly 2,000 tsubo (about 6,600 square meters) of city land that the government had

34. Ibid., 2120.8, 4–6.
35. Mayor Satō Etarō was chairman of the board (rijichō) of the PWS in 1927, and the county guardian was named a consultative member in 1920. See Kiirun kōekisha, Shōwa ninen, 20–21; TSTF, 6810.5, Jan. 1, 1920. On changes to the articles of incorporation, see TSTF, 2120.8.
36. TSTF, 6509.2, Jan. 1, 1918. The application required that six out of seven consultative members were Japanese.

9 賣 店 點 景 (其の一)

FIGURE 3.2. The Jilong Public Hall, center building, during the celebrations for the new city government building. Image courtesy of the National Taiwan Library, Taipei.

bestowed on the PWS provided a consistent income. In addition, the society sold water to boats in the harbor, received grants from the Jilong Club (Kiirun kurabu) and the Public Hall (fig. 3.2), profited from the cafeteria that it established in the Public Hall, and sold coal that it salvaged from the harbor. It also floated bonds and, as of 1933, held some 30,000 yen in investments.[37] In 1927, unfortunately the only year for which statistics are extant, all of these sources brought in a substantial revenue total of a bit more than 13,000 yen.[38] To put these figures in perspective, although the largest companies with offices in Jilong, empirewide giants such as Mitsui Mining and Osaka Shipping, were capitalized at more than 100 million yen, the most profitable small business in the city took in 2,700 yen in 1931, and only eight businesses

37. Irie, *Kiirun fūdo*, 169.
38. Kiirun kōekisha, *Shōwa ninen*, 10–12.

had more than 1,000 yen in revenue.[39] Its variegated sources of income gave the PWS a strong financial foundation, rooted it in the city's essential mining and commerce enterprises, and bound it to the very people whose lives it sought to improve.

During its heyday, from its founding until 1933, the PWS made multifarious contributions to building a sense of unity, of belonging to a common place, among Jilong residents. From its creation, it fired a cannon each day at noon to signal the time, to keep everyone in the compact city center on a common schedule, and it maintained several bulletin boards that were available for public use, to display news and distribute other information. One of these boards was next to the Public Hall, two were in the Japanese zone of Small Jilong, and another was near the main temples and markets in the heart of Big Jilong, locations that must have seen significant foot traffic every day. The PWS promoted business connections among its members and nonmembers in the city and elsewhere, mediated in commercial disputes, ran an employment agency, and conducted surveys of local economic conditions. In 1925 it absorbed the collection of Ishizaka Sōsaku's public library into the Jilong Library (Kiirun bunko), which it thereafter oversaw.[40] Most important, for many years it managed both the Public Hall and the Jilong Club, the latter a semi-independent organization of Japanese businessmen that provided them with a haven for relaxation and the entertainment of residents and visitors.[41] Various organizations and individuals used both of these spaces to hold a wide array of public and private events, well over two hundred events in some years, including meetings of the Imperial Veterans' Association, several youth groups, the local Women's Association, and local welfare commissioners, as well as frequent exhibitions of paintings, calligraphy, and antiques.[42] As the PWS had intended when it chose the location for its Public Hall, the entire city came together at this central crossroads.

39. Ishizaka, *Ora ga Kiirun*, 72–73, 78–79. The income disparity had something to do with the Depression, but the PWS was nonetheless a well-to-do organization.
40. Tsubamoto, *Kiirun kō daikan*; and TSTF, 10516.9, Jan. 1, 1935.
41. The Jilong Club was founded in 1913; see Tsubamoto, *Kiirun kō daikan*, 68.
42. Kiirun kōekisha, *Shōwa ninen*, 12–14.

As the city became more closely linked to trade networks within and beyond the Japanese Empire, the PWS both promoted Jilong's image to the wider world and tried to minimize the effects of external difficulties. In 1929, inspired in part by an unnamed resolution of the International Labor Organization's conference in Geneva, and in part by a sense that Jilong lacked something that major port cities should possess, the PWS launched a drive to establish a sailors' home (*kaiin hōmu*) for mariners, migrants, and travelers who arrived by sea. The idea gained support from the city and colonial governments, and thousands of sailors were enlisted to begin constructing the center.[43] The following year, after the worldwide Depression brought a sudden influx of unemployed laborers to the city, the PWS swiftly developed and publicized methods for coping with economic difficulties. Working with district leaders and other groups, it exhorted residents to use only national products (*koku sanpin aiyō*) and to economize by purchasing fewer luxury items.[44] Such a protectionist campaign was not unique to Jilong or to Japan's empire, for promoting national products became one way of promoting the nation itself.[45] This defensive, exclusionary nationalism also manifested in Manchuria around 1930, in the rise of settler politics as a mass movement in Dalian and in the agrarian settlement drive.[46] Much like Japanese settlers in Dalian, members of the PWS led the way in linking the local, colonial, and national economies in their effort to advance their own fortunes and those of the Japanese Empire.

However, it was the more inclusionary side of its mandate that brought the PWS into its finest hour, in the summer of 1933. One weekend that July, the All-Island Business Conference (Zentō jigyō taikai) held its seventeenth annual meeting in Jilong, overlapping with the

43. "Kaiin hōmu no kensetsu," *NS*, July 5, 1929, 2; "Kakushite kaiin hōmu kensetsu michinori e," *NS*, Sept. 15, 1929, 10. According to the second article, the Geneva conference mandated that "All port cities should construct a sailors' home."

44. "Jilong gongyishe pingyihui," *TNS*, June 17, 1930, 4; "Jilong gongyishe bujingqi duice," *TNS*, Nov. 5, 1930, 8.

45. On nationalizing, protectionist responses to the worldwide Depression, see Kindleberger, *The World in Depression*.

46. O'Dwyer, *Significant Soil*, 212–13; Young, *Japan's Total Empire*, chap. 7.

A view of Keelung Harbour Furnaces. (常州) 基隆港全景（其ノ二）
近年の發展に伴ひ港灣の諸設備も整ひ通商、交通の便日に重み島民の幸福は此處にも表はれて居ります

FIGURE 3.3. A panoramic view of Jilong's inner harbor, showcasing Small Jilong. Detail taken from image spanning two postcards. Image courtesy of the National Central Library, Taipei.

first-ever Jilong Harbor Festival (Kiirun kō matsuri).[47] The timing was not a coincidence; the PWS, which selected Jilong's representatives to the business meeting, organized both events that year to showcase its city.[48] Surviving accounts indicate that the conference was a resounding success. More than 260 business owners and other attendees came from all over Taiwan, a larger turnout than at any previous meeting, to discuss eighteen separate proposals on a wide range of topics. Almost all of the issues reflected a mixture of local, islandwide, and regional business concerns, such as improving shipping routes between Taiwan and Japan, dredging the Danshui (Tamsui) River, promoting animal husbandry in indigenous zones, and developing Jilong's outer harbor. The interplay between personal interest, locality, and colony that underlay these discussions came out most clearly when the representatives explored ways to use the upcoming 1935 Taiwan Exhibition to highlight their commercial achievements.[49]

The two-day Harbor Festival was perhaps a greater triumph, a point suggested by a prominent headline in the *Taiwan Daily News* that announced, "Morning Thunderclaps Herald the Opening of the Jilong Harbor Festival." Nagahama Makoto, a member of the Jilong Harbor Association, first proposed this event in his contribution to the 1932 collection of articles on how to improve Jilong, and the PWS, now under the leadership of Ōmi Tokigorō, brought the idea to fruition.[50] Unlike the members-only business conference, the festival was a public event attended by families and individuals of all ages from Jilong and much of northern Taiwan. The PWS made the recently completed experimental aquarium, constructed, with public funds, near the mouth of the harbor, the centerpiece of its festival, and put the city on display with events scattered throughout the downtown area (fig. 3.3). It

47. The PWS also hosted the eighth edition of this event in 1924. See "Kiirun ni okeru zentō jigyō daikai," *TNS*, Sept. 21, 1924, 7.

48. Kiirun kōekisha, *Shōwa ninen do*, 3–4.

49. The *Taiwan Daily News* published numerous articles about the conference, including "Jilong gongyishe lishi ji pingyihui," *TNS*, May 16, 1933, 4; "Kaikaku o sakebaruru jitsugyōkai no tōgi," *TNS*, July 17, 1933, 3; and "Quandao shiye dahui (di er ri): shiba yi'an quan ke jue," *TNS*, July 17, 1933, 8.

50. "Shimin no sei: Kiirun hatten saku (yon)," *NS*, 1932, 3. For 1932 proposals, see chapter 2.

planned presentations of islander plays (*hontō gi*) in Takasago Park in Big Jilong, scheduled dance performances on outdoor stages near the Public Hall and in the Denryōkō pleasure quarters, and routed a parade through the streets of Small Jilong.[51] The new aquarium, the various cultural events, and tours through the modern streets proudly exhibited the city's remarkable growth since 1895 in ways that spoke to a varied audience. Moreover, with these two events the PWS displayed its own achievements in fulfilling its inclusive mandate to improve the lives and lived environment of all residents.

Unfortunately for the PWS, these successes could not alter the fact that the organization faced a struggle for its survival. Challenges to its preeminence began as early as 1922, when other local groups successfully contested its exclusive right to coal-salvaging operations in the harbor.[52] More significantly, in 1930 it lost control of the Jilong Club and the Public Hall, which had previously supported it financially and undergirded its status. Bending to both financial and social pressures, it helped set up a new, exclusively Japanese group called the Jilong Club Association (Kiirun kurabukai), which assumed responsibility for the building. It also transferred to the city government management of the Public Hall, the very structure that had embodied its strategy for building up Jilong.[53] The following year, the local paper reported that public support for the PWS had declined, perhaps because the city government's social work office had taken over many of the society's charitable activities.[54] Its loss of status seemed complete in 1935, a mere two years after its great success with the Harbor Festival and business conference. When Taiwan held perhaps its first truly world-class event, the Taiwan Exhibition, in celebration of forty years of Japanese rule, the

51. The Harbor Festival also received an abundance of press coverage. See, in *TNS*, "Jilong gang ji: shiwu ye jiazhuang," July 13, 1933, 8; "Kiirun kō matsuri no nigihi (futsuka me): honnen hajimete no hitode," July 17, 1933, 7; and "Jilong gang ji di er ri gezhong yuxing qi kai ji cheng yishi renao," July 18, 1933, 4. According to the first report, some sixty or seventy organizations and shops were involved in the event.

52. Irie, *Kiirun fūdo*, 169–70; "Kiirun henpen: kaichintan dorobō," *NS*, May 29, 1930, 4.

53. "Jilong julebu neigui," *NS*, Nov. 5, 1930, 8.

54. "Kiirun zakkei," *NS*, Jan. 29, 1931, 4.

Jilong Public Welfare Society played no role. Some of its members sat on the planning committee, and other organizations participated, but the PWS was absent.[55]

Multiple factors caused the society's decline after two decades "at the center of Jilong's social life."[56] To an extent it reflected shifts and conflicts within the city's social fabric as the new generation of Japanese elites challenged the old. The formation of the Jilong Harbor Association, a new group that comprised solely Japanese businessmen, was partially an effort by recent arrivals to upset the dominance of their predecessors. There may have also been a measure of class conflict involved, an extension of the effort to represent middle-class interests against the big capitalists that was seen in the founding of the PCU. Indeed, the PWS received criticism for failing to fully represent the interests of the lower and middle classes in its collective solutions to the economic difficulties of the early 1930s.[57] However, neither generational nor class rivalries provide a sufficient explanation, because many of the old capitalists retained their influence and status. The head of the new Harbor Association was none other than Ōmi Tokigorō, and Ishizaka Sōsaku was never marginalized. When Kimura Kutarō and Yan Guonian, the biggest of Jilong's big capitalists, passed away in 1936 and 1937, respectively, Jilong's residents honored them in grand style, and the Yan family maintained its major enterprises.

Politics, rather than changes within elite society or class conflict, seems to have determined the downfall of the PWS. In 1934 the Jilong newspaper called on the PWS, "an organization with mysterious influence (myōyō) for advancing the island's autonomy," to represent Jilong residents in the islandwide struggle for full political participation.[58] With the drive for local autonomy gaining more support around the island, the PWS took up that task, perhaps to counteract recent criticism that it had not done enough to lead the effort.[59] The following year, the Japanese home government finally gave in to this pressure and

55. Shikamata, *Shisei yonjū shūnen*, 419–41. Key PWS representatives included Yan Guonian, Ishizaka Sōsaku, and Ōmi Tokigorō.

56. Nakajima, *Kiirun shi annai*, 124.

57. "Chū shō shōkōgyō sha kyūsai," *NS*, Sept. 23, 1933, 3.

58. "Kōeki sha soshiki kaizō ni tsuite," *NS*, May 11, 1934, 4.

59. Ibid.; "Jilong san tuanti kai zuotanhui," *TNS*, Oct. 24, 1935, 4.

seemingly fulfilled the long-deferred promise of Taishō democracy by establishing elected assemblies for the island and its cities and towns. In practice, however, this was a dead letter, for by the mid-1930s the military and political oligarchs had begun to reassert their control over the Japanese government, and the era of party cabinets and electoral power was effectively over. Thus, when the PWS took up the cause of local self-government on behalf of both Japanese and islanders, it was taking a stand against military and bureaucratic dominance of the political process, and in so doing, it set the stage for its own demise. In 1936 the colonial government created a new system, the Chambers of Commerce and Industry (Shōkō kaigisho), and established branches around the island, all under central control.[60] When the state set up the Jilong branch, with Ōmi Tokigorō as its head, it simply disbanded the multifunctional PWS in favor of this new, purely business-focused organization.

The PWS also inadvertently contributed to its own demise by embracing the more inclusive side of its mandate at a moment when Japanese nationalism shifted toward intolerance and expansionism. During the mid-1930s, in both Jilong and the Japanese Empire at large, discourses on the purity of a national essence favored starker differentiations between Japanese and non-Japanese. This disintegrative tendency was evident in the contrasting fates of the PWS and three other semiprivate organizations. Following the establishment of the Jilong Chamber of Commerce and Industry, colonial authorities allowed the Jilong Club and the Jilong Harbor Association to continue operating after they were merged in a new group, the Harbor Club (Kōwan kurabu).[61] The two surviving groups shared one thing in common, in contrast to the PWS: all of their members were Japanese. The leaders of the PWS, even with a formal preponderance of Japanese members, had selected the wrong moment to emphasize their inclusive Jilong identity, for within the Kōminka era's contradictory environment of strict compartmentalization and rapid assimilation, the colonial government simply disbanded the organization in favor of the officially supervised chamber of commerce and the purely Japanese Harbor Club.

60. Zhao Youzhi, *Ri ju shiqi Taiwan shanggonghui*.
61. "Tai hō ten," *NS*, Nov. 28, 1936.

A rising tide of militant ultranationalism in the home islands, exemplified by the abortive coup of February 1936, provided one explanation for the end of the PWS. More proximately, the Government-General and some Japanese settlers reacted against what they perceived, correctly, as the failure of gradual assimilation. During the same years that the PWS had tried to build an inclusive Jilong, the city's largest islander-only organization had been defending the content and boundaries of another identity group.

The Jilong Customs Assimilation Association

A defining characteristic of colonial regimes was that they all attempted to reform native customs. In fact, all modern states, as part of their nation-building efforts, endeavored to transform local traditions that did not conform to habits deemed acceptable by those who defined the national character.[62] The British in India surveyed and formalized the existing laws, languages, and practices they found to facilitate their control, and the French held to their *mission civilisatrice* across their empire but shifted from policies of assimilation (making the colonized French) to association (allowing the persistence of local customs).[63] The Japanese project in Taiwan was ideologically and practically more in keeping with the French approach, applying cultural reform projects in an incremental manner as part of a broader modernizing effort that closely resembled associationism, largely because Japanese officials and settlers remained ambivalent about the realities of assimilation. Islander elites incorporated a modernizing impulse into their identities, for they, too, wished to reform or eradicate such customs as footbinding, and certain burial rituals and marital and religious practices, on the basis of their perceived backwardness, unsanitary character, or expense. However, Japanese residents and islanders took different views of cultural change, a divergence that sharpened the border between the two groups.

62. Weber, *Peasants into Frenchmen*.
63. On the British in India, see Cohn, *Colonialism and Its Forms*; Dirks, *Castes of Mind*; Fischer-Tiné and Mann, *Colonialism as Civilizing Mission*. On the French, see Conklin, *A Mission to Civilize*; Cooper, *France in Indochina*.

The Jilong CAA, under the long-time management of Xu Zisang, played a crucial role in controlling the type and pace of customs reform in Jilong. That afternoon in 1927 on which a radical young heckler shouted down Xu was not a good day for the CAA or its leader, and it is unlikely that this was a solitary incident. Nevertheless, the organization was uniquely positioned to serve as an institutional gatekeeper, since it had contact with a larger segment of Jilong's residents than any other semiprivate group in the city. Four years after the failed lecture, it claimed almost 11,000 members, thanks in no small measure to a mandate from the Government-General.[64] The CAA's origins and development, and its prominent place within Jilong society, illustrate how social organizations contributed to ethnic formation, and how individuals created identities in their everyday lives. Whereas the PWS struggled to resolve the conflict between exclusive Japanese and inclusive Jilong consciousness, and expressed another version of the Japanese ambivalence toward assimilation, the CAA's history shows how islanders imagined themselves as a bounded social group at the local level and connected that community to a broader one across Taiwan through shared customs and administrative hierarchies.

During the early years of Japanese rule, Xu Zisang's rise to prominence coincided with his initial efforts at reforming islanders' customs. He made his first attempt in 1903, the same year that he became district chief and took over management of the Qing'an Temple—all developments that were likely related—when he joined the growing anti-foot-binding campaign in Taiwan and founded Jilong's Natural Feet Association (Tianranzuhui).[65] Several years later, in 1909, he established the Jilong Queue-Cutting Association (Jilong duanfahui) in order to eradicate the Manchu hairstyle that the Qing state had mandated for all Chinese males.[66] Both organizations relied on volunteer

---

64. Ishizaka, *Ora ga Kiirun*, 76. According to Ishizaka, the group had 10,778 members at this time.

65. Xu's group followed Huang Yujie's establishment in 1900 of an association of the same name, which had itself been a response to similar efforts in China. See Ts'ai, *Taiwan in Japan's Empire-Building*, 128–29.

66. In some circles in Taiwan the persistence of the queue, especially among migrants from the mainland, was seen as a political statement against the colonial

members, who arranged public discussion sessions and went door to door to educate people about how backward and unsanitary both practices were. Within three or four years, several thousand women and girls in the Jilong area had unbound their feet, and in even less time the town achieved the second highest rate of queue cutting in all of Taiwan.[67] In targeting these two practices for eradication, Xu and his islander allies broke from their Chinese roots in significant ways. Encouraging unbound feet among islander women meant rejecting what had been a marker of the Chinese cultural heritage throughout the Qing period. Furthermore, advocating short hair—the Chinese phrase *duanfahui* meant "short-hair association"—carried the subtext of rejecting the Qing state and thus accentuated the political separation from China, although in some instances it may have indicated sympathy with Chinese nationalism.[68] In both cases, islander bodies were liberated from the constraints of a supposedly unenlightened past in ways that dovetailed with the Government-General's attack on what it saw as unmodern and uncivilized practices. Modern-minded islanders viewed these steps as desirable cultural transformations and, in Jilong as elsewhere, they often took action before official programs went into effect.[69]

Over the course of the 1910s, private and public reform efforts converged to produce an islandwide collection of cultural transformation groups. In 1914 Xu turned to his former classmate, Yan Yunnian, and other locals for help in merging his original two associations into a new group, the Sincere Customs Association (Dunsuhui), which operated in

---

regime, and hence it had to be eradicated to distinguish between islanders and Chinese immigrants. See "Taiwan no danhatsu fu kaisokai."

67. NKKS, 1-2A-040-06 *zoi*-00166-100. Ts'ai indicates that only around eight thousand women had unbound their feet by 1905, thus Xu's efforts were among the most successful. See Ts'ai, *Taiwan in Japan's Empire-Building*, 129.

68. Mark Elliott argues that the Manchu dynasty manipulated these physical markers to preserve a distinction between Manchu and Han. Elliott, *The Manchu Way*. See also Ts'ai, *Taiwan in Japan's Empire-Building*, 129.

69. Wu Wen-hsing, "Ri ju shiqi Taiwan de fangzu." Wu argues that reformist islanders tended to be in the forefront and official legislation lagged behind, but Ts'ai maintains that neither the queue-cutting nor the foot-binding campaign succeeded until the full machinery of the state mobilized behind them, at least in the south of Taiwan. Ts'ai, *Taiwan in Japan's Empire-Building*, 130–32.

Jilong and its hinterland.[70] On August 17, the *Taiwan Daily* published the new organization's mission statement, core principles, and regulations. Lamenting the elaborate and excessive rituals currently practiced in the island, the statement called for rapid reforms of bad customs (*rōshū/louxi*) in a spirit that reflected the goals of the well-known Assimilation Society and emphasized the importance of local identity: "Our Jilong has extensive trade and a broad entrance, it serves as the whole island's crown. Civilization enters here, and it is the first to receive a new mood or practice."[71] That same year in Shulin, southwest of Taipei, a group of islanders and settlers established an organization they called the Customs Assimilation Association, to reform evil customs (*akuzoku/esu*), end old superstitions, and distribute public charity.[72] According to Wang Shih-ch'ing, the institutional model caught on quickly in the surrounding area, and the Government-General picked up on it as early as 1916 and encouraged its spread throughout Taiwan.[73] Following the promulgation of the 1919 Education Rescript, which raised the standards for islander schools even as it preserved segregation, elites in Taipei created a similar citywide institution that merged their existing programs to reform customs, spread the Japanese language, and promote morality. That organization responded to a state initiative in 1920 and combined with the Shulin group and Sincere Customs Associations in Jilong and Yilan to form the Taibei Prefecture United Customs Assimilation Association (Taihoku shū rengō dōfūkai).[74]

On the surface, incorporation by the state brought the previously disparate associations firmly under the control of the Government-General and aligned their activities with its assimilationist rhetoric. According to a retrospective report by the prefecture-level union, the entire CAA system began to operate under a new mandate:

70. "Jilong dunsuhui houwen," *TNS*, Aug. 24, 1914, 4. According to Ishizaka, *Kiirun kō*, 203, it had 127 members by 1917.

71. "Jilong dunsuhui chengli," *TNS*, Aug. 17, 1914, 4.

72. "Shulin tongfenghui neigui," *TNS*, Nov. 22, 1914, 3.

73. Wang Shih-ch'ing, "Huangminhua yundong qian," 7. Wang accurately describes these groups as integral to state reform policies, but the evidence indicates that the Jilong group had a high degree of independent agency.

74. Taihoku shū rengō dōfūkai, *Dōfūkai gairan*.

1) To respect the emperor and instill feelings of patriotism; 2) To practice the national language and diligently cultivate common knowledge; 3) To emphasize public morality and deepen a friendly coexistence; 4) To rectify traditions and strive for sincere local customs; 5) To spread industriousness and improve professional knowledge.[75]

The statement promoted assimilation to Japanese norms, to the limited extent to which Japanese officials and settlers supported such a goal, along with other agendas, not all of them complementary. Points three and five connected the CAA network to the self-consciously benevolent modernization that motivated the PWS; thus these groups potentially shared an inclusive agenda. However, although the rectification in point four was assimilationist in intent, it depended on the accumulation of knowledge about some of the very elements of their cultural heritage that islanders used to build their separate Taiwanese identity.[76]

Structurally, the CAA union paralleled the Government-General's formal bureaucracy, much as the PWS did. Beneath the main prefecture group there were county-level unions that in turn oversaw local-level organizations, each of which contained a number of sub-committees for heads of household (*huzhuhui*), housewives (*zhufuhui*), youths (*qingnianhui*), and young women (*chunühui*). At the local level the organizational structure consisted of a chairperson, a vice chair, and a consultative committee. High-ranking local officials either served as or appointed the leaders of the local and regional organizations.[77] The administrative framework acclimated islanders to modern bureaucratic structures and procedures, and the state had numerous opportunities to use this hierarchical network of CAA groups to implement its plans for social and cultural reform. Nevertheless, the

---

75. Ibid.

76. Prime examples of such research into islanders' traditional customs, which continued throughout the period of Japanese rule, include Okamatsu, *Taiwan kyū-kan seido*; Rinji kyūkan chōsakai, *Taiwan kyūkan chōsa jigyō hōkoku*; Suzuki, *Taiwan kyūkan kankon* (1934), translated and republished in 1978 as Suzuki, *Taiwan jiuguan xisu*; and the journal *Taiwan Ethnology* (*Minzoku Taiwan*) discussed in the introduction.

77. Taihoku shū rengō dōfūkai, *Dōfūkai gairan*; Wang Shih-ch'ing, "Huangminhua yundong qian," 8–9.

overarching system, as with the credit unions, allowed islanders to embed their local issues within an islandwide context.

The close parallel between the CAA's structure and that of the official bureaucracy was no accident, because the 1920 reorganization grafted the CAA directly onto the *hokō* system, which allowed it to reach more deeply into local society. Every islander head of household became a member—this composition accounted for its large, overwhelmingly male membership—and was assigned to a CAA committee that was formed in each of the city's forty-two wards. The CAA then worked through these heads-of-household committees to distribute both funds and instructions on how to implement its customs-reform projects and charitable works.[78] Moreover, Japanese officials and settlers sometimes attended CAA meetings, and they played a particularly overt role in managing the association's young women's groups.[79] The youth who heckled Xu Zisang might have had this close association with the state-run *hokō* system in mind when he accused the association of craven collaboration, for the *hokō* was one of the most prevalent and effective mechanisms through which the colonial state observed, engineered, and at times punished islander society.[80] It proved so useful in Taiwan, in fact, that the Japanese applied it in a similar fashion to Chinese populations in their leasehold territory in Manchuria and later, with a militaristic spirit and a deeper reach into Chinese society, in Manchukuo.[81]

Nevertheless, in spite of the top-down structure, the Jilong CAA showed that, in practice, it was possible to maintain a surprising degree of autonomy. Not long after its incorporation into the regional organization, it left its original home in the crowded space of the Qing'an Temple, but kept its physical roots in Big Jilong in a more substantial form: it moved into an iron-reinforced concrete structure that it built for itself in Takasago Park (see map 3.1). This new building served as

78. NKKS, 1-2A-014-00 *san*-02134-100, 1935.

79. On officials attending CAA meetings, see, for example, "Kiirun dōfūkai sōkai," *TNS*, April 4, 1921, 2. On the management of young women's groups, see "Jilong diyi chunühui fahui shengkuang," *TNS*, Nov. 28, 1929, 4.

80. Ts'ai, *Taiwan in Japan's Empire-Building*, 98–102, 117–18; Endō, *Kindai Nihon no shokuminchi*, 139–49.

81. Endō, *Kindai Nihon no shokuminchi*, 259–63.

its base of operations and an all-purpose meeting hall for the rest of its existence. To accord with the official mandate, it also set new objectives, many of which furthered the work that Xu had been doing for more than a decade: to reform old customs, spread the Japanese language, develop a spirit of citizenship (*kokumin seishin*), and improve life for Jilong's residents. Perhaps most significant, at least until after the outbreak of the Second Sino-Japanese War in 1937, the Jilong CAA experienced relatively little overt state control, in comparison to the CAAs in other cities and towns, perhaps because of its deep roots in the local society and the prominence of its leaders. In contrast to the CAA groups in Shulin and elsewhere, neither settlers nor officials served as officers of the Jilong CAA until the end of the 1930s.[82] Instead, self-appointed islanders such as Xu Zisang and Yan Guonian ran the organization for more than two decades. That simple organizational quirk meant that, within certain limits, Xu, Yan, and other prominent islanders could determine which issues their CAA concentrated on, and how aggressively it pursued them. In other words, they held a position from which they could monitor access to islander society and either shield it from, or subject it to, intrusive state programs.

At the level of implementation, many of the projects that mattered to the Government-General overlapped significantly with the interests of both the CAA and islanders in Jilong. For example, from the top officials to local elites, everyone was concerned with the teaching and learning of Japanese language. Gotō Shinpei, Den Kenjirō, and others designed the colonial education system to assimilate the islanders to Japanese culture and consciousness, largely through instruction in the national language. In the wake of Den's Education Rescript the CAA immediately threw itself into the task of spreading Japanese by organizing a few small language courses in 1920, and then swiftly expanding the enrollments and locations to sites around Jilong. Each course lasted one to six months and concentrated on teaching terms of etiquette and language necessary for daily use. The program reached its

82. Xu Zisang always chaired the organization, and Yan Guonian served as vice chair from 1923 until at least 1935, after which Yan Yunnian's son replaced him. For Japanese control of other local organizations, see "Tongfenghui chuanglihui," *TNS*, Apr. 27, 1919, 6.

peak in popularity in 1927, and more than 1,500 people had graduated from the CAA's Japanese classes by 1934; the majority of them were girls.[83] The CAA also opened a nursery school in 1920 to provide care and instruction for islander children. Operating on the grounds of Ishizaka Sōsaku's night school, the Japanese and islander teachers initially instructed pupils in Japanese language and Japan's national customs, through a curriculum of songs and games. Islanders funded the school, as they did many of the CAA's activities, with private donations. Xu and the Yan brothers provided the three largest contributions, but they were not alone.[84] The school quickly became very popular among islanders who had the means to pay the admission fees, in light of which it is difficult to single out the CAA as a "running dog of officialdom."[85] Even though the nursery school taught Japanese customs, it clearly emphasized functional language instruction rather than assimilation. In an environment in which knowledge of Japanese language and habits was important for personal and familial advancement, the CAA provided the city's residents with some very necessary tools.

Although its name suggested a determination to fundamentally change islanders' customs, the CAA in fact devoted remarkably little attention to that goal during the 1920s, and its efforts in that direction were as protective as they were transformative.[86] In February 1921 the association proposed changing the financial structure and spirit-veneration practices of four of Jilong's temples by merging their assets into a foundation under CAA control, and by holding all of the festivals in honor of the temples' deities on the same day.[87] It subsequently decided to further consolidate religious observances in Jilong by having that one-day, multi-deity festival coincide with the annual Shinto festival

83. NKKS, 1-2A-040-06 zoi-00166-100, and 1-2A-014-00 san-02134-100.

84. TSTF, 6887.3, Jan. 1, 1920.

85. "Youzhiyuan er kaishi muji," NS, Feb. 25, 1932, 15. According to this article, in most years the school received more than twice as many applications as it had spaces.

86. For example, the report on the Jilong CAA's very first meeting made no mention of any initiatives related to assimilation work. Instead, it concentrated on issues of funding and the supposed inadequacies of the nursery school. "Jilong duanxin," TNS, Sept. 8, 1920, 6.

87. "Jilong ge miao hebing an," TNS, Feb. 16, 1921, 6.

held at the Jilong Shrine.[88] However, there is no evidence that either of these plans took hold at this time, or were even advanced with much effort. Five years later, in August 1926, the *Taiwan Daily* published in its Chinese-language section a public service announcement from the CAA about a weeklong campaign to reduce the scale of sacrificial offerings and the overall expense associated with the annual Ghost Festival. Written with some of the same language used by the Sincere Customs Association a decade earlier, the article situated Jilong's celebrations within the context of Taiwan's lavish religious festivals:

> As for our Jilong, during the Ghost Festival ceremonies, each year the organizers compete with each other and it is extravagant in the extreme, no expense is spared. Moreover, each household displays sacrificial animals and fruit offerings, and each is as abundant as they can manage, as a means of presenting gifts [to the ghosts]. Indeed, they do not understand the universal salvation ceremony of the netherworld; it lies not in lavishness but is only in a sincere and respectful heart. The people have already forgotten the festival's roots and pursue the ends.[89]

This mild critique did not denigrate the festival itself, nor did it insist on a superiority of Japanese customs as a model, but it was couched in a Confucian morality that must have been familiar to Jilong's islanders.[90] The announcement reinforced this when it enjoined people to rely on

88. "Kiirun dōfūkai sōkai," *TNS*, Apr. 4, 1921, 2.

89. "Jilong tongfenghui xuanchuan Zhongyuan jipin zeng da feizhi," *TNS*, Aug. 25, 1926, 4. This announcement and the SCA's 1914 founding document both targeted elaborate and wasteful festivals, and both used the phrases "the people have forgotten the roots and pursue the ends," and "extravagance does not follow from things, increase their splendor, or please the senses." For the 1914 document, see "Jilong dunsuhui chengli," *TNS*, Aug. 17, 1914, 4.

90. This type of moralizing was also evident in a collection of stories about contemporary moral exemplars that the Taibei Prefecture CAA published first in 1925 and then, with a second volume, in 1928. See Taihoku shū rengō dōfūkai, *Hontō ni okeru migoto*. The role models included such individuals as an islander *hokō* head who resolutely developed his area, promoted Japanese, and established a local CAA near Taipei; a Japanese schoolgirl from Jilong who was devout in her prayers for the ailing Taishō emperor; and Yan Yunnian, who made enormous contributions to the education of islanders and to the prefecture CAA.

their "sincere hearts" because "the basis of the spirits is in virtue not in things." Moreover, it also advanced a modernizing rather than an assimilationist agenda as it called on residents to "avoid waste and avoid complications" by reducing or eradicating their offerings, because "leaving festival items out on a hot summer day causes them to rot, and so these offerings also damage hygiene."[91] The CAA pursued changes in the religious practices and other customs of local islanders, and it did so with a modernizing and moralizing discourse that coincided with the views of Japanese officials and settlers who favored gradual assimilation, but first and foremost it preserved the festivals and the institutions that supported them.

Overall, the CAA spent more effort and money on education and large-scale social welfare projects, at least prior to the 1930s. Its most high-profile act of social support was unquestionably the Fraternity Hospital (Bo'ai yiyuan), which Yan Guonian and Xu Zisang established under the leadership of the CAA, in the spring of 1929, to provide medical care to those who could not afford the regular clinics and doctors. The hospital treated most patients on-site, but it also worked through the local *hokō* heads, district leaders, and local welfare commissioners to bring medical aid to those who were too sick or too poor to make the journey. It turned out that the CAA chose a propitious time to found a new hospital, because when the strains of the Depression hit the next year and brought an influx of new migrants, the hospital had its busiest year on record.[92] Under those circumstances, the association resolved in 1930 to reduce the prices of its medicines.[93] In addition, at the end of each lunar year the CAA collected donations from its members and then gave rice and money to people in need.[94] The CAA usually collected and distributed this aid on its own, but in 1935 it began to

---

91. "Jilong tongfenghui xuanchuan Zhongyuan jipin zeng da feizhi," *TNS*, Aug. 25, 1926, 4.

92. NKKS, 1-2A-014-00 *san*-02134-100.

93. "Jilong bo'ai yiyuan yi jian yao jia," *TNS*, Oct. 20, 1930. This report on the year's activities discusses the hospital and education but makes no mention of customs reform.

94. "Jilong tongfenghui xupin," *TNS*, Jan. 22, 1930, 4. Xu, Yan Yunnian, and others had undertaken such actions as early as 1918, though not always at the new year; see "Jilong shi mi houwen," *TNS*, Apr. 20, 1918, 6.

cooperate with the city's local welfare commissioners and other social work institutions.[95] Although these acts of assistance did not expressly target a particular portion of Jilong's population, the organization's overall structure and the economic realities of Jilong, where islanders overwhelmingly constituted "the poor," meant that the CAA consistently and predominantly aided only one demographic sector.

Joining state welfare institutions to distribute charity marked the CAA's close relationship with the colonial government, but it did not mean that the Jilong CAA surrendered its limited autonomy. The rest of Taiwan's CAA network provides an instructive contrast. The Government-General took over most of the island's CAA groups in 1931 and amalgamated them into a new system of "social civilization" (shakai kyōka) organizations that functioned under direct state control.[96] The Jilong branch, however, had a different fate, for it both retained its name and leadership structure and, in 1936, became a foundation (zaidan hōjin), which made it the institutional equivalent of the semiprivate, legally autonomous (and soon-to-be defunct) PWS. It oversaw eight separate bureaus, including divisions for existing projects like the hospital, nursery school, and Japanese courses, as well as a new branch that focused on cultural transformation, the Everyday Life Reform Bureau (seikatsu kaizen ku/shenghuo gaishan ju). This division coordinated projects such as ending opium smoking, reforming marital practices like the bride price and large neighborhood celebrations, halting large-scale funeral processions, and changing or ending a number of religious rituals.[97] The overall reorganization, and the Everyday Life Reform Bureau, in particular, with its echoes of government-led reform efforts in metropolitan Japan during the 1910s, could indicate that a government takeover was under way.[98] However, the continuity of leadership, and the fact that the CAA had worked on the same sorts

95. "Jilong tongfenghui huiyi jue shi mi ji fengsu gailiang," TNS, Jan. 26, 1935, 8.

96. Wang Shih-ch'ing, "Huangminhua yundong qian," 11–13; Ts'ai, Taiwan in Japan's Empire-Building. "Social civilization" is my own, nonstandard translation of the Japanese term, which I explore further in chapter 5.

97. "Kiirun dōfūkai no kakudai kyōka," NS, June 6, 1936, 8.

98. Sand, House and Home, 181–84. I have adopted Sand's translation of the Japanese original, seikatsu kaizen, as "everyday life reform."

of reforms since its inception, suggest that the islanders retained some control.

The mid-1930s were a critical time for Jilong's islander elites as they attempted to maintain their position as gatekeepers. Xu Zisang, Yan Guonian, and others had to navigate between the pressure that the colonial regime placed on them to assimilate, the fluctuating actions of settlers who alternately accepted and rejected them, the practical realities of being subjects of the Japanese Empire, and their devotion to their cultural traditions. At a New Year's banquet Xu and Yan hosted at the CAA building in 1935, they made an overtly patriotic display before more than 140 assembled guests, including many of the city's top civil and military officials, Ishizaka Sōsaku, and other important individuals. They decorated the meeting hall with a large Japanese national flag, on either side of which hung a banner bearing a couplet: "With the same sentiments and origins, we enforce military preparations and encourage culture and learning, why should we fear that our enemies will run wild?" read one side, and the other stated, "The weather for crops is good, the world is at peace and the land is fertile, the people are happy and peaceful, the economy is vibrant, it must be that our imperial nation is prospering."[99] These words reflected the rising tide of nationalism, hinted at the racialist ideas of pan-Asianism, and displayed an affinity that the men felt for the regime under which both they and their city had flourished.

However, there was another side to this banquet and to the story of the CAA. The New Year's gathering was an annual event that local notables had attended in the past, and on this evening the representatives of the colonial state and Japanese settlers came to the CAA, on its own ground, and paid homage to it, just as it was paying homage to the empire.[100] That approach marked essentially the same way in which the Government-General had always dealt with the organization, which it needed to meet goals that neither it nor any other group was able to accomplish. The relationship was to an extent symbiotic, because the

99. "Jilong guanmin xinnian yanhui," *TNS*, Jan. 10, 1935, 8. I thank Fann Meeiyuan and Torsten Weber for helping to refine my understanding of this couplet.
100. For a prior such occasion, see "Jilong tongfenghui chun yan," *TNS*, Jan. 8, 1929, 4.

association required official approval and access to the *hokō* system in order to maximize its connections with islander-Taiwanese society. In contrast to the PWS, which took the entire city and all of its residents within its purview even as it oscillated between tolerant and exclusionary versions of the Japanese vision of Jilong, the CAA consistently acted only with and for one segment of the city. State policies had confined the CAA's work to the islanders, and over time it forged strong connections with its assigned group through programs that frequently sustained its members in both material and spiritual ways. In short, the Jilong CAA closely identified itself only with the islander community and, as a sort of counterpart to the all-Japanese Jilong Harbor Association, it helped to define the imagined border between islanders and Japanese.

In light of this islander-oriented framework, the language of the celebratory couplet reveals something other than simple patriotism and dedication to imperial expansion. Even as Yan Guonian and Xu Zisang applauded the empire's prosperity and the cultural and racial characteristics that they purportedly shared with the Japanese, they did so in terms that displayed an overriding concern for the welfare of Jilong, and that resonated more closely with the Chinese cultural tradition in which they had been raised. As members of both the PWS and the CAA, the two men consistently pursued a multilayered objective: creating a modern city in which residents benefited from its economic prosperity and, when needed, social welfare programs. To achieve that goal, they sought to rationalize their cultural roots with their contemporary business interests and the demands of the Japanese colonial state to reform and adapt. The couplet expressed the influence of both their Chinese heritage and their accommodations to Japanese rule. The references to an active business environment, peaceful world context, and the serenity of the people all highlighted their dedication to Jilong and the successful construction of a prosperous, modern port. The common sentiments and origins expressed the inclusiveness of Jilong identity as well as pan-Asianist ideals, whereas the martial ethos and cultural and educational development represented an acknowledgment of Japan's priorities.

The reference to "enemies" (*hu'er*), a term with an ancient application to supposedly uncivilized groups beyond the state's borders, was perhaps the most telling statement of their independent consciousness. On one level was the question of just who these enemies were. Just across the Taiwan Strait lay Republican China, where the central government did not have firm control over all of the provinces, but the centralizing regime at times threatened Japanese interests; to the north of the area under Nationalist Chinese rule lay Manchuria, an ancient homeland for China's enemies, including some historical *hu'er*, where the Japanese Army ran a puppet state through the last Manchu emperor and challenged Chinese sovereignty. Which group corresponded to the enemies who might run wild? At no time had Yan and Xu overtly displayed the sort of anti-Japanese Chinese nationalism that flourished across the strait and motivated the "half-mountain people" (*banshanren*) who left Taiwan to fight Japan in China.[101] They would certainly not have risked referring to Manchukuo as an enemy in the presence of Government-General representatives. It is more likely that both the ongoing fragmentation in China and the potential danger of a more unified nation under Nationalist control sparked the metaphor, but even so the message did not favor expansion, since these enemies gave no real cause for concern. Yan and Xu subtly challenged those who saw Taiwan as a bastion for further imperial conquest, and they did so by relying on an old Chinese worldview of external threats, and on the language of literary Chinese, which connected them to their cultural background rather than to contemporary Japanese nationalism.[102]

Xu and Yan were not alone in their efforts to determine the best way to manage the intensifying pressures to assimilate without abandoning core aspects of their evolving identity. Roughly eighteen months after this banquet, the CAA faced deep divisions that threatened to tear

---

101. Jacobs, "Taiwanese and the Chinese Nationalists."

102. One linguistic choice might have prioritized Chinese culture within the pan-Asianist unity. The final phrase, "*huangguo longxing*" 皇國龍興, I have translated as "our imperial nation is prospering." The penultimate character should more likely have been written as the "long" in Jilong (隆), but if this phrase is not a misprint, a more literal translation would be "our imperial nation is flourishing like the dragon," with the dragon being deeply linked to China. Xu also displayed his cultural roots in his role as the distinguished chairman (*mingyu shezhang*) of an important Chinese language literary journal, the *Poetry Bulletin* (*Shi bao*), which was published in Jilong in the 1930s and 1940s.

the association apart. At that time, three factions struggled for control over the pace at which the organization should seek to reform native customs. The radicals (*jijinpai*) sought a rapid transformation that would swiftly accommodate some state directives; the gradualists (*jianjinpai*) supported some reforms but at a slower rate; and the conservatives (*baoshoupai*) raised the most overt resistance to any further transformation. In 1937 the radicals, led by Xu Zisang, attempted to stamp out the practice of burning ghost money—gold and silver colored paper with monetary denominations written on it—as an offering to the spirits. This was one of the islanders' most important devotional practices and the gradualists and conservatives temporarily withdrew from the organization in protest, with the widespread support of local islanders. Xu and the other radicals recognized that they had gone too far and endangered their organization's connections to the islander community, and thus its ability to occupy the borderlands between Japanese settlers and islanders. They quickly reached a compromise with the other factions and preserved the practice, the association, and the bonds between the CAA and its core constituency.[103] As this episode showed, many members were willing to accept reform up to a certain point, but they also resolutely tried to protect from the intensifying state-run assimilation projects certain traditions that they held to be central to their vision of themselves.

Nevertheless, even though the CAA did not engage in politics as the PWS did, this dispute and the changing regional context proved fatal to the organization's autonomy.[104] Just when these divisions broke out into public view, in July 1937, the Marco Polo Bridge Incident outside of Beijing led quickly to full-scale hostilities in China. At this time, the city government seized control of the CAA and directed it to form a new youth group, even though it already had loose affiliations with some of Jilong's seven existing youth associations and the state

103. "Kin chō haishi ni tan o hasshi dōfūkai naibu no funjō bakuhatsu," *NS*, July 3, 1937, 9, and "Dōfūkai no funjō sai hatsu," *NS*, July 31, 1937, 7.

104. The CAA held informational meetings about the reforms associated with the arrival of local self-government in 1935, but it expressly refrained from entering politics and instead concentrated on social and cultural reform. See "Jilong tong-fenghui xuanchuan zizhi," *TNS*, Sept. 28, 1935, 4; "Ichiji wa kaisan o mei seraren to shita Kiirun dōfūkai no sono ato no katsudō," *NS*, June 19, 1937, 14.

controlled a majority of the groups, since municipal and public school officials had established most of them in the late 1920s or early 1930s.[105] Now, however, colonial officials saw in the war an opportunity to use the CAA to raise the patriotic spirit of local youths and to wipe away what they referred to as moral corruption that had resulted from bad external influences.[106] The new group's manifesto clearly illuminated its purpose: "With the great spirit of the Imperial Nation as our basis, we reveal our true feelings of the sincerity of loyal and courageous service by encouraging the cultivation of indomitable resolve. We look forward to enhancing the national prestige."[107] The phrasing here echoed the "spirit of the Imperial Way" that settlers had instilled in their East Asia Co-Prosperity Association three years earlier, as well as the 1920 mandate that created the CAA union. Even though Xu Zisang and Yan Qinxian, the son of Yan Yunnian, retained their positions at the head of the CAA, the Japanese leaders of this new component, many of them city officials, imbued it with their expansive nationalism. Their insertion of themselves into the CAA mirrored the Japanese military's invasion of China and Southeast Asia, albeit in a much less violent way. Although Xu remained the nominal head of the organization and it continued to function into the 1940s, from late 1937 onward it lost its ability to shape and defend islander society.

Conclusion

Local elites and the organizations that they established and ran contributed in fundamental ways to the creation and propagation of Jilong identity. They provided structure and support for a rapidly expanding population that faced both hardships and numerous opportunities associated with oscillating periods of economic expansion and contraction. These groups concentrated their efforts on promoting capitalist accumulation, urban development, Jilong's reputation, social welfare, and the reform of native customs. They served as forums within which

105. Ishizaka, *Ora ga Kiirun*, 77–78.
106. Kiirun dōfūkai, *Kiirun dōfū seinen*.
107. Ibid.

elites from different demographic groups could interact with each other while developing and implementing their visions of what Jilong should be, sometimes advocating for inclusivity in the cases of the PWS and the PCU. Moreover, because they stood at the intersection of state and society, they both facilitated the imposition of state plans for control and reform and, conversely, defended the interests of local residents from some of those same programs. In fact, each of the organizations addressed above displayed both an autonomous position, within the structural confines established by the Government-General, and a willingness to make demands on the colonial state or even contest its priorities, as seen in the PWS's advocacy for local self-government or the CAA's defense of particular customs. They were social organizations in the sense of being principally of society, rather than primarily agents of the state, and as such they manifested a form of the public sphere that resembled the highly circumscribed versions that emerged in Japan and China in the early twentieth century.

Elite-led organizations also facilitated the differential reterritorialization of Jilong and clarified the imagined border between identity groups. In part because of the fundamentally ambivalent Japanese view of assimilation, and in part because of the attachment that islanders evidently felt to the norms and practices rooted in their Chinese background, cultural transformation faced obstacles from multiple sides. In practice, most of the organizations in Jilong worked primarily or exclusively with one demographic group, from the first credit unions that served either settlers or islanders, and the PWS, which enshrined a Japanese leadership even as it sought to benefit the lives of all members, to the CAA that was institutionally bound to the islander community. Thus through both structural and operational features, these groups forged strong bonds to their respective sectors of society. Although the organizations and their founders received criticism from both a rising generation of elites and more radical members of society, their stature and the limited support of the state enhanced their power and authority in local society, and thus their ability to shape the identities of its members. Perhaps most significant, because many of these groups were embedded in prefectural and colonywide institutions, or addressed cultural material that extended across Taiwan, they connected Jilong's imaginary geography to a broader terrain.

The credit unions furthered localization in both Jilong and Taiwan by enhancing financial ties to those places, and they also promoted a self-consciously modern mindset by updating old gentry functions through a new organizational model designed to ameliorate class struggle. They also traced divisions between islanders and Japanese, even as one transcended those borders. The PWS expressed inclusive and exclusive strains of both Japanese and Jilong identity, but it never abandoned its fundamental Meiji-Taishō vision of urban modernity. Even so, it was insufficiently nationalistic and vanished in the march of intolerant imperial expansion. During the decades of relative tolerance for islander customs and autonomy, the CAA interposed itself between the colonial state and islander society, building the strength of the latter through social welfare and a shifting balance of customs reform and preservation. In sum, these groups introduced a strong sense of in-group connectivity and a similar awareness of out-group separation, and they concentrated on the translocal cultural content necessary to create a modern ethnic identity. They therefore contributed to the reterritorialization of Jilong as both Japanese and Taiwanese. In fact, with these pieces in place, it is now possible to begin speaking of "the Taiwanese," at least within the chronological setting of the early 1930s and after, as an ethnic group that obtained cohesion and sought survival within the confines of the Japanese Empire.

CHAPTER FOUR

Sacred Spaces
Religions and the Construction of Identities

On the afternoon of June 15, 1937, a group of city officials, temple managers, prominent Taiwanese and Japanese, journalists, and the head of the Jilong Shrine paid visits to three important Taiwanese institutions, the Qing'an, Dianji, and Chenghuang Temples. That day, all three were to hold a key festival for their principal gods. The group had come to remove the large censers, or ovens, in which people burned "ghost money" to honor the spirits, implementing a recent directive from the Jilong Customs Assimilation Association that banned the practice. At each stop, the head of the Jilong Shrine performed a Shinto exorcism ceremony (*shūfutsu*) to spiritually sanitize the ground where the censers had stood. When the group reached the narrow street outside of the Dianji Temple, a small crowd blocked its entry to the grounds. An altercation seemed likely, until the police arrived and arrested those who attempted to prevent this limitation of their custom, and the colonial authorities and local elites completed their mission, taking away all three of the temples' ovens.[1] This episode put on display the intense conflict over Taiwanese religion that took place throughout the colony, with Japanese officials and settlers attempting to wipe away all of its manifestations, and the Taiwanese

1. Jilong CAA, "Wa ga Kiirun shi ni okeru kingin kami shōkyaku haishi no keika," *SJT* 104 (Jul 1937): 9–12.

accommodating some modifications while they built their ethnicity around a religious core.

Religion can be a key component of both ethnic and national identities, and it certainly served this role in Japanese-era Taiwan, and after.[2] The process was similar to one Thomas DuBois has traced across Asia in the age of imperialism: the Government-General and settlers studied, categorized, and tried to transform the islanders' spiritual lives, and islanders used those "technologies" for very different ends.[3] Islanders forged group solidarity through their pursuit of a voice in local governance and their social organizations, but religious institutions and practices became the foundational cultural components of their new collective identity. As a result, the cults and rituals transported to Taiwan by generations of Chinese settlers made primary contributions, from the Chinese cultural sphere, to Taiwanese ethnicity. Islanders recognized the Chinese origins even as they reterritorialized those sacred spaces as Taiwanese. By supporting temples and facilitating their ceremonies, elite islanders displayed their allegiance to their main constituencies—other elites and the islander masses—even as they reshaped the religious terrain according to their modernizing sensibilities and the demands of the colonial state. Similarly, Japanese officials and settlers held their religious institutions and beliefs as central components of their national consciousness, and sought to replace the so-called backwards customs of the islanders with purportedly modern and civilized Shinto and Japanese Buddhism.[4] These opposing trends made religion a spiritual borderland within which the Taiwanese-Japanese boundary took shape. Japanese attempts to reterritorialize the islanders' religious domain proceeded slowly because officials and settlers remained relatively tolerant of all religious behavior into the 1930s. However, the aggressively nationalistic projects before and during the Kōminka period enlisted both Shinto and some Japanese Buddhist sects in their intolerant, and unsuccessful, conquest of the sacred

2. See Katz and Rubinstein, *Religion and the Formation*.

3. DuBois, "Introduction."

4. Japanese sources used a variety of terms for the islanders' customs, all with negative connotations, including "wicked customs" (*akuzoku*), "evil customs" (*rōshū*), and "Chinese religion" (*Shina shūkyō*).

realm.[5] The pressure that the Japanese applied during the 1930s in fact strengthened the bonds between islanders and their religions, making religion a key feature of Taiwanese ethnicity.

Religions in Japanese-Era Taiwan

Between 1895 and 1945 two distinct and yet overlapping religious traditions inhabited Taiwan, one brought by migrants from China's southeastern coast and the other imported by Japanese colonials.[6] The islanders practiced the syncretic tradition of southern China, a relatively open conglomeration of beliefs, deities, and rituals from disparate sources. Contemporary Japanese scholars, and many others before and since, viewed this syncretism as a combination of discrete branches of Confucianism, Daoism, and Buddhism, but in fact the internal divisions had long since become blurred in a setting that stressed ritual practice over doctrine.[7] As Michael Szonyi described, Qing-era elites responded to the imperial distinction between orthodox and heterodox by conflating their Daoist deities with imperially sanctioned cults that emphasized loyalty to authority, or by using the orthodox deities as shields to protect their ongoing worship of heterodox gods.[8] Thus Confucian shrines in Taiwan represented the product of long-term mingling with Daoist cults, temples devoted to Daoist deities also paid homage to Buddhist figures, and what Japanese observers described as Buddhism combined Buddhist doctrine with cults dedicated to local deities. To give one example, the "vegetarian teaching" (zhaijiao) that Japanese scholars denigrated as popular Buddhism had in fact grown

5. This two-stage periodization differs from the more common three-phase division, which outlines a hands-off phase, 1895–1914; a phase of study, 1915–30, that was sparked by the 1915 rebellion that had ties to an islander Buddhistic sect; and a phase of amalgamation and suppression, 1931–45. See Cai Jintang, *Nihon teikoku shugi shita*, 10–11.

6. Indigenous belief systems constituted a third, internally diverse category, but they are omitted here because they did not play a significant role in Jilong.

7. Marui, *Taiwan shūkyō chōsa*, 6–7. For a fuller discussion of how Japanese scholars and officials carried out some research through schools and police bureaus, see Jones, *Religion in Modern Taiwan*, 21–22.

8. Szonyi, "Illusion of Standardizing the Gods."

out of the Ming-era Longhua sect, a group classified as heterodox by
the Qing for its amalgamation of Amitabha Buddha worship with
non-Buddhist practices.[9] At a broader level islander religion resembled
Robert Hymes's conception of Southern Song religion, as something
shaped by both bureaucratic and personal models of the spiritual
realm, and human interactions therewith.[10]

Japanese settlers brought a similarly multifaceted religious tradition with them, one in which the recent emergence of State Shinto had
dramatically altered Japan's spiritual landscape. As Helen Hardacre
has shown, what the Meiji oligarchs defined as Japan's indigenous religious tradition had neither an independent institutional existence nor
a uniform set of practices or doctrines that were followed across a wide
area, prior to the late nineteenth century. The beliefs and rituals that
became Shinto had long been practiced within Buddhist temples, on
which they were entirely dependent for their development and survival.
However, during the nineteenth century participants in the nativist
(kokugaku) movement and the search for a pure Japanese essence began
to criticize the polluting influence of foreign Buddhism. The renova-
tionist Meiji leaders joined with a group of similarly minded priests to
create a unified and uniform Shinto out of older forms of spirit (kami)
worship and linked it to the modern nation-state through the imperial
institution (kokutai).[11] They intertwined nation, emperor, and Shinto
in the popular consciousness during Japan's first two wars of imperial
expansion, against China in 1894–95 and Russia in 1904–5.[12] Shinto
rose at the initial expense of Buddhism, whose adherents responded by
embracing a modern sensibility and a new activism for proselytizing.
Proponents of Shinto attacked Buddhist temples and persecuted their
priests, and according to James Ketelaar, in the 1880s and 1890s Japanese Buddhists responded by redefining their religion. Picking up on
both nativist and modernist trends, they framed Buddhism as a

9. For Japanese views, see Marui, *Taiwan shūkyō chōsa*, 6–7. For the Longhua
sect, see Seiwert and Ma, *Popular Religious Movements*, 216–60; Wang Jianchuan,
Taiwan de zhaijiao, 3–18, introduction 61–62; de Groot, *Sectarianism and Religious
Persecution*, chap. 7.

10. Hymes, *Way and Byway*.

11. Gluck, *Japan's Modern Myths*.

12. Hardacre, *Shintō and the State*.

foundation of the Japanese essence and a modern religion that Japan could export to the rest of the world.[13] They imported Buddhism into Taiwan through eight main sects, each of which was centered on a large temple-monastery in or near one of Japan's urban centers and had widespread local branches: Jōdo (or Pure Land), Jōdo Shinshū, Nichiren, Hokke, Tendai, Shingon, and the Zen sects of Sōdō and Rinzai.[14] Many of the sects' leaders saw themselves as both religious and national emissaries; thus their followers entered the colony with a missionary zeal.[15]

From the beginning of Japanese rule, Japanese and islanders viewed each other's religions in significantly different ways. The creation of Shinto and reformation of Buddhism suggest that, by the end of the nineteenth century, Japanese viewed "modern religion" as something that was pure and unalloyed, rationally organized with clear lines of connection and authority between parent and branch temples, and representative of the nation. Even at their most tolerant, Japanese settlers and officials looked down on the islanders' tradition as a collection of backward, uncivilized beliefs and rituals based in irrationally organized and highly localized institutions, often run by lay clergy rather than centrally ordained priests and monks. To reform the supposedly "wretched" (nagekawashii) state of islander religion, and to make "twentieth-century religionists" (nijū sekai no shūkyōsha) out of the islanders, Japanese settlers and officials established temples for their own use and as exemplars for the natives.[16] However, they did not actively try to eradicate the religions that they denigrated until the last decade of their rule. In contrast to this transformative agenda, islanders treated Shinto and the Japanese Buddhist sects in much the same way that they approached Japanese language and education: they used Japanese religion when it brought benefits but did not convert in order to become Japanese.

---

13. Ketelaar, Of Heretics and Martyrs.

14. Jiang, Taiwan Fojiao bainian, 127n1.

15. Yoshiko Okamoto, "Buddhism and the Twenty-One Demands: The Politics behind the International Movement of Japanese Buddhists," in Minohara, Hon, and Dawley, Decade of the Great War, 394–414.

16. Kiirun jinja, Kiirun jinja shi, 1; "Hontō no shūkyō kai," TNS, Mar. 2, 1901, 1.

Temples and the Imagined Borders of Jilong

When Japanese forces marched into Jilong in 1895, they took up residence in one of the newest and most important temples in town, located
right on the southern edge of the harbor.[17] This act, which they repeated
across Taiwan, combined the practical need for a temporary barracks
with the overarching goals of undercutting resistance and reshaping
Taiwan's social and cultural milieu.[18] Soon after, the Government-
General of Taiwan shuttered all existing temples and banned all religious festivals. These prohibitions, which paralleled the actions of the
early Meiji government within the home islands, constituted a serious
attack on the everyday lives of the islanders. Although they removed
potential obstacles to the application of state power, they heightened
the danger of destabilizing society and complicated the imposition
of colonial rule.[19] After a year, the Government-General reconsid-
ered its strategy and expressed a different view in the *Taiwan Daily*:
"In regard to the leadership of the people's hearts, this is something
that must have originated with the long-established system of temples. Now that Taiwan has become a part of Japan, we must of course
maintain this system."[20] It reversed the ban and allowed the islanders
to reopen their temples, as part of a new effort to advance its control
through stability.

In Jilong, this "long-established system" revolved around three
main temples that sat within a few blocks of each other near the
harbor—Qing'an Temple (Qing'an gong), Dianji Temple (Dianji gong),
and Chenghuang Temple (Chenghuang miao) —and contained a broad
array of religious associations and institutions (map 4.1). According to

17. "Xiusu shenxiang," *TNS*, July 16, 1897, page illegible.

18. According to Paul Katz, the Japanese turned sixty-nine temples into military
barracks and another sixty-three into police stations. See Katz, *Religion in China*,
65–66.

19. Prasenjit Duara argued that local religious associations and temples were key
elements in the "cultural nexus of power" that defined state-society relations in late
imperial China. Taiwan's society differed from his North China cases, but his point
about the centrality of local temples carries over. See Duara, *Culture, Power*, 5, 148–57,
250–55.

20. "Taiwan no shaji," *TNS*, Nov. 12, 1896, 2.

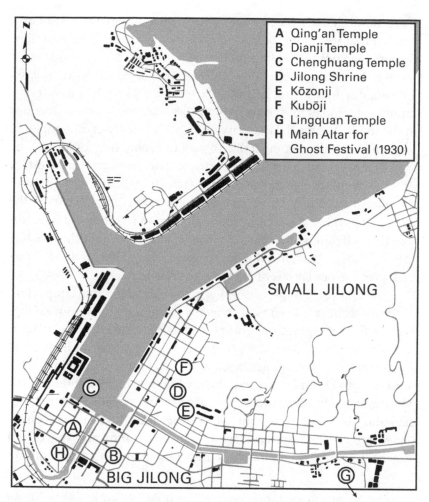

A Qing'an Temple
B Dianji Temple
C Chenghuang Temple
D Jilong Shrine
E Kōzonji
F Kubōji
G Lingquan Temple
H Main Altar for
   Ghost Festival (1930)

SMALL JILONG

BIG JILONG

MAP 4.1. Sacred spaces in Jilong. Map created by Scott Walker, based on a map designed by the U.S. Army Map Service, AMS L991, 1945, held in the Geography and Map Reading Room at the Library of Congress, Washington, DC.

a survey of Taiwan's temples published in 1919, Jilong had nineteen, four of which were built after 1895, whereas a second survey of northern Taiwan from 1933 reported only fourteen. The decline was unexplained, but it could indicate that some temples had closed or, more likely, that the earlier study had included more of the surrounding countryside. The 1933 study classified two as popular Buddhist temples, or *zhaitang* ("vegetarian halls"), listed a third that had originated as a *zhaitang*, another that was more "orthodox" Buddhist in nature, and described the rest—including the Qing'an, Dianji, and Chenghuang—as sites for the practice of "traditional religion."[21] In comparison to other cities on Taiwan, during the first half of Japanese rule Jilong had an average number of temples for the north of the island but fewer than locations in the south. The much larger city of Taipei had forty-eight temples in 1919, and Gaoxiong, comparable in size to Jilong, had forty.[22] Yet by 1933, Jilong had fallen behind its northern neighbors in terms of establishing new places of worship; at this time Taipei had sixty-one, and the smaller town of Yilan surpassed Jilong with around twenty.[23] The declining number and concentration of temples in Jilong did not indicate that religion mattered less to local islanders, or that the city was insignificant in Taiwan's religious sphere; rather, it meant that its spiritual prominence lay elsewhere than in statistics.

The Qing'an Temple (fig. 4.1) was the oldest and most important of the three, having been established by Chinese settlers from Zhangzhou in the late eighteenth century.[24] They dedicated it to the goddess Mazu, who was a patron deity for the sea-faring people of Fujian and a member of the official pantheon approved by the Qing court.[25] Indeed, as both David Jordan and Murray Rubinstein have observed, the Mazu cult is a fundamental aspect of Taiwanese identity.[26] Qing officials and Chinese settlers from both Zhangzhou and Quanzhou established around one hundred temples in her honor across western Taiwan, within clearly hierarchical networks. Some had direct links to

21. See Marui, *Taiwan shūkyō chōsa*, 7–8; Taiwan shaji shūkyō kankōkai, *Taihoku shū shita ni okeru*, 31–32.

22. Marui, *Taiwan shūkyō chōsa*, table 2, 1–6.

23. Taiwan shaji shūkyō kankōkai, *Taihoku shū shita ni okeru*, 219, 65.

24. Most accounts say it was established on the west side of the harbor in 1780, and that local elites moved it to its current location and gave it its current name in 1815. See Liu Qingfan, *Qing'an gong zhi*, 10; "Jilong Qing'an gong Xu guanliren jian yu citui," *TNS*, June 3, 1930, 4. A 1911 land survey states, probably more accurately, that it grew out of a temporary lodging place for fishermen and was supported by fees paid by these fishermen. See Wang and Li, *Taiwan Mazu miao*, 63–64.

25. See Watson, "Standardizing the Gods."

26. Jordan, "Changes in Postwar Taiwan," 157; Rubinstein, "'Medium/Message,'" 213.

THE MATSUMYO, KIIRUN.
(打算前路難原所)
廟　祖　媽　隆　基
(清可許號一〇二郵部令司某要陸年恒正六)

FIGURE 4.1. The Qing'an Temple in 1915. Image courtesy of the National Central Library, Taipei.

parent temples on the mainland, whereas others traced their lineage to prominent temples in Taiwan, through chains of dividing incense (*fenxiang*). The most important center in Taiwan was the Chaotian Temple in Beigang, although other temples claimed prominence in their own right. Pilgrims from the branch temples returned to their parent temples to burn incense at important festivals in their deity's honor, or to restore their spirit images (*shenxiang*).[27] The Qing'an Temple's early history is not well documented, but it belonged to either the Chaotian's network or that of another central temple in Taiwan.

All three of the Jilong temples were dedicated to local or imperially sanctioned deities. The Qing'an was devoted to Mazu, but Jilong's Zhangzhou natives had also long enshrined their patron deity, the "Sage Lord who Opened Zhangzhou," Kaizhang Shengwang, within its walls.[28] However, in 1875, perhaps motivated by Jilong's growing

27. Wang and Li, *Taiwan Mazu miao*, 26–42; Sangren, *History and Magical Power*, 213–15. According to Sangren, branch temples retain ritual power only if they periodically renew the relationship with the parent temple.

28. Wu Huifang, "Xu Zisang yu Ri," 162.

TAMADAGAI KIIRUN.   廟公皇聖街田玉瑩基 (錐可許部令司寓要廣基)

FIGURE 4.2. The Dianji Temple, undated. Referred to in the original caption on the front of the postcard as "Shenghuang Temple," a misprint for "Shengwang." Image courtesy of the National Central Library, Taipei.

status among Taiwan's ports, a group of local elites, using land donated by the eminent Banqiao Lin family (also from Zhangzhou), established the Dianji Temple (fig. 4.2) to house Kaizhang Shengwang.[29] Similarly, during the wave of late-Qing self-strengthening, in 1887 two local degree holders took it upon themselves to establish the Chenghuang Temple to honor the City God, Chenghuang Ye.[30] Chenghuang Ye, who held protective powers if local residents correctly observed the rituals, occupied one of the highest ranks within the official pantheon; thus the Qing government consecrated official Chenghuang temples only in important administrative locations.[31] Gaining such an institution, even through private initiative, gave Chinese religion a stronger physical presence in Jilong and elevated the town's status within Taiwan's

29. Ke, *Jilong Dianji gong*, 3–5; Taiwan shaji shūkyō kankōkai, *Taihoku shū shita ni okeru*, chap. 3.7; Ishizaka, *Ora ga Kiirun*, 30.

30. Ishizaka, *Ora ga Kiirun*, 30. The temple founders both taught Xu Zisang. See TSTF, 6837.3, Jan. 1, 1920.

31. Sung, "Religion and Society," 228–30.

spiritual hierarchy, at the same moment that Liu Mingchuan sought to make it an emblem of modern reforms.

The bonds forged among deity, temple, and locality before 1895 only became stronger thereafter.[32] Early in the Japanese era, an internal dispute over the Qing'an Temple's assets erupted when its head, a monk named Wang Liuzhuan, clandestinely sold some of its property to the government for use as a graveyard. Some incensed local leaders convinced the government to ban Wang from the temple, and in 1903 Xu Zisang was installed in his place as manager.[33] This appointment simultaneously confirmed and enhanced Xu's status, which he used to reinforce the temple's social and territorial position. In 1911 he and some of his earlier proponents began to sell parcels of land the temple owned to the Government-General, probably at the request of officials who wanted to expand the harbor and enlarge Takasago Park. These sales augmented the temple's finances, which ultimately included revenue from land it leased to both Japanese and islanders, dividends from investments in the Jilong Credit Union, and donations from Chinese sailors who came to Jilong.[34] More significantly, having sold the city land that it wanted, Xu obtained higher-value plots that bordered the temple itself.[35] These property moves placed the temple on a stronger financial foundation, in greater control over its immediate surroundings, and more firmly under the leadership of a man favored by the Japanese authorities and some prominent islanders.

The Qing'an forged its first direct link to a mainland temple and established itself as a center of Taiwan's black-faced (heimian) Mazu cult, in 1914.[36] That spring, for the first time in the temple's history, Xu

32. Lin argues for "strong territorial and social ties" in popular religion at the village level in postwar Taiwan, although she minimizes the importance of temples themselves. Lin Wei-Ping, Materializing Magic Power, 15.

33. See "Jilong Qing'an gong Xu guanliren jian yu citui," TNS, June 3, 1930, 4; "Guanggao," TNS, Aug. 18, 1903, 4; and "Jilong Mazu Qing'an gong qu zhuseng Wang Liuzhuan dui Cai Tianpei wai shi shu ming guanliquan fensong shijian," TNS, Sept. 11, 1904, 6.

34. TSTF, 1796.16, 1936.29, and 2126.17, Apr. 1, 1913.

35. Ibid., 6225.2, Jan. 11, 1916; "Jilong Qing'an gong Xu guanliren jian yu citui," TNS, June 3, 1930, 4.

36. At temples that belong to this cult, the statues of Mazu are painted black, for reasons I could not discern.

Zīsang led a group of nine across the Taiwan Strait to the island of Meizhou, in Fujian, the original home of the Mazu cult, to burn incense and restore the temple's spirit image.[37] The group returned to Jilong with a portable shrine—a palanquin with Mazu's likeness inside—which they subsequently used at their annual festival in her honor.[38] When the Government-General mounted a campaign near Hualian in 1915 to pacify indigenous peoples, a number of Jilong's islanders joined the effort. Before departing, they prayed before the temple's black-faced Mazu icon, and subsequently credited her with their swift victory. As a result of this triumph, the black-faced Mazu gained popularity across Taiwan, with the Qing'an Temple as its source.[39] Linking Jilong directly to the origin of the Mazu cult through this institution made the city a central location in Taiwan's spiritual realm.

When islander elites repaired and renovated Jilong's temples, they reinforced the significance of popular religion and manifested the connections between those institutions and their Jilong identity. After temples were reopened in 1897, islanders quickly repaired damage that some of them, such as the Chenghuang and Dianji Temples, had sustained during the Japanese conquest. In the case of Chenghuang, they replaced the image of its patron deity, which Japanese soldiers had destroyed when they occupied the temple.[40] According to Lin Wei-Ping, spirit images are physical representations of a deity's power, and they are necessary to demonstrate that the worship of that deity is effective.[41] Replacing a protective deity like Chenghuang Ye, especially at a moment when disease was prevalent in northern Taiwan, was an important act.[42] In 1912, Xu, Yan Yunnian, and the manager of the Dianji Temple, Lin Rongqin, began renovations on the Qing'an Temple. To mark

37. Wang and Li, *Taiwan Mazu miao*, 49–50. Over the next fifteen years, representatives from three other temples (the Tianhou Temple in Lugang, Wanchun Temple in Taizhong, and Tianmu Temple in Taipei) followed suit.

38. Ibid., 66; "Jilong Qing'an gong Xu guanliren jian yu cuitui," *TNS*, June 3, 1930, 4.

39. Wang and Li, *Taiwan Mazu miao*, 49.

40. "Xiu su shenxiang," *TNS*, July 16, 1897, 1, and "Pudu ping'an," *TNS*, Sept. 5, 1897, 1. The Dianji Temple also had damage repaired; see Taiwan shaji shūkyō kankōkai, *Taihoku shū shita ni okeru*, chap. 3.7.

41. Lin Wei-Ping, *Materializing Magic Power*, 10.

42. Katz, "Local Elites"; Sung, "Religion and Society," 180, 189–98.

the opening of the new structure, they inscribed a stele to express their feelings about their city: "At the head of the leviathan's back [i.e., Taiwan], it is called Jilong. Surrounded by the sea and embraced by mountains, it alone is cherished by the spirits. In former times it was simply a shore on a rocky frontier, but now it has become a port in a key location. It has become densely populated, and the market is bountiful."[43] With these words, they connected the former, decayed temple to Jilong's relative insignificance in the Qing era, and linked the rebuilt facility with its current prominence and prosperity. Some years later, in 1921, the new manager of the Dianji Temple, Lin Rongqin's son Lin Guanshi, used funding from Xu, Yan Guonian, and others to complete a full renovation.[44] The occasion was marked with a stele that once again stressed the bond between the institution and the city: "Calamities cannot invade a place with a bright spirit, and animals will not experience disease. That being the case, the temple's appearance must be dignified. How can it be only for the sake of admiring it that it is built?"[45] Here, islanders embraced as the city's true defenders the sacred icons and spaces that Japanese forces had damaged.

Islanders enhanced their bonds to their deities and temples primarily to distinguish themselves from the Japanese, but in the process they also deepened their separation from China. The renovation of the Dianji Temple should be viewed in light of both Governor-General Den Kenjirō's 1920 proclamation that assimilation was the official policy, and the fact that it played host to many of the culture lectures and political events that took place in Jilong during the 1920s.[46] In these contexts, the stele expressed a form of territorial control that rejected assimilation by asserting the authority of Kaizhang Shengwang in Jilong. Similarly, Xu led the journey to Meizhou in conjunction with

43. He and Lin, *Taiwan diqu xiancun beijie*, 202–3. I believe that the stele currently at the temple's entrance is a post-1945 reconstruction of the original, because of variations in the rendering of dates. The date of the start of construction, May 1912, is given as Meiji 45.5, but the date of its completion, June 1913, is ROC (*Minguo*) 2.6. Japanese authorities would not have allowed the Republican calendar to be used, nor would the elites who financed the renovation have preferred it.

44. Taiwan shaji shūkyō kankōkai, *Taihoku shū shita ni okeru*, chap. 3.7.

45. He and Lin, *Taiwan diqu xiancun beijie*, 208–14.

46. Tsurumi, *Japanese Colonial Education*, 93.

the renovation of the Qing'an Temple, reinforcing the fact that islanders' religion was rooted in their Chinese heritage, rather than in Japanese traditions. However, this connection was to a key pilgrimage site,
not to a larger imagined Chinese national community. Both temples'
renovation inscriptions also clearly articulated an identification with
contemporary Jilong, and therefore a certain distancing from the
China in which the temples' leaders or their ancestors had lived.

Islanders had to reassert their existence outside the Japanese
sphere because the colonial regime inserted itself into their religious
institutions and practices, even during the decades of relative tolerance. Much like their counterparts in other empires, Japanese officials
and scholars, either employed by the Government-General or working
on their own, catalogued, studied, and classified indigenous religions.
Most well known in this regard was Inō Kanori, who conducted some
of the earliest and most extensive research on islander and aboriginal
customs.[47] In the process, Inō and others created the categories of
"Taiwan religions" (*Taiwan shūkyō*) and "islanders' religions" (*hontōjin no shūkyō*), unprecedented groupings that opened the spiritual
realm to colonial policies.[48] Moreover, the Government-General altered the administrative structure of islanders' temples to assert more
direct control. Historically, management at most local temples fell to
either a resident monk or to the master of incense (*luzhu*), an individual whom the prominent local lineages selected on a temporary
basis.[49] Lay clergy administered the *zhaitang* that constituted the vast
majority of Taiwan's Buddhistic institutions. Since Taiwan had very
few temple-monasteries before 1895, in contrast to both Japan and
China, it did not have a strong tradition of management by Buddhist
monks or abbots. The Government-General created the posts of temple manager (*kanrijin/guanliren*) and representative (*daihyōsha/
daibiaozhe*), bureaucratic positions at the top of islander temples that
were often held by neighborhood administrators, as conduits through

47. Barclay, "An Historian among the Anthropologists," 117–36; Matsuda, "Inō
Kanori's 'History,'" 179–96.
48. See Marui, *Taiwan shūkyō chōsa*, and Masuda, *Taiwan hontōjin no shūkyō*.
49. Wang Shih-ch'ing, "Religious Organization in the History of a Taiwanese
Town," in Wolf, *Religion and Ritual*, 76, 85.

which it could observe and potentially reform the "Taiwan religions" into more rationally organized, Japanese-style faiths.[50] The customary leaders did not disappear, but at many institutions the new temple managers supplanted them.

However, these mechanisms of control could also be used against the colonial state. The process of studying and classifying customs and rituals employed many islanders around Taiwan and, in contrast to official intentions, allowed them to see their practices and institutions as fundamentally linked to and rooted in the island. Moreover, much as Kodama Gentarō and Gotō Shinpei decided to moderate the pace of assimilation in the school system, the colonial government allowed islanders to select those who served as intermediaries between their temples and the regime. As spiritual and social outsiders, Japanese authorities required a mediator to transmit information upward and official policies downward. In Jilong, elites selected Xu Zisang to manage the Qing'an and Chenghuang Temples, and they also appointed him as a representative of the Dianji Temple.[51] These positions gave him a potentially dramatic degree of influence over all of Jilong's most important islander spiritual institutions, since they put him in position either to push through state-mandated reforms or to mediate them. During the years when the Government-General called for few changes to the material or ritual aspects of islander religion, Xu displayed his devotion by partially or fully renovating the three main institutions, and founding a fourth. The new one was created to honor a popular deity, the Divine Emperor of Broad Protection (Fuyou dijun), whom islanders frequently invoked to oppose official policies such as the opium monopoly.[52] These acts by Xu preserved and strengthened the temples that were most important to Jilong's islanders, and thus enhanced his status as a gatekeeper.

Japanese settlers and bureaucrats did more than just impinge on islanders' institutions, they sought to transform the spiritual terrain

---

50. Jiang, "Riben diguo zai Tai," 106.

51. Taiwan shaji shūkyō kankōkai, *Taihoku shū shita ni okeru*, 31–32.

52. This opposition took the form of spirit-writing rituals that invoked the aid of the deity Lü Dongbin, one of the Daoist Eight Immortals. See Wang Shih-ch'ing, "Ri ju chuqi Taiwan," 111–51.

of Taiwan by importing Japanese religious institutions into the colony, much as they did in Korea.[53] Owing to their fundamental connections with the formation of Japanese national identity and Japan's overseas empire, Shinto shrines were the most prominent spiritual vehicles for making Taiwan Japanese, for they ostensibly brought modern, civilized religion to Taiwan and challenged the islanders' backward practices.[54] The colonial government established the Taiwan Shrine (Taiwan jinja) in 1901, on a site well north of Taipei's city walls.[55] Appropriately, the Government-General consecrated the first shrine in Japan's first colony to three spirits of pioneering and reclamation that had previously been enshrined in Hokkaido, and to Prince Kitashirakawa, who had died pacifying the island.[56] It gained classification as an imperial shrine (kanpeisha) and thus received funding directly from the national treasury and sat within the same category as, but at a much lower rank than, the Grand Shrine at Ise, center of the cult of Amaterasu, the sun goddess and legendary ancestor of the Japanese imperial line.

Although the colonial authorities quickly established a shrine in the capital, private individuals took the lead in localities like Jilong. In January 1902, an early settler founded Jilong's first Shinto institution when he dedicated a small shrine to the deity Inari.[57] However, his compatriots felt that this minor shrine was both too small to meet the needs of the growing settler population and not commensurate with Jilong's position as the gateway to modern Taiwan. Beginning in 1903, a small group that included Kimura Kutarō, Akabi Sanehira, and others drew up plans, gathered funding, and applied to the Government-General. The official who granted approval lamented, "It is a great pity that Kiirun has no protective deity (shugoshin) associated with it at this time."[58] Evidently, Chenghuang Ye did not count. When the Jilong Shrine finally opened in 1911, it did so as an unranked shrine, which

53. Henry, *Assimilating Seoul*, chap. 3.

54. "Jilong yulan shenghui ji," *TNS*, Sept. 16, 1898, 3.

55. Joseph Allen argues that this location would serve variously, over time, as a sign of separation, integration, and imperial conquest. See Allen, *Taipei*, 30–33.

56. Cai Jintang, *Nihon teikoku shugi shita*, 4.

57. Wen, *Taiwan zongdufu zongjiao shiliao*, 198.

58. Kiirun jinja, *Kiirun jinja shi*, 2–3.

meant that it sat slightly apart from the official shrine hierarchy.[59] Its origins and status bore many similarities to the Seoul Shrine, according to Todd Henry's description.[60] What it lacked in connections to the structure of State Shinto it made up for through its patron deity, Koto-hira, a spirit originally known as Konpira that offered prosperity and safe voyages, much like Mazu did. Kotohira was an especially good choice for a colonial city because, as Sarah Thal outlines in her excellent study of the deity, its prominence in Meiji Japan resulted from the purification process that extracted State Shinto from Buddhist temples. Moreover, the priests and elite parishioners of the parent shrine in Kagawa Prefecture had used their patriotism during the Sino-Japanese War to promote their deity.[61] Thus the Jilong Shrine expressed both the discriminating character of modern Japanese religion and the nationalist goal of imperial expansion.

Throughout the Japanese empire, settlers frequently took the lead in building and managing local shrines.[62] A broad range of individuals and groups supported the expansion of the Jilong Shrine in 1912, financing new buildings that honored Amaterasu and the pioneering spirits enshrined at the Taiwan Shrine. The Jilong Women's Association (Kiirun fujinkai) donated money for trees and part of one of the gates (torii), and the Hiroshima Residents' Association (Hiroshima ken dō-shikai) and Okinawa Residents' Association (Okinawa kenjinkai) donated lanterns and cloth, respectively.[63] Ishizaka Sōsaku, Kimura Kutarō, and other prominent residents established two committees that managed the shrine and oversaw its maintenance and renovation. In fact, much like temples and other islander institutions, popular management of shrines was a matter of official policy. In the metropole, the ranks of shrines matched the official bureaucracy, so each level of government oversaw its corresponding shrine. Taiwan's administrative designations did not match Japan's, however, and Gotō Shinpei wrote

59. State Shinto classified shrines according to seven types: imperial, national (kokuheisha), prefecture (kensha), district (chōsha), village (gōsha), hamlet (sonsha), and unranked (mukakusha). See Hardacre, Shintō and the State, 84–86.

60. Henry, Assimilating Seoul, 63–67.

61. Thal, Rearranging the Landscape, chaps. 10, 12.

62. For the Korean case, see Uchida, Brokers of Empire, 79–80.

63. Kiirun jinja, Kiirun jinja shi, 11–13, 25–32.

to Tokyo in 1901 for instructions on how to classify them. He was told to use the regular classifications, and that clergy should be selected by the parishioners themselves, subject to official approval.[64] According to a report in the Jilong paper, "Taiwan is very different from the home islands, especially in a port city like Kiirun, where the task is not entrusted to the city government, it is the citizens who must gird themselves" to establish and sustain shrines.[65] Settlers used Shinto shrines to bind themselves to their colony, to make the unfamiliar territory more familiar, and, to a greater degree than in the metropole, to express their Japanese national identity.[66]

Achieving a full Japanese transformation, or reterritorialization, of Taiwan's religious realm meant more than just building shrines; it meant that islanders had to absorb the national ideology of Shinto. Islanders indeed attended shrines in substantial numbers, with as many as 75,000 visiting the Taiwan Shrine in Taipei in a single year during the 1920s, a decade before the enforced observances of the Kōminka period.[67] During the early 1930s, the Jilong Shrine received, on average, about nine thousand Taiwanese visitors each year, up to one-sixth of the local Taiwanese population (fig. 4.3).[68] More significantly, Xu Zisang, Yan Guonian, and other islanders served with Japanese elites on the shrine committees and financially supported its ongoing construction. However, one wonders if they did so out of sincere faith or the need to work with settlers and officials. For example, in 1932 the shrine installed a cannon as a sign of respect to the military. According to the shrine committee's report, after the plan was

64. Wen, *Taiwan zongdufu zongjiao shiliao*, 181–87.

65. "Ikuta no kuroshimi o tatte chikaku umareru Kiirun jinja," *NS*, July 15, 1929, no page.

66. Okinawans occupied a somewhat ambiguous space within Japan; they had been legally incorporated into the Japanese nation around 1880 but were viewed as backward and uncivilized by "real" Japanese. Thus their donation to the Jilong Shrine can be seen as intended to identify them as Japanese and to raise their status vis-à-vis the Taiwanese. See Christy, "Making of Imperial Subjects."

67. In 1922, 54,000 islanders visited this shrine, in 1926 almost 75,000 did, and the following year it had more than 63,000 visitors. See Taihoku shū yaku sho, *Taihoku shū yōran 3*, "Shūkyō."

68. The exact counts for 1931, 1932, and 1933, respectively, were 9,200, 8,300, and 10,800 Taiwanese visitors. Kiirun jinja, *Kiirun jinja shi*, 21–22.

FIGURE 4.3. The Jilong Shrine, probably between 1933 and 1945. Image courtesy of Special Collections and College Archives, Skillman Library, Lafayette College, and the East Asia Image Collection, http://digital.lafayette.edu/collections /eastasia/.

announced, "the sound of official and popular support spontaneously erupted, and with deep emotion the work began." However, the only individual donors to the cannon's installation were thirteen Taiwanese, who paid almost half of the 2,700-yen cost.[69] It is unlikely that Japanese elites were indifferent toward the shrine, or that the Taiwanese donors embraced it—and Shinto—with greater patriotic zeal. Rather, it is probable that Japanese settlers and officials conserved their finances and pressured the Taiwanese elites to pay, and that the Taiwanese responded for pragmatic reasons. Most important, the Japanese faced a basic difficulty in using Shinto as a tool of assimilation: Shinto rites came out of the Meiji-era construction of Japan as a family-state, with the emperor and empress as the national parents; so long as Taiwanese were

69. Ibid., 11–13, 25–32, quote on 25. The rest came from the local branch of the Imperial Veterans' Association, to which settlers would have contributed, but none gave in their own name.

kept outside of that family, they could never fully incorporate Shinto into their religious lives.

Many Japanese thought that Buddhism and Buddhist institutions were even more important than Shinto for purifying and rationalizing the religious environment of Taiwan. Japanese Buddhist temples sat in hierarchies that connected parent temples to branch and sub-branch temples not through the division of incense, as with most islanders' institutions, but through the transmission of doctrine and the ordination of monks. Many of the Japanese Buddhist sects contributed to the colonization of Taiwan through the conquest and reconsecration of sacred ground, as they occupied islanders' religious institutions and established their branch temples on the same sites, sometimes temporarily and sometimes permanently. The Pure Land sect used the Chenghuang Temple until it moved to a location near the Jilong Shrine, and the local branch of the Shinshū Honganji occupied an existing temple before establishing its own, the Kōzonji Temple, to the east of the harbor.[70] The Sōdō sect then took over that prime location, in the northern part of Small Jilong, and established its home, the Kubōji Temple (fig. 4.4), in the recently vacated building.[71] Settlers, rather than the parent institutions in the home islands, provided most of the funding, replicating the localizing process that occurred with the Shinto shrines.[72] These acts of occupation and transformation replaced what the Japanese saw as irrational and superstitious institutions with purportedly rational and modern temples.

However, the Government-General apparently grew uneasy with the repeated incidence of reconsecration, and in 1908 it halted the

---

70. Wen, *Taiwan zongdufu zongjiao shiliao*, 197–98. This Shinshū temple traced its lineage through a major temple located in the Tsukiji district of Tokyo, back to the original Western Honganji Temple (Nishi honganji) in Kyoto. The permanent location for the Pure Land temple is listed in Taiwan shaji shūkyō kankōkai, *Taihoku shū shita ni okeru.*

71. Wen, *Taiwan zongdufu zongjiao shiliao*, 262.

72. Kimura Kutarō donated as much as 10,000 yen for the Kubōji, and Ishizaka Sōsaku joined with four others to contribute 2,000 more. "Sōdō shū Kubōji no kenritsu," *TNS*, June 23, 1906, 5. Kimura's biography says that he contributed only 5,000 yen to this project, but either sum was a large amount at the time. See Nomura, *Kimura Kutarō ō*, 150–51.

基 隆 久 寶 寺 全 景

FIGURE 4.4. The Kubōji Temple, after the construction of its new buildings. Image courtesy of the National Taiwan Library, Taipei.

practice, claiming that it wished to preserve the independence of the islanders' religious institutions. At this time, the government informed Jilong's Sōdō leaders that they would thereafter have to construct new buildings for any future branch temples.[73] On one hand, the colonial authorities might have recognized that displacing islanders' temples could destabilize society, and so they chose to constrain the Japanese sects. On the other hand, the new policy indicated an administrative decision to draw a sharper distinction between islanders and Japanese. The government's choice must have come out of Japan's recent history of religious separation, for in cases where the native institutions had not been Buddhist, or not sufficiently Buddhist, allowing a Japanese sect to inhabit the same space would have led to precisely the sort of blending of religions that defined pre-Meiji Japan and made the

73. Jiang, *Taiwan Fojiao bainian*, 140.

Chinese tradition appear irrational and nonmodern. Although the Government-General remained tolerant of Taiwan's religions, it never-theless decided to clarify the divisions between the Japanese and non-Japanese realms.

Japanese Buddhists were at that time motivated by an expansionist zeal that echoed the surge of missionary activity among Europeans and Americans.[74] Embracing what DuBois terms "the organizational and proselytizational techniques of religious mission," the Sōdō, Pure Land, and Shinshū sects quickly established proselytizing centers (*fukyōsho*) in Jilong, where the monks sought converts among both Japanese and islanders.[75] In the first four months of 1902 the Sōdō sect held ten public sessions for religious training at its main mission station and branches; the Shinshū sect held sixty-nine sessions for Japanese participants and sixteen for islanders; and the Pure Land sect led about a dozen gather-ings, many for the islanders working in the gold and coal mines to the east of Jilong, near Jiufen and Jinguashi.[76] These missionaries resolved to "break down the old customs of the islanders" to ensure that they "receive the corrective influence bestowed by Buddhist doctrines."[77] Although they faced persecution in the metropole, the Buddhist sects established a strong presence among Japanese in Taiwan. However, they did not bring in many islanders. By the late 1910s, seven sects had established temples in Jilong—of the sects listed earlier, all except Hokke—along with eight new missionary centers. They reported al-most 4,000 Japanese members, or close to 70 percent of all Japanese in Jilong, but only 1,480 islanders, or about 8 percent of the population. In comparison to other cities, Jilong ranked fourth in the numbers of both Japanese and islanders who belonged to these sects, behind Taipei, Tainan, and Taizhong.[78]

The institutional distribution of islander converts highlights the failure of Japanization through conversion. The vast majority of island-ers who joined Japanese temples were recruited not by Japanese monks,

74. For the Western cases, see DuBois, "Introduction," 8–11; Hutchison, *Errand to the World*.

75. DuBois, "Introduction," 6.

76. Wen, *Taiwan zongdufu zongjiao shiliao*, 262–63.

77. Ibid., 227–28.

78. Marui, *Taiwan shūkyō chōsa*, 175–87.

but through the efforts of a local islander who converted to Chan/Zen, later joined the Sōdō sect, and made his temple-monastery, the Lingquan Temple (Lingquan si), one of its local branches. This institution accounted for almost 85 percent of the islander adherents of Japanese Buddhism in Jilong before 1920, a pattern that prevailed throughout Taiwan, as the vast majority who joined Japanese sects did so either through preexisting institutions or by joining two sects that doctrinally most closely resembled the Buddhism they already practiced, Sōdō and Shinshū. Both Shinshū and the popular lay sects worshipped Amitabha Buddha, whereas the few Qing-era Buddhist monasteries practiced Chan/Zen, as did the Sōdō sect.[79] Thus, instead of converting to Japanese Buddhism or adopting its emphases on doctrinal purity and a Japanese essence, islanders added another layer of affiliation and practice to their religious lives at the points of closest intersection with their existing beliefs and behaviors.

Nevertheless, the Lingquan Temple exemplified the contributions that both Chinese and Japanese religious traditions made to the development of Taiwanese ethnicity.[80] A Chinese Chan monk who came to Jilong in 1900 from the Yongquan Temple in Fujian gained a local disciple who took the name Shanhui after his ordination, and together they founded the Lingquan.[81] After soliciting contributions from Xu Zisang, Yan Yunnian, and Taipei businessman Gu Xianrong, they began construction in the hills southeast of Jilong, near Ruifang. Before it opened in 1908, when a monk from the Yongquan arrived to consecrate the temple, Shanhui met with an abbot of the Sōdō sect and promised to make the Lingquan one of its branches.[82] Shanhui later became a Sōdō follower himself, but because he had already been ordained in the Chan/Zen

79. Ibid. In 1917 Ishizaka Sōsaku divided the islanders between the Lingquan (Sōdō) and Kōzonji (Shinshū) Temples. See Ishizaka, *Kiirun kō*, 150–51.

80. The Lingquan Temple was and remains one of the four most important Buddhist centers in Taiwan, and during the colonial period in particular it exerted a tremendous influence on the growth of Buddhism. Jiang, *Taiwan Fojiao bainian*, 128–29. For a more detailed history, see Jones, *Buddhism in Taiwan*, 39–44.

81. *Lingquan si yange*, 1–4. There is no bibliographic information for this source, which is held at the Institute of Ethnology at Academia Sinica, Taipei, Taiwan.

82. "Sōdō shū Reisenji," *TNS*, Jan. 18, 1906, page number illegible; and "Reisenji an nai," in Zhang and Li, *Lingquan si tong*.

tradition, it did not require a great leap of faith for him to make this transition. His subsequent actions suggest that he did so as a strategy to both enhance the temple's prestige and maintain control over its growth.

As a location of convergence for Buddhist traditions, the Lingquan Temple also manifested an inclusive Jilong identity. Further donations from local residents enabled the construction of new buildings and other structures associated with the temple and its monastery.[83] Temple leaders used one of these new sites, a Hall of Merits and Virtues (Gongde tang), expressly to connect the Lingquan to the new Jilong, and to provide a sense of belonging for those who had recently arrived, a category that included the vast majority of the population. In other words, as the Lingquan Temple expanded, it positioned itself as a place where all of Jilong's residents could demonstrate their connection to that community. Yan Yunnian, who moved to Jilong from its hinterland around 1900, proclaimed Jilong as his home when he placed his ancestral tablets within this hall.[84]

Shanhui charted a course of development for the temple that drew from its institutional links to both of its parent traditions and placed it at the forefront of Buddhism in Taiwan. For much of the Japanese period it was one of the few places that trained and ordained monks, giving it tremendous influence over the teaching and practice of Buddhism in the colony.[85] It enhanced its position when it joined with an important metropolitan Sōdō temple, the recently reopened Sōjiji in Yokohama, to host a Patriotic Buddhist Training Course (Aikoku Bukkyō kōshūkai) in 1918. The course's month-long curriculum aimed to increase both the skills and patriotic fervor of Buddhist monks and missionaries, and thus it appeared to support the imperialist, expansionist tendencies of contemporary Japanese Buddhism. However, Shanhui blunted these nationalizing effects by bringing most of the speakers across the Strait from Fujian, rather than from Japan.[86]

83. *Lingquan si yange*, 4–8.
84. "Shan si jin zhu," *TNS*, Oct. 13, 1914, 3.
85. *Lingquan si yange*, 7–8.
86. Zhang and Li, *Lingquan si tong*, 4. Jiang Canteng argues, "Taiwanese Buddhism was one of the most important aspects of the triangular relations of China, Japan, and Taiwan, and moreover it was one that had official approval." See Jiang, *Taiwan Fojiao bainian*, 136.

Although the Lingquan Temple maintained close ties to its parent temple, it also attempted to distance itself from the lay Buddhism, or "vegetarian teaching," that predominated in Taiwan, perhaps because the leaders of the major anticolonial uprising of 1915, the Tapani (Jiaobannian) or Xilai An Incident, had close ties to the vegetarian sects.[87] By hosting the 1918 training course, the Lingquan's leaders, much like the islanders who formed the Patriotic Buddhist Association in Tainan immediately after the uprising, drew a clear line between their ostensibly pure and law-abiding teachings and the backward, polluted popular Buddhism of the 1915 rebellion.[88]

Most significantly, Shanhui became the primary advocate for a new Taiwanese Buddhism that grew out of his binational religious roots. The precise doctrinal or ritual debts this Taiwanese form owed to its parent traditions are unclear, but the relationships with both religious communities are manifest. He made multiple trips to the mainland in 1911 and the late 1920s to visit temples and ordain monks, and journeyed to the Japanese home islands in 1912 and 1925 to pay his respects to the head of the Sōdō sect and to contribute to an East Asia Buddhist Conference (Tōa Bukkyō taikai).[89] Furthermore, he actively recruited young men from across Taiwan to train as monks at the Lingquan, through an islandwide youth group he established, and via the Southern Ocean Buddhist Association (Nan'ei Bukkyōkai) that he created in conjunction with a monk from Danshui and a prominent Japanese scholar of islander religions, Marui Keijirō.[90] The temple's connections to temples in China and Japan did not make it a tool of either side, for Shanhui and other islanders ran it, and only islanders joined it in its

87. Katz, When Valleys Turned Blood Red, chap. 3.

88. Jones, Buddhism in Taiwan, 66–68. As Jones points out, the association's members did not, in practice, abandon the vegetarian halls themselves.

89. "Reisenji an nai," in Zhang and Li, Lingquan si tong, 1–2.

90. Ibid., 5. This association published a journal called Southern Ocean Buddhism (Nan'ei Bukkyō). Charles Jones examines both Shanhui's youth group and the Southern Ocean Buddhist Association (which he calls the South Seas Buddhist Association). Jones argues that the association in particular was never more than an organ of the colonial state, but I maintain that, with Shanhui's involvement, it did not always serve the interests of the Japanese regime. See Jones, Buddhism in Taiwan, 68–81.

first decade.[91] Thus, although Japanese Buddhists advanced into the spiritual terrain of Jilong and Taiwan, the Lingquan Temple carved out space for itself and its vision of Taiwanese Buddhism, and thus for a separate Taiwanese consciousness and affiliated imagined territory.

Religious Festivals, Territoriality, and Taiwanese Identity

Public religious festivals are crucial manifestations of collective identity because they bring together large numbers of people of all ages from across the socioeconomic spectrum in concrete enactments of important components of their identities. To put it another way, communal rituals are among the most meaningful events at which groups of people perform their identities for multiple audiences, particularly at a time when they are being pressured to abandon or significantly modify those practices. Catherine Bell has referred to rituals as "the very stuff of being a social group" in arguing that they are both ubiquitous across cultures and culturally specific enough to define unique societies, and she also posits "'ritualization' as a strategic *way* of acting."[92] David Kertzer similarly emphasizes the universal significance of rituals, particularly political ones, because they build organizations, create legitimacy and solidarity, and mold people's understanding of their world.[93] From Qing times to the present, the communities established by Chinese settlers in Taiwan have observed remarkably elaborate and lively religious celebrations, and during the Japanese era the most important annual events were the summer Ghost Festival (Zhongyuan pudu or Zhongyuan ji) and the deity-welcoming festivals (*yingshen ji*) associated with the main indigenous temples.[94] Japanese settlers, too, put significant energy into annual religious events, which sometimes influenced how islanders expressed their identities.

91. It had no Japanese members in 1917. Ishizaka, *Kiirun kō*, 151.

92. Bell, "Introduction," 2–3. Bell, *Ritual Theory*, 7; emphasis in quotation is in the original.

93. Kertzer, *Ritual, Politics*, 2–8, 14. I thank John Romano for this and the Bell citations.

94. Sangren, *History and Magical Power*, 88.

The annual Ghost Festival was a central event in the spiritual calendar across Taiwan, an ancient ritual with roots in Daoist cosmology
and Buddhist liturgy that is practiced in varying forms across northeast Asia.[95] The basic purpose of the festival was to appease the lonely
or hungry ghosts (*guhun* or *egui*) that roamed the land during the
seventh lunar month (*zhongyuan*), seeking release from purgatory and
temporary solace because they died without descendants to mourn
them properly, or without leaving the physical remains necessary to
perform ancestral rites. According to Robert Weller, "The ghosts of
those who died by drowning are especially dangerous. . . . Coal mines,
military bases, old battle sites, and other areas of frequent violent death
also have a high concentration of ghosts."[96] The treacherous crossing
from the mainland, the island's rich history of rebellion and native-
place violence, and its numerous dangerous mines all gave Taiwan a
particularly high concentration of such ghosts and heightened the need
to hold the festival. During the seventh month, it was believed, the gates
of the underworld opened and these spirits entered the physical world
to partake of feasts offered by the living and to participate in universal
salvation ceremonies, alternately called the *yulan penhui*, *yulanhui*,
pudu, or *pushi*, performed by Buddhist monks and other spiritual leaders. The main rituals of the Ghost Festival occurred on or around the
fifteenth day, but some continued until the gateway to the underworld
closed at the end of the month. The multireligious foundation of the
festival, as well as its essentially classless nature, gave it the potential to
unify disparate groups and ease social tensions.[97]

During the latter half of the nineteenth century Chinese settlers
ascribed particular significance to the Ghost Festival, and those in
Jilong were no exception.[98] In the early 1850s, armed conflict over land

95. Robert Weller emphasizes the festival's unifying elements. Weller, *Unities and
Diversities*, 14–21.

96. Ibid., 62. Weller places the festival within the bureaucratic framework of
Chinese religion, in which the deities mirror the social hierarchies and relationships
of the human world, and especially of officialdom.

97. Ibid., 11–21, 60–74; Sangren, *History and Magical Power*, 34–36, 81–82.

98. According to Wu Huifang, the leading scholar of Jilong's Ghost Festival,
during the Qing era the festival became larger, longer, more elaborate, more
secularized, and more important across Taiwan than it was on the mainland. A range

and harbor access erupted between the established settlers from Zhangzhou and more recent arrivals from Quanzhou. More than one hundred people died in this clash, and their remains were interred at a public monument near the battle site, south of the harbor. The dispute simmered until 1855, when local elites attempted to channel the energies of residents away from the destructive feuding and into observing the Ghost Festival. They divided Jilong's residents into eleven different surname groups, several of which contained multiple names, and established a rotating schedule whereby each year a different group assumed the role of master of the festival (*lunzhi zhupu*).[99] Other places in Taiwan followed a pattern of sharing leadership according to a set order, with considerable variation from one location to another.[100] The lead group worked under the guidance of a special master of incense and selected assistants to help prepare the festival's main elements, the Four Great Pillars (*sidazhu*): the main salvation (*zhupu*), main assembly (*zhuhui*), main ritual (*zhujiao*), and main altar (*zhutan*).[101] In fact, as Robert Weller observed, the names of these components also served as the titles of the four assistants, and applied to specific parts of a city or town, imparting an element of territoriality to the festival.[102]

In Jilong, the lead surname(s) concentrated on the most important elements of the festival, which occurred on the twenty-fifth and twenty-sixth days of the lunar month, when the tide reached its peak. The master of the festival constructed a primary salvation altar (*zhuputan*) at the Qing'an Temple and placed offerings of animals and other food

---

of official, academic, and popular sources date the festival's growth in Jilong to the mid-1850s. See Wu Huifang, *Jilong Zhongyuan ji*, chaps. 1–2.

99. Chen Yanru, "Zhongyuan pudu yu zhengshang," 76; Liu Qingfan, *Qing'an gong zhi*, 221–23. Either 105 or 108 people died; see Wu Huifang, "Jilong Zhongyuan ji li", 222n2. For an exhaustive discussion of the postwar materials that describe the origins, see Wu Huifang, *Jilong Zhongyuan ji*, chap. 2. "Master of the festival" is my translation of *lunzhi zhupu*, which more literally means "take turns on duty for the main salvation," but in the sources it frequently refers to a role, not a process.

100. DeGlopper, *Lukang*, 66; Weller, *Unities and Diversities*, 16; "Zhilan Zhongyuan," *TNS*, Aug. 15, 1897, 1.

101. Wu Huifang, "Diyuan chongtu," 51–95.

102. Weller, *Unities and Diversities*, 41–43; "Jilong yulan shenghui ji," *TNS*, Sept. 16, 1898, 3.

Lantern in the Water.   燈水放

FIGURE 4.5. Water lanterns used in the Ghost Festival parade, location unknown. Image courtesy of the National Taiwan Library, Taipei.

items before it, invited Buddhist monks to lead the salvation rituals, and built a stage on which musical and dramatic brigades (*zhentou*) engaged in a competition that diffused native-place (or other) rivalries in nonviolent acts. The main assistants built and decorated subsidiary altars in their parts of the city.[103] The high point was a parade in which representatives from all of the surname groups carried water lanterns through the downtown streets before lighting them and floating them in the harbor, to guide the souls of those lost at sea to the shore (fig. 4.5).[104] The rotating cycle for leading the festival prevented many families, including the late-arriving Yans, from heading the festival for

103. Marui, *Taiwan shūkyō chōsa*, 128–33; Huang Wenrong, *Jilong Zhongyuan ji*, 46; "Jilong yulan shenghui ji," *TNS*, Sept. 16, 1898, 3.
104. The water lanterns were constructed for just this occasion. See Marui, *Taiwan shūkyō chōsa*, 132.

decades, but it did not keep them from serving as one of the Great Pillars or participating in the water lantern parade.[105] Jilong's system of rotation diminished the significance of native-place ties by shifting the focus onto surnames instead of origins, whereas the considerable expenditure of resources and energy diverted residents away from reprising old conflicts. Thus the festival strengthened a sense of community in Jilong even before 1895.[106]

The deity-welcoming festivals bore certain ritual similarities to the Ghost Festival but were more significant for their territorial aspects. Each year, the primary god of a particular institution was invited to inhabit the temple on an appointed day, to secure the god's blessings for the community in the year to come. Celebrations of these events included animal sacrifices and a large parade, in which local residents carried portable shrines (*guijiao*) containing statues of deities through the streets. They also formed troupes of lion dancers and musical brigades, which accompanied the deities on their journey.[107] The Chinese term for this procession is *raojing*, which literally means "to move around the boundaries," thus the deity-welcoming festival was essentially a means by which a god reestablished its territorial limits and visited with members of its cult. The principal deities of Jilong's main temples—Mazu, Kaizhang Shengwang, and Chenghuang Ye—all had territorial cults that linked them to a defined zone around the temple grounds.[108] Taken together, these rituals support Hymes's point that the personal and bureaucratic models "travel together," because the Ghost Festival and the deity festivals reinforced personal connections with the spirit world, and the annual repetition of the latter indicated

105. Wu Huifang, "Diyuan chongtu," 79–81.

106. Wu Huifang makes a similar point about the displacement of native-place loyalties by surname allegiance. Ibid., 87.

107. "Jilong saishenhui," *TNS*, May 4, 1905, 4. See also Sangren, *History and Magical Power*.

108. For the territorial nature of deity cults in Taiwan, see Sangren, *History and Magical Power*, 61–77, 83–86; Chipman, "The De-Territorialization of Ritual." Chipman (32) states that "the physical act of traversing the town in ritual procession inscribes its streets as territory of the goddess and her temple[,] and by participating in temple ritual activities Beigang's residents are confirmed as members of Beigang Mazu's community."

that each god had a temporary presence, and an appointed position, that had to be renewed.[109]

The Japanese residents of Jilong felt a mixture of curiosity and disdain for the deity festivals, but those who observed the Ghost Festival recognized similarities between its universal salvation ceremony and either the Feast of Lanterns (Urabon'e, or just Bon) or a more generic festival of salvation (*podo*, or *pushi*; written with the same characters in Japanese and Chinese) practiced in Japan. Most of the Meiji- and Taishō-era reports emphasize this commonality by referring to the Ghost Festival by one of these two names rather than by its most common Chinese name, Zhongyuan.[110] Furthermore, when official and semiofficial sources described the festival, they emphasized Buddhist practices such as yoga, meditation, and reading sutras to appease the ghosts.[111] Settlers in Jilong showed their interest in the festival by attending its ceremonies in significant numbers, as welcome observers, through the early 1930s.[112] One Japanese artist, Murakami Hideo, left a striking record of the event with his 1927 painting *Burning Water Lanterns in Jilong* (*Kiirun ranbō suitō to*), which depicts a long parade snaking its way through town while a crowd watches.[113] Japanese governments, in contrast, were not entirely comfortable with the festival by any name, as the early Meiji state had attempted to ban its celebration, arguing that there should be fewer religious holidays each year.[114] The Government-General took similar action when it prohibited the Ghost Festival in 1895, but as in the home islands it was not a

109. Hymes, *Way and Byway.*

110. This conclusion is based on my survey of the *Taiwan Daily News* and official government sources. Only in the late 1920s did Zhongyuan become more common, perhaps to distinguish the Ghost Festival as non-Japanese and thus to mark it off as something to be transformed. For a postwar comparison of the two, and a Korean equivalent, see Suzuki, "Bon ni kuru rei."

111. Marui, *Taiwan shūkyō chōsa*, 128–33.

112. "Qing'an gong Zhongyuan hedeng shengkuang pudu bei yu saoxing," *TNS*, Sept. 19, 1933, 4.

113. The lively, brightly colored painting, which measures roughly six feet by five feet, is held in the collection of the Taiwan Fine Arts Museum (Taiwan meishuguan) in Taizhong.

114. Hardacre, *Shintō and the State*, 33.

permanent restriction, and the festival grew and evolved for decades with few, if any, overt restrictions.

In 1898, the year after islanders had successfully petitioned to re-open the Chenghuang Temple to make offerings for the deity's assistance amid a wave of disease, they also received permission to hold a simplified version of the Ghost Festival under the strict observation of regular and military police.[115] Once the Government-General relaxed its restrictions, residents held a lavish gathering in the streets around the Qing'an Temple, where offerings of food, alcohol, and lanterns "followed each other in abundance." At the end, they released burning water lanterns into the harbor while police officers kept a close watch on the proceedings. By a coincidence of timing, that year the cycle of leadership fell to the Xu surname group, the smallest and least well-off of the eleven.[116] Although Xu Zisang was not yet the leader of his clan, as the head of his family he would have been involved in the preparations, and the authorities observing the proceedings were almost certainly aware of his role. Perhaps as a result, Xu and the Ghost Festival remained deeply intertwined for the rest of his life.[117]

Between 1895 and 1945 Jilong's Ghost Festival expanded, gained prominence, and likely sank more deeply into the consciousness of islanders there and around Taiwan. Data on the amount that the master of the festival spent each year is spotty, but there was a marked increase of resources expended on the altars and sacrificial items. In 1913 the lead group spent 3,000 yen, and late the next decade the figure peaked in the vicinity of almost 30,000 yen before dropping back significantly and then rising slowly in the Depression-era 1930s.[118] That growth dovetailed with a development that occurred across Taiwan during the 1920s, when islanders began to form a new type of lineage group, the clan association (zongqinhui). Many of these organizations had members throughout the entire island, or at least in multiple cities, such as the one that Xu Zisang founded in 1927 with the help of a prominent

115. "Pudu ping'an," TNS, Sept. 5, 1897, 1.

116. "Jilong yulan shenghui ji," TNS, Sept. 16, 1898, 3.

117. The close relationship between Xu and the Ghost Festival is apparent from my research and is the subject of Wu Huifang, "Xu Zisang yu Ri."

118. Wu Huifang, "Jilong Zhongyuan ji li," 251.

Taipei businessman, Xu Bing, only to leave it soon thereafter. In Jilong, when the rotating cycle fell to one of the five surname groups that had a clan association, the association took on the role of master of the festival.[119] The *Taiwan Daily News*, with its islandwide circulation, enhanced the sense that Jilong had a special link to this event through multiple annual reports on the festival, including one in 1922 that stated, "Jilong's Ghost Festival is the most extravagant in all of Taiwan."[120]

Some Japanese and islander-Taiwanese saw negative aspects to the extravagance and scale of these religious celebrations, and as a result the 1920s and 1930s witnessed ongoing negotiations over how to deal with financial, institutional, and social pressures to reform. In practice, however, the deity-welcoming and Ghost Festivals went on without any significant intervention or alteration, and each year the events themselves brought huge numbers of people to Jilong. For example, during the mid-1920s the Qing'an Temple's black-faced Mazu festival alone—not merged with other temples and their deities, as the CAA had attempted in 1921—brought forty to fifty thousand people to Jilong, some from as far away as Tainan.[121] Even though these events shrank in later years, they still raised considerable logistical challenges, from transportation to crowd control. Organizers usually managed the transportation problem by arranging with the railway bureau and Jilong Light Rail for special trains.[122] To handle the crowds, they at least sometimes drew on the CAA and its youth groups to direct traffic.[123] All of these measures, not to mention the elements of the festivals

119. Chen Yanru, "Zhongyuan pudu yu zhengshang," 106–23. The Jilong branch disbanded in 1930 owing to its members' inability to pay the membership fee.

120. "Zhunbei yulan," *TNS*, Sept. 13, 1922, 6, quoted in Wu Huifang, "Xu Zisang yu Ri," 151.

121. "Shiqi ri Mazu raojing: qing fa linshi lieche," *TNS*, May 9, 1927, 4. "Jijin jin xin: saihui jisheng," *TNS*, Aug. 5, 1919, 6. The installation of this version of Mazu in 1914 drew people to the Qing'an Temple from the surrounding area to present incense. See "Jilong Mazu jidian dingli," *TNS*, Apr. 21, 1918, 6.

122. In *TNS*: "Shiqi ri Mazu raojing," May 9, 1927, 4; "Jilong shi Mazu raojing zhentou bi qiannian zengjia," May 17, 1930, 4; "Jilong Daojiang yingshen xiansheng," May 10, 1933, 4; "Qing'an gong Zhongyuan hedeng shengkuang pudu bei yu saoxing," Sept. 19, 1933, 4.

123. "Jilong Mazu raojing xiansheng: dui difang canjia yinletuan zeng yi xiuqi er jiangli," *TNS*, May 8, 1930, 4.

themselves—lanterns, musical brigades, sacrificial offerings, altars, and so on—increased the considerable expense of the events.[124] Officials and islanders attempted on multiple occasions to reduce individuals' costs of participating by issuing frequent reminders to simplify one's offerings, and by banning begging, arresting vagrants, and curtailing the practice of giving alms to monks in exchange for prayers, the latter on the grounds that it was equivalent to begging.[125] In 1928 Xu Zisang began construction of a permanent altar for the Ghost Festival in Takasago Park (see map 4.1), to save the money spent on erecting a new primary altar every year. He completed the multistory structure in 1930 with some financial assistance from the city government.[126] Later, a committee that included Xu Zisang, the new Dianji Temple manager, Lin Dexin, and a leader of Jilong's social work programs named Cai Qingyun, fulfilled the CAA's earlier vision when they decided in 1933 to merge the deity-welcoming festivals of the Qing'an, Dianji, and Chenghuang Temples into one collective display.[127]

These changes arose out of both renewed pressures from the colonial government to reform native customs and a long-standing debate within islander society over that same question. When the Taibei Prefecture government published a survey of temples in northern Taiwan in 1933, the first such study in almost fifteen years, it lamented a marked contrast between the material and spiritual realms. In the former, Japanese rule had brought remarkable progress, but in the latter, success still seemed far away, a disparity that placed a more intensive focus on

124. In 1933, for example, the three temple festivals together cost in the vicinity of 400,000 yen. See "Jilong Mazu, Chenghuang, Shengwanggong mingnian qi hebing raojing," *TNS*, Nov. 1, 1933, 8. For descriptions of the grandeur of that year's festivities, see, in *TNS*: "Jilong Daojiang yingshen xiansheng," May 10, 1933, 4; "Jilong shi Chenghuang raojing jian zhu sishinian jinian: feizhi pifa daijia chouzhuang," Oct. 3, 1933, 8; "Jilong Chenghuang raojing zhi cheng," Oct. 7, 1933, 8; and "Jilong Dianji gong yingshen shengkuang," Dec. 8, 1933, 4.

125. "Jueyi gailiang er jian," *TNS*, Sept. 19, 1933, 4. The CAA relied on members of its youth groups to spot beggars and alert the local police, who picked up the vagrants and brought them to a holding area away from the city center.

126. "Jian yinyue tang," *NS*, May 25, 1929, 18.

127. "Jilong Mazu, Chenghuang, Shengwanggong mingnian qi hebing raojing," *TNS*. Lin Dexin was a relative of the previous two managers.

Taiwanese religious practice.[128] Even before this time, the prominent surname groups, organizations like the CAA, and the islander masses in Jilong had been engaged in discussions of how to modernize, sanitize, and economize aspects of the Ghost Festival, if they were to make any changes to it at all.[129] Within both the colonial regime and Taiwanese society there was a sense that some practices no longer had a place in Jilong, with the purposely disheveled hair and wearing of the cangue that were common in the Chenghuang festival now targeted much as the queue and foot-binding had been earlier.[130] Japanese and Taiwanese in Jilong did not share motivations or objectives, but the latter unquestionably incorporated modern ideas of sanitation, economy, and civility into their new identities.

In fact, Jilong residents preserved their religious customs in the face of the transformational attitudes that underlay the 1933 report on temples. Rather than abandoning their gods for the imperial deities, Jilong's elites resurrected the CAA's old plan for a merger, which had not been needed in the relatively tolerant 1920s. During the more restrictive 1930s, it ensured that Mazu and the others could continue to visit and demarcate the boundaries of their territories. Xu's iron and stone altar fixed the Ghost Festival's celebrations even more firmly in Jilong's physical and religious landscape, and thus in the identity of its residents, even as it moved the key rituals from the cramped streets to an open space where many more people could participate. In 1934, a resident named Liu Azhen, "one of the new elites of Jilong, who initially wished to reform the festival," attempted to convince the rest of the Liu surname group, leader of the Ghost Festival that year, to forgo the traditional sacrificial animals. However, according to a chagrined news report, "there were some within the lineage who stubbornly persisted in carrying out the old traditions," and on the day of the main rituals the Lius arranged more than four hundred pigs and other animals before the main altar alone.[131]

128. Taiwan shaji shūkyō kankōkai, *Taihoku shū shita ni okeru*, see Introduction.
129. Wu Huifang, "Xu Zisang yu Ri." On the CAA's early attempts to change the Ghost Festival, see chapter 3.
130. "Jilong shi Chenghuang raojing jian zhu sishinian jinian," *TNS*, Oct. 3, 1933, 8.
131. "Jilong Qing'an gong Zhongyuan di er ri pudu shengkuang," *TNS*, Sept. 8, 1934, 4.

These efforts to protect core aspects of the emerging Taiwanese identity evidently did not go unnoticed by the settler population in Jilong. The Jilong Shrine festival was intimately tied to the growth of Japan's empire, held as it was on June 2, the date that the formal handover of Taiwan to Japan in 1895 took place aboard a ship outside of Jilong's harbor. Up through 1933 the event had been restrained in its celebrations, held in the immediate vicinity of the shrine itself. However, 1934 saw the completion of a significant renovation of the shrine, a long-awaited upswing in the local economy, and the first occasion of the joint deity-welcoming festival. That year, the shrine's managers expanded their festival into a three-day event: the first day was for honoring the spirits, the second day for the dedication of the new buildings, and the third for a large public festival with celebrations in both the Japanese core of Small Jilong and some of the mixed districts east and west of the city center, an unprecedented territorial reach.[132] The temporal and territorial extension in Jilong lagged behind the process in Seoul, where the Seoul and Korea Shrine celebrations had moved into Korean neighborhoods by the mid-1920s.[133]

This expansion of the Jilong Shrine festival exemplified the attempt to extend Japanese control over Jilong identity, and the Taiwanese community reacted in kind the following year. In 1935, on the day following the two-day Jilong Shrine festival, the joint deity-welcoming festival's parade carried the three gods into Small Jilong, passing through the heart of the Japanese settlement, beneath the Jilong Shrine, and in front of some of the most important Japanese Buddhist temples (see map 4.1).[134] Symbolically, the deities marked those districts as their territory. An image, probably from the early 1930s, indicates that deity parades had come this way before, but the Taiwan Daily had not reported on them until the scale of the 1935 event made it noteworthy (fig. 4.6). Unfortunately, this procession route proved to be a miscalculation. Although Japanese had initially supported the joint festival, once it

132. "Kiirun jinja saiten," NS, May 11, 1934, 7; "Kiirun jinja daisai," NS, May 25, 1934, 4; and "Kinrai ni nai Kiirun no omatsuri kibun," NS, June 1, 1934, 8.

133. Henry, Assimilating Seoul, 76–85.

134. "Raojing luguan," TNS, June 9, 1935, 8; "Jilong sanshen hebing raojing difang guanke yue shuwan ren," TNS, June 12, 1935, 4; and "Jilong hebing yingshen xubao," TNS, June 12, 1935, 8.

(哲晷原新) 列行祭人土街頭船哨隆甚 (深可游海合同至業充基)
PROCESSION OF THE NATIVE FESTIVAL.

FIGURE 4.6. The procession of a deity-welcoming festival past the entrance to the Jilong Shrine and the Kōzonji Temple, prior to 1933. Image courtesy of Special Collections and College Archives, Skillman Library, Lafayette College, and the East Asia Image Collection, http://digital.lafayette.edu/collections/eastasia/.

entered their territory they moved against it. Later in 1935 a group of officials and settlers, including the mayor of Jilong and Ōmi Tokigorō, met with Xu Zisang and other festival organizers to select leaders for the following year's event.[135] The inclusion of Japanese advisors in the planning meeting marked the strongest Japanese intervention in an indigenous festival since the colonial government had lifted its ban in 1897. Moreover, in 1936, after the Government-General finally granted the long-standing request of the Jilong Shrine parishioners to have their institution elevated to a prefectural shrine, to match the city's status as Taiwan's leading port, the temple leaders immediately launched a special commemoration that took place alongside the three-year-old city-wide Harbor Festival.[136] In conjunction with that secular celebration of the settlers' Jilong, the shrine festival took the unprecedented step

135. "Jilong san shen hebing jidian," *TNS*, June 14, 1935, 8.
136. "Kiirun jinja saiten, kōsai," *NS*, June 27, 1936, 7, and "Kiirun jinja no kensha shōkaku undō," *NS*, Mar. 13, 1935, 5.

of expanding into Big Jilong, intertwining city and shrine in a way that challenged the territorial zone of Taiwanese religious celebrations.

The Ghost Festival, too, experienced what amounted to a Japanese invasion of its spiritual terrain in the late 1930s. Amid the rising nationalism and militarism that brought the radical Japanization of the Kōminka movement and war with China, neither the economizing reforms nor the Buddhist elements of the festival proved sufficient to forestall a massive act of state intervention. Local authorities strongly criticized the system of rotating leadership, claiming that it bred competition and waste, and then passed an ordinance banning it altogether in 1937. A few years later, the city government prohibited the construction of the auxiliary altars and limited the scope of the celebrations to Xu's permanent structure.[137] Jilong's festival fared better than Nantou's, at least, where locals reportedly removed it from the streets and confined it to acts of ancestor worship in the home and at one temple.[138] Around 1940, municipal officials reinvigorated a Japanese ceremony to honor the dead, the *shōkon*, which originated alongside the modern Japanese nation-state and became linked to the expansion of its empire. The Meiji regime first observed this rite to honor those who died defeating the last Tokugawa loyalists in the Bōshin War (1868–69), and colonial authorities held the ritual in Jilong in 1898 to commemorate Japanese troops who had perished there in the process of taking over Taiwan.[139] However, its observance in Jilong ceased during the 1910s, according to the inscription on a stele erected in 1927 to reinvigorate the ceremony, and it was not held often thereafter, if at all, until the war years.[140] At that time, in conjunction with the efforts to diminish the Ghost Festival, it seems that colonial officials reemphasized the *shōkon* to challenge or replace the Taiwanese festival for their kindred spirits with a Japanese cognate for the Japanese war dead. However, even with the power of the modern state and the mobilization of the war years,

137. Huang Wenrong, *Jilong Zhongyuan ji*, 46–48.

138. "Nantou jie yi changzhu cui Zhongyuan jidian gaishan," *NS*, Sept. 12, 1936, 13.

139. "Kiirun no shōkon matsuri," *TNS*, Oct. 24, 1940, 2. The first *shōkon* shrine established by the Meiji government is now the well-known Yasukuni Shrine. See Ketelaar, *Of Heretics and Martyrs*, 60, 116; Hardacre, *Shintō and the State*, 90–92.

140. He and Lin, *Taiwan diqu xiancun beijie*, 199–201. The practice faded after the monument erected for the ceremony in 1898 was moved to Takasago Park in 1910.

the settlers and officials failed to achieve their goal of religious conquest. As the islanders became Taiwanese, they did so on a cultural foundation of which their festivals were essential building blocks.

Temple Restructuring and Border Defense

In September 1936 the Japanese government launched the Kōminka movement in Taiwan, and the following year extended it into Korea. This campaign's main goal was to transform Taiwanese and Koreans into good, loyal Japanese subjects of the emperor through social mobilization. It represented the full realization of the assimilationist, civilizing strains that had been present within Japanese colonialism from the beginning, even as it completed the shift away from the moderate, tolerant policies that had earlier prevailed. A core aspect of Kōminka was to spread Shinto over the full extent of Taiwan's spiritual realm. To this end, in 1937 and 1938 the Government-General issued policies to establish more public shrines, replace ancestral altars within the home with Shinto altars, and amalgamate Taiwanese temples into fewer institutions before shutting them down or reconsecrating them as Shinto shrines.[141] These plans marked the apogee of Japanese efforts to reterritorialize Taiwan's religious spaces and, on the local stage, they reinforced the attempts by Japanese settlers and local officials to make expansive Japanese nationalism coterminous with Jilong identity, leaving no room for an alternative Taiwanese consciousness.

This program to amalgamate and shut down Taiwanese temples was called the Temple Restructuring movement (Jibyō seiri undō) and it extended across the island. The government of Gangshan (Okayama) County, near Gaoxiong, abolished all of that county's Taiwanese temples in 1939 and the county shrine took control of their resources, which it then used to construct more Shinto institutions in the vicinity.[142] In Tainan, the city government took the same step toward all Taiwanese

141. The details of this policy are explored at length in Cai Jintang, *Nihon teikoku shugi shita*, chap. 7.

142. "Jibyō o haishi shite gaishō ni jinja kenritsu," *TNS*, Apr. 20, 1939, 5.

temples in 1940 but diverted their resources to educational projects.[143] However, implementation of the rate of temple closure varied tremendously across Taiwan's prefectures, ranging from 7 percent of all temples shut down ("restructured," or *seiri*) in Taibei, more than half in Tainan and Gaoxiong, and up to 93 percent in Taidong (Taitung). No temples were formally closed in Jilong or nearby Danshui.[144] The north-south divide suggests that Japanese officials either viewed southern temples as a greater impediment or prioritized avoiding disruptions over assimilation in the north and in cities in general. All of Jilong's Taiwanese temple managers held a series of meetings with other local leaders during the summer and fall of 1940 in which they decided, no doubt under pressure, to fold their separate institutions into the Qing'an Temple rather than close them. They finally adopted the plan proposed by the CAA in 1921 and pooled their resources in a new foundation, which they placed under the leadership of the mayor of Jilong, to run the amalgamated temple.[145] Official regulations allowed for this amalgamation as it offered the Government-General some control, but it seems that in Jilong and other cities, the strength of Taiwanese identity kept the temples open, if sometimes in new forms.[146]

In fact, Japanese control was much more apparent than real. The pressure that Taiwanese elites faced to abolish their key religious institutions was an extreme version of the earlier pressure to alter specific religious practices and other customs, and they responded in similar ways. Taiwanese elites in Jilong closed ranks within their most important sacred institution, in much the same way that they had earlier combined the three deity-welcoming festivals under the leadership of the Qing'an Temple. Such expressions of unity highlighted the strength of Taiwanese ethnicity, with its religious affiliations, in Jilong. The long-standing efforts of Xu Zisang and others to accommodate the demands of the Japanese state and settlers while not simply serving as

143. "Zen jibyō o haishi," *TNS*, Jan. 31, 1940, 5.

144. Cai Jintang, *Nihon teikoku shugi shita*, 241–42.

145. "Kaku jibyō o seiri shite, Kei'an miya heigō tōitsu," *TNS*, June 8, 1940, 2; "Zen jibyō o heigō zaidan hōjin ni," *TNS*, Oct. 24, 1940, 2.

146. Cai Jintang, *Nihon teikoku shugi shita*, 254–55, 242. Of the other major cities, 2 percent of temples in Taipei, 3 percent in Gaoxiong, and 4 percent in Tainan were closed.

"running dogs" enabled Jilong's temples to avoid the fate of those in rural parts of Tainan and Taidong. The strength of Taiwanese ethnicity in Jilong, the city at the forefront of its creation, made it harder for the state to challenge key institutions there. The islandwide power of a strategy of superficial submission manifested itself when the colonial government halted the Temple Restructuring movement in 1941 and allowed Taiwanese temples more freedom of action.[147] The costs required to control and suppress Taiwanese religion, both in terms of bureaucratic resources and the potential for sparking unrest, proved to be far too high for the government to bear, especially as the war with China dragged on and the possibility of conflict with the United States increased.

The foremost Japanese scholar of religion in Taiwan, Masuda Fukutarō, offered his views of Japan's religious influence in Taiwan when he recounted his May 1942 tour of temples in the north. On the day that Masuda visited Jilong, he stopped first at the Qing'an Temple. As he approached it, he found that a "clamorous" festival in Mazu's honor—he made no mention of a joint festival—was in full swing, and that the smell of animal offerings filled the air.[148] Masuda then moved on to the Lingquan, where he found further evidence of the failures of colonial religious policies. He saw that the Buddhist temple was flourishing, which might have demonstrated the beneficial influence of the Sōdō sect. By this time, the Lingquan had expanded its reach across Taiwan through more than thirty branch temples and affiliated institutions. However, when he looked more closely at the buildings and talked with the monks, he saw little evidence of Japanization. He lamented what he saw as the continued influence of the backward, syncretist Taiwanese religion, the failure to embody the purity of Japan's Zen tradition, and the fact that the temple maintained ties to its parent temple in Fujian. He wrote, with evident chagrin, "Even among the monks there are some who completely lack in training, and there are none who, in their hearts, understand the meaning of the sutras that they chant."[149] Nevertheless, he tried to close on a philosophical note: "[This temple]

147. Ibid., 314.
148. Masuda, *Minzoku shinkō*, 216–17.
149. Ibid., 217–23, quotation on 223.

should not be criticized for the fact that a Japanese-Taiwanese Buddhist fusion is still far off."[150] Masuda grasped at straws with these words, for his report on Jilong attested to the fact that not only had Japanese policies and actions to reform islanders' religions failed, but their efforts had provoked the Taiwanese to defend their traditions and to place them at the heart of their ethnic identity.

Conclusion

Islanders and Japanese shared the physical spaces of Jilong, but they filled that territory with separate religious traditions. These sacred realms overlapped in a number of ways, with some common ritual practices, similar strains of Buddhism, and even some shared institutional structures such as hierarchies of parent and branch temples and officially sanctioned deities. Yet religion was consistently a zone of contestation and conflict for the fifty years of Japanese rule. Those tensions were caused, first and foremost, by the invasiveness of Japanese colonization. For Japanese settlers and officials, the importation of Shinto and their Buddhist sects into Taiwan was a crucial element of the larger colonial projects to civilize, modernize, and Japanize the islanders. Reconsecrating islanders' temples as the homes of Japanese sects, proselytizing by Buddhist missionaries, establishing Shinto shrines and expanding their festivals, and restructuring Taiwanese temples out of existence, all of these were acts of reterritorialization, efforts to make Jilong and Taiwan wholly Japanese. However, at the heart of this spiritual transformation was a contradiction: being Japanese required following Shinto, and even though islander-Taiwanese served on the Jilong Shrine committee and attended ceremonies there, Shinto's close affiliation with the familial structures of the Japanese nation-state kept the islanders, almost by definition, on the outside. That internal conflict limited the degree of assimilation that could be achieved through religious means in Taiwan, as Henry has also observed in Korea.[151]

150. Ibid., 224.
151. Henry, *Assimilating Seoul*, 63, 73.

The islanders held themselves outside of the Japanese religious realm, as they built their ethnic identity around a core of religious institutions and practices and demarcated the boundary around it. The Chinese origins of the deities Mazu, Kaizhang Shengwang, and Chenghuang Ye, and the Ghost Festival, outlined the basic distinctions between islander and Japanese religions, and the territoriality of the deity cults, deity-welcoming festivals, and Ghost Festival all delineated the islanders' spiritual terrain. During the decades of relative Japanese tolerance, islander-Taiwanese strengthened their connections to this terrain, and as Japanese attempts to conquer it intensified during the 1930s, they fiercely protected it. Through strategic modifications to temples and festivals, elites in Jilong played their role as gatekeepers, acceding to some of the demands of the colonial regime but ensuring the survival of institutions and rituals. Even in the areas of greatest overlap, Taiwanese succeeded in keeping the Japanese out of the spaces that they had reterritorialized. The performance of Jilong's Ghost Festival was organized by surname, which meant that Japanese residents could never be more than observers. In the Lingquan Temple, Shanhui and the other leaders did not produce the Taiwanese-Japanese fusion of Buddhism that Japanese hoped to see, but rather created and promoted their own vision of a specifically Taiwanese Buddhism. As seen in the incident with which this chapter began, aggressive attacks on the religious core of Taiwanese ethnicity served as a rallying point for the defense of this newly formed identity.

Religion facilitated the expansion of this Taiwanese ethnicity beyond just the city of Jilong. Temples and especially festivals, as manifestations of personal connections to the spirit world, held strong connections to a specific place, and they also connected worshipers to wider networks through incense-division, pilgrimage routes, and similar practices. Thus, as the island's center of the black-faced Mazu cult, the Qing'an Temple was bound to a geographically broad community, and the Lingquan Temple forged links across Taiwan by recruiting and training monks. Prominent coverage of Jilong's Ghost Festival helped to connect place and practice for an islandwide audience. In addition, after the crackdown on political movements with nationalistic leanings in the late 1920s, most Taiwanese turned to religion as they constructed their own group consciousness outside of the nation-state model. This process of ethnic construction defined borders between Taiwanese and Japanese, and also set those who became Taiwanese apart from mainland Chinese. After building and maintaining rigid borders around their ethnic identity under Japanese rule, the Taiwanese people would face new religious challenges in the postwar world.

CHAPTER FIVE

Realms of Welfare
Social Work and Border Defense

In 1935, social workers from Jilong joined a group from Taiwan on an annual trip to the home islands. This tour usually provided an opportunity for colonial social workers to learn from programs in the metropole, and this year they visited welfare projects designed to raise national consciousness through patriotic training. One highlight was the Rokuhara Youth Center in Iwate Prefecture, where boys and girls practiced moral improvement, self-discipline, and battle formations. The ultimate goal of these youth programs was to strengthen and expand the empire.[1] A Japanese member of the group focused on the military and patriotic education of boys and girls—the "Rokuhara spirit" (*Rokuhara seishin*)—but the two Taiwanese delegates from Jilong, both welfare commissioners and Customs Assimilation Association officers, connected the Japanese national spirit to religion and religious institutions. The crowds of people they saw praying at local

Some of the material in this chapter appeared previously in Evan Dawley, "Expanding Japan: Reforming Society through Social Work in Colonial Taiwan," in *Tumultuous Decade: Japan's Challenge to the International System, 1931–1941*, edited by Masato Kimura and Tosh Minohara (Toronto: University of Toronto Press, 2013). Copyright University of Toronto Press. Reprinted with permission of the publisher.

1. Nakajima Ichio, "Iwate ken no sui: Rokuhara seinen dōjō shisatsu ki," *SJT* 80 (July 1935): 69–70. Nakajima was the Japanese secretary for social work in Jilong, and it was his hope that the girls who internalized the Rokuhara spirit would go on to marry heroic settlers in Manchuria and Mongolia.

Shinto shrines, major Buddhist temples, and the imperial Ise and
Meiji Shrines favorably impressed them, as did the employment offices, clinics, housing settlements, and other welfare projects managed by those temples and shrines. They noted a sharp contrast
between Japanese and Taiwanese institutions, the latter of which they
felt almost completely shirked their welfare responsibilities. Except
for the Qing'an Temple, which donated 1,000 yen a year to the Jilong
CAA for social work, they said that the Taiwanese temples in Jilong
merely consumed needed resources in extravagant annual festivals
and other activities. They advocated curtailing these wasteful customs and redirecting the efforts and finances of Taiwanese temples
toward social work.[2]

Social work in Taiwan began as a system that provided assistance
to those in need and a measure of social control from the grassroots
level up, but over time its purpose merged with larger goals of cultural
reform and modernization. As that shift took place, officials, settlers,
and islander-Taiwanese transferred the practice of social work from a
shared imagined space, in which both Japanese and Taiwanese residents acted for the greater good of the local society, into an arena
starkly divided by the borders between groups. To be sure, specific
assistance projects manifested distinct identities from their inception,
but until the late 1930s the strength of Jilong consciousness enabled all
local residents to engage in welfare provision, even as Japanese settlers
and officials increasingly used the system to reterritorialize the city's
imagined geography and control the population. As in the religious
realm, the late-colonial attempts to impose Japanese national identity
provoked a strong defense of Taiwanese ethnicity by local social workers and their community.

Although it may not be immediately apparent how social work, in
contrast to religion, contributed to ethnic formation, it nonetheless
fundamentally shaped Taiwanese consciousness. As with social organizations, social work significantly reinforced the islanders' collective
sense of self and strengthened in-group bonds because it institutionalized patterns of providing assistance to other islanders that crossed

---

2. He Peng and Lin Shuanghui, "Naichi shisatsu zakkan," *SJT* 80 (July 1935):
81–84.

lines of class, gender, generation, and native place. It also gave local elites another opportunity to perform their roles as leaders and supporters of their local community. Moreover, the colonial structures of social work and their persistent attention to customs reform ethnicized the islanders; that is, the Government-General's policies treated them as a unified ethnic group with shared social behaviors and cultural characteristics. The system's hierarchical model, and the trans-island connections and discursive mechanisms it promoted, allowed the boundaries that formed locally to reterritorialize Jilong and the island as Taiwanese. Finally, social work linked Taiwanese consciousness to modern ideas of professionalization and hygiene. In much the same way that doctors, as Ming-cheng Lo's work shows, brought modern medicine into their construction of Taiwanese nationalism, social workers used this new form of social welfare to shape their identities.[3] Taiwanese social workers appealed to elite and nonelite constituencies by sustaining their society and defined their ethnic group as internally unified, geographically dispersed, and explicitly modern, rational, and scientific in its view of the world.

Social Work in Global and Local Perspectives

Imperial Japan sometimes absorbed models from Europe and the United States and presented them to its colonies in modified form, and social work was one example of the phenomenon of the transnational circulation of ideas initially reaching Taiwan through Japan.[4] Social work first emerged in modern cities in Western countries during the late nineteenth and early twentieth centuries, where urbanization brought new possibilities for individual and collective action, but also the perception of new ills like competitiveness, deviancy, social sickness, self-aggrandizement, and crime. Reformers on both sides of the Atlantic believed that resolving these problems and maintaining social order

3. Lo, *Doctors within Borders*, 74, 109, chap. 5.
4. See Shiyung Liu's argument that the Taiwan Government-General imported a Japanized version of the German *Staatsmedizin* system. Michael Shiyung Liu, *Prescribing Colonization*, chap. 1.

required a scientific and professionalized form of welfare. Their views gave birth to the case worker, a trained, usually middle-class, often female social worker who worked with poor, lower-class clients on an individualized basis.[5] Although the precise routes of transmission are not clear, some Japanese social reformers adopted elements of these models, such as the emphasis on social surveys, urbanization, and the scientific outlook that made modern social work (*shakai jigyō*) a supposedly advanced form of the older social welfare (*shakai kyūsai*, or *shakai fukushi*). However, certain characteristics displayed Japan's historical legacy, such as a hierarchy of assistance in which the state gave aid only in the last resort, to people who could not be helped by family members or neighbors. The dominant model reflected the thinking of early nineteenth-century rural reformer Ninomiya Sontoku, who stressed thrift, self-reliance, and mutual assistance through village or neighborhood organizations. According to Sheldon Garon, these basic traits persisted into the Meiji era and beyond, when "Japanese style welfare was to be administratively simple, strongly didactic, relatively immune from taxpayers' opposition to public assistance, and embedded in the traditional relationship between the benevolent ruler and his subject."[6]

Key figures, such as Gotō Shinpei, had paid close attention to foreign models since the early Meiji period, but social work did not emerge in Japan until the middle of the 1910s. At that time the state provided more funding, although still not as much as needed, and reformers adopted a more scientific approach to treating social ills. However, social work never became fully professionalized in Japan, nor was it dominated by women, as it was in the United States in particular. It continued to rely instead on primarily untrained male volunteers and appointees to do most of the work.[7] The form of social work that Japan exported to its colonies stressed state oversight and definition of goals,

5. Lees, *Cities, Sin, and Social*, 1–3, 15–17; Walkowitz, *Working with Class*, prologue, chap. 1. The highest profile manifestation of early social work was the large, multifunctional, urban settlement house, such as Chicago's well-known Hull House, where Jane Addams was a pioneer in the field; see Addams, *Twenty Years at Hull House*.

6. Garon, *Molding Japanese Minds*, 49.

7. Ibid., chap. 2.

along with reliance on private institutions and mostly nonprofessional social workers to develop local solutions. Officials and settlers employed a tacit formula that emphasized moral assistance first, and material assistance only when absolutely necessary. To highlight the changes that took place around 1920, in this chapter "social welfare" refers generally to the provision of assistance in all eras, whereas the terms "social work" and "social workers" refer specifically to the systematic form of welfare that took shape after World War I.

Practices of social welfare that reflected Chinese patterns of elite activism took root in Taiwan during the Qing period. Japanese-era sources emphasize that the mostly ad hoc institutions that existed before 1895 were "half official, half private" (hankan hanmin) initiatives. They addressed a wide range of issues, including aid to infants, children, and the aged, and provided for public burial grounds and defense against bandits. In addition, a number of organizations throughout the island cared for vagrants and assisted travelers who became sick or died while in Taiwan.[8] Given what we know about late-Qing elite behavior, it seems likely that local gentry in Taiwan consistently played active roles in a variety of welfare and other projects, particularly in the late nineteenth century when the demand for action on the part of the gentry rose.[9] Therefore, in spite of Japanese claims to the contrary, Taiwan was not a blank slate onto which officials and settlers could inscribe entirely unprecedented welfare practices. Instead, islanders approached the social work system designed by the Government-General, which combined the older welfare organizations with a broad range of new institutions that penetrated deeply into local society, with their own ideas on how to give aid to those in need. The legacy of Chinese elite leadership helps to explain both a high level of islander participation in the new system and how the Taiwanese employed social work to define and preserve their ethnic community.

8. This description is drawn from several different accounts, including: Kinebuchi, *Taiwan shakai jgyō shi*, 1129; Taiwan sōtokufu, "Taiwan shakai jigyō yōran," in Nagaoka, *Shokuminchi shakai jigyō 1*, 47; Taiwan sōtokufu, "Taiwan shakai jigyō yōran," in Nagaoka, *Shokuminchi shakai jigyō 5*, 44; Taihoku chō, *Taihoku chō shi 2*, 591–93.

9. Rankin, *Elite Activism*, 3, 93–100; Rowe, *Hankow: Commerce and Society*, chap. 9.

Creating Modern Social Work in Taiwan

During the first decades of their rule, the Japanese used social welfare to address some of the problems they faced in adapting to and reterritorializing their new environment. The first governors-general adopted essentially the same attitude toward social welfare institutions as they did religious ones: they shut them down as part of a larger strategy to undercut resistance to Japanese rule.[10] However, within a few years the Government-General began to reauthorize many of the same institutions it had so recently closed.[11] Local problems exerted tremendous influence on the types of institutions that were reopened first. One of the main obstacles faced by the early Japanese government, military, and settlers was disease. Unaccustomed to the climate and local ailments, many early arrivals in the colony, from Prince Kitashirakawa to the brother of Jilong's mining giant, Kimura Kutarō, fell victim to tropical pathogens, which endangered the success of the colonial project. To address this, in 1899 Kodama Gentarō reopened some institutions that provided health care, starting with a large clinic (*jikei in*) in Taipei and then expanding out to six others, one in each of the colony's new prefectures. In this way, from the beginning social welfare was linked to the colonial reconfigurations of administrative spaces that later facilitated Taiwanese identity construction. These clinics apparently quickly proved their utility, because soon thereafter the state reauthorized other institutions throughout the island and allowed for the establishment of new ones. In the following months and years, it issued regulations governing disaster relief, assistance to travelers who fell ill or died, aid to veterans, and youth reformatories.[12]

Gotō Shinpei spearheaded the government's attention to social welfare as head of the Civil Administration under Governor-General Kodama. Gotō opened several initiatives to transform Taiwan into a modern colony through the application of so-called "scientific

10. Imai, "Nihon tōji shita," 24.
11. Ibid.; Taihoku chō, *Taihoku chō shi 2*, 597.
12. Imai, "Nihon tōji shita" 24; Kinebuchi, *Taiwan shakai jigyō shi*, 1120, 1129; and Taiwan sōtokufu, "Taiwan shakai jigyō yōran," in Nagaoka, *Shokuminchi shakai jigyō 1*, 48.

colonialism." He had studied social policy in Germany, where he observed the growth of modern social work and Bismarck's creation of the foundations of the welfare state. Motivated in part by what he saw there, in the early 1890s he launched a drive to reform Japan's Relief Regulations (Jukkyū kisoku) of 1874 to increase state assistance to those in need, especially the working poor. The effort failed, but his interest in public welfare carried over to his new job in Taiwan. In 1899, he imported the existing Relief Regulations and issued them in a modified form in Order 95 as the Taiwan Poor Relief Code (Taiwan kyōmin kyūjo kisoku). To expand the role of the state in welfare, he extended the range of eligible age groups, standardized the amounts of aid, and funded assistance through taxes and levies rather than just through donations.[13] Gotō's policies highlighted the administrative differences between the colony and the metropole and, more significantly, showed that Japan's social welfare system was very much in flux.[14] The Government-General did not apply it from the home islands fully formed but rather adapted it to prevailing local conditions. Nevertheless, as social work developed within social welfare in metropolitan Japan, the shifting ideas filtered out to Taiwan. One thing, however, remained constant in the Japanese approach to welfare in the colonies: they saw it as one mechanism for separating Taiwan from its backward, Chinese past and civilizing it with Japanese modernity.

Jilong contained very few welfare institutions prior to 1895, but residents developed them quickly in the following years. Existing records confirm the presence of only one Qing-era institution, a temporary accommodation for the poor established near the Qing'an Temple in 1881 through an official initiative and substantial donations from local elites.[15] However, as Jilong grew in size and importance, the practice of social welfare expanded dramatically. At around the time that

---

13. Imai, "Nihon tōji shita."

14. The Meiji state distributed seven types of aid in the home islands, but in Taiwan there were five different categories of imperial aid for people or institutions: misfortune (kikkyō), disaster (saigai), encouragement (shōrei), assistance (josei), and medical care (iryō). Imperial charity included donations for the poor or sick, aid to the elderly, disaster relief, and special assistance given at important festivals or to honor the dead. See Kinebuchi, Taiwan shakai jigyō shi, 1120.

15. Taihoku chō, Taihoku chō shi 2, 595.

the Government-General anointed him with the status of "Taiwan gentry" and appointed him district chief, in 1903, Xu Zisang solicited financial support from local elites to reestablish the old home for vagrants. A few years later they moved it to make way for Takasago Park, and redirected its purpose to caring for sick travelers.[16] Xu and Yan Yunnian's Sincere Customs Association engaged in social welfare through its charitable activities, and also set a precedent for linking assistance with reforming social practices. Ishizaka Sōsaku founded the Jilong Night School and the Ishizaka Library, acts that replicated the educational focus of some of Germany's early social workers. However, the local government lagged behind these individuals and groups. City officials established only a single welfare institution before World War I, a shelter that provided assistance to new arrivals that it set up in 1898 and enlarged in 1911.[17] Taken collectively, these early initiatives responded to the difficulties that accompanied urbanization in a rapidly growing port, where the state had few resources to devote to welfare provision.

During the 1920s the Government-General implemented an extensive and intensive system of modern social work that grew out of the need to address the problems of urbanization, and that drew on models and experiences in the metropole.[18] Japanese municipal and national officials, prompted by economic and social fluctuations during and after World War I, reformed welfare institutions and sparked a florescence of social work in the early interwar years.[19] Soon thereafter, Governor-

16. Ibid.; Taihoku shū hōmen iin rengōkai, "Shakai jigyō gaiyō Shōwa jūgo nendo," in Nagaoka, *Shokuminchi shakai jigyō 40*, 80–81. The first source connects Xu's actions to the vagrants' home set up in 1881, but the second says that the home's purpose had always been to help visitors who fell ill. Both call it a temporary residence center (*qi liu suo*) and both mention that it had to be moved to make way for the park, but the latter source says that it was reformed as a clinic called the Yangming Hall (Yangming tang). The reformation seems likely, but the source seems to have missed the original purpose.

17. Taihoku chō, *Taihoku chō shi 2*, 601.

18. Kristin Stapleton details parallel developments in Chengdu, China, where a local official, inspired by his observations of Japanese cities, used the municipal police force to build and run "beggar workhouses" for adults, orphanages, and medical centers, and to conduct detailed social surveys. His concern was less with welfare and more with creating an orderly, civilized (*wenming*) city. Stapleton, *Civilizing Chengdu*, 125–38.

19. Garon, *Molding Japanese Minds*, 49–52.

General Den Kenjirō mandated the alteration of the existing practices of social welfare to promote modern social work in the colony. He launched a major survey of social conditions and ordered the creation of a new system to fulfill a greater number and variety of goals, including to provide medical assistance, support and educate children, sanitize existing markets, facilitate employment, construct or subsidize inexpensive or even free lodging, encourage the observance of official holidays, and establish public baths and pawnshops. Den retained some elements of the public-private cooperation that had characterized earlier social welfare in both Japan and China by relying on local organizations and companies to make the plan a reality.[20] Yet he combined the old and new when he envisioned a centralized hierarchy that roughly paralleled the colony's bureaucratic structure.[21]

One of the architects of Taiwan's social work system published a comprehensive record of the project in 1940, a massive 1,200-page tome called *A History of Social Work in Taiwan (Taiwan shakai jigyō shi)*. The author, Kinebuchi Yoshifusa, settled in Taiwan in the early 1920s to design new welfare policies for the Government-General, based on his experience managing the Japan Social Work Association (Nihon shakai jigyō kyōkai). On top of his official duties, he conducted extensive research into Taiwan's Qing-era social welfare that he began to publish in the early 1930s, serving as a precursor to the 1940 volume.[22] Sometimes explicitly and sometimes implicitly, Kinebuchi framed social work as one means for introducing modern civilization into Taiwan and remaking the colony in Japan's image. His vision reflected other

20. Kinebuchi, *Taiwan shakai jigyō shi*, 1130–33.

21. At first, the colony's Home Affairs Bureau (Naimukyoku) delegated authority to local government offices. In 1924, as part of a full bureaucratic reorganization, the local social work officers (*shakai jigyō kei*) and the existing offices for education (Gakumu ka), censorship (Henshū ka), and shrine management (Shaji ka) were combined within the new Office for Education and Culture (Bunkyō ka), in the Home Affairs Bureau. Control over social work activities shifted from the local offices to the central one. Two years later that office was elevated to the status of a bureau (*kyoku*) that contained a new Office for Social Affairs (Shakai ka), which oversaw all of the social work offices at the prefecture, county, city, town, and village levels. Ibid., 1134–35.

22. He published a series of articles titled "Taiwan shakai jigyō shi" in the monthly journal *The Social Work Companion (Shakai jigyō no tomo)* in 1933 and 1934.

ideas of improvement through colonization, such as the French ideal of *mise en valeur*, the British civilizing mission in India, and the American sense of benevolent and humanitarian rule in the Philippines.[23] *A History of Social Work in Taiwan* also showed the influence of Kōminka-era ideology, but even before that time Japanese authorities, and to a lesser extent settlers, used social work to change Taiwan's social structure and practices.

Den, Kinebuchi, and others designed the social work system to facilitate the gradual assimilation of islanders to Japanese social and cultural norms through large institutions and a few key fields of operation. They built the structure around, and under, the Social Work Conference (Shakai jigyō taikai; SWC), first held in 1928, and the Social Work Association (Shakai jigyō kyōkai; SWA), which the SWC established to commemorate the second anniversary of the Shōwa emperor's ascendance to the throne. Both the SWC and SWA facilitated information distribution and provided leadership for ongoing research and surveys of Taiwan's society, but they sought to prevent duplication of efforts.[24] From 1928 to 1943, the SWA published the monthly journal *The Social Work Companion* (*Shakai jigyō no tomo*), which knit geographically dispersed social workers together and provided a crucial record of their work. Moreover, the contents of this journal displayed clearly the transnational and transactional nature of social work in Taiwan. The authors made frequent references to developments in the United States and Europe, occasionally translated articles by Western social workers, and also wrote about Japanese participation in international meetings and discourses.[25] The state created and oversaw these islandwide umbrella organizations and the journal, but most of the members, contributors, and readers were not government officials.

---

23. Cooper, *France in Indochina*; Fischer-Tiné and Mann, *Colonialism as Civilizing Mission*; Kramer, "Empires, Exceptions, and Anglo-Saxons."

24. Kinebuchi, *Taiwan shakai jigyō shi*, 1136–38. Coordination became increasingly important as the number of institutions rose from 748 in 1926 to around 1,300 a decade later. Ibid., 1137, and Taiwan sōtokufu, "Taiwan shakai jigyō yōran," in Nagaoka, *Shokuminchi shakai jigyō 5*, 34.

25. I base this description of *The Social Work Companion* on my extensive survey of the contents of the journal for its entire run. Its name made it a partner of the journal of the Japan Social Work Association, *Social Work* (*Shakai jigyō*).

Den's 1921 edict directed social workers to engage in multiple types of welfare, which can be divided into four areas of activity deemed central to the civilizing process: medical assistance, economic assistance, cultural reform, and social control.[26]

Jilong joined Taipei and other major cities as central locations for social work. As one of the island's fastest growing urban centers, and its gateway port, it was a locus of many of the social ills that the modern welfare programs were designed to cure: unemployment, housing shortages, poor health, poverty, transience, and supposedly backward customs.[27] In addition, some residents believed that their Jilong had to be a model for the rest of the colony in how it managed the problems of urbanization, much as they held up their city as Taiwan's leader in beneficial modernization.[28] External entities including the Government-General, the Taibei Prefecture authorities, and the SWA defined the context for modern social welfare in Taiwan, and a combination of local initiative, government co-optation of existing institutions, and new state-created organizations formed its structure and praxis.[29] Given Jilong's strong organizational culture, the engagement of local leaders, and the propensity of the state to minimize its expenses and responsibilities, Japanese and islander elites rose to implement the concrete programs that gave practical form to the state's abstract plans.

State and private groups shaped the system in stages, beginning in 1921 when the municipal government mandated a public clinic and its first public housing project, the housing being primarily for Japanese residents. Two years later the prefecture authorities recruited a cadre of local welfare commissioners, and the city opened several public pawnshops designed to protect people from the supposedly unscrupulous

26. Kinebuchi, *Taiwan shakai jigyō shi*, 1130–33. This quadripartite division is my own; Kinebuchi discussed seven categories of welfare: social administration, connected research, promotional assistance, relief, economic protection, child protection, and social civilization. Ibid., 1119.

27. Kiirun shi yakusho, "Kiirun shakai jigyō yōran," in Nagaoka, *Shokuminchi shakai jigyō 45*, 268.

28. Cai Qingyun, "Kiirun shi seikatsu kaizen no gaikō to tōmen no jigyō," *SJT* 96 (Nov. 1936): 26.

29. Kiirun shi yakusho, "Kiirun shakai jigyō yōran," in Nagaoka, *Shokuminchi shakai jigyō 45*, 268.

practices of their private counterparts. After these modest beginnings, during the late 1920s and 1930s public and private initiatives either created or incorporated over two dozen agencies in a growing network of welfare institutions, more than in Gaoxiong and about the same as in Taizhong.[30] These institutions included five agencies that offered inexpensive housing, four that gave medical assistance, four that provided economic assistance (including another employment office), seven groups that performed multiple functions (everything from counseling to customs reform), and four others.[31] This particular constellation of organizations demonstrated that social work grew out of existing institutions and practices even as it threatened to violate one of the main principles of the SWA and SWC—to avoid duplication of efforts—but in Jilong there was certainly no shortage of work for them to do.

Four groups constituted the core of social work activity in Jilong: the CAA, the Jilong Fraternity Group (JFG), the city's welfare commissioners, and the Social Hall (Shakai kan). With the exception of the local welfare commissioners, these institutions originated through private initiatives and were subsequently taken over by the state. The commissioners owed their existence to state planning but in practice relied almost entirely on the activism and skill of local social workers. Thus all four groups embodied the intersection of, and clash between, public and private interests. With so many different entities attempting to provide assistance, reinforce the social fabric, and reform native religious practices and other activities, these four stood out for their physical and numeric size, the fact that they addressed a variety of problems in urban society, and their manifestations of efforts to reterritorialize the city and colony as either Japanese or Taiwanese.

Most of these organizations were prominent physical fixtures in Jilong's cityscape and engaged significant numbers of people as members or as targets of social work. The CAA occupied a sizable building in Takasago Park and had an enormous membership of roughly eleven

30. Ibid., 253–64, 268–69; Nakajima, *Kiirun shi annai*, 88; Taihoku shū yaku sho, *Taihoku shū yōran 3*, 75. For Gaoxiong, see Takao shi yaku sho, *Takao shi sei*. This volume contains several annual editions, see pp. 12–18 for 1929, pp. 13–18 for 1934, and pp. 39–46 for 1936. On Taizhong, see Ujihira, *Taichū shi*, 635–704.

31. Kiirun shi yakusho, "Kiirun shakai jigyō yōran," in Nagaoka, *Shokuminchi shakai jigyō 45*, 1–2.

基 隆 博 愛 團

FIGURE 5.1. The headquarters of the Jilong Fraternity Group. Image courtesy of the National Taiwan Library, Taipei.

thousand by 1931, thanks to its links to the *hokō* system. It also appeared frequently in the pages of *The Social Work Companion*, where local social workers rated it as one of the most important social work institutions in all of Taiwan, especially for economic relief and customs reform, and the leader of its Social Work Division, a licensed opium and tobacco seller named Cai Qingyun, served as codirector of the SWA in 1933.[32] Even more impressive, the JFG filled an entire city block in Big Jilong with its hulking structure (fig. 5.1), could house around one thousand people at any given moment in inexpensive accommodations, and provided medical and other services for its residents and other locals.[33] The Social Hall, though something of a latecomer, took

32. He and Lin, "Naichi shisatsu zakkan," *SJT* 80 (July 1935): 88; "Jilong tongfenghui zhucui shehui shiye lianhe weiyuanhui," *NS*, May 23, 1936, 13. Multiple editions of the *Social Work Companion* list Cai Qingyun as head of the SWA.

33. O-sei, "Daisanhan Kiirun shisatsu ni ka harite," *SJT* 85 (Dec. 1935): 92–94.

up residence at the southwest corner of the harbor in the building formerly occupied by the city government, after the latter moved to its new home in 1933.[34]

The significance of Jilong's local welfare commissioners derived from their historic origins and local establishment. The system of commissioners originated in the Japanese home islands in 1917, when an official in Okayama Prefecture, supposedly inspired by a conversation he had with the Taishō emperor, launched a survey of Okayama's social conditions and formulated a mechanism to deliver aid. The following year, that official moved to Osaka, where he established the first network of unpaid commissioners, who were responsible for gathering information and distributing aid to residents of their specific districts.[35] After the unrest of Japan's 1918 Rice Riots struck cities as well as villages, the system spread to other urban centers, where municipal governments recognized its potential for studying and controlling society. Furthermore, the commissioner system was inexpensive for the state to run because it guided people away from public financial assistance.[36] The commissioners arose from Japan's specific conditions but nonetheless resembled the professional social workers of the United States and Europe, in that they provided assistance mostly on a case-by-case basis.

The welfare commissioner model arrived in Taiwan in 1923 and quickly became the colony's preeminent social work institution. After the Government-General established the first programs in Taipei and Jilong, it swiftly extended them to the other major cities, including Taizhong, Tainan, and Gaoxiong, and then more slowly to the smaller cities and towns. In 1925, only the second full year in which the system operated, the commissioners in Taipei handled 1,346 cases, whereas in Tainan they managed almost twice that many. The commissioners registered local residents, helped children in need, counseled individuals and mediated disputes, gave medical and financial aid, and performed

34. Taki Ryūji, "Umare iden to suru Kiirun shi Shakai kan," *SJT* 60 (Nov. 1933): 64.

35. Kinebuchi, *Taiwan shakai jigyō shi*, 1124; Garon, *Molding Japanese Minds*, 52–58. Kinebuchi suggests that the officials in Osaka relied on a German model in designing this system.

36. Garon, *Molding Japanese Minds*, 52; Namae Takashi, "Hōmen jigyō," *SJT* 26 (Jan. 1931): 85–90.

a range of other services. By the end of 1937, when 2,611 commissioners worked in Taiwan, aiding a population of just over 5 million, the system had handled almost 1.3 million cases since its inception.[37] These raw numbers do not indicate what constituted a case, but it likely meant a discrete instance of commissioner activity rather than a unique individual recipient of aid. At the all-island level, the Local Welfare Commissioners Conference (Hōmen iin taikai) facilitated communication between the mostly locally controlled groups of commissioners. It met once every year, starting in 1929, to share knowledge and coordinate activities across Taiwan, and in the process brought local actors into a broader, regional affiliation.

Jilong stood at the forefront of Taiwan's welfare commissioner system, both for its early arrival there and its scale of operations. Initially, the organizers divided the city into five districts, each with three commissioners, and they added two more districts by 1931. Soon thereafter, twenty-five regular commissioners worked in the city, supported by a roughly equivalent number of staffers and advisors. Jilong had the highest concentration of commissioners per district, and also the largest supporting staff, of any city in northern Taiwan. By way of comparison, in 1936 it had a total staff of 51, which meant that each staff member corresponded to 389 households, whereas Taipei had 111 members, creating a ratio of 1 for every 591 families. Other cities in the north had much smaller groups of commissioners.[38]

The Jilong commissioners kept very busy. In the first half of the 1930s they dealt with five thousand to ten thousand cases annually, the great majority of which had to do with medical, financial, or counseling

37. Kinebuchi, *Taiwan shakai jigyō shi*, 1223-25; Taiwan sōtokufu, "Taiwan shakai jigyō yōran," in Nagaoka, *Shokuminchi shakai jigyō 1*, 247; Taihoku shū yaku sho, *Taihoku shū yōran 3*, 84–85. In comparison, in the home islands there were 10,545 welfare commissioners in 1925; 27,907 in 1931; and 74,560 in 1942. Garon, *Molding Japanese Minds*, 52.

38. Taihoku shū hōmen iin rengōkai, "Shakai jigyō gaiyō Shōwa jūgo nendo," in Nagaoka, *Shokuminchi shakai jigyō 40*, 32–33; Taihoku shū hōmen iin rengōkai, "Shakai jigyō gaiyō Shōwa jūichinen," in Nagaoka, *Shokuminchi shakai jigyō 39*, 16; Kiirun shi yakusho, "Kiirun shakai jigyō yōran," in Nagaoka, *Shokuminchi shakai jigyō 45*, 278. Taipei had a better ratio of citizens per welfare commissioner, at 677:1 compared with more than 800:1 in Jilong. Neither city approached the ideal ratio established in Osaka in 1918, of 1 commissioner for every 200 households.

5.1. Numbers of cases handled by welfare commissioners in Jilong and northern Taiwan

Aid type	Cases in Jilong					Total cases to 1940			
	1930	1931	1932	1933	1934	Jilong	Taipei	Luodong	Yilan
Counseling	511	972	682	865	681	66,029	34,607	4,985	7,637
Child aid	23	7	154	22	154	950	2,539	200	151
Medical	1,311	1,564	4,234	5,260	4,234	92,951	74,383	113,671	44,061
Mediation	254	605	1,070	1,093	1,061	16,628	17,822	132	1,265
Donations	2,588	1,333	2,185	1,558	2,185	10,797	17,015	204	353
Registration	355	443	442	532	442	20,214	48,203	6,321	7,916
Other	170	254	947	1,229	947	16,413	16,762	287	2,923
Total	5,212	5,178	9,714	10,559	9,695	223,982	211,331	125,800[a]	64,306

SOURCE: Data from Kiirun shi yakusho, "Kiirun shakai jigyō yōran," in Nagaoka, *Shokuminchi shakai jigyō 45*, 278–79; for the 1940 figures, see Taihoku shū hōmen iin rengōkai, "Shakai jigyō gaiyō Shōwa jūgo nendo," in Nagaoka, *Shokuminchi shakai jigyō 40*, 48–49.

NOTE: The welfare-commissioner system arrived later in Yilan, in 1927, and Luodong (Lotung), in 1932.

[a] The original source states a total 125,900 cases for Luodong, which does not match the numbers listed for each category of cases

assistance (table 5.1). By 1940 they had processed more cases than the commissioners in any other city in northern Taiwan, even Taipei.[39] The roughly five thousand cases in 1930 did not mean that the commissioners reached one out of every sixteen of Jilong's roughly seventy thousand residents in that year, but the large numbers of cases, and the relatively high concentration of commissioners and staff per district, gave them a high profile, especially in the densely packed islander neighborhoods. The commissioners also provided the most convenient source of medical and counseling assistance for many residents. Although there were two hospitals in Jilong, as well as some small clinics, the commissioners gave crucial medical supplies to people who did not, or could not, visit those centers. By contrast, Taipei residents had more health care options and so the commissioners worked on a smaller number of medical cases. The data also indicate that the commissioners

39. Taihoku shū hōmen iin rengōkai, "Shakai jigyō gaiyō Shōwa jūgo nendo," in Nagaoka, *Shokuminchi shakai jigyō 40*, 48–49.

were not simply local, but were institutionally embedded in broader geographic networks.

The table highlights the multifunctionality that gave social work organizations such dominant positions in local welfare practices. The commissioners concentrated their efforts in economic protection work and social control, but likely also promoted customs reform through counseling, mediation, and medical assistance. In fact, in the health care area they worked with the CAA's Fraternity Hospital to deliver medicine throughout the city.[40] The CAA had long provided material assistance to the poor, and three of its eight divisions—Social Work, Social Civilization, and Everyday Life Reform—launched a welfare movement for the betterment of society in the spring of 1936.[41] Much like settlement houses in the United States, the JFG combined its inexpensive lodging with employment placement, job training, some medical care, and other functions.[42] Ultimately its facilities expanded to include a public bath, midwifery care, a sanitation union, a pawnshop, a purchasing cooperative, and an employment service (*jusan*).[43] The Social Hall was established as a direct result of separate trips that Ishizaka Sōsaku and an official in the Jilong Education Office made to Japan, Korea, and Manchuria in the late 1920s and early 1930s, where they were favorably impressed by the concentration of multiple social work functions into single organizations. Ishizaka wrote glowingly of the Social Hall that he visited in Dalian, through which Japanese and Chinese managed, and made use of, multiple programs designed to improve residents' moral fiber. Inspired by this example, and those observed in Pusan and Fengtian, a group of officials and settlers established Jilong's own Social Hall, with an initial focus on housing, feeding, and employing Jilong's poor residents and the many transients who

40. In 1929 Xu Zisang brought the two together for the distribution of medical aid. See "Kiirun shi hōmen iin kondankai," *SJT* 13 (Dec. 1929): 123.

41. "Jilong tongfenghui zhucui shehui shiye lianhe weiyuanhui," *NS*, May 23, 1936, 13.

42. Katsuya Kentarō, "Kiirun haku'aidan: rinbō jigyō no dendō tare," *SJT* 39 (Feb. 1932): 33–34. The resemblance to settlement houses might have been coincidental, and the JFG might have been modeled at least in part on Qing-era benevolent halls (*shantang*). See Naquin, *Peking*, 652–53, 668–69.

43. TSTF, 10748.8, 1938, 12, 15, 25–32.

came to the city. It thereafter expanded its operations and came to be seen as a center of social work.[44]

With their functions, members, and clients spread across the city, and in some cases their substantial physical edifices, these four groups recreated Jilong's concrete and imagined space through social work. Whereas the CAA's role in building the islander community has already been explored in terms of religious customs and practices, the JFG's history reveals competing attempts to reterritorialize Jilong through welfare. Yan Yunnian founded the JFG in 1920, with the aid of the prominent businessmen Gu Xianrong and Lin Taizheng, and the centerpiece of their project was the organization's enormous modern brick building in Big Jilong, a few blocks away from the Dianji Temple and beside the city's largest public market. Construction was finished within a few years, but in spite of the initial promises of generous funding—in the vicinity of an astounding 350,000 yen in 1920—the JFG quickly ran into financial difficulties when the post–World War I boom came to an abrupt end.[45] To make up for the sudden shortfall, the JFG took out a loan that it never fully repaid, despite subsequent private donations and grants of imperial assistance.[46] Financial difficulties became so severe in the early 1930s that Yan Guonian had no choice but to sell the main structure and all of its assets to the city government. The municipal authorities dissolved the JFG

44. Ishizaka Sōsaku, "Bokoku Man Chō shakai jigyō kan ken," *SJT* 2 (Jan. 1929): 50–59, 63; Taki, "Umare iden to suru Kiirun shi Shakai kan," *SJT* 60 (Nov. 1933): 64–67. The Social Hall was mentioned only briefly in a Dalian-based journal. See Arikura, "Dairen shi no shakai jigyō," 46–47. The journal was originally called *Manshū no shakai* (Manchurian Society) and later changed its name to *Shakai kenkyū* (Social Research). I thank Emer O'Dwyer and Tatiana Linkhoeva for this reference. O'Dwyer discusses social welfare in Dalian, including Japanese settlers' challenges to excessive spending on such programs; see O'Dwyer, *Significant Soil*, 172–80.

45. Yan Yunnian, Lin Taizheng, and Gu Xianrong pledged 200,000 yen, 100,000 yen, and 50,000 yen, respectively, but actually contributed much less. An article from 1932 says that, between them, Yan and Lin donated 120,000 yen, which agrees with both a local gazetteer and one Government-General document that states that Yan provided roughly 100,000 and Lin 20,000. However, another report from the Government-General lists the contributions as Yan 115,500, Lin 25,000, and Gu 15,000. See Katsuya, "Kiirun haku'aidan," *SJT* 39 (Feb. 1932): 30; TSTF, 10682.2, Aug. 1, 1935, 14, and 10748.8, 1938, 15. See also Irie, *Kiirun fūdo*, 181.

46. Katsuya, "Kiirun haku'aidan," *SJT* 19 (June 1930): 76.

foundation, took over all of its properties, and assumed its 170,000-yen debt.[47] At this time, a number of Jilong residents joined with city officials to form the Jilong Fraternity Association (Haku'aikai; JFA), which then ran many of the institution's welfare activities and enhanced its transformational reach with a nursery school and a Japanese-language training center.[48] When the city government took over this important social work institution, it both preserved it and, perhaps more important, opened a new avenue for state efforts to assimilate the Taiwanese. However, most of those who ran the association's day-to-day activities were Taiwanese, and they retained positions of influence over the JFG's activities.

The roughly contemporaneous rise of the Social Hall, the Japanese-run counterpart to the JFG, indicated that the Taiwanese social welfare elites faced increasing pressures from settlers and the state. The Social Hall encapsulated all of the modernizing, transformative, and expansionist elements of Japanese imperialist ideology. For more than a decade after its establishment, the JFG dominated the field of multifunctional social welfare in Jilong, but it evidently did not inspire Japanese settlers and officials to launch a similar initiative, even though both tapped into similar global trends in welfare. Instead, Ishizaka and others looked to a Japanese-created model in Dalian, which they imported to encroach on both the operational and physical space of the JFG.[49] Not only did the Social Hall Japanize the work that had previously been the purview of the JFG, it subtly invaded Taiwanese space. The location, on the southern edge of the harbor and the northern edge of Big Jilong, just a stone's throw from the train station and the wharves, was a prime location from which to both monitor and access the core of Jilong's Taiwanese community.

The welfare commissioners led a more concerted effort to make Jilong—and everywhere they operated—Japanese space. They worked across the entire city, but their geographic distribution meant settlers

47. TSTF, 10682.2, Aug. 1, 1935, 14–16, and 10748.8, 1938, 2. The latter source provides the figure of 170,000 yen. The transfer of the JFG to the city made the islandwide news; "Jilong shishunian xuan'an bo'aituan yuanman jiejue," TNS, Aug. 29, 1935, 8.

48. TSTF, 10748.8, 1938, 12, 28–32.

49. Ishizaka, "Bokoku Man Chō shakai jigyō kan ken," SJT 2 (Jan. 1929): 50–59, 63; Taki, "Umare iden to suru Kiirun shi Shakai kan," SJT 60 (Nov. 1933): 64–67.

were overrepresented in both the Japanese and Taiwanese districts and they held an absolute majority on the oversight committee.[50] Settler preponderance throughout the commissioner system suggests that it could become a tool of transformative Japanese nationalism. This trend was evident by the middle of the 1930s, when the local welfare commissioners assumed total responsibility for the year-end rice distribution from the CAA and launched two separate Sympathy Weeks (Dōjō shūkan), one just before the end of the solar year for Japanese residents and the other just before the lunar new year for Taiwanese. For each week, the commissioners went door-to-door to assess the living conditions of all of the households within their jurisdiction and gathered donations by distributing thousands of leaflets and "sympathy bags" (dōjō fukuro).[51]

These four institutions show that the social work system, conceived by its Japanese architects as a mechanism to make Taiwan more like the metropole by bringing civilization and modernity to the colony, ultimately shaped the borders and content of Taiwanese ethnicity. Even before the 1920s, welfare organizations targeted clearly defined communities. Ishizaka opened his school and library to both islanders and Japanese, and he particularly emphasized educating the former. In contrast, although no legal code prevented islander Taiwanese from aiding poor Japanese settlers, Xu, Yan, and others directed their welfare operations toward other members of their assigned demographic category. Meanwhile, social work established crucial pathways for regular

50. Taihoku shū, *Taihoku shū hōmen iin meibo*, 13–17. In parts of Jilong where Japanese settlers made up less than 20 percent of the population, they nonetheless held one-quarter or one-third of the commissioner positions, whereas in a district where Taiwanese islanders constituted up to 50 percent of the population, four of five commissioners were Japanese. The ratios of commissioners per district are based on a correlation of neighborhoods with the population distribution maps cited in chapter 1; see Cheng-siang Chen, *Port City of Keelung*, 20–21. The commissioners were overseen by a committee of eighteen members, all Japanese, including one woman who served as a midwife for the settler community. There were also six advisors, three Taiwanese, including Xu Zisang and two prominent doctors, and three Japanese. In Yilan, all of the commissioners were Taiwanese, and the oversight committee contained six Japanese and two Taiwanese.

51. Kiirun shi yakusho, "Kiirun shakai jigyō yōran," in Nagaoka, *Shokuminchi shakai jigyō 45*, 9–12.

direct and indirect interactions through which social workers forged connections beyond the local level, even to the extent of engaging Taiwan with this manifestation of global modernity. Nonetheless, even though it began as an arena in which islanders and Japanese cooperated on objectives and shared information and experiences, social work promoted sharp divisions. A system in which the Japanese felt empowered, or even obligated, to assist islanders, but islanders were constrained from crossing out of their social group, contained inherent power differentials that enhanced contestation over who would define the islanders.

Building Community through Economic Welfare

"Economic protection work" (*keizai hogo jigyō*), as it was formally known, covered a wide variety of activities aimed at achieving one of the highest goals of social work: to retrieve people from, and prevent them from falling into poverty.[52] In practical terms it involved relieving economic distress, providing inexpensive housing, and finding jobs for the unemployed. The state encouraged and supported private groups, corporations, and banks that contributed the logistical and financial bases for these sorts of projects.[53] The late 1920s and early 1930s saw numerous examples of discontent with the political and economic status quo in Taiwan, including the movement for local self-government, the petition movement, and the growth of the Taiwanese People's Party. The worldwide dislocations and unemployment accompanying the Great Depression exacerbated tensions between Taiwanese and Japanese, between the colony and metropole, and between imperial subjects and the state. In that context, social workers viewed economic assistance as crucial for minimizing the dangers of social instability and unrest.

The head of Jilong's Pure Land Buddhist temple, who was an active participant in social welfare, summed up the connection between

---

52. Kinebuchi, *Taiwan shakai jigyō shi*, 1184–85.
53. Taiwan sōtokufu, "Taiwan shakai jigyō yōran," in Nagaoka, *Shokuminchi shakai jigyō* 1, 52–53.

economic problems and social unrest with an organic, recursive model of society. Regarding the origins of the problems that social work cured, he wrote, "When the society which I inhabit is out of balance, this will cause social ills to arise." In this scheme, imbalance was seen to come from within. He equated people with the cells of the social body and stated that, much as a tumor in one cell or group of cells can damage the health of the entire body, so, too, could the difficulties of one individual or small group hinder the progress of a whole society.[54] Extrapolating from this scientifically inflected model, difficulties such as unemployment or vagrancy destabilized society, which in turn gave rise to more serious problems. Therefore, it was crucial to solve economic difficulties before they could cause any problems for society at large.

As seen in conjunction with the Ghost Festival and individual temple festivals, vagrants and a surplus population caused particular anxiety in Jilong. Not only did they clutter the streets, these rootless elements could fall under the influence of dangerous political forces. In an essay in *The Social Work Companion*, one Japanese resident recounted the story of a friend who graduated college with a degree in commercial science and training in English, and found work as an accountant. When he lost this job after the Depression hit, he came to Taiwan with a letter that identified him as a port construction coolie, not a university graduate, and he soon landed in jail and was deported to Japan. He quickly returned to Taiwan, disembarking in Jilong with his belongings on his back, an unemployed intellectual in search of a new life; the author compared him to a snail. Although he sympathized with his friend, the author saw three dangers lurking in the man's unemployment: crime; mental illness, possibly leading to suicide; and, worst of all, social or proletarian movements (*musan undō*). During the early 1930s, people saw Jilong as especially vulnerable to the bad influence of the lumpen intelligentsia and lumpen proletarians who flowed through the city.[55]

54. Akeyama Sei'en, "Shakai jigyō to sono seishin," *SJT* 4 (Mar. 1929): 87–88.
55. Katsuya Kentarō, "Kiirun kō runpen sōkan ōrai chō," *SJT* 37 (Dec. 1931): 65–76.

This fluid population posed two major challenges for the island's main port: housing and employing the new arrivals. Almost four hundred Japanese and Taiwanese elites had earlier established the Jilong Social Work Assistance Association (Shakai jigyō joseikai), which tried to minimize the problem of new arrivals by quickly repatriating undesirables to Japan or Korea, or sending them on to other points in Taiwan.[56] However, many people stayed, exacerbating Jilong's chronic housing shortage. The JFG provided the largest concentration of inexpensive housing, with three hundred rooms available for a cost of just a few yen a month, plus all of its additional services, for which it received justifiable praise in Taiwan's social work journal.[57] Beginning in 1921, the city government built a substantial number of single-family units in planned neighborhoods, complete with sports grounds and swimming pools, on the eastern edge of the city. However, critics such as Ishizaka Sōsaku argued that these projects were too expensive for the lower classes and that only middle-class government clerks and company office workers could afford to live in them.[58] He and others took it upon themselves to establish inexpensive or even free lodgings. In the mid-1920s the Buddhist Youth Group opened a free dormitory within the grounds of the main temple of the Shinshū sect, but demand quickly outstripped supply, so the managers of the Social Hall established a new dormitory on its premises in 1933 that housed several thousand people each year. In combination with its other functions, the housing project made the Social Hall, much like the JFG, a halfway house for new immigrants before they moved into more permanent

56. The Social Work Assistance Association was established to provide general financial support, mostly from membership fees, for social work in Jilong. Taihoku shū hōmen iin rengōkai, "Shakai jigyō gaiyō Shōwa jūgo nendo," in Nagaoka, Shokuminchi shakai jigyō 40, 67. By 1935 it had 384 members, who contributed close to ten thousand yen for operations in that year. See "Jilong zuchenghui deng zhu hui," TNS, July 13, 1935, 4.

57. See O-sei, "Daisanhan Kiirun shisatsu ni ka harite," SJT 85 (Dec. 1935): 90–92.

58. Kiirun shi yakusho, "Kiirun shi shakai jigyō yōran," in Nagaoka, Shokuminchi shakai jigyō 45, 297–301; Ishizaka Sōsaku, "Kiirun ni okeru shakai jigyō," SJT 10 (Sept. 1929): 80.

housing or left the city.[59] In terms of the social model proposed by the Pure Land temple's abbot, these various housing plans served to maintain Jilong's internal balance and promote its prosperity by keeping the poor off the streets.

Social workers also sought to ensure social stability by solving the city's unemployment problem with job training programs and employment agencies.[60] The Jilong Night School, the Public Welfare Society, the city government, the JFG, and the Jilong Women's Association all provided vocational training or job placement to local residents.[61] These agencies worked directly with companies, banks, shops, and other employers to connect those with job openings to those who sought work. Ishizaka Sōsaku drafted ambitious plans for two new institutions: a household industry center (*katei kōgyō denshūsho*) to train women and the elderly in productive work for the city's benefit; and an independent labor cooperation center (*rōshi kyōchōsho*) to promote harmonious relations between local workers and businesses.[62] All of these initiatives paralleled developments in the home islands where the state-sponsored model of femininity, the good wife and wise mother (*ryōsai kenbo*), promoted a family-oriented vision of women's labor, and the growing labor movement sparked fears of social unrest.[63] Recent strikes in Jilong and Taipei heightened the interest in dispute mediation.[64] Although Ishizaka's plans never came to fruition, by the early 1930s there was a great need for such programs. Prior to the Great Depression the

59. Kiirun shi yakusho, "Kiirun shi shakai jigyō yōran," in Nagaoka, *Shokuminchi shakai jigyō* 45, 301–5.

60. I was unable to locate unemployment rates or other statistics for Jilong, but unemployment was discussed in the local press and other sources as a serious issue from the early 1920s to the late 1930s.

61. Kiirun shi yakusho, "Kiirun shi shakai jigyō yōran," in Nagaoka, *Shokuminchi shakai jigyō* 45, 145–49.

62. Ishizaka, "Kiirun ni okeru shakai jigyō," *SJT* 10 (Sept. 1929): 80, 82–85.

63. On labor cooperation in Japan, see Garon, *Molding Japanese Minds*, 53–59, 195–96; Gordon, *The Evolution of Labor Relations*, 425–26.

64. Ishizaka, "Kiirun ni okeru shakai jigyō," *SJT* 10 (Sept. 1929): 84. On a strike against Mitsui in Jilong, see "Bantanfu kaishi zong bagong: Mitsui Jilong zhuren zhan shouwan guyong tiaojian guoyu kebo," *TMB*, Apr. 21, 1929, 3; "Bantanfu zong bagong houwen: Mitsui jili nongfan jiance gongren bei pian yijian fugong," *TMB*, Apr. 28, 1929, 4.

employment agency run by the PWS, which the city government took
over in 1926, often had more jobs than applicants.[65] However, in 1933
there were about twice as many job seekers as opportunities, and fewer
than half of those who applied eventually found work. The vast majority of people who got jobs were Japanese, as were the firms looking for
employees.[66]

Local, ethnic, and national identities all intersected with issues of
economic welfare. Ishizaka displayed a primary concern with local
workers when he recommended that the city's employment agency
should be open only to long-term residents, to improve their position
vis-à-vis the contracting job pool.[67] This Jilong-centric fortress men-
tality took an ethnocentric turn in 1936 when, in the face of both the
persistent job shortage and the apparent bias in favor of Japanese workers, the CAA Social Work division called for a ban on Chinese workers
to reduce labor competition.[68] In sum, ongoing economic pressures
clarified and strengthened multiple borders. The city government's
employment agency heavily favored Japanese workers, and the experience of being largely shut out of official employment assistance forced
islanders to rely more on islander institutions like the JFG and the
CAA. In addition, by the 1930s many Taiwanese had no direct memory
of being a part of China but knew only the conditions and institutions
of Japanese rule; this generational change promoted the exclusion of
those with whom they may have shared language and customs but not
a primary identification. Such economic policies in the interest of social
work thus strengthened their sense of being Taiwanese, as distinct from
both Japanese and Chinese nationalities.

65. Nakajima, *Kiirun shi annai*, 90–91; Kiirun shi yakusho, *Kiirun shi shakai
kyōiku*, in Nagaoka, *Shokuminchi shakai jigyō 45*, 295–97. In 1928 employers sought
workers for 423 positions, but there were only 264 applicants and in the end 178
positions remained unfilled.

66. Kiirun shi yakusho, *Kiirun shi shakai kyōiku*, in Nagaoka, *Shokuminchi shakai
jigyō 45*, 295–97. About thirteen hundred people applied, and around five hundred
found jobs. The ratio of Japanese to Taiwanese, both among those who found work
and those offering jobs, was roughly 6:1.

67. Ishizaka, "Kiirun ni okeru shakai jigyō," *SJT* 10 (Sept. 1929): 80.

68. "Jilong tongfenghui zhucui shehui shiye lianhe weiyuanhui," *NS*, May 23,
1936, 13.

Customs Reform and Ethnic Construction

Economic social work contributed to a sense of group cohesion, and cultural forms buttressed the identification and defense of some of the key components of Taiwanese ethnicity. The inclusion of customs reform—that is, the transformation of religious rituals, personal behaviors, observances of major life events, and so on—within the purview of social work beginning in the late 1920s suggests that Japanese, and some Taiwanese, came to view aspects of islander culture as a type of social "disease" that, through diagnosis and treatment, could be cured. They did not have purely clinical motivations; rather, they grounded their views in a sense of cultural hierarchy that distinguished between advanced and uncivilized (*shizenteki jōtai*) individuals and groups in society, and impelled the former to impart their modernism to the latter.[69]

Government officials in the metropole as well as the colonies worked on social reform, but those in the colonies acted out of a heightened sense of civilizational superiority. The policies of "cultural rule" (*bunka seiji*) in both Taiwan and Korea had tolerated multicultural variation within Japan's empire, but increasingly the Japanese in Taiwan targeted purportedly evil customs within islander-Taiwanese society that they believed hindered progress, endangered good customs, and caused unrest in society. Social workers critiqued the abuse of alcohol, tobacco, and opium, all of which they framed, somewhat preposterously, as problems peculiar to the islanders or—in the last case—attributed to a flaw within Chinese culture. They also sought to stamp out practices they identified as purely Taiwanese, such as arranged marriages, brideprices, and extravagant, unsanitary funerals.[70] These ideas resonated with a much larger, empirewide project to construct Japan as a "moral

---

69. Kinebuchi, *Taiwan shakai jigyō shi*, 1212–13.

70. Ibid., 1226–35. Kinebuchi's description of arranged marriage correlates with what was practiced widely in postwar northern Taiwan. See Wolf, *Women and the Family*, chap. 11, which is titled "Girls Who Marry Their Brothers." As for opium smoking, the colonial government deserved as much responsibility for its persistence as the Taiwanese, because its opium monopoly, though intended to control and eradicate the problem, left the government dependent on this form of revenue. See Ka, *Japanese Colonialism in Taiwan*, 54–55.

nation," as described by Miriam Kingsberg.[71] At their most extreme, state plans used this realm of social work to mandate common practices throughout the colony by replacing native with Japanese practices and, in the process, imposing Japanese national identity.

Social workers applied the words *shakai kyōka*, a term that has several possible English renditions, to their transformative operations. Sheldon Garon translates the phrase as "moral suasion," whereas Patricia Tsurumi renders it "acculturation."[72] Garon demonstrates that moral suasion campaigns and organizations were the key components of state-initiated programs to mobilize, reform, and manage Japanese society, especially during the interwar period. By incorporating private citizens, especially women, in these projects, the state sought to clamp down on unorthodox religious sects and regulate morality throughout society, beginning within the home.[73] However, in contrast to women in the metropole, women played a very small role in Taiwan, a fact that highlighted the masculinity of both Japanese colonial ideology and the imagined terrain in which Taiwanese consciousness took shape.[74] Also, in the colonial setting the term assumed a culturally hierarchical aspect in implying the Japanese brought something the islanders lacked. That sense of superiority was akin to the spirit if not the letter of "acculturation," which Tsurumi frames broadly to include civilizing and evangelizing impulses. However, to stress the inequalities inherent in the programs instituted in Taiwan, and to emphasize the connection to social work, I use the more literal translation, "social civilization."

The Government-General linked social civilization with the expressly transformative objectives of another of its key programs, social education (*shakai kyōiku*). The education project had three main goals for resolving social problems throughout Taiwan: 1) to spread the spirit of national citizenship (*kokumin seishin*) and strengthen national consciousness (*kokumin teki jikaku*), 2) to train people as good citizens with a sense of self-reliance (*jichi teki kannen*), and 3) to develop practical

71. Kingsberg, *Moral Nation*.
72. Garon, *Molding Japanese Minds*, 7; Tsurumi, *Japanese Colonial Education*, 146.
73. Garon, *Molding Japanese Minds*, chaps. 2–4.
74. Japanese women settlers contributed in significant ways to the colonization of Taiwan, especially in their attention to female islanders, in particular, and education in general. See Dawley, "Women on the Move."

knowledge and remove the nonessentials from life.[75] Government officials launched similar projects during the early 1930s in the home islands, where promoting self-reliance and nationalist fervor gained increasing importance, but in the colony they concentrated on the islander-Taiwanese, not the settlers. Social education and social civilization in Taiwan aimed at the complete social and cultural assimilation of those who were becoming Taiwanese.

Japanese officials and settlers applied this pedagogical and discursive project unevenly across Taiwan. In 1931 the Government-General replaced all of the island's Customs Assimilation Associations with Social Civilization Associations, except in Jilong. There, even though the Jilong CAA maintained its autonomy, officials established a network of organizations beneath the umbrella of the new Jilong Social Civilization Union (Kiirun shakai kyōka rengōkai; SCU). The SCU set as its goal "the achievement of a national society," which it would accomplish by instilling in city residents an emperor-centered vision of the nation (*kokutai kannen*), expanding Japanese language proficiency, and reforming local customs.[76] A small committee of nine Japanese ran the SCU, including the city mayor and Ishizaka Sōsaku as the chair and vice chair respectively, but other residents did much of the real work through several affiliated organizations. To run the affiliates, the SCU relied on schools, youth groups, language training centers, Japanese religious institutions, the Jilong Women's Association, and the Jilong CAA.

The social civilization network covered Jilong's physical terrain with a peculiar ethnic-national mosaic. The SCU divided the city into thirteen different civilization wards (*kyōka ku*) and six settlements

---

75. Kiirun shi yakusho, *Kiirun shi shakai kyōiku*, in Nagaoka, *Shokuminchi shakai jigyō 45*, 2–4. The term rendered as "self-reliance" is the same one (*jichi*) translated in chapter 2 as "self-government." In the present context, the state clearly did not intend to foster the political autonomy of its citizen-subjects but rather wanted to wean them from state assistance.

76. Ibid., 78. *Kokutai kannen* is a difficult term to express in English. *Kokutai* is generally rendered as "national polity," and it is equated with the imperial institution, thus a more literal translation could be "national polity idea." In practice, the SCU taught people to revere the emperor as the leader and embodiment of the Japanese nation.

(*buraku*). The settlements were located around the periphery of the city, in the northern coastal districts and on the eastern and western edges, and the civilization wards were distributed throughout the city center, although the solidly Taiwanese part of Big Jilong did not become a civilization ward.[77] It appears that the ongoing strength of the CAA through most of the 1930s worked in concert with the ambivalence that Japanese settlers felt about the assimilation of Taiwanese to keep the state-run SCU out of that part of the city. Elsewhere, however, the invariably Japanese-run local neighborhood committees managed the civilization wards, regardless of the wards' ethnic composition, and Taiwanese residents oversaw all of the peripheral settlements. The SCU also appointed a group of fifty-six civilization commissioners (*kyōka iin*), many of whom were also welfare commissioners, to institute policies and coordinate activities throughout the city. The vast majority of these commissioners were Japanese men; eminent Taiwanese, such as Xu Zisang and Cai Qingyun, filled about a quarter of the posts, but they worked with fewer people in the less densely populated peripheral neighborhoods.[78] The discontinuities between the ethnic and national distribution of the civilization commissioners, on the one hand, and residents, on the other, highlighted how the Japanese attempted to use social civilization to redirect social work toward their goal of incorporating Jilong and Taiwan as Japanese space.

Nevertheless, Taiwanese residents played important roles in certain parts of the social civilization project and consistently focused on the modernization, rather than the cultural reorientation, of their community. For example, the JFG implemented the latest standards of personal hygiene when it installed public baths and opened them to the entire city, but it is not clear if the association's leaders shared the view of Kinebuchi Yoshifusa, who classified bathing as a tradition (*fūzoku shūkan*), or of the Government-General, which proclaimed

77. Ibid. For Japanese, the term for settlement (*buraku*) evoked the *burakumin*, an underclass caste that many Japanese considered to be separate from the rest of society. For Taiwanese, the same word (*buluo* in Chinese) was one term for an indigenous group. It is not clear if the SCU intended to reference either of these purportedly semicivilized populations, but the term must have implied a group with a greater need for social civilization.

78. Ibid., 88–93.

that the JFG acted "in order to plant the tradition of bathing in the Taiwanese."[79] Cai Qingyun brought contemporary ideas of gender equality to his efforts to stamp out the bride-price system and the practice of selling girls into marriage. In an article in *The Social Work Companion*, he railed against the harmful effects of what he called "bride-price-ism" (*pinjin zhuyi*), saying that it oppressed women and damaged society at large. The continuation of this tradition, which he said he regrettably found in his own city as late as 1931, prevented Taiwanese society from becoming civilized, Cai claimed.[80] These examples, much like Xu Zisang's earlier campaigns against foot-binding and the queue, suggest that Taiwanese elites sought to create a modern society, whereas officials and settlers tried to build a Japanese one. In this regard, Taiwan closely resembled other colonies, such as India, where native elites embraced aspects of the British civilizing mission and used it to critique the imperial project, and Vietnam, where educated Vietnamese adopted the French language to promote their equality with the French.[81]

Religious beliefs sat at the heart of Japanese views on modern social work. Some Japanese traced the origins of social welfare in Japan to the Buddhist temples and sects. As early as the sixth century, Buddhist institutions supposedly manifested the ideal of giving aid to those in need through charitable acts, and in modern times, large temples like the Kyoto home of the Shinshū sect, and organizations such as the Buddhist Social Work Association (Bukkyō shakai jigyō kyōkai), financially supported the welfare commissioners and other social work institutions. Private individuals inserted Buddhism directly into the practice of social work through the Imperial Way of Buddhism (Kōdō Bukkyō), which, they said, required its adherents to engage in charity

79. Kinebuchi, *Taiwan shakai jigyō shi*, 1133; TSTF, 10748.8, 15.

80. Cai Qingyun, "Hontōjin no hei kin seido no heigai wa wakaki danjo o shiro e yūdō," *SJT* 37 (Dec. 1931): 56–59.

81. Mani, *Contentious Traditions*, and Fischer-Tiné and Mann, *Colonialism as Civilizing Mission*, especially the essay by Fischer-Tiné on education in colonial India. On Vietnam, see Goscha, "'The Modern Barbarian.'"

for the benefit of society.[82] Yamamuro Gunpei, the Christian founder of Japan's Salvation Army and a well-known advocate for the poor, also explored the relationship between social work and religion in two articles published in *The Social Work Companion* in 1929.[83] Yamamuro sharply criticized most contemporary social work, which he said officials performed with all of the spirituality of a factory assembly line. Instead, in terms that resonated with the ideas of the Social Gospel that motivated American Christian missionaries in the late nineteenth and twentieth centuries, he argued that for social work to be effective, for it to be extended to everyone in need and heal the spirit as well as the flesh, social workers absolutely required a core of religious faith.[84]

By the mid-1930s, many Japanese also linked social welfare to Shinto. One contributor to *The Social Work Companion* manufactured an ancient pedigree by tracing the practice of tree planting as social welfare in the Tokugawa period back to tree planting as a devotional act in a more distant age. The author argued that the non–State Shinto new religions that emerged in the late Tokugawa years, such as Tenrikyō and Konkōkyō, reinforced this heritage through their frequent practice of charitable acts. Most important, after the reclassification of shrines in 1898, many local institutions organized day-care centers and neighborhood assistance programs, and some social workers established their own altars to Shinto deities.[85] The bonds that the Japanese forged between Shinto and social welfare in the home islands carried over to Taiwan.

When social work concentrated on religion, it became intertwined with a larger battle over belief and identity. Social workers addressed a number of religious practices in the context of customs reform,

---

82. He and Lin, "Naichi shisatsu zakkan," *SJT* 80 (July 1935): 84; Hori Hideo, "Hontō jiin shakai jigyō ka ni yokosu," *SJT* 98 (Jan. 1937): 41; and Okabe Kaidō, "Shūkyō to nichijyō no kinmi o taiken shite Bukkyō shin taisei no kakuritsu o sakebu," *SJT* 145 (Dec. 1940): 48.

83. Rightmire, *Salvationist Samurai*.

84. Yamamuro Gunpei, "Shakai jigyō to shūkyō," in *SJT* 10 (Sept. 1929): 3–14 and *SJT* 11 (Oct. 1929): 1–12. On the Social Gospel movement and its influence, see Hutchison, *Errand to the World*; Dawley, "Changing Minds."

85. Hashimoto Shirō, "Jinja to shakai jigyō," *SJT* 81 (Aug. 1935): 10–17.

including wearing the cangue, renovating spirit idols, and so-called superstitions, such as divination and geomancy.[86] In 1928, the first islandwide social work conference issued a statement of principles that proclaimed: "We must guide religious organizations and public festivals to emphasize social work activities. As for the social work activities of these organizations, we must make them more efficient and advance their social work to the highest level."[87] However, the prevailing context had changed by the mid-1930s, when a Japanese social worker from Jilong extolled the virtues of the "Rokuhara spirit," and two Taiwanese welfare commissioners wrote a positive report on the welfare activities of Japanese shrines and temples in the home islands.[88] The increasing intolerance of Japanese nationalism in the 1930s, and the intensifying pressure to assimilate, suggest that complex motivations underlay the enthusiasm displayed by Taiwanese social workers for religious social work.

A multipronged effort to eradicate the burning of ghost money revealed the intimate and complex linkages between religion, social work, and ethnic formation. During the summer of 1937, a Taiwanese employee of the Government-General's social work bureau exemplified the precarious position of social workers engaged in customs reform when he criticized the practice. He used an epithet for burning ghost money common to Japanese commentaries—rōshū, one of several terms translatable as "evil custom"—but his primary critique was based on economic and social grounds. He lamented that the Taiwanese expended so much real money on this practice, as much as three million yen a year, instead of devoting those resources to aiding their compatriots by supporting social work. He lauded the Jilong CAA for promoting just such a redirection of personal finances, in part because it would keep Taiwanese money in Taiwan rather than sending it across the strait in order to purchase ghost money from Chinese producers.[89]

86. "Kiirun dōfūkai kingin kami shōkyaku o danko haishi," *SJT* 104 (July 1937): 79–80.

87. "Dai ikkai zentō shakai jigyō taikai," *SJT* 1 (Dec. 1928): 101.

88. He and Lin, "Naichi shisatsu zakkan," *SJT* 80 (July 1935). See the opening of this chapter.

89. Chen Quanyong, "Kingin kami shōkyaku haishi ni tsuite," *SJT* 104 (July 1937): 6–8. The article stated that local producers could provide only about one-third of the

In fact, the CAA led an islandwide effort to address this important ritual. The association began internal discussions of the issue at least as early as 1936, and late the following spring it hosted a meeting of central and prefecture social work officials, delegates to prefecture and city assemblies from all over the island, local government officers, all of Jilong's temple managers, and some sixty members of the CAA itself. The mostly Taiwanese delegates approved a three-part plan for dealing with the practice in Jilong. The first step provoked the incident described at the opening of chapter 4: a committee of elites and officials removed the large ovens used for burning ghost money from the three main Taiwanese temples on the day of their deity-welcoming festivals, and later from all the rest of the city's temples. Second, the plan called on all members of the CAA to promptly cease the practice within their own homes and turn in their personal burners. Third, it recommended that the local sellers and manufacturers of ghost money voluntarily turn to other forms of business. The CAA publicized these measures throughout Taiwan, thereby placing itself and the city at the intersection of social work and reform.

Taiwanese residents of Jilong resisted the ban almost immediately, most publicly outside of the Dianji Temple, where citizens tried to halt the removal of the temple's censer until the local police arrived and removed them. They also directed personal attacks against many of the CAA officials who had formulated the plan. For example, they boycotted the alcohol and tobacco store of a Taiwanese commissioner named He Peng, resulting in the loss of some six hundred yen for his business. Discontented Taiwanese verbally abused a director of the CAA Everyday Life Reform division at that year's municipal council elections, and a small crowd looted his fishery products store. Perhaps most significant, the majority of the CAA's membership refused to abide by the prohibition: only ten members turned in the burners from their homes in the first month of the ban. Given that the CAA overlapped with the *hokō* system, the plan's failure indicated the limits of the power of the security apparatus. Faced with such opposition, and

---

ghost money burned across Taiwan each year. The rest of it came from China, largely through clandestine trade.

to prevent the CAA's internal collapse, the officers lifted the prohibition after only a few months.[90]

The ghost money dispute revealed that the formerly shared arena of social work had become a battleground for competing identities by the mid-1930s. At this time, Japanese social workers were using their activities to push a radical agenda of cultural transformation on the Taiwanese, framed in terms of the persistence of backward, uncivilized practices. They had imposed this new agenda because of the rising tide of expansionist nationalism in Japan, and because they recognized the failure of long-standing programs for gradual assimilation. What they observed in fact, in that failure, was the existence of a strongly bounded modern Taiwanese ethnic identity. Faced with these new attacks on local customs, Taiwanese social workers defended their ethnicity through a variety of means. Some engaged in defense through modification, and made a show of abolishing the ritual burning of ghost money on the grounds that it wasted resources that should be used for the social development of the Taiwanese community. Others rejected this accommodation and refused to eliminate something of such evident importance. Ultimately, they all closed ranks and defended the border.

Overcoming the Local:
Wartime Social Control and Japanization

When the social reform official Kinebuchi Yoshifusa published the fruits of his long years of research in 1940, a vice minister of the Imperial Household, Baron Shirane Matsusuke, wrote an introduction to the enormous volume. The baron juxtaposed Japan's supposedly successful efforts in transforming Taiwan with the establishment of a new order (shin chitsujo) in East Asia. He stated that the imperial system of social work had been created in the home islands, then developed and refined in Taiwan in preparation for a much larger project that would

---

90. Jilong CAA, "Wa ga Kiirun shi ni okeru kingin kami shōkyaku haishi no keika," SJT 104 (July 1937): 12. See also "Kin chō haishi ni tan o hasshi dōfūkai naibu no funjō bakuhatsu," NS, July 3, 1937, 9; "Dōfūkai no funjō sai hatsu," NS, July 31, 1937, 7.

soon extend over all of China.[91] To put it another way, wartime leaders of the Japanese Empire replaced their predecessors' concerns for charity and assistance with an overriding emphasis on using social work for the transformation and control of the societies under their rule, especially in their overseas territories. Baron Shirane based his vision on a flawed premise, however, because as Japanese social workers and officials in Taiwan recognized, they still had much work to do there. Nevertheless, within the framework of wartime mobilization, they shifted social work policy to deemphasize local problems in favor of meeting supposedly empirewide wartime objectives.[92] Downgrading local issues drove a wedge between social work and the Jilong identity, and the greater devotion to empire building and increasing reliance on Japanese-run programs threatened to make social work purely a tool for the Japanization of Taiwanese consciousness.

The predominance of Japanese nationalism as the ideological guide for social work, along with its religious focus, coincided with the intensification of the Kōminka movement and the launch of the Temple Restructuring movement in 1937, resulting in an islandwide assault against so-called Taiwanese superstitions (*Taiwan meishin*). Social workers looked beyond their urban bastions and targeted the thousands of "wish-granting temples" (*youying gongmiao*) throughout rural Taiwan that, they argued, epitomized backward beliefs and practices.[93] The Temple Restructuring movement tried to replace Taiwanese temples with small Shinto shrines, ignoring the irony that the deities or spirits in both sacred spaces offered similar services, but social workers also zealously promoted Japanese Buddhism. A Japanese social worker wrote in *The Social Work Companion* that Japan's establishment of the Greater East Asia Co-Prosperity Sphere in 1940 brought a number of dramatic changes, including a Shōwa religious revolution (*Shōwa no shūkyō dai kaikaku*) that heralded the unification of all Buddhist

91. Kinebuchi, *Taiwan shakai jigyō shi*, Introduction, 11.

92. From August 1937 until *The Social Work Companion* closed in 1943, the vast majority of the journal's articles addressed home-front defense and support for military forces in action, as well as general issues of health and hygiene; articles about local programs appeared only rarely, especially compared with their prevalence prior to 1937.

93. Zeng Jinglai, "Taiwan meishin," *SJT* 106 (Sept. 1937): 10–14.

branches and sects. He insisted that the social civilization of Taiwan depended on the conversion of the Taiwanese people, so that they could join together to make Taiwan a bastion of a new form of imperial Buddhism.[94] The engagement of social workers across Taiwan in these projects linked the social work system with the massive wartime effort to inscribe Japanese nationalism in the lives and minds of the Taiwanese.

The merger between social welfare, social civilization, and cultural transformation had other facets as well. One of the most important Kōminka programs was linguistic reform via intensive Japanese instruction, removing the Chinese language from newspapers, and banning the use of Taiwanese in public. In August 1937, as part of its social civilization agenda, the Government-General set an ambitious goal of raising Japanese proficiency levels among Taiwanese to 50 percent by 1940.[95] With only a third of Taiwanese people able to comprehend Japanese in 1937, that appeared to be an unreachable target in three years, but by 1945, roughly 70 percent of Taiwanese had Japanese proficiency.[96] This attention to language appeared everywhere, including in Taiwan's flagship institution for curing opium addiction, the Taipei Healthy Life Institute (Taibei kangshengyuan), where the director, islander Du Congming (Tu Tsungming), promoted Japanese instruction alongside treatment.[97] Locally, changes within the CAA highlighted the increasing exclusivity of Japanese nationalism. The CAA remained a key social work organization into the 1940s, and Xu Zisang served as its nominal leader throughout the war. However, beginning with the establishment of its new patriotic youth group, Japanese authorities asserted greater control over its activities. Their influence emerged when the CAA launched a campaign that stressed public duties (hōkō) such as raising money for national defense, sending care packages to soldiers, and

94. Okabe, "Shūkyō to nichijyō no kinmi," *SJT* 145 (Dec. 1940): 42–46.

95. "Kōminka wa kokugo fukyū kara jikyoku no han'ei ka, hontōjin no kokugo shūtoku netsu wa monosugoi ikioi," *TNS*, Aug. 28, 1937, 7.

96. The percentage of Japanese-speaking Taiwanese rose from 38 percent to 71 percent islandwide during the Kōminka movement. See Chang Mau-kuei, "On the Origins and Transformation of Taiwanese National Identity," in Katz and Rubinstein, *Religion and the Formation*, 39–40.

97. Kingsberg, *Moral Nation*, 165.

adopting Shinto worship practices.[98] Both the coercive language program and the use of the CAA to support the Imperial Army and spread Shinto reflected the attempted Japanization of institutions and identities. The fact that the Taiwanese in Jilong and elsewhere adopted some of these practices indicates that the borders of Taiwanese ethnicity faced concerted attack and required new types of identity performance to defend them.

As the local faced greater pressure from the national, officials relied more and more on the Japanese-dominated welfare commissioners, instead of organizations founded by the Taiwanese, to carry out social work. The objectives of control and Japanization were inherent to the origins and local composition of the commissioners. The system had emerged out of Japan's post–World War I Rice Riots, as a tool for preventing the recurrence of such unrest, and Jilong's commissioners, a cross-section of elite men, were closely allied with the state. The Government-General appointed top-tier figures like Ishizaka Sōsaku, Yan Guonian, and Xu Zisang to serve as the city's first commissioners and to help establish the system, later adding second-tier businessmen such as Cai Qingyun and Akabi Sanehira. In 1940, the twenty-five commissioners included fourteen Japanese and eleven Taiwanese, and almost all came from the professional class: they were merchants, company officials, shipping agents, contractors, business owners, doctors, school principals, and bureaucrats. The lone exception was an abbot of the Sōdō sect.[99] Many were members of the CAA and of Jilong's numerous credit unions, but the most common shared characteristic was their involvement with the civilian and police bureaucracies. A majority of Jilong's commissioners were members of the city assembly, held semi-bureaucratic positions as district or ward officers, and served as leaders in the hokō system. Almost all were second-generation elites for whom Japanese rule of Taiwan was the only governing system with which they had direct experience.[100]

98. Taihoku shū hōmen iin rengōkai, "Shakai jigyō gaiyō Shōwa jūgo nendo," in Nagaoka, Shokuminchi shakai jigyō 40, 149–50.

99. Taihoku shū, Taihoku shū hōmen iin meibo.

100. This summary is based on my survey of the biographies of many local welfare commissioners, not just those from 1940. I reviewed biographies of the following individuals, sixteen Taiwanese and six Japanese: Cai Qingyun, Pan Rongchun, Lin

During the late 1930s and 1940s the commissioners focused on both religious reform and home front mobilization in the service of imperial goals. At a meeting in the fall of 1937, the welfare commissioners addressed their progress, or lack thereof, in supporting the Temple Restructuring movement by controlling, amalgamating, and shutting down Taiwanese temples, as well as in eradicating customs such as burning ghost money.[101] As Japanese forces expanded the scope of the so-called China Incident—that is, the Second Sino-Japanese War—the growing conflict endangered the stability of Taiwan itself. Many Japanese and Taiwanese fled China for the colony, and many from the colony—at first only Japanese, but later Taiwanese and indigenous islanders—prepared to go off to fight. The commissioners received special instructions to increase their efforts to care for refugees, aid the families of draftees, and put the island on a wartime footing.[102] Within a few months, a call went out to strengthen the commissioner system: "As for the general mobilization of the commissioner spirit, because it is the ideal spiritual activity for elevating neighborhood assistance to its highest level, it fully acknowledges the true nature of the commissioner spirit, and it manifests the responsibilities of local welfare commissioners, it is important, or even vital."[103]

From this point on, the work of the commissioners revolved around the war. Medical assistance, charitable donations, counseling, and other tasks all received a new urgency, because social ills had to be cured quickly and cheaply in order to direct every available resource

Shuanghui, He Peng, Wang Tusheng, Song Yuantai, Xiao Zongrong, Ye Shuijian, Lin Tianwang, Lin Yingshi, Zhang Fuyun, Yang Taishan, Zhang Shiwen, Liu Qilin, Jian Aquan, Guo Qinrong, Akabi Sanehira, Tajiri Shinji, Yoshiwara Tasaburō, Honda Toshihiro, Kojima Teizō, and Inomata Keizō. I relied on the biographical database *Taiwan renwu zhi ziliaoku*, tww.ith.sinica.edu.tw/login_whoswho.htm, accessed Apr. 2017; the database is compiled by researchers at Academia Sinica, Taipei, from Japanese-era biographical compendiums. The database is accessible only from within Academia Sinica.

101. "Dai jū kai Taihoku shū hōmen iin sōkai yōmō," *SJT* 108 (Nov. 1937): 79.

102. Mori Hiroshi, "Nichi-Shi jihen to hōmen iin no katsudō," *SJT* 106 (Sept. 1937): 1.

103. Suzuki Etake, "Hōmen seishin sōdōin o motte taishosu," *SJT* 108 (Nov. 1937): 13.

to the all-important war effort. The commissioners also acquired new tasks as part of an attempt to fulfill the potential for social control that had helped spread the commissioner system after unrest in Japan in the early 1920s. Under the terms of the recently passed Military Assistance Law (Gunji fujo hō), the state empowered local commissioners to register all military families in their districts and determine appropriate levels of aid for them. Since imperial refugees from China, who numbered more than five thousand in Taibei Prefecture alone, fell outside of this new law, the commissioners lobbied for the extension of the existing Aid Law (Kyūgo hō) of 1929 to provide for their support.[104] Commissioners also raised money during the now nationwide Sympathy Week, which gained a higher profile when the holiday celebrated in honor of the Taishō emperor, December 25, was renamed Commissioner Thanksgiving Day (Hōmen kansha hi) in 1937.[105]

The war unquestionably enhanced the sense of purpose, and at times the strength and reach, of the welfare commissioner system. Since its inception, the system had stressed moral and spiritual assistance rather than material aid. Therefore, in the context of wartime Japanese nationalism, social workers encouraged people to be independent and self-reliant (*jiritsu jikatsu*) by helping individuals and families develop plans for self-support.[106] Commissioners also pulled neighborhoods and even entire cities together through mutual assistance activities to ameliorate wartime shortages, in the name of conserving state resources for the war effort and building and strengthening the Japanese nation-state.[107] Their potential for social control emerged more clearly with the surge in wartime nationalism, as local commissioners made a special effort to gather new information on all the needy families within their jurisdiction and to update the data on the existing special assistance cards (*hogo kaado*), in an effort to monitor the local

104. Ibid., 12–13; Mori, "Nichi-Shi jihen to hōmen iin no katsudō," *SJT* 106 (Sept. 1937): 1.

105. "Sentō hōmen iin dōjō shūkan kaisai yōmō," *SJT* 109 (Dec. 1937): 73–74.

106. Suzuki, "Hōmen seishin sōdōin o motte taishosu," *SJT* 108 (Nov. 1937): 14–15.

107. "Dai jū kai Taihoku shū hōmen iin sōkai yōmō," *SJT* 108 (Nov. 1937): 75–76; "Taihoku shū hōmen iin sōkai yōmō," *SJT* 121 (Dec. 1938): 67.

population.[108] They established several centers in Taibei Prefecture to hold beggars in state custody after removing them from the streets of cities and towns.[109] Finally, the local committees took on a much greater role in coordinating social work activities. Even though they did not take control of other social work institutions, they did keep track of each group's activities and finances.[110] The local welfare commissioners became overseers of Taiwan's entire social work apparatus.

When the commissioner system came to Taiwan, its architects were primarily seeking a more effective and efficient way to distribute aid; social control and assimilation had been secondary and tertiary concerns. The early focus on the efficient provision of welfare enabled the system to establish itself as a crucial piece of the social work superstructure in Jilong, and from this central position it brought together islanders and Japanese in a shared operational space in which they assisted local residents, and developed and enacted their strong sense of being Jilongese. However, following the emergence of the Taiwanese ethnic identity and the outbreak of war, social work officials reshuffled their goals and reframed the provision of aid wholly in the service of supporting expansive Japanese nationalism. The commissioner system now emphasized dissolving the local into the national; thus Jilong consciousness mattered, to settlers and officials, only to the extent that it supported imperial goals. The sources do not reveal how Taiwanese residents reacted to these changes, or if Taiwanese social workers resisted the nationalization and imperialization of welfare. They surely enacted behaviors associated with Japaneseness—speaking Japanese, visiting shrines, sending care packages to soldiers—but perhaps they did so only for self-protection. What seems likely is that they continued to aid their in-group members as best they could, enhancing the ties that bound them together as an ethnicity while performing the social responsibilities associated with their elite status.

108. "Hōmen kanshi hi settei no shushi narabini hōhō," *SJT* 109 (Dec. 1937): 74.
109. "Dai jū kai Taihoku shū hōmen iin sōkai yōmō," *SJT* 108 (Nov. 1937): 77–78.
110. TSTF, 10873.13, Jan. 1, 1940.

Conclusion

Islanders constructed their Taiwanese ethnic identity along multiple pathways, not least through their social work. This self-consciously modern practice provided them with semiprofessional training, an ideology of rational welfare, and institutional structures that connected them to extralocal networks of peers. Just as medicine influenced the nationalism of Taiwanese doctors, social work, through economic assistance, customs reform, and social control, promoted ethnic construction by strengthening islanders' sense of group identification through the provision of needed relief, or via complex defenses of the practices targeted for reform.[111] The system's institutions and personnel demarcated the city's physical terrain in ways that sometimes reflected its demographic divisions and at other times attempted reterritorialization through the insertion of Japanese into islander-Taiwanese districts. It also reinforced the position of islander-Taiwanese elites as gatekeepers, situated between their own socially, culturally, and officially designated community and the Japanese settlers and officials who, with much ambivalence, sought to assimilate them to Japanese practices, norms, and traditions.

Although the early prominence of locally created institutions and the local welfare commissioners reinforced a shared Jilong identity, the social work system's increasing attention to cultural transformation and national affairs during the 1920s and 1930s sharpened the borders between Taiwanese and Japanese. That system's divisiveness came in part from different mindsets about the work itself. Japanese social workers saw their activities as a means of civilizing the islanders, and facilitating the fusion of Taiwanese and Japanese (*naiTai yūgō*), or the merger of metropole and colony.[112] The Taiwanese people embraced contemporary standards of hygiene and movements for equal rights for women, as well as expanding the welfare activities of their temples and organizations, but they defended the religious practices and other traditions at the core of their ethnicity. As social civilization and social control programs became more prominent, particularly during

---

111. Lo, *Doctors within Borders*.
112. Katsuya, "Kiirun haku'aidan," *SJT* 39 (Feb. 1932): 30.

wartime, the Government-General redirected social work to meet the overriding goals of strengthening the Japanese nation-state and expanding its empire. The system that had been created for local needs now had a single-minded focus on the nation-state and its empire. When Japanese colonial officials disassociated social work from the local sphere, and tried to fully reterritorialize the city's imagined terrain, they removed one of the few shared interests that had tied Japanese and Taiwanese together. Moreover, opposition from Japanese settlers meant that the Taiwanese could never become full members of the Japanese national family. As a result, although settlers could extrapolate from their local to their national identity, the Taiwanese had no such option, nor could they safely imagine a Taiwanese nation-state. Thus Taiwanese ethnic consciousness became much more significant even as it came under greater threat.

This process of ethnic construction through social work had important implications for the postwar encounter between Taiwanese and Chinese peoples. Remaining Taiwanese in the face of Kōminka required the defensive, accommodating performance of certain behaviors—such as attending Shinto shrines or using Japanese—that would become important markers of distinction under a new regime. In addition, the explicitly modern nature of social work, with its deep linkages to global discourses of modernization, its professionalization, its concern with hygiene, and its professed separation from the past, influenced the character of the group sense of self that it helped formulate. That is, it helped to make Taiwanese ethnicity a self-consciously modern identity. Finally, because islander elites appealed to multiple constituencies, including other elite islanders who shared their views and nonelite islanders who received their aid, social work was one of the most important factors that transcended (though it did not erase) older ties to native place, to Hokkien or Hakka. It also helped to break down the boundaries between disparate classes and social groups. In short, social work unified most of the islands' inhabitants as Taiwanese. Therefore, in-group assistance was one of the defining characteristics of the Taiwanese ethnic community. The strength of that community surfaced quickly when Taiwan was added to a Chinese state after Japan's defeat in 1945.

CHAPTER SIX

Defining New Boundaries in the Reconstruction of Jilong, 1945–1947

The Nationalist Chinese incorporation of Taiwan, heralded from the mainland as a "glorious recovery" (*guangfu*) and initially welcomed with zeal on Taiwan, quickly reached a moment of crisis. The heavy-handedness of Nationalist rule combined with a rapidly expanding list of economic and political grievances to breed discontentment among the Taiwanese. On the evening of February 27, 1947, a dispute broke out between police and Taiwanese citizens in the streets of Taipei. Acting under authority of the Taiwan administration's tobacco monopoly, police officers harassed a woman they thought was selling contraband cigarettes in the streets. Their ensuing argument sparked a clash with some passersby, who acted out the frustrations many Taiwanese felt over the similarities they saw between Chinese and Japanese sovereign control. Word of this unrest quickly spread north to Jilong, where violence erupted a few hours later, and Taiwanese in other cities soon followed suit. Within a few days, the Nationalist authorities

Some of the material in this chapter appeared previously in Evan Dawley, "Closing a Colony: The Meanings of Japanese Deportation from Taiwan after World War II," in *Japanese Taiwan: Colonial Rule and its Contested Legacy*, edited by Andrew Morris (London: Bloomsbury Academic, an imprint of Bloomsbury Publishing PLC, 2015). Used with permission of the publisher.

faced an islandwide uprising; antigovernment activities had not been seen on such a scale in Taiwan since the 1890s, and perhaps not since the major rebellions of the eighteenth century. Less than eighteen months after Taiwan's reunion with China, a place for which many felt a strong ancestral and cultural affinity, the Taiwanese people explosively expressed the stark differences in power, position, and identity between themselves and the Nationalist Chinese who now governed them.

The 2-28 Uprising, as these events have come to be known, exemplified the tensions that coalesced in retrocession-era Taiwan. It revealed just how far the communities on either side of the Taiwan Strait had diverged from each other in terms of their primary senses of group consciousness, in their views of the proper relationship between government and people, and in how they defined modernity. More specifically, the uprising and its suppression showed that the Taiwanese shared neither the Nationalists' vision of the Chinese nation, nor the loyalty and willingness to sacrifice themselves for that nation that the new regime demanded. Instead of quickly assimilating themselves to a new national identity, Taiwanese across the island defended their ethnicity, and Jilong residents reclaimed their local consciousness from the recent Japanese efforts to colonize the city as a purely Japanese, and fully nationalized, space. The new rulers and their agents attempted to inscribe their national identity on Taiwan, much as their Japanese predecessors had done, and they framed it as a process of re-Sinicization, or restoring Chinese political, social, and cultural norms to the Taiwanese. Huang Yingzhe has explored this "cultural reconstruction policy" (*wenhua chongjian zhengce*) as a defining feature of postwar Taiwan, but it seems that the policy had few if any parallels in mainland areas reclaimed from Japan after the war.[1] They launched a project of deterritorialization, to remove the Japanese presence, and reterritorialization, to remake the island in a Chinese mold. Moreover, because these new Chinese transplants saw themselves as modern and the

---

1. Huang Yingzhe, *Qu Riben hua*. Huang focuses on the policy and its associated institutions, with less attention to how the Taiwanese addressed it. In my brief survey of scholarship on postwar China, I located no comparable cases in other areas recovered from the Japanese.

Taiwanese as backward, re-Sinicization also meant bringing civilization to the island. In fact, the tremendous overlap between the two
regimes in terms of their monopolies on political power, imbalanced
distribution of economic opportunity, and plans for the physical and
mental transformation of Taiwan and all of its residents supports
Emma Teng's point that it is impossible to speak of the "postcolonial"
in Taiwan's history.[2] Early governance by the Nationalists was, in essence, a recolonization of Taiwan and, as with the Japanese, their vision
for re-creating Taiwan outstripped state capacities in part because of
contestation and demands from the Taiwanese.

Important differences existed between Chinese and Japanese rule,
but from the perspective of the Taiwanese, the initial similarities mattered more. Physical geography still defined Taiwan's main social
groups, although the terms had shifted from "islanders" and "metro-
politans" (*hontōjin* and *naichijin*) to "insiders" (*benshengren*) and "outsiders" (*waishengren*).[3] The first category corresponded to Taiwanese,
and the second denoted mainlanders or transplanted Chinese.[4] As a
result of the shift in the national language from Japanese to Mandarin
Chinese, from this point onward, I rely more on the Mandarin pronunciations for transliteration. Terminology aside, the quality of interactions remained essentially continuous: contestations over who
defined the identity of the insiders, and how they constructed it,
shaped relations between the two groups. For their part, the Taiwanese
employed many of the same strategies for operating within the Nationalist system as they had during the Japanese period. The sources from
the early retrocession years do not permit as fine-grained an exploration of Jilong society, nor of the motivations and actions of the Taiwanese, as was possible for the Japanese era. Nevertheless, it is clear that,
as mainlanders imposed their vision of the nation and their plans for

2. Teng, *Taiwan's Imagined Geography*, 250.
3. Both Taiwanese and Chinese made use of these terms, which literally mean
"people of the province" and "people from outside the province."
4. As discussed in the introduction, I use a range of terms to denote the same
group of people. "Chinese," "mainlanders," "transplants," "agents of the state," and
(from 1949) "refugees" are all umbrella terms for the same group of people, those who
came to Taiwan from the mainland after the end of World War II. I use "Nationalists"
specifically for the subset of this group that served in the government and military.

national reconstruction in Taiwan, the Taiwanese sought a larger role in local governance and greater influence over the rebuilding of their city after the destructive war, goals that preserved the connections among members of their ethnic community. In their efforts, they defined borders between themselves and the Chinese transplants, and reinforced the ethnic identity that they had forged over the previous five decades.

Redefining Boundaries during Regime Change

One of the most durable results of the long and bloody Pacific War was the apparent reversal of what had taken place fifty years earlier in the waters off of Jilong, as Japan surrendered the island to the Republic of China. With the war over, completing the transfer of jurisdiction was relatively easy but what followed was significantly more complicated. In the months and years that succeeded the formal end of the Taiwan Government-General and the official beginning of Nationalist Chinese governance in late October of 1945, the new regime and its agents had to remove the old, and incorporate the Taiwanese into their vision of modern China. This involved remapping and reterritorializing the imagined terrain of Jilong and Taiwan in ways that could accommodate their new demographic context.

Chinese nationalism was a new element in the postwar environment, but it had roots in the earlier transfer of Taiwan's sovereignty. In the wake of the Qing dynasty's defeat by Japan, Chinese reformers and revolutionaries envisioned China in the form of a nation-state with a strong centralized government that would be the locus of Chinese identity formation and loyalty.[5] Revolutionaries such as Zou Rong, Zhang Binglin, and Sun Yat-sen at first imagined Chinese national identity through the lens of virulent anti–Manchu Han ethnocentrism, but after the 1911 Revolution, Sun and others fundamentally embraced both the multiethnic and territorial legacies of the Qing Empire.[6] Thereafter, in the context of warlord rivalries, interparty competition, Nationalist

5. Zarrow, "Reform Movement," 17–47; Zarrow, *China in War*, chap. 3.
6. Gang Zhao, "Reinventing China," 19–21.

unification, and urbanization, Chinese nationalism became self-consciously modern. From the end of the Qing through the New Life Movement of the 1930s, nationalists of all ideological stripes placed cultural or social transformation at the center of their evolving Chinese consciousness.[7] Some emphasized "the material transformation of everyday life" for the masses, and others sought to break from the past by eradicating the backward treatment of women, superstitious religion, and unscientific and undemocratic viewpoints that had plagued old China.[8] The Nationalist Party, especially during the Nanjing Decade (1927–37), stressed the construction of a strong state that would transform national politics as well as personal lives.[9] Once the people were mobilized for that national entity, they would be willing to mete out mortal punishment on those who transgressed and betrayed the nation.[10]

If Chinese national identity was firmly united around the idea of a strong central state that commanded the loyalty of its citizens, it was historically more ambivalent regarding Taiwan. According to Shi-chi Mike Lan, Chinese both within and outside the government consistently placed Taiwan beyond China's territorial, or external, borders. Moreover, when Chinese spoke of Taiwanese as compatriots (*tongbao*) or family members, they used terminology—usually referring to brothers who were sold, daughters who were married out, abandoned orphans—that placed these fictive siblings and children outside of China's mental, or internal, boundaries.[11] Two survey teams that the governor of Fujian Province, Chen Yi, sent to Taiwan in 1934 and 1936 highlighted the island's externality by referring to Taiwan as a "mirror of *modernity*" into which officials in the Republic of China could gaze

7. Harrison, *The Making of the Republican Citizen*, 60–92; Chow, *The May Fourth Movement*; Kirby, *Germany and Republican China*, 176–85.

8. Yeh, *Becoming Chinese*, 7. In the quotation, Yeh refers to Leo Ou-fan Lee's chapter in the volume on print modernity in Shanghai. On the goal of eradicating old ideas, see Judge, "Reforming the Feminine"; Suisheng Zhao, *A Nation-State by Construction*, 56–64; Duara, *Rescuing History*, chaps. 3, 5; Duara, "Of Authenticity and Woman."

9. Strauss, "The Evolution of Republican Government," 335.

10. Wakeman, "*Hanjian* (Traitor)!"

11. Lan, "The Ambivalence of National Imagination."

to learn how to improve their own state.[12] Only during the second half of the war did China's nation builders reframe the territory of Taiwan as belonging within China's external borders; on the subject of the Taiwanese people, however, the Chinese retained their ambivalence.[13] Late in 1944, following the Cairo Declaration, Chen Yi led the Taiwan Investigation Committee (Taiwan diaocha weiyuanhui) in planning for the takeover of Taiwan. The committee's blueprint for establishing Nationalist Chinese rule covered a comprehensive set of political, social, and economic factors. Its main principles emphasized wiping away Japanese influence (*diguo shili*), promoting rapid economic recovery, practicing Sun's Three People's Principles, and establishing a strong civil administration and constitutional government.[14] This foundational document summarized the Nationalists' view of their multiple roles in Taiwan as liberators, rulers, transformers, and modernizers.

A primary manifestation of the Japanese presence in Taiwan was the roughly 350,000 Japanese civilians living there at the end of the war.[15] For many, Taiwan was their homeland and the Japanese settlers had played a large role in building Taiwan's cities and societies. It was in part owing to their economic activities, their devotion to urban and social construction, and their pressure on the Government-General and the metropolitan government that Taiwan had gained its modern infrastructure, a limited measure of popular participation in governance, widespread mass media, and a dense network of modern social organizations. Of course, their presence had also limited the range of educational, commercial, and political opportunities for the Taiwanese. For reasons both suppressive and salutary, the impact the Japanese

12. Ibid., 190; original italics. Governor Chen wrote prefaces to both reports.

13. Ibid., 197. See also Kirby, "The Internationalization of China," 433–58.

14. See Taiwan diaocha weiyuanhui, "Taiwan jieguan jihua gangyao caoan," in Kirby et al., *State and Economy*, 107–21.

15. Zeng, *1945 poxiao shike*, 206–7. Zeng provides estimates ranging from around 350,000 to 390,000 Japanese in Taiwan, a number that was small in comparison to Manchuria, where almost 2 million mostly civilian Japanese resided at the war's end, and China, where there were about 1.5 million, although a larger proportion of the Japanese in China were in the military. A similar number of Japanese had to be repatriated from Korea after the war. See Watt, "Imperial Remnants," 245, 254n7.

had on Jilong and other urban centers in Taiwan cannot be overstated. Therefore, understanding the ROC reconstruction of Taiwan and the deterritorialization of the island after 1945 begins with exploring the process by which Japanese people were removed from the island. Taiwan's case contrasts markedly with both the rapid removal of Japanese residents from Korea and the extreme hardships experienced by the Japanese in Manchuria and Siberia, as described by Lori Watt.[16]

The emperor's August 15 surrender announcement struck Japanese settlers like a lightning bolt. On top of the frequent air raids that had overcome Japanese defenses and devastated Taiwan's major cities, the war's abrupt end fundamentally destabilized the worldview of the Japanese colonizers. On hearing the emperor's speech on the radio, a young man named Itō Keisuke, a native Jilongese who had served in a student military brigade outside of Taipei, wrote in his diary: "I don't understand anything. I cannot write anything. Whether it is true, or if it is a deception, what is true is that it is a disaster."[17] His views reflected the profound sense of dislocation experienced by the Japanese in Taiwan, a sentiment that no doubt intensified when it became clear that they would have to leave. Chen Yi's administration formalized their imminent departure that winter, when it announced a multistage deportation plan for all Japanese residents of Taiwan, to take place in 1946 and 1947. The forced removal of Japanese settlers dramatically transformed Taiwan's social framework and devastated many of the deportees, and it also served as one mechanism through which Taiwanese and Chinese defined themselves in contrast to each other (fig. 6.1).[18]

The deportation authorities designated Jilong as the main embarkation site for much of the island, thus in the early postwar period the city became a gathering place for tens of thousands of Japanese who were

16. Watt, *When Empire Comes Home*.

17. Itō Keisuke, "Gakuto dai no owari," in Taiwan kyōkai, *Taiwan hikiage shi*, 30.

18. I make this argument in a lengthier survey of the process of Japanese deportation, where I also explain my rationale for selecting "deport" rather than the more commonly used "repatriate." Briefly put, since the Japanese settlers had never left Japanese territory, and many were being sent to a place where they had never lived, the sense of return inherent in the word "repatriation" did not apply to those living in Taiwan. See Dawley, "Closing a Colony."

FIGURE 6.1.   A Japanese family selling their belongings in Jilong prior to deportation. Image courtesy of the Library of Congress, Washington, DC.

leaving their lives behind for an uncertain future in Japan. Ideally, they spent only a few days in Jilong, living in a demarcated and restricted zone among the warehouses on the west side of the harbor. Deportees arrived by train, walked a short distance to the holding area, where they were given physical and medical exams, and then remained within that zone, almost completely cut off from the world until a ship appeared to carry them away (fig. 6.2). Before they left, their luggage was searched to make sure that they were not trying to remove any contraband, such as Taiwanese cultural artifacts (*Taiwan no fūbutsu*) or precious metals. A committee of Japanese settlers managed most of these arrangements, whereas Ryukyuan Japanese were assigned the tasks of constructing temporary housing, carrying luggage, and feeding the waiting deportees.[19] The entire deportation process literally and figuratively quarantined the

19. Kawahara, *Taiwan hikiage ryūyō*, 2:209–14, diagram on 244–45.

FIGURE 6.2. Japanese deportees awaiting transportation out of Taiwan, near the Jilong Station. Image courtesy of USS *Block Island* Association, http://ussblockisland .org/Beta/V2-PhotoGallery/Photos_-_POW.html.

deportees, so that their contagious disease—Japaneseness—could not further infect the island and its people. When the Japanese departed, they closed the circle of their colonization: Jilong was both the first and last place in Taiwan that many of them saw.

Under Chen's plan, the vast majority of Japanese settlers in Taiwan were sent to Japan in the spring of 1946, but one group complicated the Nationalists' vision of creating a Chinese Taiwan, because they provided lingering evidence of Japan's impact. This group encompassed some 7,000 individuals whom the new government relied on to assist with the reconstruction of Taiwan's economy, government, and education system.[20] Including family members, there were about twenty-eight

20. John Dower notes that in China, both Nationalists and Communists retained tens of thousands of Japanese residents for technical or other purposes; see Dower,

thousand of the so-called "kept-on Japanese" (*liuyong Riqiao/ryūyō Nikkyō*) living, working, and attending school in Taiwan much as they had during the colonial period. They provided expertise in medicine, science, railroads, education, agriculture, port construction, and commerce.[21] As of early 1947, the 133 remaining Japanese residents of Jilong included an employee of the city government planning bureau, a number of people involved in both the production and management sides of the fishing industry, and a handful of technicians and engineers working for the Taiwan Fertilizer Manufacturing Company, Taiwan Electric Company, and Jilong Port Authority. Gaoxiong then held about twice as many Japanese, indicating a greater need for assistance in reconstructing the southern port.[22] To sequester this Japanese community from the rest of society, the provincial authorities also retained Japanese teachers and religious leaders to attend to its educational and spiritual needs.

The ROC's reliance on so many of its recent bitter enemies indicates that multiple concerns mediated the removal of Japanese influence. Japan had, for half a century, provided a model of modernization for Chinese officials and elites. From Qing sponsorship of study in Japan to Sun's and Chiang's reliance on Japanese advisors, China's political leaders had long looked to Japan for practical guidance. More immediately, the Nationalists viewed the Taiwanese with greater suspicion than they did their wartime adversaries, perhaps because of the unknown and potentially invisible effects of their prolonged contact with Japanese culture. For these reasons, the ROC government on Taiwan appeared reluctant to let go of its Japanese educators and technicians: the last official deportation ship left Jilong for Japan in the summer of 1949, and a few Japanese instructors continued to teach at National Taiwan University—the former Taihoku Imperial University—into the early 1950s.[23]

Embracing Defeat, 51. Watt does not indicate that the postwar authorities in Korea kept any Japanese there to assist with reconstruction. Watt, *When Empire Comes Home*.

21. Kawahara, *Taiwan hikiage ryūyō*, 1:5.

22. Ibid., 8:60–63, 104–12, 138–40.

23. Ibid., 1:12–13. The last deportation ship arrived in Sasebo on August 14, 1949.

A second group presented another obstacle to the Chinese efforts to de-Japanize Taiwan, the people involved in Taiwanese-Japanese unions and their offspring. The existing ROC citizenship law claimed all people of Chinese descent, anywhere in the world, as citizens according to the jus sanguinis principle.[24] Nevertheless, confusion lingered for several years over the nationality of Taiwanese women married to or living with Japanese men, Japanese women similarly linked to Taiwanese men, and their children. The low rates of pre-1945 intermarriage meant that very few people fell into these categories, although one report from November 1946 indicated that a sudden flood of people sought passage to Japan, perhaps to escape the deteriorating conditions, suggestive of a larger population of mixed couples and their offspring.[25] China's Ministry of the Interior issued regulations in February 1946 that sought to prevent most Japanese in Taiwan from naturalizing but claimed all Taiwanese (*Taiwan renmin*) as historical citizens who had temporarily been cut off by Japanese imperialism.[26] However, it was clear in early 1948 that the ROC government had adopted a more flexible position. Japanese men and women who had married Taiwanese spouses before the end of the war could gain Chinese citizenship if they applied for it. However, any Taiwanese who was married to a Japanese spouse and had previously acquired Japanese citizenship had to go to Japan. Gender and nationality mattered in regard to the children of these mixed marriages, in that a child's citizenship followed that of the mother, not the father. Those born to Taiwanese mothers who had not gained Japanese citizenship were considered Chinese, but children of Taiwanese women who held Japanese citizenship, and children of Japanese women who had married Taiwanese men, could apply for Chinese citizenship if they wanted it but did not automatically receive it.[27] These particular circumstances reveal how the ROC government defined its citizens. The ruling

24. Li Yinghui, *Huaqiao zhengce*, chap. 3.

25. XZZG, 3642, Riqiao guanli weiyuanhui, "Dian wei guiding bensheng renmin yu Riqiao renmin hunyin guanxizhe shenqing bu Ri banfa xi zhi zhao," Nov. 16, 1946.

26. XZZG, 1722, Taiwan xingzheng zhangguan gongshu, "Zhun neizhengbu han fu youguan Riqiao ji Taibao guoji yiyi sanxiang ling xi xunzhao banli," Feb. 26, 1946.

27. Taiwan sheng xingzheng zhangguan gongshu, *Taiwan xingzheng zhangguan gongshu gongbao* 2, no. 4 (Apr. 5, 1948): 51.

suggests that officials in Taiwan assumed that men were unlikely to give up their original citizenship whereas women might switch nationality to remain with their husband, so the state tried to lay claim to the offspring and thus keep the mothers in China.

The ROC took a greater interest in the assets of Japanese residents than in their technical skills. Even before the formal handover, it paved the way for state expropriation of assets by issuing a freeze on all Japanese-owned finances and property so that they could not be sold or otherwise transferred. However, Japanese and Taiwanese residents widely ignored this directive, in response to which the central authorities issued a more stringent regulation on October 15, outlawing the sale of property to Taiwanese individuals and ordering the return of anything that had changed hands since August 15.[28] A number of factors made it difficult to register and seize Japanese assets, such as the absence of records that clearly stated the date on which Taiwanese buyers had gained ownership, the unwillingness of Nationalist authorities to recognize claims that conflicted with their own plans, and instances in which Taiwanese disregarded official policies to pursue financial gain.[29] Difficulties such as these prompted the Jilong municipal authorities to slow down their seizure of Japanese property and proceed in a more discreet manner, to avoid disputes.[30] As a result, in April 1948 the provincial government reissued a directive for the immediate registration of all formerly Japanese property.[31] In spite of these difficulties, the early yield from this policy suggested that the seizure of Japanese assets provided a great boon for the state, which took in 9.5 billion yuan islandwide during the first four months of 1946.[32] In Jilong, addressing

28. "Riben gongsi caichan bude shanzi maimai," *MB*, Oct. 16, 1945, 1.

29. For examples of the first two difficulties, see GSG, Ministry of Finance (Caizhengbu; CZB), 275-1:00646, "Cao Heshi chan quan." There is no date on this collection of documents, but the document that lists the questionable cases, including four in Jilong, is from March 1952. For an example of the third case, see "Riqiao yi wu de yubo," *MB*, Nov. 14, 1946, 3.

30. "Jilong shi canyihui yu niansi ri kai disanci linshi huiyi," *MB*, Oct. 26, 1946, 4.

31. Taiwan sheng xingzheng zhangguan gongshu, *Taiwan xingzheng zhangguan gongshu gongbao* 2, no. 13, 4 *zi* 2144 (Apr. 15, 1948): 198.

32. Lai, Myers, and Wei, *A Tragic Beginning*, 71. A note on currency: as part of the takeover, the Chinese government banned the Japanese yen, and in May 1946 the Bank of Taiwan began issuing a new Taiwanese yuan (*Taibi yuan* 台幣元), valued at a

a number of illegal transfers in May and June provided the state with undeveloped land, 705 houses, 185 shops, 7 factories, 15 warehouses, almost 18 million yuan in savings, and an additional 9 million yuan in bonds, shares in credit unions, and cash.[33]

The relatively smooth process of deportation suggested that Taiwanese and Nationalist Chinese agreed about the need for decolonization of territory and society, but the instances of contention over the dispersal of Japanese assets hint at a battle that Taiwanese residents and Chinese transplants waged against each other. It was a struggle for control, not simply over resources, but over who would play the dominant role in governing Taiwan. More fundamentally, it was also a process of contestation for the identity of the island's residents. If there was agreement on the broad outlines of deterritorializing Japanized Taiwan, the manner of its reterritorialization was in much greater dispute. The Japanese were going, but how would their presence be remembered? Would local identities matter, or would they be erased in a new nation-building project? How would competing understandings of what constituted modernity be rationalized with each other? And would Taiwanese people exchange their ethnicity for a hegemonic Chinese nationalism, or would they hold to the identity they had forged under colonial rule? Some answers to these questions emerged in the processes of urban reconstruction and port redevelopment between 1945 and 1947.

Reconstructing Jilong, Phase 1 (1945–1947)

When the Nationalists arrived to complete the recovery (*huifu*) or "glorious retrocession" (*guangfu*) of Taiwan, their developmentalist mindset strongly colored their approach to the island in general and Jilong in particular. Mainlanders crossed the Taiwan Strait in sizable numbers during the last months of 1945. The great majority of the 100,000 who

---

one-to-one correspondence with the yen, or 30 Chinese yuan. This was used on the island until 1949, when a new Taiwanese yuan (*xin Taibi* 新台幣), or New Taiwan dollar (NT) was issued with an exchange rate of 1 NT to 40,000 old Taiwanese yuan, and 5 NT to 1 U.S. dollar. Ibid., 230n77.

33. Jilong shi zhengfu, *Jilong shi nianjian*, 165–66.

landed on the island by the end of the year had official roles as bureaucrats and soldiers, but almost 8,000 civilians arrived to pursue business and work opportunities.[34] The bulk of the military forces came ashore at Jilong on October 16 and 17, and Chen Yi, the first governor of the Taiwan Provincial Administration, flew to Taipei a week later. He formally took control of the island from the last Japanese governor-general, Andō Rikichi, on October 25, 1945. A mainland-based state once again governed Taiwan, although unlike the Qing, the Republic of China was a nation-state that espoused a complete integration of people, regime, and territory and an agenda of modernization through central planning. As William Kirby states, prewar ROC bureaucrats, and the engineers and technicians with whom they worked at the National Resources Commission (Guojia ziyuan weiyuanhui; NRC), were "consumed with the industrial metamorphosis of *national* life, planned by a central—and centralizing—government."[35] J. Megan Greene, in her crucial study of the developmental state in Taiwan, confirms that Chiang Kai-shek and the NRC directors embraced this vision both as a means to mobilize resources for the defeat of Japan, and to prepare for postwar reconstruction.[36] The new agents of the state faced the same questions that the Japanese addressed in 1895: How would they occupy, rule, and incorporate Taiwan? How would they impose their own national identity and deal with the identities of Taiwan's residents?

Jilong desperately needed rebuilding, a condition that it shared with Taiwan's other urban centers, particularly Gaoxiong and Taipei. During the late stages of the war, U.S. military forces in the Pacific worked their way northward toward Japan, driving the Japanese back from the areas they had conquered in Southeast Asia. This island-hopping strategy reached Taiwan in 1944 and 1945, bringing massive aerial bombing of the island's primary ports and military installations, rather than a land battle like the one later waged on Okinawa. The air war rained down devastation on Jilong, as U.S. planes dropped bombs on the city

---

34. See Lai, Myers, and Wei, *A Tragic Beginning*, especially chap. 3; Phillips, *Between Assimilation and Independence*, chap. 3. The figure of 100,000 comes from Lai et al., *Tragic Beginning*, 73; the 8,000 is from Lin Shengwei, "Zhengzhi suanshu," 45.

35. Kirby, "Engineering China"; quotation on 137, original italics.

36. Greene, *Origins of the Developmental State*.

FIGURE 6.3. The bombed wreckage of the Osaka Shipping Company building, near the Jilong Station. Image courtesy of USS *Block Island* Association, http://uss blockisland.org/Beta/V2-PhotoGallery/Photos_-_POW.html.

on twenty-five separate occasions beginning in the fall of 1944.[37] By the estimate of George Kerr, a U.S. official who served in Taiwan both before and after the war, the bombing destroyed more than 50 percent of the city's existing structures (fig. 6.3). Many of those that survived, such as the elegant dome-capped post office building, were so badly damaged that they had to be replaced. The wharves and dock facilities were barely operable, and several of the ships that had been moored in the harbor now sat on its bottom. Although statistics indicate fewer than 400 deaths in Jilong, Kerr estimated that almost half of the population suffered from the bombing campaign.[38] Gaoxiong, perhaps because it directly supplied

37. Jilong shi zhengfu, *Jilong shi nianjian*, 59.
38. Kerr, "Ports and Harbors—Keelung, 1946," Box 6, Folder 6.12, George Kerr Collection, Hoover Institution Archives, Stanford, CA.

the Japanese war effort in Southeast Asia, suffered more severe damage. Allied bombing destroyed around 90 percent of the port facilities there, causing extensive damage to the rest of the city as well.[39]

Jilong's population fluctuated considerably late in the war and in its immediate aftermath. It had more than 100,000 residents in the early 1940s, but during 1944 and 1945 there was a mass exodus as many fled to safety in the countryside, and by some accounts, when the war ended a mere 40,000 people remained in the city.[40] Afterward, people returned to Jilong at a rapid rate (table 6.1) and the population again reached close to 100,000 in late 1947, thanks in part to the addition of Qidu as a new city district.[41] Although most of the early-arriving Chinese passed through Jilong, they initially constituted a very small portion of Jilong's population. At the end of 1947, roughly 4,000 Chinese lived in Jilong, representing 4.07 percent of the total population. However, that number rose dramatically to 27,736 (or 20 percent) in 1949, and 50,851 (27 percent) in 1955.[42] By comparison, the Chinese constituted almost 10 percent of Taipei's population in 1947 but only 2 percent in Taizhong and 0.4 percent in Gaoxiong, although those percentages

39. Taiwan sheng xingzheng zhangguan gongshu minzhengchu mishushi, *Taiwan sheng canyihui diyiju diyici*; GSG, Ministry of Transportation (Jiaotongbu; JTB), microfilm 79, Jilong gangwu ju, ed., *Jilong gang*, Nov. 9, 1946, 0749.

40. Jilong shi zhengfu, *Jilong shi nianjian*, 24; GSG, Ministry of the Interior (Neizhengbu; NZB), microfilm 16, "Taiwan sheng Jilong shi ziran ji renwen gaikuang diaocha ziliao baogao shu," Sept. 1947, 0801; and Kerr, "Ports and Harbors—Keelung, 1946." These sources all cite the same number of residents, 40,454, in Jilong at the end of the war. No source is given for this number, and one source may in fact be the basis for the other two.

41. Different sources disagree on Jilong's immediate postwar population, deriving in part from the difficulty of keeping accurate records amid the chaos, and in part from the city's geographic expansion in 1947. The figures in table 6.1 are taken from data collected by the city government in 1946, but elsewhere the city lists a higher figure, 69,956, for the middle of that year, and another source gives even higher numbers for 1946. See Jilong shi zhengfu, *Jilong shi nianjian*, 26; GSG, NZB, microfilm 16, "Taiwan sheng Jilong shi ziran ji renwen gaikuang diaocha ziliao baogao shu," Sept. 1947, 0801–2. The latter source states that in mid-1947 the population had recovered to a total of 99,139. A 1988 edition of the city gazetteer lists a population of 99,465; Jilong shi zhengfu, *Renkou pian*, 34–35.

42. Jilong shi zhengfu minzhengju, *Hukou pian*, 211 and 216. This source uses the term *ta shengshi* ("other province or city") rather than *waishengren*.

Table 6.1. Jilong's wartime and postwar populations

Date	Taiwanese population			Foreign population			Total population
	Male	Female	Total	Male	Female	Total	
12/1944	36,229	32,453	68,682[a]	12,451	12,406	24,857	93,539
8/15/1945			31,084			9,370	40,454
12/1945	31,689	30,843	62,532	6,800	7,288	14,088	76,620
6/1946	32,692	32,445	65,137	1,277	1,265	2,542	67,679

SOURCE: Jilong shi zhengfu, Jilong shi nianjian, 24–26.

NOTE: In the original source, the Taiwanese were classified as Chinese, but there were at most a handful of mainlanders on the island in 1945 and just over a thousand by mid-1946, so I use "Taiwanese" for consistency.

[a] The original source states a total Taiwanese population of 67,682 for 12/1944, which does not match the sum of the parts.

rose to 38, 19, and 22 percent, respectively, by 1957.[43] Defeat by the Communists in China's civil war meant that, within a decade, Chinese affiliated with the Nationalists made up a portion of the population in Taiwan's main cities that was comparable to the earlier Japanese presence, and by some measures interethnic relations seemed less fraught after 1945. Intermarriage between Taiwanese and mainlanders occurred very rarely before 1955, which had as much to do with regulations against marriage among soldiers as it did the gulf between the two groups. Over time, however, such unions would constitute more than 10 percent of all marriages in Taiwan among those born before 1950.[44] That percentage was an order of magnitude above the rate of Taiwanese-Japanese unions.

Amid the disruptions following World War II, residents faced a resurgence of disease and crime, or "social ills" in the parlance of social work, both of which had been largely controlled during the latter part of the colonial period. Over the course of a few weeks in September and

43. Jilong shi zhengfu, Renkou pian, 35.
44. According to detailed research published by Wang Fu-ch'ang, marriage rates among all mainlanders was low until the 1960s, and most cases of intermarriage occurred between Taiwanese women and Chinese men. Wang Fu-ch'ang, "Guangfu hou Taiwan Hanren tonghun"; the figure of 10.62 percent is on 67.

October 1946, the local sanitation bureau reported sixty-eight cases of cholera, with thirty-three deaths; at the peak of the outbreak in early October, the mortality rate was much higher. However, the official report describes a successful mobilization of doctors, nurses, and assistants, including many high school students, to locate the epicenter of the disease, quarantine those afflicted, and launch a major inoculation drive to protect the city.[45] Crime, too, was on the rise after the war, with more than 250 instances of robbery, murder, assault, and endangerment reported between June and October of 1946.[46] These cases followed an earlier wave that swept the island in late 1945.[47]

Crime and disease were symptomatic of the severely depressed economic conditions.[48] A combination of bombing damage and loss of trade with Japan brought the local economy almost to a standstill for a time, as seen in a steep decline in the number of operating shops and markets, and a rise in prices for goods. Before the war there were more than 2,200 shops in the city, whereas afterward the number was down to 1,071. Despite the one-to-one exchange ratio for Japanese yen and Taiwan dollars, which should have controlled prices, the cost of pork, for example, quintupled from about 6 yuan (or yen) a half kilo in 1944 to 30 yuan in January 1946, and rice shot up astronomically from 2.25 yuan a deciliter to 99 yuan in the same time period. Prices continued to rise throughout 1946, although they may have stabilized at the new high levels by the late fall.[49] In short, Jilong entered the postwar period as a shattered version of its former self, with fifty years of physical, social, and economic construction largely reduced to rubble. The city's

45. Taiwan sheng xingzheng zhangguan gongshu minzheng, *Guanyu chengsong Jilong.* According to the report, from September 27 to October 5 the campaign gave injections to 70,522 people; if true, that would have been close to the entire population of the city. See also, in *MB*: "Jilong huoluan zheng," Oct. 1, 1946, 4; "Jilong bingshi qiwei xiaomi: qing fu faxian bingren duo ming," Oct. 3, 1946, 4; and "Jilong huoluan xufa: xian zheng jiajin fangbing," Oct. 5, 1946, 3.

46. "Jilong fanfei tongji," *MB*, Nov. 18, 1946, 4.

47. Fix, "Reading the Numbers."

48. Fix argues that economic concerns drove the 1945 crime wave; see ibid.

49. Jilong shi zhengfu, *Jilong shi nianjian*, 106–13. Recent authors describe a worsening economic collapse through the end of 1946 and into early 1947, which they blame to a large extent on the statist economic policies of Chen Yi. See Lai, Myers, and Wei, *A Tragic Beginning*, 80–89.

FIGURE 6.4. Rebuilding
Jilong after the devasta-
tion of war. Image cour-
tesy of the Library of
Congress, Washington,
DC.

reconstruction became one of the most important projects of Taiwan's
postwar renovation (see fig.6.4).

Initially, it appeared that the integration of Taiwan into ROC territory would be smooth, and that urban reconstruction was an issue
that would unite Chinese and Taiwanese. When the Seventieth Brigade
of the Nationalist Chinese Army arrived in Jilong on October 17, 1945,
they received a greeting diametrically opposite to the one that met the
Japanese army led by Prince Kitashirakawa in 1895. The Japanese forces
had landed up the coast, well out of range of Jilong's cannons, and then
fought their way into the city. In contrast, a large crowd met the Nationalist troops at the docks, waving flags and shouting, "Long live the
Republic of China!" One news article likened it to the reunion of two
long-lost siblings.[50] The influence of pre-1895 history remained strong
among the Taiwanese, but as Steven Phillips argues, their immediate

50. In *MB*, see "Wanren kong xiang huansheng leidong kangzhan zhuangshi an
di Taiwan," and "Jilong quan shi ru kuang," Oct. 18, 1945, 1. See also the account of

reactions covered a range from excitement to indifference to criticism of the slovenly appearance of the soldiers.[51] A number of sources indicate that at least parts of the new regime held Jilong in high regard, including publications about Taiwan that appeared between 1945 and early 1947, numerous government reports on Jilong and its harbor, and the detailed surveys produced by the NRC regarding Jilong's port and enterprises. Much like the Japanese colonial government before it, the Nationalist regime needed a conduit through which to move people and materials necessary to ruling and rebuilding the island, and it settled on Jilong as the first place to focus its efforts.

In fact, port cities held a position of special importance within the overall Nationalist vision of nation building and China's postwar reconstruction. In 1946, the government commissioned a New York engineering firm to survey China's thirteen most important ports and outline the measures and costs necessary to renovate and expand them. When Song Xishang, a maritime scholar and transportation official who fits Greene's description of the technicians who helped build China's developmental state, published a translation of these reports in 1958, he wrote in the preface: "Seaports occupy the gates of the country, and in regard to national defense, economy, transportation, and for promoting the people's livelihood, they are very significant."[52] Another study by a shipping scholar and long-time official in the Transportation Bureau, Wang Guang, originally published in 1951, described ports as essential for helping both national politics and the economy to flourish, and for controlling markets. Therefore, he said, nation-states devoted extra attention to their development.[53] These mainland-oriented experts did not include Taiwan's ports in their rankings—even the 1957 edition of Wang Guang's book listed the section on Taiwan as "temporarily omitted," although it counted Jilong and Gaoxiong among China's international harbors—but Taiwan-specific sources express the same set of ideas and plans.

noted pro-Taiwanese independence leader Peng Min-min, in Lai, Myers, and Wei, *A Tragic Beginning*, 155–56.

51. Phillips, *Between Assimilation and Independence*, 55.

52. Meiguo gang gong diaochatuan, *Zhongguo zhongyao haigang gaiyao*, preface, 1.

53. Wang Guang, *Zhongguo gangkou lun*, 2. I thank Shirley Ye for directing me to this source as well as to Song's translation.

The Chinese-dominated Jilong Municipal Government (Shi zhengfu) and Jilong Port Authority (Gangwuju), established in November 1945 on the basis of the Japanese-era institutions, expressed high hopes that the city could become a major node for international import and export, and for transshipment of goods from the mainland. One study compared it to Shanghai and another said that it was "the third best port in the East."[54] Variations on this statement appear with such frequency that they seem to have become a sort of mantra. A 1947 guide to Taiwan targeted at secondary school students said, "Jilong has attained the same position for Taiwan that Shanghai holds for the heartland," and a year later another guidebook referred to Jilong as "Taiwan's most important port."[55] In his opening remarks to the first meeting of the Taiwan Provincial Assembly in May 1946, delegate Yan Qinxian, the son of Yan Yunnian, described Jilong as "Taiwan's port of entry" and outlined a plan for regenerating the city through public and private initiatives.[56] These statements may have exaggerated Jilong's potential, but there is no question that during the first years of Nationalist rule, it was the principal point of ingress and egress for the island, and its reconstruction was essential to the incorporation of Taiwan. In 1946 Chen Yi endorsed the vision of city leaders to turn Jilong into a city of global importance.[57] The new Port Authority planned to clear the inner harbor, restore the wharves and other facilities to working condition, expand the outer harbor, and complete a breakwater that had been begun in the last years of Japanese rule.[58]

The harbor was the centerpiece of reconstruction, but urban planners in the city government drew up an ambitious long-range agenda. They called for a major alteration in land-use patterns that reserved the current downtown area for maritime activities, and shifted the political,

54. GSG, JTB, microfilm 79, 0722; Jilong gangwuju, *Jilong Gang*, 13; and Jilong shi zhengfu, *Jilong shi nianjian*, 185–87. The top two ports are not named.
55. Song Jiatai, *Taiwan dili*, 116; *Taiwan zhinan* (*Taiwan Guidebook*), in Yang and Chen, *Minjian sizang, chanye pian yi*, 293.
56. Taiwan sheng xingzheng zhangguan gongshu minzhengchu mishushi, *Taiwan sheng canyihui diyiju diyici*, 18.
57. "Chen zhangguan shicha Jilong," *MB*, 1946.8.15, 2.
58. GSG, JTB, Microfilm 79, 0846-47, 0797-800; and Jilong gangwuju, *Jilong gang*, 143–46.

residential, and cultural center southward into less developed regions away from the harbor. The new city center would contain the city hall, police headquarters, museum, library, athletic stadium, a public hall named in honor of Sun Yat-sen, schools, markets, parks, and tree-lined boulevards. The plan also remodeled the core of Big Jilong to hold branches of the city government and police, and new light-rail lines extending north and east along the coast, and east alongside the canal, which was to be widened and lengthened into the hinterland. It mentioned new schools, housing, parks, hospitals, telephone lines, markets, and a passenger rail station, and designated the area around Takasago Park as the new commercial center. The planners' ambitions even extended to a zoo, a botanical garden, a golf course, and a two-runway airport.[59] It is not entirely clear who designed this remarkable blueprint, although the Chinese dominance of the city government and the strong similarities between this outline and the practices of urban development in Chengdu, Nanjing, and Shanghai during the 1920s and 1930s suggest that it epitomized the Nationalists' attempt to inscribe their vision of urban life on the Taiwanese landscape.[60] Their radical, and radically compartmentalized, conception of urban development, had it been fulfilled, would have advanced de- and reterritorialization by largely erasing the Japanese city plan and replacing it with a Nationalist Chinese urbanism that had, ironically, been shaped by the earlier study of Japanese models.[61]

The NRC brought its developmentalist mindset to Taiwan in the form of a major effort to survey, catalog, and manage Jilong's human, natural, and industrial resources. It was active nationwide in the immediate postwar years, producing well over 10,000 files of reports, plans, and other documents, and Taiwan was by no means the center of its attention. Still, dozens of files from the years 1945–47 addressed conditions in and plans for Jilong, and dozens more connected to the city in more tangential ways through general requests for information

59. Jilong shi zhengfu, *Jilong shi nianjian*, 223–29.

60. Stapleton, *Civilizing Chengdu*; Musgrove, *China's Contested Capital*; Lipkin, *Useless to the State*, 9 and chap. 1; Henriot, *Shanghai*, chap. 7.

61. There is a contrast here to Taipei, where the new government planned the city largely in keeping with the unfulfilled designs of the Japanese Government-General. See Allen, *Taipei*, 41.

or widely broadcast reports. The planners at the NRC devoted more attention to Gaoxiong, perhaps because it was in more dire need of attention, and the commission's early concern presaged the ultimate rise of the southern port as Taiwan's primary maritime link to the outside world. Nevertheless, the NRC's interest in industrial enterprises and resources such as electric power, coal and copper mining, shipbuilding, chemical fertilizers, and cement meant that Jilong figured significantly in its plans for renovating Taiwan and incorporating the province into the overall process of centrally planned and scientific national reconstruction.[62]

A few examples from the NRC files illustrate its plans for Taiwan in general and Jilong in particular, and also reveal the colonialist, expropriationist nature of the postwar Nationalist governance of Taiwan. A study of the Taiwan Electric Power Company prepared in October 1946 outlined an overall economic plan that, in its emphasis on industrial self-sufficiency, bore an uncanny resemblance to the Japanese Government-General's objective of making Taiwan pay for itself. The document encouraged production in the sugar, mining, paper-making, cement, and fertilizer industries, all of which could expand through locally available materials. It further noted that, whereas the largest native power supply was the war-damaged Sun-Moon Lake hydro-electric plant, Jilong's existing thermal plant had the highest generating capacity on the island, so its restoration and expansion were crucial for helping Taiwan Electric complete its planned mission, "to fulfill the demand for the orderly economic development of the island."[63] A survey of Japanese-built fertilizer factories in Jilong and Gaoxiong indicated that the NRC intended not merely that Taiwan should become

62. A search of the digital archive of Academia Historica (GSG-SD), made on July 14, 2014, found that the NRC opened 12,011 files between 1945 and 1947, many of which extended beyond 1947. Of these files, 1,259 were sent to or received from Taiwan; 180 contained reports from or instructions to Jilong; and 415 addressed Gaoxiong in some capacity.

63. GSG-SD, 003-020200-0374: NRC to Ministry of the Economy (Jingjibu; JJB), "Taiwan dianli ziliao," 1948, quote on page 7. The report was written in English, which supports Megan Greene's conclusion that China's postwar technicians used foreign expertise to justify their plans to the government. See Greene, *Origins of the Developmental State*, 142.

self-reliant, but that it should contribute to the nation as a whole. "Due to the large demand for chemical fertilizers in China," the authors wrote, "the rehabilitation and expansion of the present phosphate plants in Formosa will be the most effective means of partially relieving the situation." The foreign technicians who completed the survey viewed Jilong as the most important center of fertilizer production on Taiwan, although they suggested that Gaoxiong would ultimately become more productive and thus more significant.[64] The NRC envisioned Jilong and its industrial enterprises as important pieces in its centrally driven initiative to rapidly reconstruct Taiwan, incorporate it into China, and accelerate its contributions to building and modernizing the Chinese nation.

The Nationalist regime's transformative agenda went beyond the technocrats' plans to embrace a reterritorialization of the island. It announced its intentions to nationalize Taiwan at both the industrial and cognitive levels in the weeks before and after its formal assumption of sovereignty, by publishing excerpts of Chiang Kai-shek's *China's Destiny* in one of the new Chinese-language papers, *The People's Press* (*Minbao*).[65] The physical reconstruction of Jilong reflected the larger effort at re-Sinicization, although the Nationalists frequently built with remnants from the Japanese era. For example, the new administration renamed each of the city's fourteen bridges and consolidated the city's previous sixteen wards (*ku*) into five much larger districts (*qu*; indicated with the same character but representing a different area) that it subdivided into 103 hamlets, or neighborhoods (*cunli*). Although the Nationalist authorities undertook this administrative reorganization as part of their plan for remaking Taiwan, the previous era remained written in the city's jurisdictional geography. The Irifune and Gijū areas,

---

64. GSG-SD, 003-020200-0343: "Ziyuan weiyuanhui jishuyuan beiwanglu ji Taiwan linsuanyan gongchang chongjian jihua," NRC to JJB, 1947; report in English. See also GSG-SD, 003-010301-0117: "Ziyuan weiyuanhui Taiwan ge shiye gongzuo jihua deng an," from NRC to JJB, 1946–47, for an overview of NRC plans for several nationalized companies, including Taiwan Electric, Taiwan Cement, Taiwan Fertilizer, and Taiwan Shipbuilding, all of which had significant operations in and around Jilong.

65. Beginning around October 11 and ending on November 14, the paper printed Chiang's treatise in thirty-two sections, each on the paper's first or second page.

located in the formerly Japanese-dominated Small Jilong, and the Takasago neighborhood around the park south of the harbor, all retained the same characters but with Chinese pronunciations: Ruchuan, Yizhong, and Gaosha, respectively. The new Bo'ai neighborhood was named for Yan Yunnian's Jilong Fraternity (*bo'ai*) Group, which had its home there.[66]

The Nationalists' approach extended to a cultural reformulation of the Taiwanese. Echoing the Japanese Government-General's emphasis on education, the new civil administration devoted considerable attention to revising school curricula and teaching the new national language (*guoyu* instead of *kokugo*), Mandarin Chinese. Across Taiwan, Chinese officials faced a populace within which Hokkien/Minnanese was almost ubiquitous, Japanese widespread, Hakka prevalent, and indigenous languages scattered, but for whom Chinese played almost no role in daily life. This linguistic profile presented a serious obstacle for the Nationalist officials, most of whom spoke sometimes heavily accented Chinese and something other than Hokkien, and many if not most civilians and soldiers spoke their local language or dialect and maybe Chinese, especially after 1948.[67] To bridge the language gap and promote its transformative agenda, Chen Yi's government stressed language training in the curriculum of the new national schools (*guomin xuexiao*), and established numerous extracurricular Chinese language courses for both children and adults.[68] Officials explicitly stated that their goal was to free the Taiwanese from the colonial education that had enslaved them and separated them from their ancestral homeland.[69] However, the Chinese government placed too great an emphasis on language as a determinant of identity, because most Taiwanese viewed learning Chinese, as they had

---

66. Jilong shi zhengfu, *Jilong shi nianjian*, 16–17.

67. Cheng, "Language Unification," and Wachman, "Competing Identities," 53–54.

68. During the war, all elementary schools within the Japanese empire, including both common and elementary schools in Taiwan, had been renamed National Schools (*kokumin gakkō*); see Tsurumi, *Japanese Colonial Education*, 112. Chen Yi himself was an exception, as he spoke both Hokkien and Japanese.

69. Jilong shi zhengfu, *Jilong shi nianjian*, 121.

Japanese, in functional terms.[70] Thus what Phillips has described as a "mania" among the Taiwanese for Chinese language was likely no more than the recognition of the utility, or necessity, of speaking it.[71]

Both local and provincial governments issued plans for educational and cultural reform. The state implemented a variety of methods and media—education, newspapers, movies, public lectures, and so on—to change practices that displayed Japanese influences. Late in 1947 the provincial government received a report from the Taiwan New Life Movement Promotion Committee (Taiwan xin shenghuo yundong tuijinhui), an association that extended one of the Republican regime's most important programs of the 1930s to Taiwan. The document stated that many shop signs and public announcements in Taipei were still written in Japanese, and added that, if things were bad in the provincial capital, they must be much worse in other locations. The provincial government followed the committee's recommendations forcefully and banned the public use of Japanese because it feared that such a "poisonous remnant" (yudu) could endanger the people's national consciousness (minzu yishi).[72] This threat mattered because strengthening national identity was a cornerstone of Nationalist rule in Taiwan.[73]

Chen Yi explicitly expressed the congruence between urban construction, modernization, and re-Sinicization when he told Jilong's elites that the renovation of their city depended on removing the pernicious influence of Japan. During an official visit in mid-1946, the city's leaders spoke to Chen of their hopes for public and private cooperation to transform Jilong into a global port city. Chen responded with his own vision: the Taiwanese government employees must be patriotic,

70. Alan Wachman argues that the Taiwanese came to feel a sense of inferiority because they did not speak Mandarin, but I did not find evidence of that for this period. See Wachman, "Competing Identities," 53.

71. Phillips, Between Assimilation and Independence, 43.

72. Taiwan sheng xingzheng zhangguan gongshu, Taiwan xingzheng zhangguan gongshu gongbao 2, no. 20 (Jan. 26, 1947): 310–11; no. 23, 3 zi 8659 (Jan. 29, 1947): 360–61; and no. 53, zi 109328 (Dec. 2, 1947): 819–20. The last document refers to the poisonous or pernicious remains of the Japanese.

73. It was one of the main principles listed in the Draft Outline for the Takeover of Taiwan. See Kirby et al., State and Economy, 115.

and "must eliminate their bad bureaucratic habits . . . and erase the bad practices left by the Japanese."[74] For Chen and other Nationalists, the Taiwanese were not fully modern, and as such they constituted a drag on Chinese nation building. This harsh critique of the Japanese period represented a sharp change of opinion for Chen, who as governor of Fujian had lauded Japan's accomplishments in its colony during the 1930s. Evidently, the war and the difficulty of incorporating Taiwan had caused a shift in his thinking. His specific criticism of Taiwanese elites displayed a substantive division between islanders and mainlanders that would become much more starkly defined in the coming months.

Reconstruction and the Struggle
over Local Governance

The key institution responsible for designing and implementing Jilong's reconstruction was the city government, which quickly took shape in the fall of 1945, although formal regulations for the administrative agencies of Jilong, and Gaoxiong as well, were not issued until 1948. Islandwide, the government shrank dramatically, to roughly half of what it had been under the Japanese, a reduction that took jobs away from some thirty-six thousand Taiwanese and gave them a much smaller share of the remaining positions.[75] To help fill that administrative vacuum and facilitate reconstruction, local officials set up ad hoc municipal councils that drew on Taiwanese individuals who had either been involved with the previous municipal body or were prominent local citizens. Following the model deployed to rebuild Taipei, the city and provincial governments jointly established a new company, the Rejuvenation Corporation (Fuxing gongsi), designed to lead residents in repairing war damage and providing housing for the people

74. "Chen zhangguan shicha Jilong," *MB*, Aug. 15, 1946, 2.
75. See Lai, Myers, and Wei, *A Tragic Beginning*, 65. Prior to 1945 Taiwanese workers had held almost half of government offices, but that fraction dropped down to one-fifth.

who moved into the city.[76] City and provincial authorities also mandated the establishment of a number of collaborative organizations (*hezuo tuanti*) to further mobilize people and resources. By the end of 1946, officials and citizens had created eight of these organizations, all built from previously existing credit unions and other groups. Gaoxiong's nine postwar collaborative organizations also emerged out of prewar cognates, but both Taipei and Tainan saw the creation of multiple entirely new organizations.[77] The local institutions joined the interim Port Authority in assuming primary responsibility for rebuilding Jilong.

Jilong's elite society, and the individuals who played leading roles in it during the retrocession period, differed from society in the Japanese era in a number of ways. Perhaps most significantly, because of the rapid departure of Japanese settlers and the tumultuous climate of the late 1940s, it is not as clear as it was in the earlier period precisely who were the key pillars of local society. In addition, the sources on this era do not provide substantial information on the Chinese who settled in Jilong, outside of naming those who held positions in the city government. It is, therefore, not possible to provide the same balanced picture of Jilong society for the postwar years as it was for the Japanese period. Nevertheless, a few Taiwanese men emerged as important figures who took on the role of gatekeeper as they helped define imagined borders between Chinese and Taiwanese. Much like their Japanese-era counterparts, they held prominence in the context of local politics, specifically through debates that took place in the Jilong City Council (Jilong shi canyihui), a body that residents formed in the fall of 1946 to convey their concerns to the city government, over who would have a say in how the city was rebuilt and reterritorialized. Many of these individuals also led key local institutions, and

76. "Chuangshe fuxing gongsi," *MB*, July 10, 1946, 2, evening edition. The Jilong city government was supposed to provide 40 percent of the funding, but owing to financial shortfalls at the city level the provincial government paid almost all of the cost. See also "Jilong fuxing gongsi wei baoban ye dongjia," *GSB*, Nov. 12, 1946, 2.

77. Taiwan sheng xingzheng zhangguan gongshu, *Taiwan sheng tongji yaolan*, table 151; "Ge xian shi yi chengli hezuoshe," 190. Jilong's collaborative organizations were re-formed (*gaizu*), whereas others were newly established (*xin chengli*).

some served as delegates to the National Assembly. Although municipal and colonial assemblies had existed under Japanese rule, their apparently greater significance after retrocession highlighted a break between pre-1945 and post-1945 conditions, as the Nationalist government, even at its most authoritarian, allowed some manifestations of its democratic ideology to operate.

The individual men who served as gatekeepers in the postwar era— it was, again, men who filled this role—were not the same as those who had led under the Japanese, although this was not the result of a conscious effort on anyone's part. With the notable exception of the head of the Yan family, Yan Qinxian, few of the old top-tier elites played important roles after the handover. Most of them had either died or were sent to Japan. Xu Zisang lived to see the end of the war and the first days of retrocession but not much more, and Cai Qingyun assumed a much less public role as a contributor to Jilong's first postwar gazetteer.[78] However, there was no effort to overturn Taiwan's social order by targeting collaborators with mass arrests and punishment.[79] Nor do we yet have evidence in Taiwan of popular discourse like the debates that Yun Xia has found on the mainland that targeted Chinese women who had engaged in intimate relations with Japanese men or male Chinese collaborators.[80] Some Taiwanese initially sought retribution against those who had grown rich working with the Japanese, the so-called imperial running gentry (*yuyong shenshi*), but those sentiments faded amid the realities of dealing with the Chinese state, an entity that acted with ambivalence in arresting and prosecuting traitors to the nation (*Hanjian*).[81] It held high-profile trials to convict and execute leaders of the wartime puppet regimes in Nanjing, but even though some three hundred Taiwanese were arrested, not many saw trial, and those who did received lenient sentences.[82]

78. For Cai, see Wu Huifang, *Jilong Zhongyuan ji*, 33.

79. Phillips, *Between Assimilation and Independence*, 65–66, 86.

80. Xia, "Engendering Contempt."

81. Lo, "Trials of the Taiwanese," 279–315. See also Xu, "'Taiwan guangfu zhijingtuan,'" 121–24, 139. Pepper, *Civil War in China*, 9–16.

82. Zanasi, "Globalizing Hanjian"; Brook, "Hesitating before the Judgment of History"; Lo, "Trials of the Taiwanese," 305, 308.

Jilongese of the generation born and raised under Japanese rule had the opportunity to follow two paths to elite status.[83] One, exemplified by the city council's chair, Huang Shushui, derived from prominence in the establishment institutions of Japanese-era Taiwan. Huang's antecedents made a fortune in gold mining east of Jilong before moving into the small port just before the Japanese arrived. His father quickly gained stature as a business associate of Xu Zisang's and through his social service as a local welfare commissioner, and Huang himself graduated from Ishizaka Sōsaku's night school, received further schooling in Japan, and then began working for Xu and his father. He developed commercial ties to the Yan family, served on the Jilong municipal council, and was even elected to the mock city assembly in 1930. After retrocession, his earlier success apparently aided his advancement because he became a delegate to the National Assembly and chair of the Jilong Chamber of Commerce (Jilong zongshanghui), and advised the government when it sent trade delegations to Japan.[84]

The other route to elite status, followed by the council's vice chair, Yang Yuanding, depended on one's prior opposition to the Japanese regime. Yang received his education in Taoyuan, after which he moved to Jilong, quickly became a leader in the local branch of the Taiwan People's Party, and out-polled Huang to get his own seat in the mock assembly. With fewer opportunities under the stricter policies of the 1930s, Yang went to Shanghai after the war began, where he reportedly engaged in anti-Japanese resistance. Those credentials got him his positions in the city government and on the board of the Jilong Chamber of Commerce, and enabled him to join Huang and Yan Qinxian as delegates to the National Assembly.[85] In contrast to the harsh

83. Phillips looks at four categories of postwar elites, at least two of which overlap with those I describe here. See Phillips, *Between Assimilation and Independence*, chap. 6.

84. See Huang Shushui's biography in Tang Yu, "Bei Tai renwu zhuan," 125–28, and that of his father, Huang Xiangchi, in Jilong shi wenxian weiyuanhui, *Renwu pian*, 20–30. His presence on the colonial municipal council is noted in "Shin shi kyōgiin no nentō kan," *NS*, Jan. 8, 1931, 4; his election to the mock assembly comes from "Moni xuanju zhou yiyuan dangjuzhe ru zuo," *TMB*, Jan. 17, 1931, 17–18.

85. Jilong shi wenxian weiyuanhui, *Renwu pian*, 25–26. According to this biography the Japanese colonial police frequently imprisoned him, including for one

anti-Japanese rhetoric of the Nationalist Party, postwar Taiwan's first group of elites contained both individuals who had thrived under Japanese control and those who had struggled against it. The realities of governance forced the Chinese regime to be more flexible in practice than in rhetoric.[86]

Although these and other Taiwanese individuals held important positions and played significant roles, mainlanders, such as the new mayor, Shi Yanhan, quickly dominated the top layers of local government. By the end of 1946, Nationalists held the position of bureau chief in every single division of the city government and police, as well as most of the second-tier positions. A few Taiwanese served as government technicians and a number held positions as junior officers; a small handful of Japanese at those ranks also continued to work for the government, before they were deported. At the lowest level, most government employees and police officers were Taiwanese, and Taiwanese leadership was also strong at the district level.[87] To carry out the crucial work of swift reconstruction, the Nationalists had to employ some Taiwanese, much as the Japanese had relied on islanders to assert control and implement programs. In return, the Taiwanese elites gained a certain amount of status and power. There was, however, a key difference between the Chinese and the Japanese. Although Japanese such as Ishizaka Sōsaku and Kimura Kutarō swiftly established themselves within a Jilong society that was small, weakly unified, and relatively porous to Japanese colonial power, Chinese like Shi Yanhan and his associates in government stood outside of the social framework that had solidified over the preceding decades. Thus, Chinese dominance replicated the earlier boundaries between the ruling minority and the ruled majority, and the connections between the governing state and Taiwanese elites, but with less immediate direct involvement in the social life of the city.

---

ten-month stint after the People's Party was disbanded. For his various political activities, see "Difang tongxin, Jilong: Minzhongdang yuan zangshi," *MB*, Oct. 4, 1930, 8, and "Moni xuanju zhou yiyuan dangjuzhe ru zuo," *MB*, Jan. 17, 1931, 17–18.

86. Lo points out that Taiwanese doctors also retained their pre-1945 prominence after the change of regime. See Lo, *Doctors within Borders*, 24.

87. "Jilong shi renshi qingxing: benshengren jie ju xiaceng," *MB*, Nov. 21, 1946, 4; "Jilong quzhang xuanju," *MB*, Nov. 11, 1946, 4.

In spite of some remarkable early progress on urban renovation, increasingly evident tensions in Jilong reflected the sharpening divisions between Taiwanese residents and the Chinese arrivals. By early 1947 officials and residents could point with pride to a list of successes: they had restored the harbor and repaired wharves and warehouses to accommodate trade; cleaned up most of the rubble left by the aerial bombing; restarted basic necessities like plumbing and electricity; and rebuilt roads, floodwalls, and reservoirs.[88] In addition, they had repaired and reopened many schools, and set up programs for teaching Mandarin Chinese.[89] These efforts set the city on the road to recovery, but they failed to assuage the enmity that began growing between Chinese and Taiwanese leaders during 1946. A dispute flared at a three-day meeting of the Jilong City Council that fall, and Shi Yanhan bore the brunt of it. One councilor expressed the frustration of his colleagues when he complained that too many of the schools were still damaged, and that one still had no working toilet. The mayor assured him that school renovation would be completed the following year. Others asked about a planned Charity Center (Jiuji yuan), wondering when it would open, how large its budget would be, and how many people it would employ, in light of the city's massive unemployment problem. Shi replied that it would be larger and better funded than initially planned.[90] A Taiwanese businessman named Ye Songtao spoke more accusingly: "It appears that the city government does not care about the economic problems of the city residents." Mayor Shi responded simply, "The city cares."[91]

88. "Gang zheng zhongxin fenwei liang an," *GSB*, Jan. 1, 1947, page illegible. Pictures in the city yearbook for 1946, though of poor quality, show dramatic progress in removing wreckage and rebuilding many damaged structures. See Jilong shi zhengfu, *Jilong shi nianjian*.

89. The City Council launched a special initiative for school repair in October 1946. See "Jilong shi canyihui yu niansi, ri kai di san ci linshi huiyi," *MB*, Oct. 26, 1946, 4.

90. Officials and residents disagreed on the size of the unemployment problem. One council member said that Jilong then had 20,000 unemployed workers, but the city government's survey found a mere 1,104 jobless workers in Jilong in the month of August. See Jilong shi zhengfu, *Jilong shi nianjian*, 132.

91. "Ge shi canyihui shizheng guozhong xingshi," *MB*, Dec. 7, 1946, 4. Some of the information in this paragraph and the next is from "Ge shi canyihui zhuijiu renshi

Some Taiwanese residents made more pointed comments about the exalted status of the Chinese in Jilong. One representative complained that mainlanders filled all of the high-class restaurants and businesses, and summed up his feelings rather bluntly: "It is like the difference between heaven and earth."[92] The councilors agreed that the root of such problems was Chinese dominance of the bureaucracy, at the expense of positions for Taiwanese. Yang Yuanding stated that at the end of the Japanese period, 134 Taiwanese worked for the city government, but a year later there were just over half as many, 74, compared with 76 mainlanders. "The current employment policies of the city's government," he stated, "are exactly like the enslavement policies of Japanese imperialism." Yang's goal had long been to give Taiwanese islanders a larger voice in local affairs, and to him this situation was all too familiar. The mayor responded, weakly though not incorrectly, that the size of the government itself had contracted, and added that the number of positions for Taiwanese would expand, but he said that for the time being Chinese dominated in leadership positions because he wanted to work with those whom he most trusted.[93]

Within a short time, the Taiwanese began to clarify the boundary between themselves and the Chinese transplants in the context of rebuilding Jilong, where they saw most clearly their limited opportunities and the lack of state attention to their needs. Steven Phillips has argued that they welcomed the change of regime as a chance to finally have greater influence over events in their homeland, but they soon became disillusioned with the realities of working under the Nationalists.[94] Furthermore, at some point in the reconstruction process priorities diverged. All agreed on the importance of restoring the city, but the agents of the state were primarily concerned with consolidating their position and used harbor renovation purely in the service of strengthening their state and building their nation, to facilitate Taiwan's self-sufficiency and its ability to provide a surplus for projects across the strait. In contrast,

wenti," *MB*, Dec. 4, 1946, 4; and "Youling zhiyuan ruo wenti," *MB*, Dec. 6, 1946, 4. At this time city councils were meeting all over the island and dealing with many similar issues.

92. "Ge shi canyihui zhuijiu renshi wenti," *MB*, Dec. 4, 1946, 4.
93. Ibid.
94. Phillips, *Between Assimilation and Independence*, chap. 7.

the Taiwanese residents were much more concerned with the well-being of their social community. To put it another way, conflict arose over the difference between protecting national (Chinese) and ethnic (Taiwanese) identities. By the end of 1946 the simmering tension was approaching a flashpoint. The spark that briefly ignited the island came precisely two months into the new year.

Localism and Ethnicity in the February 28th Incident

When violence broke out in Taipei on February 27 and 28, 1947, it fanned discontent into a major conflagration. Taiwanese residents directed their attacks against mainlanders in general, and particularly against members of the police and military, and elites called for major political reform. After a few days of escalating demands and unrest, Chen Yi agreed with the suggestion of his superiors in Nanjing that reinforcements should be dispatched to the island. The troops came ashore at Jilong and spread out across the island, arresting or killing anyone who appeared to resist. The Nationalist forces swiftly crushed the main urban uprising, but their mopping-up campaign in the countryside continued into May. Thousands died in the crackdown, and thousands more were imprisoned, which effectively put an end to such acts of overt resistance.[95] The uprising has generally been treated as an almost inevitable clash arising out of the different goals of Chinese and Taiwanese factions, and the unsettled atmosphere of political transition and modernization. It has been interpreted as the genesis-moment for Taiwanese nationalism, and the brutal suppression is often used as justification for Taiwanese independence. However, a

95. The general course of events is well laid out in the first major work in English on the subject. See Lai, Myers, and Wei, *A Tragic Beginning*, chaps. 4–5. This book explores the numbers of dead according to then-available sources, with estimates ranging between the extremes of five hundred and one hundred thousand, and settles on something in the vicinity of ten thousand killed. See also Phillips, *Between Assimilation and Independence*, chap. 4.

close examination of the 2-28 Incident in Jilong, based on government reports and the reminiscences of witnesses and participants, suggests an alternate interpretation. Rather than marking the transformation of Taiwanese ethnicity into Taiwanese nationalism, the clash represented an expression of the border defense that Taiwanese people had been engaged in since the 1930s and early 1940s.

What began with police harassment of a cigarette seller revealed the islandwide breadth of Taiwanese consciousness and frustrations, as the incident sparked uprisings in all major cities and large towns. Word of the unrest spread quickly to Jilong, first to the army garrison and then to the general population, and some people immediately took to the streets as February twenty-seventh turned into the twenty-eighth. The demonstrators, who likely included both Jilong and Taipei residents—the official report emphasized the influence of "ruffians from Taipei"—directed their attacks against the Jilong military outpost, police, and those civilians they identified as Chinese.[96] Local security officials declared martial law in the morning and held an emergency meeting with the police, members of the City Council, and local district heads in an effort to keep the peace. The civilian officials were charged with convincing local citizens to remain calm and not take part in the unrest.[97]

These initial measures had little impact, and the violence escalated. Reports spread through Jilong that so-called hooligans were preparing a major demonstration on the following afternoon, March 1. Police, military police, and regular soldiers went out to halt any unrest, resulting in violent clashes throughout the city, especially around the harbor. One newly arrived Chinese man learned of the unrest while at a barbershop downtown and hurried back to his rooming house in the west of the city, pretending to be a local to avoid being beaten. On his way, he saw crowds he identified as Taiwanese attacking civilians and soldiers gathered in Gaosha Park and near the train station. He made it back to his residence unscathed, but three of his roommates, also

96. "Jilong shi 'Ererba' shijian rizhi," in Jian Shenghuang, *Ererba shijian dang'an huibian*, 2:150.

97. Ibid., 149–50; and Chen Fangming, *Taiwan zhanhou shi ziliao xuan*, 182–83.

Chinese, returned in the evening bearing injuries.[98] Earlier that day, in the nearby town of Ruifang, a mob of youths marched on the train station shouting, "Beat the deficient corrupt officials!" and "Mainlanders wake up! Taiwan has nothing to eat because of you!"[99] Similar activities occurred across the island in the early days of March, with violent unrest arising in Taizhong, Tainan, Jiayi, and Gaoxiong by March 3, all of it targeting mainlanders on the streets, on trains, and wherever they had taken refuge.[100] Not all Chinese were wealthy, and ties of class or acquaintance could bridge the ethnic-national divide, but all transplants nonetheless faced real danger.

A brief calm came to Jilong on March 2, and the following day the authorities lifted martial law. The City Council set up a local branch of the 2-28 Resolution Committee (Ererba chuli weiyuanhui), under Yang Yuanding's leadership, to respond to the recent events. However, this early peace was simply the eye of the storm, and in the following days crowds continued to gather. On March 4, Jilong's Resolution Committee requested 5,000 sacks of flour from the government to alleviate a food shortage. The next day, as unauthorized crowds continued to gather, it requested the creation of an independent security maintenance team (zhi'an weichi dui) and asked that all security agents not carry guns while on patrol, to help reduce tensions.[101] A few days earlier, near Ruifang, some two thousand people had gathered to discuss matters of local security. According to an official report, most of those present spoke Japanese.[102] These efforts to quell the unrest had little effect, for on March 7 and 8 things reached another crisis point, at least from the state's point of view, when a group of protestors in Jilong briefly occupied both the city government and Port Authority offices

---

98. "Jilong wenjian," in Taiwan zhengyi chubanshe, Taiwan Ererba shijian, 91–96. The author, writing under what was likely a pseudonym, Zhan Zhou ("develop the continent"), referred to the Taiwanese acquaintance as a local friend (bendi pengyou).

99. Jian Shenghuang, Ererba shijian dang'an huibian 2:150; "Jilong qu shu Ererba shibian jingguo qingxing baogaoshu," in Jian Shenghuang, Ererba shijian dang'an huibian, 11:353.

100. Lai, Myers, and Wei, A Tragic Beginning, 124–31.

101. Jian Shenghuang, Ererba shijian dang'an huibian, 2:152–53.

102. Ibid., 11:353–55.

and again attacked the military garrison.[103] Events in Jilong paralleled those elsewhere, such as in Gaoxiong, where locals demanded the surrender of the military garrison, and Taizhong, where activists seized weapons and established their own militia.[104]

By this time troops were already on their way from the mainland, and on March 8 and 9 units of Fujian military police and soldiers from the Nationalist Army landed in Jilong harbor. This time no one welcomed them with flags and cheers of "Long live the Republic of China," and they came ready for battle. Up until that point, the authorities in Taiwan had merely tried to control the demonstrations, not completely suppress them, and at times they had been conciliatory toward Taiwanese demands. From the moment the reinforcements landed, however, the state's response became systematic destruction of the resistance. In Jilong, soldiers went door to door in search of able-bodied men, who were brought before the police. As had happened in 1895, military forces quickly defeated the open resistance, and within two days the Nationalist regime had, by its own account, restored peace to the city.[105] By March 11, the military had suppressed the uprising in other cities, although the pacification efforts continued in the towns and mountainous regions well into the spring.[106] From the point of view of the Nationalist government, it had swiftly, effectively, and most of all, justifiably crushed the opposition.

Eyewitness accounts and published surveys of the events in Jilong emphasize the indiscriminate nature of the violence, and they shed light on the identities that came into conflict in the uprising.[107] Oral

103. Ibid., 2:154–55.

104. Lai, Myers, and Wei, *A Tragic Beginning*, 127–28, 130.

105. Jian Shenghuang, *Ererba shijian dang'an huibian*, 2:155–56. According to this report, by March 10 "the entire city glowed brightly," a phrase that belied the fact that March was the bloodiest phase of the crackdown, as the majority of deaths occurred between March 8 and March 20. Zhang Yanxian, "Ererba minzhong shiguan," 11–13.

106. Lai, Myers, and Wei, *A Tragic Beginning*, 124–31; and Jian Shenghuang, *Ererba shijian dang'an huibian*, 11:147–50.

107. A wave of 2-28 oral histories hit the shelves in Taiwan beginning in 1989, with multiple volumes produced for most major cities. For Jilong, there are two major collections, Zhang Yanxian, *Jilong yugang Ererba*, and Zhuang, Chen, and Zhou, *Yi jiazi*. The first was part of an islandwide project begun soon after restrictions were

histories describe chains of people, bound to each other by wire, lined up along the harbor and shot—one bullet per chain—and suggest that most of those killed in Jilong were dockworkers or boatmen who just happened to be out on the streets when the troops arrived.[108] One person recalled the fate of about one hundred repatriated Taiwanese who had served as soldiers in the Japanese Army. They arrived by boat in Jilong on the morning of March 8 and boarded a train for transfer to their homes further south. They spent the day awaiting clearance from the military command, which was preoccupied with a major clash that afternoon at a key intersection just south of the canal, across from the Public Hall and city government offices. The order to depart never came, and late that night Nationalist troops took the returned soldiers off the train, led them behind the station, and shot them.[109] In a less brutal case, the police arrested Yan Qinxian's son Huimin and may have brought Yan himself in for questioning as well. It seems most likely that Huimin's associations with Japan, where he had been a student during and after the war, made him seem suspicious. Regardless, following the arrest, his father purchased his freedom and later smuggled him to Japan.[110] The Allied occupation authorities in Japan had closed Japan's borders to its former colonial subjects; nonetheless,

---

lifted on open discussion of the event, whereas the second was produced by locals who felt that their stories had not yet been fully told.

108. Zhang Yanxian, "Ererba minzhong shiguan," 12, account of Lin Muqi. He was at one end of a human chain, and when no bullet struck him he was able to disengage himself from the rest and swim away. Across Taiwan, intellectuals and other elites made up perhaps half of those killed. See Lai, Myers, and Wei, *A Tragic Beginning*, 160.

109. Zhuang, Chen, and Zhou, *Yi jiazi*, 114–16, account of Lai Youfu.

110. Zhang, "Ererba minzhong shiguan," 12. Yan Qinxian's name appears on a list of people interrogated in Taipei immediately after the initial clash. See Chen Fangming, *Taiwan zhanhou shi ziliao*, 167. Huimin's story is a fascinating footnote to the history of Japan's empire. According to an article in the *Asahi News*, he did not return to Taiwan until early 1947 and was smuggled out in 1949. See "Hitoto shimai to Gan ka (2)," *AS*, Oct. 29, 2008, 2. He spent most of the rest of his life in Japan, where his elder daughter, Hitoto Tae, gained a reputation as an author of books that address lingering issues of Japanese colonization, and his younger daughter, Hitoto Yō, became a well-known pop singer. Both daughters—Yan Yunnian's great granddaughters—were born in Taiwan but work professionally in Japan under the family name of their Japanese mother, Hitoto Kazue.

many Taiwanese entered the country clandestinely.[111] The Nationalist regime displayed less concern with carefully seeking out those responsible for the uprising and showed greater interest in rapidly removing the stain of Japanese influence.

The uprising and crackdown were not simply the result of conflict over recent events; rather, they reflected tensions across the boundaries that had emerged from the divergent trajectories of Taiwanese and Chinese identity formation. In its assessment of events in Jilong, the provincial government placed some blame on taxation policies that favored mainlanders, but more immediately it found fault with the use of Taiwanese police officers in the early phases of suppression and, most significantly, with the Taiwanese elites who had been unable to assert effective control because they sympathized with the local demonstrators. The official report criticized by name city councilors Huang Shushui, Ji Qiushui, and Ye Songtao, all of whom had originally been supportive of the new regime but had strongly criticized the government at the City Council meeting in late 1946. When postwar elites placed the interests of local society above those of the nation in this manner, the government saw them as part of the problem. Even more telling was the fate of Yang Yuanding, the advocate of Taiwanese involvement in government who had gone to Shanghai to fight the Japanese during the war. His pointed criticisms made him a target for the Nationalist forces, which were apparently not completely indiscriminate in their killing. When they swept through Jilong on the night of March 8, they took him to a bridge over the canal, shot him, and dumped his body into the water. The structure had only recently been renamed Independence Bridge (map 6.1).[112]

---

111. Morris-Suzuki, "Invisible Immigrants."

112. The official report of Yang's death, from 1947, says that he was secretly arrested and judged (*mibu micai*) before being executed, whereas his biography in the first postwar city gazetteer simply mentions that he "unexpectedly met with difficulties." The latter version was repeated in the revised edition of the gazetteer from 2001. The oral histories are more explicit, as is an unofficial report from around the time of the event. See, respectively, Jian Shenghuang, *Ererba shijian dang'an duibian*, 2:155; Jilong shi wenxian weiyuanhui, *Renwu pian*, 26; Li and Zheng, *Renwu liezhuan pian*, 43; Zhuang, Chen, and Zhou, *Yi jiazi*, 118–19; and Zhang Yanxian, "Ererba minzhong shiguan," 10. In an indication of more recent shifts in views of 2-28, a picture of Yang

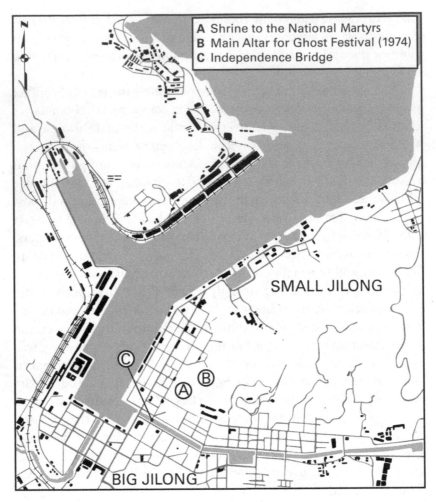

MAP 6.1. Postwar Jilong. Map created by Scott Walker, based on a map designed by the U.S. Army Map Service, AMS L991, 1945, held in the Geography and Map Reading Room at the Library of Congress, Washington, DC.

When the Taiwanese assessed the event, they drew fundamental distinctions between themselves and the Chinese. Almost all of the seven

Yuanding hangs in the 2-28 Memorial Museum in Peace Memorial Park, Taipei, and in the museum of the National Archives in Nantou, Taiwan, along with images of other martyrs of the incident.

million Taiwanese yuan in damage caused by the protestors in Jilong was done to government buildings or to the private property of mainlander officials.[113] Early in 1948, the Taiwanese Native Place Associations (Tongxianghui) of Beijing and Tianjin concluded that the difficulties of retrocession stemmed in part from differences that had emerged between China and Taiwan in the previous fifty years, and in part from the "fundamentally imperialist oppression" that the "traditional" (guqiande) and "feudal" (fengijiande) Nationalists brought to the island.[114] This particular perspective, of China as traditional and oppressive and Taiwan as modern and oppressed, was also articulated in retrospective views of the Nationalist takeover in 1945 that emphasized the slovenly, almost subhuman character of the first troops that arrived.[115] The 2-28 Incident itself and the subsequent imposition of martial law did not create this sense of distinction, because the Taiwanese directed their anger at the new regime and its representatives both before and during those events. Their rage derived in part from the economic downturn that most severely affected Taiwanese islanders, in part from Nationalist dominance of local governance, and in part from the plans that the new regime instituted to transform the Taiwanese into Chinese. Together, these elements reinforced Taiwanese ethnic identity as something apart from Chinese national identity.

Conclusion

The Nationalist Chinese era dawned in Taiwan with a combination of devastation and hope. Jilong, a centerpiece of Japan's colonial modernization, lay in rubble, as did other Taiwanese cities. The Japanese settlers who had contributed so much to the city's institutional structures,

113. Chen, Qi, and Ma, Taiwan "Er-erba" shijian, 367. The remaining damage was directed toward people on the City Council, such as Huang Shushui, whose shop was heavily vandalized. See Jian Shenghuang, Ererba shijian dang'an huibian, 2:153.

114. Tang, "Pingjie 'Ererba,'" 49–51.

115. See, for example, Zhuang, Chen, and Zhou, Yi jiazi, introduction, 9, which talks about the unhygienic soldiers (quefa weisheng guannian de junren) who plundered the storehouses of Jilong and polluted the harbor (biancheng chouqi chongtian de chougang).

identity, and prevailing inequities were now powerless and soon to depart. Jilong's Taiwanese population met the uncertain transition from Japanese to Chinese rule with an initial burst of enthusiasm as new elite gatekeepers sought to assert themselves in the reconstruction of the city that they had helped build, a self-appointed task through which they appealed to the needs of the Taiwanese community. It seemed that regime change would allow a resurgence of the localism suppressed during the war and, as in the earlier period, that local identities could be extrapolated to regional ones through common institutions and experiences. However, the new Chinese transplants—mostly officials, soldiers, and businessmen—arrived with a strong sense of nationalism and a vision of modernization that did not leave much space for alternative identities. These features of Jilong's physical and imagined landscape created a range of possibilities for restoring the city to its prewar position as one of Taiwan's leading urban centers, but they also held the potential for discontent and conflict. As Taiwanese residents and mainlanders surveyed the task of reterritorializing Jilong as a non-Japanese place, its future form hung in the balance. Ultimately, factors both internal and external to the city and province pushed the Taiwanese and Chinese populations toward the conflagration of 1947, but the conflict was not an inevitable outcome.

Taiwanese and Chinese interests overlapped considerably on the general subject of physical and economic reconstruction, and if the two groups did not view the deportation of the Japanese in precisely the same way, at least they agreed on the overall need to remove that population. However, where their visions were not contiguous they drew new imagined borders that separated them as erstwhile siblings. The similarity in the objectives of planners in the Nationalist regime, especially in the NRC, and natives of Jilong was most noticeable in the blueprints for urban reconstruction drawn up by the municipal government in 1946. The bustling modern city that those plans would have created represented perhaps the highest degree of convergence between national Chinese, ethnic Taiwanese, and local Jilong identities. Nationalist objectives, however, did not stop at physical reconstruction but extended to a thorough cultural rejuvenation and spiritual cleansing that would purify the Taiwanese of their Japanese influences and mold them into patriotic Chinese citizens. Thus, for the Chinese, Japanese deportation was a part of re-Sinicization, and urban reconstruction was a means to nation and state building. The Taiwanese shared neither of these objectives, and in fact objected to the premise of the first, for it portrayed them as backward and uncivilized. Moreover, when the need to extract sugar, fertilizer, and other resources from Taiwan to sustain the war against the Communists destroyed the local economy, Chen Yi's administration sacrificed its developmentalist agenda in favor of enforcing loyalty to the state above all else.

The particular shape of the imagined boundaries that emerged in the process of rebuilding Jilong revealed that the Chinese and the Taiwanese people held different views of modernity. For the mainlanders, the highly centralized nation-state, with its tight controls over economic planning and its position as the locus of identity, was the epitome of the modern world. Thus any plans for renovation and new construction had to emerge from the center, and the people had to adopt the centrally defined vision of national culture. The Taiwanese, however, viewed modernity as something that to an extent revolved around scientific standards of hygiene and urbanization, but was inherently more pluralistic and allowed for participation from outside the party-state, as in postwar Japan. Thus when a Taiwanese assessment of the 2-28 Incident referred to the Nationalists as feudal, it condemned them for reproducing the autocratic practices of China's dynastic past. Given that Chinese national identity had been formed expressly in opposition to Qing rule, and that the Nationalists viewed themselves as the bearers of modernization, it is hard to imagine a more damaging epithet. Although the suppression of the 1947 uprising seemingly settled the question of political involvement against pluralism, its brutality and the fear and punishments of the subsequent White Terror hung over later attempts by the Taiwanese and Chinese to negotiate the borders between them. Disputes over what was modern underlay the contestation between national and ethnic identities.

CHAPTER SEVEN

Ethnicity, Nationalism, and the Re-creation of Jilong, 1945–1955

On May 22, 1947, less than three months after the explosive events of February 28, the Jilong City Council held its fourth meeting. Council chair Huang Shushui, who had been singled out for criticism in an official report on the uprising and had his property vandalized by demonstrators, opened the session with an apology for the meeting's postponement as a result of the "2-28" incident. According to Huang, the unrest had not seriously affected Jilong: "Social order was quickly reestablished, and the good people were able to maintain peace." His words ignored the random and not-so-random killings, but they paralleled the account given in the city government's report, delivered at the meeting by Mayor Shi Yanhan. Indeed, Shi used stronger language and referred to the incident as a nightmare, even as he tried to distance Jilong from the worst of the violence. In the immediate aftermath, it seemed that both long-time city residents and newly arrived agents of the state wanted to get on with other business. Huang expressed the main shared objective in his concluding statement: "We hope to be a genuine bridge between the city government and the people, and all of our issues and inquiries will not only be appropriate, they will be constructive proposals, rejuvenating issues, and encouraging questions that will soon make this city a model city, not only for this city's benefit, but for the benefit of all of Taiwan."[1] With words that echoed the inclusivity of the Jilong identity of the Japanese era, Huang delineated common ground with the Nationalist government.

However, between his minimization of what actually occurred in Jilong during the uprising and his hopes for the future, Huang also subtly traced some of the boundaries that divided Chinese from Taiwanese. Recent events forced him to choose his words carefully, using established Nationalist terminology to get his points across. He said the appointment of Wei Daoming, recently ambassador to the United States, as the first governor of Taiwan Province was "one step on Taiwan's road to democracy, and a manifestation of the establishment of constitutional government," for it would allow the Taiwanese to learn true democracy and establish a government of the people.[2] Nationalist ideology suffused his brief speech: democracy (*minzhu*) was the endpoint of Sun Yat-sen's stages of national construction, and Wei's leadership referenced the period of tutelage that Sun had seen as necessary for preparing the people to participate in a constitutional democracy. Yet Huang himself understood the electoral process and the tasks of governance, as he had been selected as a delegate in Jilong's mock election of 1930, and had served on the municipal council under Japanese rule before leading it afterward. He and others like him did not need tutelage from the authoritarian Nationalist state. Therefore, his use of sanctioned terminology indicates a continuation of the Taiwanese habit of adapting to prevailing circumstances even while seeking a voice in matters that affect their lives and livelihoods.

Huang and other Taiwanese islanders reinforced the imagined boundaries around their ethnic identity by working within the limits on permissible discourse established by the Nationalist Chinese regime. In addition to Huang's comments on democracy, other participants talked repeatedly about defending the people's livelihood (*minsheng*), the third of Sun's Three People's Principles. The Taiwanese in Jilong did not raise what was arguably the most important of Sun's

1. Jilong shi canyihui, *Jilong shi canyihui diyiju disici*, 73–74; original quotation marks around "2-28."
2. Ibid., 73.

principles, nationalism (*minzu*), which at the time unambiguously referred to membership in the Chinese nation-state. Their silence on this
topic suggests that, although the Taiwanese challenged the Nationalists
on their own ideological ground, they skirted issues that might bring
their ethnic identity under greater scrutiny. This chapter examines how
Taiwanese people reset the borders of their ethnic consciousness in the
spaces and practices of everyday life, through distinctive approaches
to the ongoing reconstruction of Jilong, the establishment of a new
range of social organizations and social work activities, and the redef-
inition and reinterpretation of sacred spaces and religious practices.
Within the context of Chinese recolonization and attempted reterritorialization, processes that intensified after Taiwan's second political
separation from mainland China in 1949 and the arrival of more than
one million Chinese refugees on the island, competing visions of modernity facilitated, and even necessitated, the differentiation of Taiwanese and Chinese identities.

Reconstructing Jilong, Phase Two (1947–1954)

National, provincial, and international conditions all encouraged the
reemergence of the local as a site for overt cooperation and subtle contestation. From the spring of 1947 onward, China's concern with dissent
within Taiwan; the declining fortunes of Nationalist forces in the civil
war, leading to the mass abandonment of the mainland; and the crys-
tallization of global anticommunism under the polarization of the Cold
War and its hot manifestation in Korea all combined to promote the
Nationalists' authoritarian rule on Taiwan. The 2-28 crackdown, the
proclamation of martial law, and the mass arrests and executions
during what became known as the White Terror, which Jiang Jingguo
(Chiang Ching-kuo) launched in mid-1949, all pushed the Taiwanese
into defensive positions.[3] Most proponents of Taiwanese nationalism

---

3. The official statistics cite 29,407 arrests during the era of martial law, with
roughly 700 convictions in each year of 1951, 1952, and 1954, and some 14,000 prisoners
incarcerated on Green Island in 1955. See Taylor, *The Generalissimo's Son*, 211–12. These

either fled Taiwan or remained underground rather than face the punitive powers of a colonizing regime exiled to its colony.[4] Meanwhile,
although they held all the levers of political and military power, the
Nationalists had to consider ways to develop Taiwan as a bastion if they
were to achieve their primary goal of recovering the mainland. Although Taiwan remained peripheral to state goals into the mid-1950s,
the flight to the island around 1949 meant that the government focused
more on enlisting the local population in its causes. To the Nationalist
government, urban renewal served as a counterpart to the largely successful land-reform program under way from 1949 to 1953.[5] In that
context, rebuilding Jilong appeared to be a process to which all could
contribute.

Although the government achieved substantive progress by early
1947 in clearing away the wartime wreckage and restoring the port
facilities to a functional condition, Jilong remained a work in progress.
For example, over a few weeks in September 1949 the city government
sent two requests to the National Resources Commission on behalf of
the local education committee, regarding the need for five thousand
yuan to repair bomb-damaged school buildings. Official support had
been so slow in coming that the school board had either solicited or
been offered the money by the China Oil Company, and it now asked
permission to accept the donation to support its "Save food, build
schools movement."[6] Jilong's new mayor, Xie Guanyi, made these requests at what was an inopportune moment, to say the least. The Nationalist government and armed forces were in full-scale retreat and
the NRC would understandably have been focused on conserving and
allocating resources for the flight to Taiwan. Nonetheless, at the local
level functional school buildings mattered, and the city government's
efforts in fact indicate convergence between official interests and the
aspirations of the Jilongese.

---

figures are likely far below the reality, given other high estimates of 90,000 arrests
and some 45,000 executions; see Manthorpe, *Forbidden Nation*, 204.

4. Phillips, "Building a Taiwanese Republic."

5. On land reform, see Gold, *State and Society*, 64–67.

6. GSG-SD, 003-010404-1244: NRC to JJB, "Jilong shizhengfu qing juanzhu
xiujian xiaoshe jingfei an," 1949, 3–5.

Objectives and visions for Jilong's future overlapped only to a limited extent, however, as revealed at the May 1947 City Council meeting. There, Ye Songtao was elected to replace the recently killed Yang Yuanding as vice chair, Huang Shushui made his comments on democracy, and Mayor Shi Yanhan laid out a sweeping four-point vision for rebuilding and remaking Jilong.[7] His key elements included creating a new environment (*xin de huanjing*), new policy making (*xin de juece*), accelerating progress on construction, and locating financial support for the construction work. The last two points were relatively straightforward, as Shi both outlined the need for new buildings to house a population that he expected to reach 100,000 that year and evinced support for the ambitious 1946 urban reform plan, for which he had received approval from Governor Wei Daoming but not financing.[8]

The limits of congruence between his vision and that of the city councilors emerged as he explained this new environment. Mayor Shi emphasized that Taiwan had made tremendous progress since the low point of late 1946, which he attributed to the national declaration of martial law in December 1946; the reorganization of the government in April; the "major incident" of February 28; and the establishment of a formal provincial government on May 16. As a result, he said, Jilong's residents now lived in fundamentally improved circumstances. According to Shi, these structural factors created an environment that contained a measure of both political democratization (*zhengzhi minzhuhua*) and Taiwan's incorporation into the ancestral nation (*Taiwan zuguohua*). He called on the councilors to recognize this new reality, and to cast aside their old ways of thinking, which stood as impediments to the completion of democratization and nationalization.[9]

Turning to new policy making, he outlined three ways in which the government's approach had changed, and needed to change, in the

7. On the position of vice chair, see Jilong shi canyihui, *Taiwan sheng Jilong shi canyihui diyiju disici*, 25. Ji Qiushui, a long-time member of Jilong's business community and a participant in the Nationalist Party Central Reform Committee (Guomindang zhongyang gaizao weiyuanhui), had been appointed as temporary vice chair but received no votes in the formal selection. See Jilong shi wenxian weiyuanhui, *Renwu pian*, 26–27.

8. Jilong shi canyihui, *Taiwan sheng Jilong shi canyihui diyiju disici*, 41–43.

9. Ibid., 34–35.

wake of 2-28. The principal lesson he drew from the recent uprising was not that Chen Yi's policies had been flawed, but that the people had not understood them, largely because the state had insufficiently mobilized them through officially sponsored organizations. According to Shi, if "the people do not understand the government's policies, that is not modern governance." His second point stressed urban renovation by taking full advantage of Jilong's position "at the entryway of transport between Taiwan Province and mainland China." This idea was not particularly original—it had been circulating since Liu Mingchuan's term as governor of Taiwan—but his recommendations for enhancing maritime contacts with the mainland and around Taiwan, as well as intraisland land transport, all of which had diminished in recent years, suggested a reorientation of priorities to cement Taiwan's place in China. His third area echoed Huang Shushui's opening remarks, in that he said the government must "nourish a true democratic spirit" through a pedagogy of political tutelage that encouraged more students to attend school, improved dissemination of government policies, and taught the national language, literature, and political skills.[10] Shi Yanhan described a plan for the reconstruction of Jilong that was firmly situated within a larger project of Chinese nation building and state strengthening, although his words could also have described the policies of the Japanese Government-General. The Jilong city councilors did not directly criticize the municipal authorities in the spring of 1947 as they had the previous December; instead they confined themselves to clarifying points about specific development projects.

When the municipal assembly met for the tenth time almost two years later, in February 1949, the discussions revealed fissures that lay below the overt agreement on urban renewal. By this time provincial authorities had replaced the provisional institutions of local governance and harbor management in Jilong, as in Gaoxiong, with a formal city government and port authority.[11] Taiwanese councilors remained circumspect, but their repeated references to promoting the people's

10. Ibid., 35–41; quotations on 36, 38, 40.
11. See Taiwan sheng xingzheng zhangguan gongshu, *Taiwan xingzheng zhangguan gongshu gongbao* 2, no. 7 (Apr. 8, 1948): 98; no. 11 (Apr. 13, 1948): 156–57; and no. 13 (Apr. 15, 1948): 187–88.

livelihood represented a more dedicated effort to protect their ethnic community through urban and social reconstruction. Huang Shushui, who opened and closed the meeting, called for "establishing a first-rate social atmosphere" through improving the quality and quantity of productive work, which would ultimately lead to the "completion of the principle of people's livelihood." He stressed enhancing scientific and technical skills, "destroying bad customs," and improving education, methods that largely overlapped with the plans of elements of the Nationalist state. Yet his critique of the ongoing deterioration of economic and social conditions displayed a firm defense of the Taiwanese people against the failings of national policies.[12] State officials, too, used the discourse of people's livelihood, a concept that the Nationalists viewed as "a distinctly Chinese path toward modernization," in the words of Margherita Zanasi.[13] The new mayor, Deng Bocui, deployed it in a report that ranged widely over such issues as strengthening the household registration system (*huji* or *hukou*); orienting social welfare toward society as a whole rather than individuals; and financing public projects, like housing and the water system, through improved tax collection. Much as Sun himself had advanced the principle to enhance political stability, Deng now raised it to fix the population in space and heighten state control.[14] The Jilongese councilors, however, employed it to highlight the government's failures in urban reconstruction and the divisions of postwar Taiwan; to target inequities in modes of transportation available to the city government and the people; and to demand greater attention to the people's daily needs. One councilor, Zeng-Lin Liangcheng, insisted that more Taiwanese teachers be hired to teach Taiwanese students, in part because of the poor training and incorrect accents of the Chinese instructors.[15] Both central and local government officials saw reconstruction as a means to national welfare and enhanced control, but the Jilongese pursued it for the benefit of their city and ethnic community.

12. Jilong canyihui, *Taiwan sheng Jilong shi canyihui diyiju dishici*, 55–58.
13. Zanasi, "Fostering the People's Livelihood," 7.
14. Jilong canyihui, *Taiwan sheng Jilong shi canyihui diyiju dishici*.
15. Ibid.

Regardless of the gaps between these visions, during the years following this council meeting, Jilong largely recovered from the devastation of the war and the uneven attention of the national, provincial, and local governments during the advent of Nationalist rule. To be sure, the recovery proceeded haltingly. An April 1949 workforce survey by the NRC indicated that the Jilong branches of the major nationalized companies restored their labor forces more slowly than those in other cities.[16] Nevertheless, over the next few years Jilong once again became one of Taiwan's most important cities. In 1948 its trade was worth less than 13 million yuan, a paltry sum by comparison to the Japanese period, but by 1950 it had skyrocketed to almost 1.5 billion yuan, or $300 million.[17] During the early 1950s it consistently accounted for more than half of Taiwan's total trade, although that figure represented a decline in most years from a peak of 84 percent in 1947.[18] Jilong's population also rapidly expanded during this second phase of reconstruction. A city of fewer than 70,000 people in the middle of 1946, following the first wave of Japanese deportation, Jilong's population surpassed 100,000 during 1948, 150,000 in 1951, and stood at a total of 180,431 residents in 1954.[19] As noted in chapter 6, an influx of Chinese refugees beginning in 1948 radically altered the demographics of Taiwan's major cities.[20] As a result, the percentage of Chinese in Jilong in 1957 bore an uncanny resemblance to the earlier presence

16. GSG-SD, 003-010102-2784: NRC to JJB, "Taiwan sheng ge jigou Ri zhi shidai yu xian you yuangongren shu bijiao," 1949. Among the companies that responded to the request for information, Taiwan Cement, Taiwan Paper, Taiwan Sugar, and Taiwan Alkali had all attained, or nearly attained, their wartime workforce. Of those, only Taiwan Cement had major operations in Jilong. In contrast, both Taiwan Gold and Copper Ore and Taiwan Shipbuilding, which were concentrated in or near Jilong, were still far below their pre-1945 employment levels.

17. Jilong shi wenxian weiyuanhui, *Shangye pian*, 127–29.

18. Jilong shi wenxian weiyuanhui, *Gaishu pian*, 2, 7. The value of trade in 1950 provided here is about half the amount stated in the volume cited in the preceding note, an odd discrepancy given that the gazetteers are part of the same series. Either editors of the later volume uncovered new amounts of trade or they inflated the numbers to accelerate the rapidity of the recovery by a year. I assume the former, but even if the latter were true it would still indicate an enormous increase in two years.

19. Jilong shi zhengfu, *Renkou pian*, 11–12.

20. See table 6.1 and the discussion in chapter 6 of Taiwan's postwar population.

of Japanese settlers, who had constituted 25 to 30 percent of the city's population for most of the preceding five decades. Accommodating this massive expansion of the population, and managing the associated potential for ethnic tensions as Chinese began to fill the city, required more than just urban renovation.

Rebuilding Society: Competing Modernities and Social Welfare

The combination of wartime dislocation, the departure of the Japanese, and the massive population increase left Jilong desperate for social reconstruction and significant assistance for those who sought to rebuild old lives or start new ones in the city. Prior to the outbreak of war in 1937, a dense network of social organizations and the zealous practice of social work had provided a foundation for the formation and stabilization of Jilong's society, even with its ethnic divisions and numerous social ills. Moreover, the institutionalization of social welfare had steeped much of urban Taiwan in an avowedly rational, scientific, and state-initiated form of collective assistance. In 1945 that system's institutions were in disarray, if not ruins, but the Taiwanese retained their organizational experience and their training in rationalized welfare, two factors that marked their identity as self-consciously modern. Put another way, social work during the period of Japanese rule had helped to define a Taiwanese modernity.

The Nationalist regime had its own experiences with conceptualizing social problems and delivering aid that gave Taiwan's new rulers a strong sense of their own modernity. As both Zwia Lipkin and Janet Chen have shown, the definition of poverty as a social problem, and the subsequent efforts to isolate, punish, and reform the urban poor, had been central to the creation of a modern Chinese state and modern citizens. Lipkin and Chen agree that modernizing Chinese elites of the twentieth century, like elites elsewhere, viewed poverty as a threat to the nation. They also concur that defining the poor and building the nation went hand in hand through a politics of inclusion—determining who was part of the newly defined civilized society—and exclusion—deciding who was not a member and had to be quarantined until such a time as they could join.[21] The close links drawn here between nation and modernity, on the one hand, and the possibility of being granted membership in both, on the other, would have important ramifications for the Nationalists as they sought to reterritorialize Taiwan. The respective backgrounds that the Taiwanese and mainlanders brought to organization-building and welfare provision meant that these would be arenas in which they could cooperate, but also that their separate histories could sharpen boundaries between their identity groups.

The Nationalist regime portrayed itself as an innovator as it attempted to install a form of social welfare that was even more state-centric in structure and self-representation than the Japanese-initiated version. The Social Office in Chongqing issued social welfare regulations in 1943 as part of a larger project of mobilization through social control, which matched the vision that underlay the Japanese system. According to those guidelines, welfare existed to "safeguard social life in order to promote peace in the social order."[22] Still, despite the fact that Chinese officials had previously acquired their views of poverty and how to handle it from Japan, in the wake of the anti-Japanese war of resistance the Nationalists made every effort in Taiwan to distinguish their views and policies from those of the Japanese Government-General.[23] The authors of *Taiwan Today* (*Jinri Taiwan*), the first postwar guide to Taiwan, began the section on social work by saying, "While Taiwan was under Japanese control, in order to appease the Chinese and aboriginal peoples, they exerted all effort to promote various types of social work."[24] A decade later, when the Jilong City Historical Materials Committee (Jilong shi wenxian weiyuanhui) published a volume of its city gazetteer on social organizations (*Shehui zuzhi pian*), it proposed that the structure for providing assistance had improved dramatically since retrocession. It had become broader, incorporating new facets such as social welfare (*shehui fuli*) instead of just social assistance (*shehui fuwu*), and expanding the range of activities and aid recipients,

21. Lipkin, *Useless to the State*; Janet Chen, *Guilty of Indigence*.
22. GSG, Executive Yuan (Xingzhengyuan; XZY), 061:949, "Shehuibu sanshier niandu shehui xingzheng fangzhen," n.d..
23. Janet Chen, *Guilty of Indigence*, 9, 44.
24. Xu and Pan, *Jinri Taiwan*, 432.

and it had come under a much higher degree of regulation and control by the state.[25] The detailed discussion of Japanese-era social work in *Taiwan Today* revealed a complex, interactive system that tended to undercut the authors' critiques, but under both Chen Yi's civil administration and the formal Provincial Government, the Nationalist regime attempted to distinguish itself from its predecessor by proclaiming, though not always fulfilling, a greater role in all areas of social work.

Beginning in early 1946 the central government issued new policies governing social organizations that it applied to all regions of the re-unified, but disintegrating, country. It revised a number of existing statutes concerning people's organizations (*renmin tuanti*), a broad category that included labor associations (*gonghui*), commercial and trade associations (*shanghui tongye gonghui*), women's associations (*funühui*), and cooperatives (*hezuoshe*). These regulations particularly emphasized creating new organizations and registering old ones, especially registering those in areas recovered from the Japanese (*shoufu qu*) on the mainland. Moving swiftly to catalog organizational activities in its territory, the government registered almost 5,500 social, artistic, cultural, religious, and welfare associations in Nationalist-held areas, not including Taiwan, by the end of 1946.[26] These policies reflected the state's attempts to extend its reach and enhance its power.

Chen Yi's administration and the Jilong authorities devoted considerable attention to enforcing control through registration during 1946. According to the report on the Taiwan Assembly meeting that May, the civil authorities had already imposed a series of measures for reformulating people's associations and directing them onto the right path. Chen ordered all groups to register with the proper authorities at the province, county, or city level, after which they would be reorganized to fit into a hierarchical administrative structure. Any organizations that had not registered by April 20 of that year were to be disbanded. It is unclear how many groups failed to meet the deadline,

25. Jilong shi wenxian weiyuanhui, *Shehui zuzhi pian*. The theme of post-retrocession improvement runs through the entire 170-page volume, but see specifically the section on social welfare for its depiction of Nationalist innovation.

26. GSG, XZY, 124:1416, "Shehuibu sanshiwu niandu gongzuo bao'an juan," n.d.

but it is evident that, although existing provincial-level associations were "revised" into twenty-nine new units, no agricultural associations had yet registered, an astounding fact for a mostly agricultural province.[27] In Jilong, the process moved in a manner that dissatisfied the local authorities. By the end of 1946, only fourteen associations had completed the registration protocols and another thirteen were in process. Of those that had formally registered, most lacked the post of secretary, whereas many others were reportedly insufficiently organized to be of use to the state.[28] Even though the regulations allowed people's associations to adopt whatever organizational structure they saw fit, the absence of a secretary apparently caused concern, indicating that the state expected such a post to facilitate its access to and control over each group.[29]

Chinese Nationalist officials at the city and provincial levels largely followed these central directives when they referred to using people's associations as an extension of state power. For example, when Shi Yanhan discussed his vision of new policy thinking, he specifically stated that people's associations must be tied to the state to realize their full potential, and that neighborhood organizations—a system outside of the regular bureaucracy, in which prominent locals were given quasi-official status, much like the district heads of the Japanese era—could more efficiently spread government directives by word of mouth.[30] Similarly, during the bimonthly meetings at which province-level associations reported on their work and received guidance from the state, officials from the Taiwan Province Social Office framed people's associations as messengers of the state. In his speech opening the October 1948 meeting, the assistant director stated that people's organizations existed primarily to propagate government policies. Two months later, a representative from the Taiwan military headquarters addressed the assembled representatives of the various associations and essentially

27. Taiwan sheng xingzheng zhangguan gongshu minzhengchu mishushi, *Taiwan sheng canyihui diyiji diyici*, 94–95.

28. XZZG, 00301200091005, Xingzheng zhangguan gongshu minzhengchu, "Jilong shi sanshiwu niandu chengli zhi renmin tuanti baogao biao cui baoan," Dec. 30, 1946.

29. Jilong shi canyihui, *Taiwan sheng Jilong shi canyihui diyiji disici*, 37.

30. Ibid.

ordered them to use their organizations to spread the message that Chinese and Taiwanese people belonged to one family (*neiTai yijia*), inseparably bound through an intimate union (*qin'ai tuanjie*).[31] The urgency of that statement reflected the increasingly dire position of ROC forces after their defeat in the Huai River campaign, as well as Chiang Kai-shek's decision to proclaim martial law that same month. Moreover, it showed that officials viewed state-led social organizations, with their potential for broad and deep access to the Taiwanese people, as a key mechanism for achieving control within Taiwan.

Although government policies for registering and organizing people's associations to meet the needs of nation building applied to all ROC territory, Taiwan received specific treatment because of its special status. These policies carried a special intensity on the island because the Nationalists fundamentally did not trust the Taiwanese. Shi-chi Mike Lan's distinction between Taiwan as a territory that had been fully brought within China's external and internal boundaries just prior to 1945, and the Taiwanese as a people whose position in the Nationalist Chinese view of China's imagined geography remained uncertain, is relevant here.[32] Also significant was the state's agenda of re-Sinicization, a policy that was almost unique to Taiwan and that entailed both purifying and civilizing the Taiwanese. Officials like the assistant director of the Social Office simply did not have faith that the Taiwanese would be able to forge and manage associations that were robust enough to meet the state's needs, hence they required bimonthly meetings to facilitate closer supervision.[33] Nationalists often expressed their critiques of the Taiwanese in terms of a purported Communist influence, in spite of the fact that, as Steven Phillips has shown,

31. GSG-SD, 003-010102-2760: NRC to JJB, "Taiwan sheng zhengfu shehuichu renmin tuanti gongzuo huibao," 1948–1949. The similarities between written Chinese and Japanese highlight deep ideological continuities between the successive regimes: the phrase used to connote familial unity also appeared in pre-1945 official pronouncements, the principal differences being the pronunciation (*naiTai ikka* instead of *neiTai yijia*) and the meaning of *nai/nei* (Japan, rather than China).

32. See Lan, "The Ambivalence of National Imagination," and discussion of Lan in chapter 6.

33. GSG-SD, 003-010102-2760: "Taiwan sheng zhengfu shehuichu renmin tuanti gongzuo huibao."

communism had never gained a strong foothold in Taiwan, least of all during the immediate postwar period.[34]

That absence of trust highlights a second point, which is that mainlander officials did not understand how the Taiwanese had forged an autonomous identity under Japanese colonization, a failing that had multiple facets. Since the dominant Nationalist Chinese narrative of Japanese rule was that it had enslaved the Taiwanese and stunted their modernization, the Taiwanese could not, therefore, operate modern institutions, a conclusion that ignored their deep embrace of modern social work. In this view, since Japanese rule had essentially locked the Taiwanese out of evolutionary time, Taiwan's society must have remained as it had been under Qing rule, with social organization and welfare provision undertaken on an ad hoc basis by local elites. Therefore, these people would have been the same sorts of elites against whom the Nationalists had spent the previous three decades struggling for control over local society.[35] In short, the transplants fundamentally misunderstood the modern ways in which Taiwanese elites organized and assisted their society, a failing that significantly complicated the process of achieving the goals of correspondence between the people and the government, and providing for the people's livelihood.[36]

These basic incongruities did not, however, prevent the Nationalists and the Taiwanese from creating a substantial network of people's associations that surpassed the Japanese era in its breadth and density. A centerpiece of this effort, both nationwide and in Taiwan, was a dizzying array of cooperative associations. In 1946 alone, across China the government registered a staggering 162,337 cooperatives, including 1,200 for the management of recovered areas like Taiwan, with a collective membership of almost twenty million and total assets of 7.5 billion yuan.[37] This apparent mania for cooperatives came to Jilong as well, where 25 cooperatives of one sort or another were set up between

34. Phillips, *Between Assimilation and Independence*, 32, 84–87. Communist ideology motivated some, such as Xie Xuehong, but their numbers were few.

35. Duara, *Rescuing History*, chap. 3.

36. GSG-SD, 003-010102-2760: "Taiwan sheng zhengfu shehuichu renmin tuanti gongzuo huibao."

37. GSG, XZY, 124: 1416, "Shehuibu sanshiwu niandu gongzuo bao'an juan," n.d.

1946 and 1951. That number is small in comparison to the total for Taiwan, but it closely parallels circumstances in Gaoxiong, which had 26 cooperatives in 1951, suggesting that the focus in Taiwan was on rural areas.[38] These included open-membership credit associations, as well as organizations that pooled resources and extended financial assistance on the basis of enterprise or activity (for example, housing, warehouses, construction, tea production, even soy sauce making), or by location in the city. Authorities established one credit association for each of the city's five new core districts: Zhongzheng, Xinyi, Ren'ai, Anle, and Zhongshan.[39] These names, which rapidly appeared on urban maps across Taiwan, represented the Nationalist state and its ideology: the first and last, on opposite sides of the harbor, were named for Chiang Kai-shek and Sun Yat-sen, and Xinyi and Ren'ai reflected the party's interpretation of Confucian principles.[40]

In many cases, the government relied on Japanese-era unions as the roots of the new cooperatives. For example, Jilong's city government took over the three main existing credit unions—the mostly Japanese membership Jilong Credit Union, the mixed Jilong People's Credit Union, and the mostly Taiwanese Jilong Commercial and Industrial Credit Union—and merged them into two new organizations early in 1946.[41] The first two became the First Jilong Credit Cooperative (Jilong diyi xinyong hezuoshe), and the third became the Second Jilong Credit Cooperative (Jilong dier xinyong hezuoshe).[42] The majority of

---

38. Zhao and Wang, *Gaoxiong shi zhi*, 1562–64.

39. Jilong shi wenxian weiyuanhui, *Shehui zuzhi pian*, 125–27.

40. Joseph Allen notes similar circumstances in Taipei; see Allen, *Taipei*, 82–86. "Anle" as a district name could be unique to Jilong in Taiwan.

41. Several members of the Yan family and Cai Qingyun were major shareholders in the Commercial and Industrial Credit Union, and Xu Zisang was a small shareholder. See GSG, CZB, 275: 0652, "Jilong shanggong xinyong zuhe qingsuan an: qingsuan zhuangkuang baogao shu," Dec. 1948.

42. Jilong shi zhengfu, *Jilong shi nianjian*, 115–16. Initially these groups were called the Guaranteed Jilong Liability Credit Cooperative (Baozheng Jilong shi zeren xinyong hezuoshe), and the Limited Jilong Commercial and Industrial Liability Credit Cooperative (Youxian Jilong shi shanggong zeren xinyong hezuoshe), but the simpler names came into use within a few years. It seems that locals continued to use the Japanese-era names, as seen in an article about a meeting of the city's cooperatives in July 1946. See "Jilong hezuo huiyi," *MB*, July 18, 1946, 2.

the shareholders—1,315 in the First Credit Cooperative, and 1,159 in the Second—were undoubtedly Taiwanese, in part because in the spring of 1946 there were only about one thousand Chinese in Jilong. Moreover, it is highly unlikely that the government would have prevented Taiwanese individuals who had belonged to the earlier unions from joining the new ones, given that the credit unions required their resources if they were to be financially viable and useful to the state. Aside from the district-level and transport workers' groups, these two credit associations were far and away the largest cooperatives in Jilong, thus their significance continued across the 1945 divide.[43]

However, although the state legislated the creation of these organizations with relative ease, and Taiwanese joined them in significant numbers, the connections between new cooperatives and the old credit unions that held significant Japanese assets complicated their financial operations. When the city government formed the First Credit Cooperative, it found that Japanese members held the majority of shares in both of its parent groups, not to mention the property and other assets the organizations owned.[44] Acting on instructions from the provincial authorities, the Jilong city government allowed departing Japanese shareholders to reclaim a portion of their shares from the People's Credit Union, up to around 120,000 of the total 825,000 yuan held by the organization.[45] It made no such stipulation for the Jilong Credit

43. Jilong shi wenxian weiyuanhui, *Shehui zuzhi pian*, 126–27. In 1953, the largest of the district cooperatives, for Zhongzheng District, had almost 5,000 members. The transport laborers' cooperative had more than 2,700 members, and the two credit unions had 1,259 members (First) and 1,916 (Second).

44. GSG, CZB, 275: 0646, "Jilong xinyong zuhe qingsuan an: qingsuan zhuang-kuang baogao shu," Dec. 1948, 119; and 275: 0647, "Jilong shumin xinyong zuhe qing-suan an: qingsuan zhuangkuang baogao shu," Dec. 1948, 197. In the Jilong Credit Union, 1,073 Japanese members held 12,241 shares, valued at almost 350,000 yuan; 1,593 Japanese members held 8,096 shares, appraised at 91,000 yuan, in the Jilong People's Credit Union. By comparison, 310 Taiwanese held 2,403 shares, appraised at 66,000 yuan, in the first institution, and 1,093 Taiwanese held 4,541 shares, worth 51,000 yuan, in the second. Although the accounting was made in early 1946, no report was submitted to the provincial authorities until almost three years later, perhaps because it took time to resolve all disputes over the Japanese assets.

45. GSG, CZB, 275: 0647, "Jilong shumin xinyong zuhe qingsuan an: qingsuan zhuangkuang baogao shu," Dec. 1948, 15.

Union. In theory, the rest of the Japanese shares reverted to the Chinese government, but when disputes arose over what was and was not a Japanese asset, Taiwanese shareholders at least sometimes managed to assert their interests against the state. For example, in 1948 a question arose over property that the First Credit Cooperative acquired from the PCU, which had received the property in question as collateral for a loan in 1936. However, it was not clear if the Japanese settler who took the loan had retained ownership until the provincial government assumed control from him. In the final assessment, completed in 1951, the city government confirmed that the property was not a Japanese asset and approved its transfer from the PCU to its postwar descendant, the First Credit Cooperative.[46] Although the provincial government attempted to claim everything that Japanese shareholders might have owned, Taiwanese members sometimes successfully defended their rights to portions of that property. The Chinese-controlled local government, rather than harm a group that was crucial to the reconstruction process, at least sometimes supported those rights.

As this one case suggests, social organizations and social welfare became realms where Taiwanese islanders asserted their modern identity without challenging the overall structure of the new order. When the provincial administration issued its call for registering people's associations, and made it clear that privately initiated groups were welcome so long as they fit themselves into the state-sanctioned framework—indicating, in other words, that the new laws were not very different from the old—Taiwanese residents of Jilong responded by creating approximately twenty new groups by the end of 1946, and almost sixty more the following year. The vast majority were commercial or occupational groups, such as the huge Longshoremen's Association (Gangbu qixie tongye gonghui), which had more than fourteen hundred members in mid-1946, or the elite-membership Jilong Commercial Association (Jilong shi shanghui). Others, such as the Women's Association and the Jilong branch of the Three People's Principles

46. GSG, CZB, 275-1: 00584, "Jilong diyi xinyong hezuoshe chanquan diyi zong," 1950–52. This document gives no explanation for why the provincial Japanese Assets Management Committee (Richan guanli weiyuanhui) requested a review in 1952, but it indicates that the city government was surprised at being asked to revisit the case.

Youth Organization (Sanmin zhuyi qingniantuan), concentrated primarily on social reform and education. Although some of these organizations were branches of provincial or national associations, the majority were local initiatives run by prominent figures, such as Yang Yuanding, Huang Shushui, Yan Qinxian, and others.[47] The process of creating a formal institution complete with a leadership structure, operational and membership regulations, set meetings, and authorization from a national government was not new for the Taiwanese, but it was a modern act.

It also quickly became clear that transplants from the mainland used these associations to establish imagined terrain where Chinese identity could take root in Taiwan. This practice had antecedents in the Nanjing government's use of social relief institutions for national reconstruction.[48] It also had strong parallels in the temporal coincidence between the continuation of trans-war Japanese nation building through moral suasion and the complex postwar construction of an "ideology of monoethnicity" by Japanese intellectuals of divergent ideological positions.[49] In contrast to the People's Republic of China after 1949, where nation building involved the construction of multiple ethnic identities, in Taiwan the goal was to simultaneously nationalize and Sinicize.[50] Moreover, both the early-arriving mainlanders and the post-1948 refugees used these groups to build and sustain their own Chinese consciousness and to exclude Taiwanese from their social group. For example, although Taiwanese residents established the new youth organization, provincial officials took control of it and linked it

47. I derived this information from several sources, including Jilong shi zhengfu, *Jilong shi nianjian*, 48, 129–31; Zhu and Chen, *Jilong shi zhi*, 2140; and several articles from *MB*, including "Jilong renmin tuanti tongji," Aug. 6, 1946, 2; "Jilong tieqi gongye chengli gonghui," Sept. 16, 1946, 2; and "Jilong renmin ziyou baozhang weiyuanhui chengli," Sept. 19, 1946, 2.

48. Janet Chen, *Guilty of Indigence*, 90–116. See also Harrison, *China*, 200–206, for a survey of the larger project of spreading national culture within which these charitable and punitive relief efforts occurred.

49. Garon, *Molding Japanese Minds*; Lie, *Multiethnic Japan*, 130–36.

50. Gladney, *Muslim Chinese*, 87–93, 96–98; Mullaney, *Coming to Terms*, 92–94.

to the nationwide network to aid the diffusion of national agendas.[51] New settlers from different parts of Fujian and Guangzhou set up four different native-place societies between 1946 and 1948, the first such groups in Jilong since Chinese residents founded the China Guild in the mid-1920s.[52] The state took an aggressive approach in late 1946, when the city government held a series of public discussions on the legal framework for, and management of, people's associations. The government stated that Taiwanese people had a poor understanding of these matters, and thus the organizations themselves were unable to fulfill their appropriate functions.[53] The irony is that the Nationalist officials who claimed sole prerogative to determine what qualified as an "appropriate function" were so out of touch with local needs that they mandated the establishment of an agricultural association (*nonghui*) in Jilong, which did not have enough agricultural laborers to meet the legal minimum for membership.[54] By establishing native-place associations that may or may not have been updated versions of a premodern form, forcing the creation of groups that fit with their vision of Taiwan rather than local conditions, and absorbing organizations established by the Taiwanese, the new regime attempted to enhance its control over local society and impose on it the government's vision of national identity.

When it came to providing welfare for the city's many needy residents, there seemed to be significant common ground, but even there divisions manifested along identity lines. The case of the Social Hall, a crucial social welfare institution created by Japanese settlers in the 1930s and reborn in the late 1940s under Chinese state management, is

51. According to Steven Phillips, Taiwanese themselves began to form Three People's Principles Youth Organizations (he translates *tuan* as "corps") as early as September 1945, as a way to learn about China, display support for the Nationalists, and maintain public order. See Phillips, *Between Assimilation and Independence*, 43. Nevertheless, the Jilong branch was under government control and thus might not have been a Taiwanese-led organization.

52. Zhu and Chen, *Jilong shi zhi*, 2197–99.

53. "Jilong juban jiangxihui," *MB*, Oct. 31, 1946, 4.

54. Officials had planned five district branches within Jilong, but given the small numbers of farmers in each district, they merged them into one so that the association could survive. See Zhu and Chen, *Jilong shi zhi*, 2141.

instructive. The city government's Civil Affairs Bureau took over the Social Hall by early 1946 and retained its multifunctionality, so that the successor institution provided inexpensive housing, ran public lectures and training sessions, and operated Jilong's main unemployment agency. However, when it assumed control of the old institution the city moved it from its prior location in the old municipal government building into the edifice that housed Yan Yunnian's settlement house.[55] Apparently the name Social Hall (Shehui guan) had a more modern sound to it than Fraternity Group (Bo'aituan). Other documents reveal that the person in charge of the day-to-day operations of the institution, Lin Shiyi, not only sought to separate it from state control but also tried to use it to aid Taiwanese residents in particular. In early December 1946, Lin responded to a request from the provincial government that he reduce the Social Hall's staff by stressing the tremendous amount of work that the Social Hall and its staff performed, highlighting both that it housed some eight hundred people and that the organization had been essentially forced by the city government to assume management of the main unemployment agency. He also defended the Social Hall as an autonomous, self-supporting association, to protect its current staffing numbers. In a note accompanying Lin's message, the city government supported him.[56] Lin had previously asked the provincial authorities to intercede with the city government to make sure that it hired Taiwanese workers for openings that met their qualifications. To illustrate his point, he appended a table that outlined the experiences of dozens of Taiwanese men and women who had sought jobs through his agency, to show that they were indeed qualified for the jobs they had pursued.[57] The parallels here between Lin's efforts

55. Jilong shi zhengfu, *Jilong shi nianjian*, 133.

56. XZZG, 00307230080016, "Jilong shi shehui guan bian zhi tiaozheng an," Dec. 2, 1946.

57. XZZG, 00303100041020, "Jilong she zhengfu zhiye jieshaosuo qing luyong zaidi rencai an," Nov. 26, 1946. His list included just a sampling of the 1,368 people, all but 140 of them Taiwanese, who had come to the agency looking for work in November 1946, only a quarter of whom found jobs by mid-December. See "Jilong jieshao zhiye da sanbailiushi ming," *DMB*, Dec. 15, 1946, 2. The number of unemployed given here suggests that the figure of 20,000 cited by a Taiwanese city councilor was probably an exaggeration, even assuming that the number of people using the

and Xu Zisang's management of the Customs Assimilation Association to resist Japanese state intervention and work only with Taiwanese residents, as well as the practice of Taiwanese local welfare commissioners to help only other Taiwanese, are too strong to ignore.

The most significant aspect of social welfare provision in the early years of retrocession, particularly regarding the expression of competing visions of who was modern and who was not, was the re-creation of a true social work system in Jilong. Initially the Nationalist regime viewed assistance primarily as a means to minimize instability, so from 1945 until early 1948 its welfare projects were mostly emergency measures that dealt with problems in the short term. In spite of Chinese protestations of being advanced and modern compared with the Taiwanese, the Nationalists did not swiftly restore something akin to the scientific and semiprofessional social work that had been a hallmark of the Japanese period. Only in the spring of 1948 did the state begin to institute such a system. That April, the city's Social Bureau set up the Jilong Social Relief Work Association (Jilong shi shehui jiuji shiye xiehui). Jilong's mayor was the nominal head, but the membership comprised representatives of public and private social welfare groups and charitable organizations, religious leaders, and local notables. Many of these individuals were Taiwanese, suggesting that the municipal officials recognized they could not meet their objectives solely by relying on the small Chinese population. These were exactly the sorts of people who, twenty years earlier, became local welfare commissioners, and the new organization functioned much as the commissioner system had: it conducted social surveys, distributed various forms of aid, created and implemented plans for relief, and coordinated relief activities throughout the city. Individuals with the title of district commissioner (*quyu weiyuan*) performed much of this work. Their title was a cognate of the Japanese term *hōmen iin*, which I have rendered as "local welfare commissioners," but "district commissioners" is also an appropriate translation.[58]

---

unemployment agency was only a fraction of those out of work. See Jilong shi zhengfu, *Jilong shi nianjian*, 132.

58. Zhu and Chen, *Jilong shi zhi*, 2203–4.

The origins of the Social Relief Work Association are murky to say the least, since records of its founding do not exist in the main postwar archives or published materials, but the balance of historical precedent and contemporary evidence suggests that the idea originated with Taiwanese in the city government. The comprehensive, manifestly non-punitive nature of Jilong's organization stands in stark contrast to the disciplinary, isolationist workhouses that Janet Chen describes as a hallmark of the Nationalist approach to poverty and other social problems.[59] Nor did it overtly spread nationalistic, state-building propaganda, a primary function of social welfare during the Nanjing Decade, according to Zwia Lipkin, and also evidently the paramount concern of provincial and local officials in postwar Taiwan.[60] The almost complete functional overlap between this institution and the social work system of the prewar years, as well as between both manifestations of the Social Hall, strongly suggests that officers of the Jilong Social Bureau drew heavily on their prior experiences as they developed at least parts of Jilong's new social work structure. If these officials were mainlanders, then perhaps they had rapidly internalized the extensive description of Taiwan's prewar conditions contained in *Taiwan Today*. The potential for providing broad assistance with minimal state expenditure, as well as the possibility for social control, would have appealed to nationally oriented ROC officials who sought to keep Taiwan passive while its resources were extracted for the civil war. However, the absence of a dedicated system for providing welfare was one of the issues for which Taiwanese members of the City Council most severely criticized city officials. Therefore, even in the absence of specific documentation, it is almost certain that Taiwanese individuals, such as Huang Shushui, who had experience in the old system, influenced the creation of a new one that mirrored what they had helped develop under Japanese rule. The transference of Japanese-era expertise also appeared in other settings, such as the manner in which the doctor Du Congming built on his pre-1945 experience managing a clinic for opium addiction

---

59. Janet Chen, *Guilty of Indigence*.
60. Lipkin, *Useless to the State*.

to shape National Taiwan University's medical school as its dean between 1945 and 1953.[61]

Most of the foregoing discussion of postwar social organizations and social work has focused on the earliest years of Nationalist rule, precisely because that was the period in which the Taiwanese and Chinese established the patterns of activity, and claimed the imagined territory, that would define those arenas at least into the 1950s. After the major influx of refugees in 1949, both Chinese influence and the hand of the state became heavier. The extension of state power is seen in the numbers of registered people's associations, which grew from 97 in 1949 to 131 in 1953. Of greater significance than the numerical increase is the fact that the vast majority—90 in 1953—were labor and commercial associations that enabled the government to keep track of the city's economic activity and potentially prevent labor activism and unrest. Only one-fifth of the groups were nominally social organizations (*shehui tuanti*) and of those, roughly one-third were native-place associations (*tongxianghui*) established by mainlanders to the exclusion of the Taiwanese.[62]

In addition, when the city government set up a new Social Welfare Office (Shehui fuwu chu) in 1951, it designed the office to achieve the sweeping social control and re-Sinicization that, apparently, had so far eluded the Nationalist regime. Among the eight responsibilities for the new administrative entity were managing social drama troupes (*shehui jutuan*), holding mass weddings (*jituan jiehun*), establishing control over job placement, and setting up "cram schools" (*buxiban*), with the express purpose of helping the government extend education and raise

---

61. National Taiwan University Medical College, "NTUMC—Deans." Du's work with opium addicts is noted in chapter 5. He was temporarily removed as dean in March 1947 but returned to the post in July 1948. I thank Miriam Kingsberg for alerting me to Du's postwar success.

62. Jilong shi wenxian weiyuanhui, *Shehui zuzhi pian*, table opposite 14, 69–78. The numbers in the table are ambiguous because they are divided by type of organization (occupational, commercial, independent, and social), with an overall total for each category and figures for subsidiary types within each broad grouping. However, the sum of the types of occupational groups never adds up to the much larger total given for that category, thus a summation of the four categories is significantly larger than the comprehensive amount for each year. I elected to use the stated annual total because that matches the amounts given for each subsidiary type of organization.

the cultural level of city dwellers.[63] During the early 1950s, within the context of martial law and the grim insecurity of the White Terror, ROC officials also tried new ways to reform the Taiwanese population. That they did so indicates their recognition that, decades before the Taiwanese took over the Nationalist Party from within, they had at least temporarily occupied a significant portion of the social welfare system by asserting their identity as modern social workers who promoted the well-being of their ethnic group. Although Nationalist officials sought to reterritorialize welfare institutions to meet the goals of the Chinese nation-state, the Taiwanese people at first redirected that effort to achieve alternate ends.

Rebuilding Society: Contesting Sacred Spaces

Nowhere in social life are the overlapping processes of deterritorialization and reterritorialization more apparent than in the religious realm. A curious aspect of temples and other sacred spaces in twenty-first century Taiwan is seen in the dates inscribed on them. When the temples were built or renovated, and when specific items (plaques, guardian statues, steles, and such) were added, the dates of their construction and names of their donors were carved on the temple walls or on the donated piece. These dates follow the official format of both the Chinese and Japanese states, meaning that they include the reign name—such as Qianlong for the Qing, Meiji for Japan, and Minguo for the ROC—followed by the year, month, and day. What makes these mundane facts so instructive for understanding the relationship between Taiwanese and Chinese identities in the postwar years is that dates from all eras remain on structures across the island, but those pertaining to the Japanese period have been treated in varying ways. For example, at the Confucius Temple in Tainan, on a series of metal plates listing contributors to the temple's reconstruction that are set into a stone monolith just inside the compound's eastern entrance, the reign name Taishō has

---

63. A news article from 1952 indicates that the government saw mass weddings as a means of both customs reform and social control. See "Ji shi juban jituan hunyin," *LHB*, Mar. 7, 1952, 5; Jilong shi wenxian weiyuanhui, *Shehui zuzhi pian*, 111–12.

been almost completely effaced in one place but left untouched in another location on the same plate. At the Longshan Temple in Taipei, which is among the city's oldest and most important, a highly motivated visitor can locate "Taishō" inscribed in a low corner to the right of the inner entrance, difficult to find but not defaced.[64]

In Jilong, the presentation of dates through particular regimes, which have been closely tied to national identity since the late nineteenth and early twentieth centuries, is even more complex. For example, at the Ciyun Temple, the reign name Shōwa was covered with cement; it remains hidden in some places, whereas in other places the cement has either fallen off or been chipped away. At the Dianji Temple, the characters for Meiji on a stele off to the side of the entrance have been left untouched except by the elements, and the name Taishō has been recut and repainted gold in the base of one of the lions guarding the entrance to the main building. On the site of the old Jilong Shrine are two stone dogs that were donated by Japanese businessmen during the Taishō era, a fact that is clearly legible on one but has been obscured with cement on the other. At the Qing'an Temple, a stele erected to commemorate the 1912 renovation of the temple was, in a subsequent renovation, either sanded down or entirely resurfaced (or both) and then reinscribed with a date that matches the ROC style.[65] These different methods of erasing, preserving, and re-creating the Japanese-era past at Taiwan's temples exemplifies the complex interplay of ethnic and national identities the Taiwanese people experienced as they attempted to protect their religious institutions by modifying them—or not—in order to adapt to the intensity with which a Chinese national identity was imposed at particular moments in time.

When the Nationalists surveyed Taiwan's religious terrain following retrocession, they determined that changes had to be made. Their primary goal was to remove all traces of Japanese religion, an objective partially fulfilled through the deportation of Japanese settlers. However, the agents of the state also had to deal with the distribution of the

---

64. These conditions were true as of 2016 for the Confucius Temple in Tainan and 2017 for the Longshan Temple in Taipei.

65. This was true when I visited the Ciyun Temple in 2004 and the Dianji, Qing'an, and former Jilong Shrine in 2018.

land, buildings, and financial holdings of the Japanese temples, and adapt the structures for different uses, two processes that dragged on well into the 1950s. Their second goal was to transform Taiwanese religious practices by, at the very least, introducing new elements with the intent to improve the overall quality of religious life in the province. In light of the rhetoric of reunion that accompanied the Nationalist takeover of Taiwan, one might not have expected the Chinese authorities to find fault with the religions of their brethren, but in fact they discovered much to criticize as uncivilized and not suitable for modern China. As Rebecca Nedostup's masterful study of the invention of religion in modern China has shown, modernizing Nationalists developed a deep suspicion of what was newly defined as superstition (mixin) and sought to eradicate all activities that they deemed superstitious, to preserve modern, rational religion and to replace religious belief with faith in the Chinese nation-state. She argues that the antisuperstition campaigns of the Nanjing Decade were "meant to facilitate both the creation of a nation (jianguo) and the governance of the party (yidang zhiguo) by cleansing society of its deleterious aspects and fundamentally reordering it."[66] The Taiwanese were generally amenable to the removal of Japanese religions, but the clear danger posed to the religious core of their identity by the Nationalists' attack on superstitions was another matter entirely. Yet, as they had in the face of the attacks on their religious practices in the 1930s and 1940s, they maintained and strengthened this part of their ethnicity even as they modified aspects of its performance.

After Japan's surrender, the Japanese temples, both Shinto and Buddhist, were in a state of limbo. They possessed considerable wealth and occupied valuable property that had to be assessed and expropriated by the state, but in the meantime Japanese settlers continued to use them while they awaited deportation. It took some years to determine the fate of the Japanese temples in Jilong (table 7.1). Although the government had closed them all by the end of formal deportation in 1947, the first accounting of their assets was not made until 1950. Most of the moribund temples sat unused for at least several years, and they remained outside of city control as late as 1957. Even those designated

66. Nedostup, *Superstitious Regimes*, quotation on 15.

Table 7.1. The fate of Japanese temples in Jilong, 1950s

Old name	New name	City management	Current status
Kōzonji (Shinshū sect)	Jile Temple	no	housing, for rent by city residents
Jilong Shrine	Zhonglie Temple	yes	city park
Bitou Shrine[a]	Bizitou Shrine	no	housing, for rent by city residents
Yebisu Shrine	unnamed	land: yes; buildings: no	housing, for rent by city residents
Kinkōkyō Temple	private city kindergarten	yes	kindergarten for city residents
Renkōji (Nichiren sect)	unnamed	land: yes; buildings: no	public bath

SOURCE: GSG, CZB, 275-5: 01883-1, 1950, and 275-1:00096-1, 1957. Data in columns one and four come from a 1957 Ministry of Finance (CZB) survey, while columns two and three come from a 1950 survey.

[a] The temple called the "Bitou Shrine" is a misprint and should read "Bizitou Shrine."

as "housing for rent by city residents" were not always truly renovated for that purpose.[67]

The case of the Shinshū sect's Kōzonji, one of the first Japanese Buddhist temples in the city, shows how identities affected the disposition of Japanese religious institutions. In 1945 or 1946 the city closed the temple and seized its assets, but soon a representative of the Lingquan Temple, which formerly had ties to the Sōdō sect, moved into the space and began to repair it. What happened next revealed that local and provincial governments did not always agree, and that the private institutions that had helped create and sustain Taiwanese ethnicity held some power. The city government granted the Lingquan representative permission to hold Buddhist rites, but in 1950 the provincial government attempted to take control of the temple buildings and land, under authority of a 1947 regulation requiring that the assets of all

67. GSG, CZB, 275-1: 00096-1, "Ge xianshi jieguan simiao, diyi zong," 1950. People moved into some Japanese temples immediately after the war, but they were told this was illegal and were subsequently removed.

unused temples revert to state control.[68] The abbot of the Lingquan Temple objected on the grounds that the land had been previously owned by a private company and had been improperly taken over by the city in the first place. With support from the neighborhood head (*lizhang*), district head, and municipal council, he forced the city government to review the land registration records. It found that a Taiwanese company had purchased the property before the end of the war, that the city should not have assumed ownership, and that the Lingquan Temple should retain use of the buildings.[69] The documents do not record the response of the provincial government, but the long-term presence of a major Buddhist temple on that site indicates that the Lingquan Temple retained the former Kōzonji as a branch temple.[70] Such developments were not unique to Jilong, as Taiwanese claimed the sites of former Japanese temples in Taipei and other cities.[71]

The new regime attempted to remap the religious landscape to accord with a Chinese national identity through its transformation of Shinto shrines throughout the island. In early November 1945, the government assumed control of the Taiwan Shrine in Taipei, which had been rededicated late in the war as the Gokoku Shrine (Gokoku jinja) in honor of Japan's war dead, and planned to transform it into

68. GSG, NZB, 128: 2188, "Xiuzheng jiandu simiao an," July 10, 1947.

69. The key piece of evidence was that the land had been purchased in 1944 by the Taiwanese-owned Jilong Purchasing Group (Baozheng zeren Jilong goumai liyong zuhe), which was re-formed after retrocession as the Jilong Public Housing Cooperative (Jilong zhuzhai gongyong hezuoshe). GSG, CZB, 275-1: 00096-1 and 275-1: 00096-2, "Ge xianshi jieguan simiao, di'er zong," 1951. In the first document, the Purchasing Group is also referred to as the Housing Use Group (Zhuzhai liyong zuhe), and it is unclear which name is correct.

70. This temple, which the Lingquan named the Jile Temple (Jile si), remained the largest Buddhist institution in downtown Jilong into the twenty-first century. It went through another change when it became a branch of the important Foguang Mountain Temple (Foguang shan), a major world center for Pure Land Buddhism located outside of Gaoxiong. Thus this physical site began its sacred existence as a Japanese Pure Land temple, then became a branch of one of the most important Taiwanese-Japanese Zen Buddhist temples, and was finally reborn as a part of an international Pure Land network based in Taiwan.

71. GSG, CZB, 275-5: 01883-1, "Jieguan Ri simiao caichan," 1957, Winter, and 275-5: 01883-2, "Jieguan Ri simiao caichan," July 11, 1957. It seems that a larger percentage of the Japanese institutions in Jilong remained temples of some sort after retrocession.

the Taiwan Province Shrine to the National Martyrs (Taiwan sheng zhonglie ci).[72] This plan for reconsecration set a model for major Shinto institutions throughout the island. The Jilong city government decided to replace the Jilong Shrine with a Shrine to the National Martyrs by late 1946, and budgeted 60,000 yuan for the project (see map 6.1).[73] Given the timing, this decision must have seemed to the Taiwanese municipal councilors to be a misdirection of resources that should have been used to aid local citizens, and some Taiwanese met the government's takeover with at least personal objections.[74] The main shrines in Tainan and Taoyuan were similarly repurposed, although others, like the one outside of Jinguashi, were abandoned in ruins. Meanwhile, the Nationalists searched for and memorialized Taiwanese islanders who had displayed appropriate dedication to their ancestral nation (*zhong ai zuguo*). By mid-1947 the provincial administration had enshrined eighty-four people as "the glorious martyrs and honorable patriots of Taiwan province."[75] This enshrinement was partially an act of revenge against the wartime enemy, as the Nationalists both physically and mentally replaced the Japanese national heroes and deities with their own, and it was an attempt to incorporate Taiwan into the Chinese nation-state at the fundamental level of self-sacrifice for the national good. It also displayed what Nedostup has described as

72. TWG, Taiwan xingzheng zhangguan gongshu, "Jieshou Huguo shenshe gaicheng sheng zhonglie ci," 129.2–7. The file itself is undated, but documents within it are from 1945 and 1946. This plan was not fulfilled; the site became home to Taipei's Grand Hotel and the Shrine to the National Martyrs sits a short distance to the east.

73. "Difang tongxun: Jilong," *MB*, Nov. 3, 1946, 4.

74. Yan Qinxian submitted his family's claim to a portion of the former shrine's property, a sizable piece of land that had been part of the family holdings that he said the city government had forced them to sell (*qiangzhi shoumai*; literally, forced purchase), for a sizable sum, in 1943 in order to expand the shrine. Yan couched his request in terms both filial and nationalistic in his effort to regain the property: "This would achieve the goal of honoring the ancestors by expressing the national spirit, and moreover the good fortune of the national people, and the good fortune of the nation." XZZG, 00315700019006, "Jilong shimin Yan Qinxian guihuan tudi chengbao an," Jan. 4, 1946.

75. TWG, Taiwan sheng zhengfu, "Zhonglie ci xianzhe shiji an," 081-3, 1946, 80–85. Items within this file that have legible dates were written in June of that year.

the Nanjing regime's effort to inculcate its citizens with a faith in the state rather than in popular religion.

The disposition of Japanese sacred spaces reveals some aspects of the struggle to reterritorialize postwar Taiwan, but far more significant was the Nationalist approach to the Taiwanese religious landscape. The Nationalist regime viewed religion with no small degree of suspicion, and had spent much of the prewar decade trying to stamp out practices it viewed as out of step with its modernizing goals.[76] Much like the radical phase of Japanization in Taiwan, the New Life Movement sought the eradication of old superstitions and promoted a more modern, rational form of religion. As Nedostup argues, certain religions, if shorn of their superstitious elements and merged with state objectives, could be admitted as part of the modern Chinese nation. Of the available options, the ROC state was most amenable to Christianity, certain forms of Buddhism, and, in particular, state-centric Confucianism.[77] Frederic Wakeman has described Nationalist ideology as "Confucian fascism," a merger between the mass-mobilization techniques of the European and Japanese fascists and what Chiang Kai-shek described as "the highest culture of our people."[78] Chiang placed four Confucian virtues—*li, yi, lian, chi*—at the heart of his New Life Movement, a campaign that he intended to fundamentally reform and modernize Chinese society.[79] Li Shiwei, writing on Confucianism in postwar Taiwan, argues for continuity into the postwar era, stating that it was "the main line of the national culture."[80]

What this Nationalist attitude toward religion meant for its colonization of Taiwan is that different aspects of religious life would be treated with different measures, some supportive and others suppressive. The Ministry of the Interior (Neizhengbu) clarified the postwar

76. In addition to Nedostup's work, see also Oldstone-Moore, "The New Life Movement."

77. Nedostup, *Superstitious Regimes*.

78. Wakeman, "A Revisionist View," 424.

79. *Li* is regulated attitude, *yi* is right conduct, *lian* is clear discrimination, and *chi* is real self-consciousness. See Chiang Kai-shek, "Essentials of the New Life Movement," in De Bary and Lufrano, *Sources of Chinese Tradition*, 342–44.

80. Li Shiwei, "Haibin fu sheng dao," 205–30, quotation on 205.

government's approach in a mid-1947 decree that mandated that the term "temple" (*simiao*) be used for the places of worship of all five approved religions—Buddhism, Daoism, Protestantism, Catholicism, and Islam—in place of such terms as temple monastery (*siyuan*) or church (*jiaotang*). The state ordered all temples to form an oversight committee (*weiyuanhui*) with a manager (*guanliren*) at its head, and to register with their local governments, which supposedly gained ultimate control. Perhaps most significantly, the new law banned all unorthodox temples (*yinci*) and evil rituals (*xiesi*).[81] Although this policy appeared to be impartial in its application to all religious institutions, a subsequent provincial decree displayed the ambivalence of the Nationalist state. On the one hand, the regulations affirmed the principle of religious freedom throughout the island, but on the other, they ordered the suppression of all defiled (*wumie*) religions.[82] As in other arenas, the government's capacity to enforce its policies did not match the extent of its vision, which had its own limitations in any case. Even as officials attempted to legislate appropriate religious practices for citizens of the Chinese nation-state, they failed to define what constituted a superstition, an unorthodox temple, or defiled religion.

At an aggregate level and over the long term, it is clear that Nationalist policies held to the first part of the contradictory legislation of 1948. Recent studies have described the postwar decades as a time when religious activity flourished on Taiwan. One has referred to it as the "period of freedom of popular faith."[83] Some evidence from Jilong alone supports this position. By one count, citizens and officials established forty-eight new temples in the city between 1951 and 1992, well more than had been built in the Qing and Japanese periods combined.[84] A recent survey published by the Jilong city government found more

81. GSG, NZB, 128: 2188, "Xiuzheng jiandu simiao an," July 10, 1947.

82. Taiwan sheng xingzheng zhangguan gongshu, *Taiwan xingzheng zhangguan gongshu gongbao* 2, no. 60 (Dec. 11, 1947): 947.

83. This phrase comes from Taiwan wenxian weiyuanhui, *Chongxiu Taiwan sheng fangzhi* 3-1, and it is the title of section 4, on popular religion. See also Zhu and Chen, *Taiwan sheng Jilong shi zhi*, vol. 21, section 4, on religion; and Jordan, "Changes in Postwar Taiwan."

84. Taiwan wenxian weiyuanhui, *Chongxiu Taiwan sheng fangzhi* 3-1, 1009, 1087–91.

than fifty additional places of worship in the city, many of them no larger than roadside altars.[85] In the short term, during the first six years after retrocession, people donated almost 300 million yuan islandwide to temples for festivals or when they visited to pray.[86] Seizing on the promise of religious freedom, Taiwanese in Jilong and elsewhere promoted a short- and long-term florescence of spiritual activity.

More instructive, however, is a finer-grained analysis of which of the pre-1945 institutions flourished and when they did so, as well as where officials most stringently applied restrictions against purported superstition. Certain temples benefited greatly from the new climate of openness. The Longtong Confucius Temple in Taipei, for example, became a key location where Taiwanese and Chinese Confucians came together to promote the temple's growth.[87] Jilong's Lingquan Temple did especially well in the immediate postwar period, perhaps because of its prior cross-strait connections. In addition to taking over the Kō-zonji, in 1947 it established the Jilong branch of the China Buddhist Association (Zhongguo Fojiaohui), under the leadership of the temple abbot, Yan Qinxian, and others.[88] The Nationalist government had authorized this young association in the late 1930s to enhance its control over Buddhism in China, and by allying itself to this organization, the Lingquan Temple once again joined with the Buddhist institutions of the dominant social and political groups.[89] Shared traditions and institutional connections evidently facilitated cooperation.

Even though some of the older Taiwanese temples, and thus some aspects of religious life, flourished in the new environment, Taiwan's religious institutions nonetheless faced denigration from Chinese transplants. The travel author Wu Jiaqing provided insight into mainlanders' views of Taiwanese Buddhist temples when he published a vignette about his early 1950s visit to the Lingquan. Although he found

85. Li, Lai, and Ye, *Gui fu shen gong*.

86. Taiwan wenxian weiyuanhui, *Chongxiu Taiwan sheng fangzhi 3-1*, 1009, 1087–91.

87. Li Shiwei, "Haibin fu sheng dao," 206–10.

88. Zhu and Chen, *Taiwan sheng Jilong shi zhi*, 4659.

89. For more information on the China Buddhist Association and its role in Taiwan in this period and after, see Jones, *Buddhism in Taiwan*, chaps. 4–5. Jones calls it the Buddhist Association of the Republic of China (BAROC).

it odd that there were no monks present when he visited, he stated that the facilities put him in mind of major Buddhist centers in Jiangsu and Sichuan. When his traveling companion asked him why so few people visited such a fine place, his poetic response targeted the Taiwanese for criticism: "It is because over the years mountain ranges of a thousand folds become sealed up by smoke and cloud, so the people who come are fewer and fewer." His words suggested that he felt Taiwanese people did not give the temple the respect it deserved. He concluded on a wistful note, lamenting the absence of the temple's founder, Shanhui, because had he been present then Wu could have enjoyed subsequent trips to the temple to discuss poetry and Chan Buddhism, and "view the colors of Mount Yuemei."[90] In Wu's view, what had once been a noble institution, with the potential of being one of China's great Buddhist centers, had lost its way and so it declined and was forgotten by those who should have maintained it. Moreover, in contrast to the Japanese religious scholar Masuda Fukutarō, who in 1942 expressed regret that there had not been a more complete synthesis of Japanese and Taiwanese Buddhism, Wu felt that it was not quite Chinese enough.

Chinese Nationalists, both officials and nonofficials, took a much dimmer view of what they and the Japanese before them classified as Daoism, which for them represented the locus of superstitious behavior among the Taiwanese. An early guide to the island published by the Taiwan News Office (Taiwan xinwen chu), *The Taiwan Guidebook* (*Taiwan zhinan*), began its section on the local deity festivals with a highly critical, and incorrectly gender- and age-limited, view of a firmly established practice: "Old Taiwanese women follow a superstitious spiritual path, and every year they expend considerable waste on paper money."[91] It further detailed, in an unflattering way, four particular aspects of Taiwanese religious life that required reforms: the *yulanhui* and the

90. Wu Jiaqing, *Taidao lan sheng* (Embracing the beauty of Taiwan Island), in Yang and Chen, *Minjian sizang, chanye pian yi*, 407.

91. *Taiwan zhinan* (*Taiwan Guidebook*), in Yang and Chen, *Minjian sizang, chanye pian yi*, 288. What I have translated as "superstitious spiritual path" is "*mixin shen dao.*" As a compound, *shendao* is the same as "Shinto," but it is clear from the context that the authors were not discussing Japanese religion.

water lanterns associated with the Ghost Festival, the intense devotion to Mazu, and the performance of ritual sacrifices.[92]

Faced with such opinions and the threat of the sorts of seizures that took place during the Nationalists' antisuperstition campaigns of the 1930s, Jilong's major temples maintained their defensive posture.[93] The Dianji Temple, which had been the most closely watched institution in Jilong during the 1920s because it hosted many potentially destabilizing public lectures, celebrated the end of Japanese rule by building a large wooden altar for its patron deity in 1946.[94] This might have been a unique act, however; the Dianji did not undertake further renovation at the time. Most local temples simply followed state directives to register themselves and adopt the mandated rationalizing structure, which consisted of a committee under the leadership of a managing official.[95] Taking this step was not a dramatic reform for Jilong's temples, which had been run by managers—by bureaucratic rather than spiritual figures—during the Japanese period as well; only the pronunciation of this position changed, from *kanrijin* to *guanliren*. Leaders of the Qing'an Temple delayed repairs and new construction until the 1960s.[96] They may have lacked funds, or perhaps they chose to defer renovation so as not to draw attention from the state. In light of Murray Rubinstein's work on the competition between temples and the growth of particular sites of the Mazu cult, it seems that the Qing'an was not able to retain its earlier status in the postwar context.[97] Regardless, although Jilong's residents, no doubt many of them Chinese, established a considerable number of new temples in the long run, the older ones saw at most modest refurbishment during the 1940s and early 1950s.

92. Ibid.

93. Nedostup, *Superstitious Regimes*, 15, 117.

94. The new altar built at the Dianji Temple was still there in 2016, with the date of construction carved into the front.

95. XZZG, 00308100028003, "Jilong shi Ren'ai qu simiao jiaotang diaochabiao bu song an," Dec. 27, 1946.

96. For the renovation of the Qing'an Temple, see Liu Qingfan, *Qing'an gong zhi*, 36–38.

97. See Rubinstein, "'Medium/Message,'" 181–218.

The Taiwanese were not, however, purely defensive in the face of pressure against their religious core; instead they adopted a more pro-active posture when it came to religious festivals. To be fair, it seems from the available sources that the Nationalist government attacked super-stition in Taiwan with much less energy and zeal than it had on the mainland during the Nanjing Decade, and certainly with less intensity than the Chinese Communists displayed after 1949.[98] Nevertheless, it is also clear that Nationalist Chinese did not view favorably the major-ity of local religious practices. The Taiwanese could have met Chinese critiques of superstition, backwardness, and waste by pointing out that, during the Japanese colonial era, they had already rationalized the organization of their temples, combined their main spirit-welcoming festivals into one united event, and limited the practice of burning ghost money when economic and political pressures became too great.[99] The postwar sources do not indicate that they raised any of these points, which may have had to do with either the fact that the intensity of the White Terror highly constrained public discussions, or that, in an atmosphere of de-Japanization, a positive discourse on that era would have been counterproductive.

Instead, the Taiwanese in Jilong relied on a performance of the religious core of their identity: the celebration of the Ghost Festival. The Japanese authorities heavily restricted, but did not fully prohibit, the festival during the 1930s and 1940s, but once Chen Yi's civil admin-istration began operating in October 1945, it issued a temporary ban on all popular religious processions, echoing the Government-General's 1895 suspension. Given the festival's persistence through the privations of the global Depression and war, it is unlikely that the local residents willingly refrained from celebrating it immediately after 1945. When the government lifted its ban in 1948, it opened a new phase in this history of contestation. That summer, for the first time in many years,

98. Johnson, *The Souls of China*, 25–27.
99. The economizing merger seems not to have continued after retrocession, but it is hard to be certain since the official documents, newspapers, and other early postwar sources make almost no references to these deity-welcoming temple fes-tivals. For Jilong, the festivals seem to have lost much significance compared with observances in the prewar era, although the Beigang Mazu festival is a major annual event for all of Taiwan.

the appointed time of year arrived without any restrictions on the manner of celebration, and the residents of Jilong and the surrounding area responded with a tremendous display. The rotating cycle of leadership fell to the Lin surname group, but it seems that everyone put forth a special effort to offer sacrifices to the spirits. So many animals were killed for the event that year that the streets of the entire area from the main altar in Gaosha (formerly Takasago) Park to the train station, roughly half of the old Taiwanese district, were filled with animal offerings. A subsequent account vividly described the area as a "forest of meat [roulin]."[100]

This elaborate celebration might have been a repetition of the lavish temple festivals held in the 1930s to ward off the Depression, or an effort to honor the spirits that had protected Jilong's residents through the war. However, the worst of the immediate postwar economic difficulties had passed, and the Ghost Festival is not an occasion to give thanks, it is a time to soothe the restless dead. The crucial rituals of the festival revolve around offerings to appease the spirits of those who died in such a way that they could not be properly mourned. When, at least according to popular memory, the residents of Jilong established their variation on this widely observed event in 1855, they did so to propitiate the spirits of both those who had died in the waters around Taiwan and those killed in a recent outbreak of factional violence. In 1948 many additional lonely ghosts roamed the island, including the spirits of those who had died abroad in Japan's war machine and, more recently, those killed by order of the Chinese government during the 2-28 unrest. These circumstances accentuated the fact that, in rapid succession, both Japanese and Chinese nationalization projects had been fatal for the Taiwanese. With the bountiful displays of that year, the Taiwanese residents of Jilong rejected Japanese rule and resisted the imposition of Chinese orthodoxy.

The ROC government did not immediately respond to this provocative collective act, but a few years later it launched its attempted suppression of the Ghost Festival. The rapid decline of Nationalist fortunes in the civil war during late 1948 and 1949, followed by the demands of establishing the displaced state on Taiwan, apparently made the event

100. Huang Wenrong, *Jilong Zhongyuan ji*, 47–48.

a subsidiary concern for a short period of time. However, in 1952 the ROC initiated a full-scale attack across Taiwan. Citing a need to "elevate an economizing atmosphere" in light of the severity of "life during wartime," the Nationalist regime decreed that all locations must hold the festival on the same day, the fifteenth day of the seventh lunar month; that the celebrations could last only one day; and that the people could not be wasteful in their observances.[101] In late August, a group of some forty individuals, including members of the Jilong government and police, the local Nationalist Party branch, the City Council, a dramatic association, and the masters of incense from each major temple, met to set limitations on local practices, at a Customs Reform Conference (Gailiang xisu zuotanhui). The results of this meeting reflected state goals to at least sanitize and regulate the festival, if not eradicate it entirely. To reduce waste, the conferees agreed to hold the festival only on the fifteenth, as mandated, rather than on the traditional date for the local *pudu* ceremony, and they determined that only one banquet could be held, with only two pigs and two sheep to be sacrificed for the occasion. The conference resolution also forbade the main surname group from raising funds through donations, although it would be allowed to apply to the city government for financial assistance, and it mandated a security brigade (*jiuchadui*) to spread out across the city to make sure that people complied with the new restrictions. The members of the brigade included representatives from the provincial assembly, city government, and city party branch; regular and military police officers as well as a contingent from the martial law headquarters; and the entire city council.[102]

These invasive measures of enforcement, at least some of which were implemented in other parts of Taiwan, aimed to bring the festival fully in line with the state's nationalizing, re-Sinicizing objectives. They resonated with techniques applied by the Japanese colonial government,

101. "Jin wei nongli Zhongyuan jie minjian baibai jin puzhang," *LHB*, Sept. 3, 1952, 3. These phrases appear in numerous newspaper reports, suggesting that they were official slogans at the time. On this date, seven articles, covering different locations in Taiwan (Jilong, Yilan, Xinzhu, Fengyuan, Hualian, Luzhou, and Dadu), appeared under this heading.
102. "Jilong shi qingzhu Zhongyuan ji: zhu yang yidui zhi Qing'an gong, jumin zhuhu bude zixing zai zhu," *ZRB*, Aug. 23, 1952, 3.

but sought a higher degree of state control than the Japanese had managed to achieve. The consolidation of the festival on the fifteenth day of the seventh month pushed it more toward its Buddhist roots, as the *yulanhui* was held on that date in the Buddhist tradition.[103] Therefore, shifting all of the local celebrations to that single day accorded with the Nationalist regime's approval of Buddhism as a relatively rational religion. By taking that step, the Chinese transplants were also able to frame their attack on the Ghost Festival as part of their general campaign against superstition and thus as one part of their modernization of Taiwan and its society.[104]

Although these acts in 1952 suggest that the Nationalist government had not missed the point of Jilong's celebration four years earlier, the new restrictions did not prove immediately effective. The initial reports on the festivities in Jilong, Taipei, Taizhong, Tainan, and elsewhere present a narrative of success, emphasizing that most people followed the new directives, reduced waste, and implemented a needed reform of customs. However, references to punishing those who violated the new regulations, and to the need to intensify the restrictions in the account of what occurred in Jilong, suggest that reality did not fully accord with official pronouncements.[105] Over the next three years the government continued to wage its offensive against the festival, using a familiar range of tactics—security brigades, sending officials door to door to pressure people into following central and local directives, and driving "broadcast vehicles" (*guangboche*) through town to spread awareness of official policies—as it expanded the range of restrictions. Beginning in 1953, Jilong's Customs Reform Conference banned water lanterns, street lanterns, and the ceremonies for opening and closing the Ghost Door, and it also prohibited temples, people's associations, and workplaces from placing their names on implements

103. Ironically, in light of the Nationalist regime's de-Japanization project in Taiwan, this was also the date on which the Bon Festival was held in Japan.

104. At least one newspaper report from 1955 specifically referred to the Ghost Festival ceremonies as superstitious. See "Zhongyuan jie pudu bude tai langfei: Ji Gao liang shi dingding banfa," *LHB*, Aug. 18, 1955, 5.

105. "Renmin zunshou quandao, shixing jieyue baibai," *ZRB*, Sept. 4, 1952, 3. Once again, numerous articles on different locations appeared under the same heading.

they provided for the festival.[106] These regulations were reprinted almost verbatim by the press in 1955, suggesting that people had continued to engage in the forbidden practices.[107] Furthermore, although the reports on Jilong's festival did not specifically discuss the numbers of animals sacrificed, reports out of Yilan and Jiayi suggested the practice continued unabated.[108] After 1955, reportage on the festival declined precipitously, but that should not be taken to indicate that the Nationalist regime had won the battle and that the Taiwanese had abandoned this core aspect of their identity. In fact, the new generation of Taiwanese elites continued the practice, developed by their predecessors in Jilong, of working within the system to defend their ethnic community. They never abandoned the Ghost Festival or the core institutions around which they built their religious lives.

Conclusion

During the years 1945 to 1955, Jilong largely recovered from the devastation it had experienced under Allied bombing, as well as the shortages and violence of the first seventeen months of formal Nationalist Chinese rule (October 1945 through March 1947). In 1954 the ROC-USA Mutual Security Treaty dramatically changed the context in which the Taiwanese lived. In the wake of the PRC's shelling of ROC-held islands off the Fujian coast during the First Taiwan Strait Crisis, it guaranteed that the United States would protect Chiang Kai-shek's regime on Taiwan and effectively prevented the president of the ROC from launching a campaign to reclaim the mainland. At the local level, it also marked the year in which Jilong's residents, both Taiwanese and Chinese, began to tell their city's history in the form of gazetteers, the first multivolume

---

106. "Shijie jin Zhongyuan jin shemi jidian," *LHB*, Aug. 14, 1953, 4.

107. "Zhongyuan jie pudu bude tai langfei," *LHB*, Aug. 18, 1955, 5.

108. In 1953 almost 400 pigs were sacrificed in Yilan, around 250 by individuals rather than temples, and an account out of Jiayi stated that the sounds of killing pigs and ducks went on for an entire day. "Quansheng yan su du Zhongyuan reng wei neng mian da baibai," *LHB*, Aug. 25, 1953, 3.

official record of Jilong's past and present ever produced.[109] Nevertheless, neither the confirmation of long-term Nationalist colonization nor
the official historical project meant that the boundaries between Taiwanese and Chinese were collapsed in the processes of Nationalist
consolidation and rebuilding the city. To be sure, the Nationalist state
was not monolithic and the actions of its local agents sometimes differed from central policies in important ways that allowed Taiwanese
residents to play a role in rebuilding their city. In fact, the physical
re-creation was incomplete, at least in terms of fulfilling the visions of
central and city planners, and as the Taiwanese engaged in social reconstruction through organization building, welfare provision, and religious institutions and practices, they performed their long-established
roles and asserted their identity as a modern ethnic group. Thus, Chinese
efforts to reterritorialize Jilong succeeded only partially through urban
reconstruction, and barely at all in remaking the imagined terrain.

Running through the disputes that occurred over local politics,
social welfare, and religion were competing versions of modernity. Taiwanese and Chinese used key elements of Nationalist ideology in their
political debates. The Taiwanese seized on the ideal of constitutional
democracy to pursue the full voice in local governance that they had
been denied under the Japanese, but the state's crackdown following
the 2-28 Incident and the oppressive White Terror made it clear that
the new regime believed that Japanese colonization had insufficiently
modernized the Taiwanese, who required further political tutelage.
Denied the promise of democratization, and with independence-minded
activists driven underground or overseas, the Taiwanese in Jilong
instead used Sun's third people's principle, the people's livelihood, to
criticize the city government, and the larger entity it represented, for
not doing enough to improve the welfare of local citizens. The Chinese
officials advanced a vision of welfare that merged new ideas of poverty
with the disciplinary power of the modern nation-state, whereas

109. Although both Japanese and Taiwanese residents of Jilong had written
numerous single-volume accounts of the city's history and conditions, the twenty
volumes published by the city government between 1954 and 1959 represented the first
official account.

Taiwanese residents called for the restoration of the scientific, semi-professional, and systematic approach to social work that had existed before 1941. Ultimately the latter group won by shaping a new welfare institution that mirrored, in function and form, the earlier system of local welfare commissioners. In the sacred realm, agents of the state attempted to enforce their antisuperstition campaign and their conception of rational "modern religion"—including Confucianism, aspects of Buddhism, and Christianity—by eradicating what they saw as backward, unhygienic, and wasteful practices. The Taiwanese, in contrast, saw no conflict between modernity and the deity-welcoming festivals, water lanterns, and rituals of the Ghost Festival that fundamentally constituted their ethnicity. By defending these elements, with some accommodations, they ensured that, amid the postwar reconstruction of Jilong, the city's imagined geography remained a predominantly Taiwanese space.

Epilogue
History, Memory, and the Usage and Utility
of Taiwanese Ethnicity

B y the mid-1950s Jilong appeared to have returned to its heyday of the prewar years. The wartime devastation, the removal of the Japanese settlers who had helped to create the physical and imagined city, and the indiscriminate killing by Nationalist Chinese forces bent on subjugating autonomous voices in their new province—these events had defined the city's darkest hours. Nevertheless, from the late nineteenth century Jilong and its residents had stood at the forefront of most if not all of Taiwan's transformations, and in 1955 the city seemed poised to maintain its vanguard position. The recovery of trade suggested that it was once again "truly an important harbor" or "a marketplace of commerce" as a Taiwanese journalist described it in 1931. The removal of wartime debris and the ongoing port construction suggested that, once again, "the light of hope [shone] brightly" on Jilong, as the city song proclaimed in 1933.[1] Although it was not quite one of the great harbors of the East, in the optimistic words of an official report of 1946, it nonetheless held pride of place as Taiwan's main port and a site for visionary urban renewal. The companies founded by the Yan brothers, Kimura Kutarō, and Ōmi Tokigorō, the society-building projects of Xu Zisang

---

1. See the epigraphs to the introduction; on commerce: Jian Wanhuo, *Jilong zhi*, introduction, 6; on the song: Kuhara, *Kiirun no uta*.

and Ishizaka Sōsaku, and the reconstructive efforts of postwar elites
had built and rebuilt Jilong, and allowed it to serve as a forge for tempering Taiwanese ethnic consciousness.

To briefly recapitulate, the historical events of the late nineteenth
to the mid-twentieth centuries shaped the intertwined emergence of
two main identities: local, urban Jilongese; and regional, ethnic Taiwanese. Historical processes of settlement, colonization, and recolonization defined these seven decades. The movement to Taiwan by people
from China's southeastern coast included a long history of conflicts
and accommodations between Chinese settlers and indigenous groups,
settlers from different home regions, and settlers and the state. Yet,
ultimately many of these settlers began to identify themselves with
particular places in Taiwan, even as they reterritorialized the island as
Chinese. However, the transfer of Taiwan and its inhabitants to Japanese colonial control, together with reterritorialization projects, fundamentally altered the history of the island and the identity trajectories
of its people. Referred to now as islanders and treated as an ethnic group
that was largely defined by its customs, language, collective genealogy,
and area of habitation, they faced policies and attitudes among Japanese settlers that, contradictorily, sought to both assimilate and exclude
them from the Japanese national family. In this setting, islanders and
Japanese found common ground for a time in the construction of
Jilong as Taiwan's preeminent port city, but the rise of expansionist and
radically assimilationist Japanese nationalism during the 1930s shattered that shared imagined space and permanently divided the two
groups. The power of Japanese national identity became a contrasting
other against which the Taiwanese constructed their consciousness.

Meanwhile, islanders joined with other islanders to advocate for
their involvement in local and islandwide political affairs, to create
organizations that undergirded their community, to protect the religious institutions and practices they held as most important, to engage
in modern methods of social welfare for the benefit—and at times
transformation—of other islanders, and to define borders between
themselves and the Japanese. They used their positions within local
institutions and businesses to develop islandwide connections through
expanding bureaucratic and economic networks and hierarchies. Thus,
both within the rapidly growing and modernizing port city of Jilong

and across urban Taiwan, the islanders became "Taiwanese," and they too reterritorialized urban and nonurban spaces to accord with their ethnicity. The fact that they created a primary identity that was ethnic but not necessarily national meant that they followed a trajectory other than the one that would be expected of them by most histories of the modern world, theories of nationalism and the nation-state, and scholarship on Taiwanese identity. Taiwanese nationalism existed, to be sure, and it drew on the ethnic community, but they were not coterminous.

Japan's defeat by the Allied forces in August 1945 resulted in a second transfer of sovereignty, this time to the modern nation-state of the Republic of China, and subjected the Taiwanese to a new phase of colonization, deterritorialization, and reterritorialization. In fact, the principal differences between prewar Japanese rule and postwar Chinese rule lay not in ideology but in temporal duration and the historical viability of claims of commonality. Many Taiwanese retained a strong Chinese cultural identity and welcomed their island's incorporation into China. Under these conditions, Jilong itself held the potential to unify, for both the Taiwanese residents and the new Nationalist rulers embraced the vision of a reconstructed port of great national and international prominence. Yet when Chinese mainlanders viewed their erstwhile siblings in Taiwan, they saw the taint of Japanese rule and the practice of backward customs—that is, they also treated the "provincials" as a premodern ethnic group—and imposed a radical program of re-Sinicization. Moreover, the civil war with the Communists demanded the extraction of all possible resources from Taiwan, and meant that the new administration of Taiwan Province was at best unable, and at worst uninterested, in addressing the basic needs of the Taiwanese. The explosion of the 2-28 Incident and its brutal suppression highlighted the enormous gulf between Taiwanese and Chinese. But even under the enforced, oppressive stability of the years that followed, the Taiwanese people continued to use religion and welfare to perform their identity and defend the carefully constructed borders around their imagined terrain. Far from submitting to the hegemony of Chinese nationalism—the new conceptual other—the Taiwanese held fast to their ethnicity.

The history that I have described and analyzed has been largely forgotten in Taiwan and among generations of scholars. Pierre Nora's point about how modern societies are condemned to forget the past is worth recalling, because the ongoing process of change in Taiwan dramatically affected the collective memory of ethnic formation. Jilong's future seemed promising in 1955, but in reality that was the moment after which it began its long slide into relative obscurity. Before 1960, Gaoxiong would eclipse Jilong's status as a port and city of significance, and Jilong has more recently become, in functional terms, a relatively distant satellite of Taipei.[2] More significant for both academic and popular understandings of Taiwanese identity as a solely national consciousness, events and contextual factors since 1945 shaped Taiwanese memories of the Japanese and early ROC eras, as well as the ways in which people in Jilong and Taiwan made use of this past to frame and mediate their interactions with the Nationalist regime and its adherents.

The earliest and most significant of these developments were, unquestionably, the violent crackdown on the 2-28 Uprising and the period of the White Terror and martial law into which it bled. The brutality of the first fell on people across Taiwan, not only those who directly engaged in acts of opposition but also those who aided the demonstrators, had previously voiced objections to the early policies of the Nationalist regime, or happened to be standing in the wrong place. Nationalist forces sometimes acted in arbitrary ways, and thus not all of the members of Jilong's municipal council who had criticized government actions or their results suffered the mortal fate of Yang Yuanding, and some who were arrested, such as Yan Yunnian's grandson, avoided imprisonment on Green Island. The violence of 1947, martial law, and the White Terror all shared the objectives of eliminating political views that lay beyond, or challenged, approved discourse, and restricting the policy-making process to a small, carefully controlled circle of mainlander power holders. More important, they all bred uncertainty, fear, and silence within the Taiwanese and indigenous populations. Although I did not have time, space, or access to sources for a more thorough examination of the White Terror in Jilong, the anxiety engendered by Nationalist policies mitigated against open

2. Other peripheral locations, such as Danshui and Taoyuan, are on the Taipei Metro rapid transit system, for example, whereas Jilong is not.

discussion of the past and promoted a view of the pre-1945 period that contrasted favorably with what came immediately after.[3] Those with stronger feelings of Taiwanese nationalism either hid underground or fled overseas to avoid punishment, and those who remained had to negotiate with an oppressive state and its agents.

The replication of the same sorts of social, political, and sometimes economic inequalities that had prevailed during the Japanese era also influenced the loss of that history. Much like their Japanese predecessors, the Nationalist Chinese initially reserved for themselves the great majority of government jobs, a position atop the social hierarchy, privileged entry into some sectors of the economy, and the power to determine who could and could not subsequently gain access to these realms. By treating the Taiwanese as a group that both shared key characteristics and sat below the transplants and refugees, the Nationalists drew boundaries between *waishengren* and *benshengren* that mirrored the distinctions of the earlier era.[4] The hierarchy was not absolute. For example, when many Taiwanese began to thrive during the phenomenal economic growth of the 1960s and after, their lifestyles sometimes contrasted with the declining circumstances of many of the retired Nationalist soldiers (*laorongmin*) in their "dependents' villages" (*juancun*).[5] Nevertheless, the evident divide between Chinese and Taiwanese, in terms of political power and social status, meant that addressing those imbalances became much more significant than examining the inequities of the Japanese era. Also, because the experiences of the period from 1895 to 1945 served as the foundation of their differences from the mainlanders who now sought to oppress them,

3. When I completed the bulk of my research for this book, relevant sources were simply unavailable. Wu Rwei-ren makes a similar argument in "Redeeming the Pariah, Redeeming the Past," 72–73.

4. This distinction was not immediate or simplistic in its creation. Stéphane Corcuff demonstrates that the identity of *waishengren*, and thus its separation from *benshengren*, emerged through a complex, dynamic process of ethnicity formation. See Corcuff, "Taiwan's 'New Mainlanders,' New Taiwanese?," in Fell, *Politics of Modern Taiwan*.

5. The living standards of individuals varied, to be sure, but over time the conditions in most of the villages themselves unmistakably declined. See Lin Qiushan, *Muqian laorongmin*; and Yang, *Luodi shenggen*, 9–12.

many Taiwanese embraced aspects of that earlier past—including speaking Japanese—as positive markers of distinction.[6] Coincidentally, following the signing of the Taipei Peace Treaty the Nationalist government derived strategic and economic benefit from closer relations with Japan and evidently saw little gain in criticizing it for its imperialist past.

The gradual process of Taiwanization within the state, the Nationalist Party, and the minds of many mainlanders also substantively affected remembrance of earlier years. The practice of local elections and the recruitment of Taiwanese into the party, the latter of which Jiang Jingguo elevated to a formal policy in the early 1970s, greatly advanced the limited political engagement that Taiwanese had experienced from the 1920s to the early postwar period, and it also resulted in a takeover of the party by Taiwanese, in terms of absolute membership and presence in local governments, by the mid-1970s.[7] Moreover, as Stéphane Corcuff, Wang Fu-ch'ang, and Mahlon Meyer have shown in different ways, the majority of those who came over after 1945 began to think of themselves as firmly rooted in Taiwan.[8] Following the haphazard and nearly abortive democratization of the martial law era, the full opening of discourse and elections from the late 1980s into the 1990s and beyond prompted a vibrant, detailed, and multifaceted examination of the past. However, this stage of remembering applied primarily to those aspects that had taken on greatest salience in the lives of the Taiwanese as a result of the most recent four decades of silence, repression, and consignment to secondary status. When Taiwanese gained the freedom to air their grievances and the ability, through access to previously classified documents, to explore the sources of their discontent, they concentrated on the more recent past: the 2-28 Uprising and its suppression,

6. Joseph Allen makes a similar point regarding recent memories of the Japanese era as a source of Taiwan's early modernization. See Allen, *Taipei*, 20.

7. The best study of this history is Jacobs, *Democratizing Taiwan*. See also the essays by Hung-mao Tien, Bruce J. Dickson, and Teh-fu Huang in Chang and Tien, *Taiwan's Electoral Politics*, especially 11–13, 53–56, and 114–17.

8. Corcuff, "Taiwan's 'New Mainlanders,'" 333–38; Wang, "You 'diyu yishi' dao 'zuqun yishi': lun Taiwan waishengren zuqun yishi de neihan yu yuanqi, 1970–1989," in Hsiau and Wang, *Zuqun, minzu yu xiandai guojia*, 181–257; and Meyer, *Remembering China from Taiwan*.

the White Terror, and the institutionalized inequities of post-1945 Taiwan. They also focused on politically charged linguistic distinctions among Mandarin Chinese (Guoyu), Taiwanese, Hakka, and indigenous languages, and the connections between language and identity. Fine-grained debates ensued over the differences among Taiwanese, Minnanese, and Hokkien. Under these circumstances, a careful examination of the decades of Japanese rule and settlement became, at best, of secondary importance.

Finally, the shifting features of the cross-strait situation affected how Taiwanese made use of their history, extending from the Japanese era to the much more distant past. During the first decades of Nationalist Chinese rule, the overarching goal of reunification meant that Taiwan had no history independent of its incorporation into a narrative of the creation of modern China. It fit into China's history through a centuries-long process of settlement, governance, and Sinicization, followed by a brief interregnum of separation and then restoration. However, as the objective of national reunion faded even from official Nationalist proclamations, it became possible to question the teleology of Chinese national construction. In addition, the rise of the more independence-minded Democratic Progressive Party (DPP) shifted both the perspective from which Taiwan's past was viewed and the purposes to which its history could be applied. Both of these trends allowed people to remember the past in a new way, as a narrative not of Sinicization but of the progressive accumulation of factors that made Taiwan distinct from China. Central to this new collective memory were the presence of indigenous peoples who did not exist across the Taiwan Strait and a sense of prolonged, successive colonization (Dutch, Spanish, Zheng, Qing, Japanese, Chinese). In this view, the Japanese era became a key marker of Taiwan's non-Chineseness, but not in a manner that demanded a careful, critical examination of that period or its influence on what it meant to be Taiwanese.

Owing to all these factors, the realms of memory created by professional and popular historians, private individuals, and government entities obscured most of the history addressed in this book. To be sure, a number of dedicated and talented scholars explored these matters and I have relied greatly on their work, but at least until after the election of the first DPP president, Chen Shui-bian, in 2000 they were a small group with little institutional backing. The enforced silence that prevented open examination of 2-28, martial law, and the White Terror, as well as the prolonged struggle to gain a voice in local and national affairs, kept those things in the forefront of Taiwanese experiences and memories. Thus, as Taiwanese consciousness evolved in the 1980s and 1990s, it did so through archives, oral histories, memoirs, museums, and monuments that revolved around the retrocession era. State-sponsored sites of memory—for example, the Chiang Kai-shek and Sun Yat-sen Memorials, the Shrines to the National Martyrs in cities across Taiwan, and the National Palace Museum—ignored the Japanese and early ROC eras, whereas they celebrated a China-based history of struggle and triumph. Both sets of national histories neglected the same past, although they did so for different reasons: the first because other matters more urgently demanded remembering, the second because the Nationalists lacked strong connections to the experiences of the Japanese era.

Historical memories began to shift in the years leading up to, and particularly after, Chen's election in 2000, although not always to favor critical, nuanced evaluations of what had been forgotten. Showcasing a careful reexamination of that past, scholars working in Taiwan's first centers for Taiwan studies, established during the 1990s, pioneered the exploration of previously unused archives and libraries, including the documents of the Taiwan Government-General, the Japanese-era collections at the Taiwan Branch Library (Taiwan fenguan, now the National Taiwan Library), Academia Sinica, Taiwan University, and Taiwan Historica in Nantou. However, as seen in the excellent work of Leo Ching, Ming-cheng Lo, Wang Tay-sheng, and others, they principally sought the origins of a more contemporary Taiwanese nationalism. Widespread practices of locating and restoring many of the remaining Japanese-era structures, both large stone and brick buildings and smaller wooden structures, preserved physical remnants, but largely in the service of highlighting Taiwan's separation from China. The policies of the Chen administration—a time that, not coincidentally, overlapped with the years in which the present work began—promoted an explosion of local histories and historical projects, museums, and exhibits that emphasized both the Japanese and early

ROC eras. In many cases, the impetus was to catalog and display, to fit the past into existing notions of the present, not to analyze or interpret it on its own terms.[9] As Shu-Mei Huang has shown, the renovation and preservation of Japanese houses and other structures fed a cultural tourism that more often led to the repurposing of old buildings as shops and restaurants than to an awareness of their colonial histories.[10]

This nostalgia for pre-1945 history produced a range of results. Most regrettably, it fed into the idea that Taiwan was Japan's good colony, a conceptual falsehood that had more to do with domestic politics in Taiwan and the efforts by some Japanese to divert vehement, historically based criticisms from China and South Korea, than it did with the realities of Japanese rule, as Barak Kushner has insightfully argued.[11] More positively, it produced an unprecedented opportunity for scholars, who gained access to official and other sources on the Japanese and early postwar periods in the improved archival and library facilities established across Taiwan. For public consumption, museums such as the National Taiwan Museum in Taipei, and the National Museums of Taiwan History and Taiwan Literature in Tainan, have embraced the era of Japanese rule as fundamental to the construction of modern Taiwan in both the contents of their illuminating exhibits and their physical structures. The first is housed in a massive hall completed in 1915 to hold the Taiwan Governor-General's Office Museum, and the last is contained behind the meticulously restored façade of the Tainan Prefectural Government building erected in 1916. On a smaller scale, some Japanese individuals have been commemorated, or even deified, for their activities in Taiwan.[12] At worst, the return of public remembrances of the Japanese era allowed observers of Taiwan to simplistically contrast the tenor of Taiwanese and South Korean relations with Japan. At best, these realms of memory enabled the Taiwanese to assess

9. Taylor, "History and the Built Environment."
10. Shu-Mei Huang, "Rediscovering the Japanese Houses."
11. Kushner, "Nationality and Nostalgia."
12. Hatta Yoichi jinianguan, "Hatta Yoichi" (Hatta Yoichi) 八田與一, www.siraya-nsa.gov.tw/hatta/, accessed May 17, 2017; Everington, "WWII Japanese Pilot." For comparison, see the monument to an American pilot in Xiangyun, Yunnan, China; "U.S. and China Honor American," *U.S. Embassy and Consulates in China.*

the complexities of their historical ties to Japan, most recently including even the sensitive subject of the comfort women, much as the opening of 2-28 archives and museums allowed them to address the difficulties of *bensheng-waisheng* relations.[13]

In Jilong, this spirit took multiple forms in the early twenty-first century. The municipal government renovated two monuments, one that had been erected in 1933 to memorialize Prince Kitashirakawa, leader of Japan's colonizing military forces, and his arrival in Jilong in June 1895; the other a cenotaph raised in 1930 to honor the more than one hundred laborers who died while building Jilong's harbor. Both markers had been defaced, their inscriptions excised, after 1945.[14] Local historians, working in conjunction with the Jilong Cultural Center (Jilong wenhua zhongxin), which fills the site once held by the Public Welfare Society's Public Hall and the Jilong Club, compiled written materials and assembled public exhibitions that commemorated some of Jilong's most important institutions and residents. Xu Zisang and the Yan brothers were featured in a 2004 exhibit called *Jilong Number One* (*Jilong diyi*), and Ishizaka Sōsaku received a display all his own in June 2005.[15] They set up plaques in the formerly Japanese neighborhood of Small Jilong that described some of the architectural remnants, and around that time a maritime history museum opened in the former outpost of the Japan Mail Shipping Corporation, with substantial coverage of the Japanese era and a "1915 Café" that is named for the year the building was built.[16] Locals reasserted other long-suppressed

13. Funü jiuyuan shehui fulishiye jijinhui, "Ama jia—heping yu nüxing renquanguan" (Ama Family Peace and Women's Human Rights Museum) 阿嬤家‒和平與女性人權館, www.twrf.org.tw/amamuseum/index.php, accessed May 17, 2017.

14. The monument to Prince Kitashirakawa is located near the former site of the Qing customs house that he used as his headquarters when he arrived, and the memorial to the laborers is on a hillside to the west of the harbor, overlooking the results of the labors of those memorialized.

15. The exhibition was based on a set of three volumes, Jilong shi zhengfu, *Jilong diyi*. The published volumes profile only Xu, but the exhibition featured both Yan brothers.

16. This is the Yang Ming Oceanic Culture and Arts Museum, established by the Jilong-based Yang Ming Marine Transport Corporation. As of 2014, the museum's exhibits cover all of China's maritime history, from nautical warfare during the Three Kingdoms period to contemporary maritime commerce.

histories with the opening of an Aboriginal Culture Hall (Yuanzhumin wenhua huiguan), and with displays on the indigenous peoples who long inhabited Jilong's shores in temporary and permanent exhibits at the Cultural Center.

The wave of memory may have been short-lived—in Jilong, the restored monuments receive few visitors today and historical plaques in the old Japanese district rapidly faded to illegibility in the city's famous rain, whereas across Taiwan, President Ma Ying-jeou launched few new commemorative initiatives during his administration, from 2008 to 2016—but in fact the developments of Japanese- and early ROC-era Taiwan had fundamentally shaped Taiwanese identities before the turn of the twenty-first century.[17] The most significant, ongoing manifestation of the history discussed and analyzed in this book is the strong religiosity of the Taiwanese. According to recent statistics from the Ministry of the Interior, Taiwan has more than thirteen thousand temples, a total that makes them an incredibly common sight in urban Taiwan.[18] Temples are ubiquitous and active, both in terms of their frequent and numerous visitors, who light incense and offer prayers before many of the deities they enshrine, and the festivals that spill noisily out into the streets around each temple at least once a year. Significantly, although temples to popular deities usually bustle with activity, the official Shrines to the National Martyrs, in contrast, receive very few visitors.[19] The origins of this religiosity probably lie in the local societies of southeastern China that sent the majority of settlers to Taiwan, but the ardent and repeated defense of local temples and festivals against Japanese and Chinese attempts to transform and even eradicate them made religion an absolutely fundamental aspect of

17. The partisan politics around preserving these plaques was evident when, on returning in the summer of 2018 when President Tsai Ing-wen and the DPP were in power, I found the plaques had been fully restored.

18. Neizhengbu, "Tongji baobiao." The total included 12,112 temples (simiao) and 1,080 churches (jiaohui/jiaotang), the former predominantly Daoist and Buddhist, the latter Christian. These figures suggest a decline since 2014, when the totals were 12,106 and 3,280, respectively, according to statistics I found on the ministry's website on May 17, 2017, but which are no longer accessible.

19. These observations are based on multiple visits to the shrines in Jilong and Taipei since 2002.

modern Taiwanese ethnicity. These institutions and events are, simply put, the most public ways in which Taiwanese perform their identity.[20] They are fundamental to the practice of being Taiwanese.

The foundational character of religion is evident in the rearticulation of both Jilong and Taiwanese consciousness through sacred spaces and activities since 1955. The two things for which Jilong is currently well known, its popular night market and its high-profile Ghost Festival, are built around the city's most important temples. The first, known in full as the Jilong Temple-Mouth Night Market (Jilong miaokou yeshi), sprawls outward for several blocks from the small courtyard at the entrance to the Dianji Temple, echoing the format of Taipei's Shilin and Raohe night markets. The Dianji Temple hosted a market during the Japanese era, and a few food stalls continued to operate at the temple's entrance even during the war years. Thereafter, the number of stalls grew through the 1950s and 1960s, and by 1980, Jilong's night market had developed a reputation for its food.[21] The current iteration, like much of Taiwan's flourishing night-market culture, is largely a product of the post-martial-law era, but it is nevertheless connected to the local prominence that the institution gained following its establishment in the 1870s.

The Ghost Festival and the Qing'an Temple are deeply entwined with each other, with Jilong, and with Taiwanese consciousness, so their post-1955 evolution sheds light on how the Taiwanese have used their earlier history in more recent times. Following a brief suspension immediately after the war, the festival resurged from 1948 into the mid-1950s, when new government regulations limited its duration and scale. Jilongese, and Taiwanese in other locations, did not bow to these restrictions but continued to hold massive celebrations. Jilong residents defied official curtailment in 1959, when they gathered more than ten million yuan for a single day of ceremonies and assembled an exceptionally large collection of food and other offerings. The Nationalist authorities apparently interpreted this impressive display in negative

20. Ian Johnson's recent work suggests that religiosity is surging in the PRC as well, but that is a very recent development and seems to be more state driven. See Johnson, *The Souls of China*.
21. Cao and Chen, *Taiwan de yinshi wenhua*, 83–103.

terms, perhaps an uncharitable recognition of the ten-year anniversary of their defeat and flight from the mainland. The following year, city officials summoned representatives from all the surname groups for the Forum on Improving the Ghost Festival (Gaishan Zhongyuan jie jidian zuotanhui). Rather than open the floor for discussion of possible improvements, city officials inveighed on the importance of economizing on religious activities and unilaterally issued a three-year plan for renovating popular customs. Subsequently, in 1961 the city government constructed a new main altar to replace the one near the center of the city that Xu Zisang built with municipal financing in 1930. Officials selected a spot overlooking the city from the east of the harbor, in a park named for Chiang Kai-shek, but even though the new altar was larger and had more surrounding space than the old one, the Jilongese did not begin to use it until 1974.[22] Their refusal to abandon the cramped downtown location for more than a decade suggests opposition to the state's efforts to dictate their celebration of the Ghost Festival.

Even with this accommodation, it seems that contention over the Ghost Festival simmered until 1984, when the Lin surname group held the role of master of the festival. By this time Taiwan had experienced more than two decades of its economic miracle; Chiang's death, in 1975; the Gaoxiong Incident of 1979, which briefly crushed the prodemocracy movement; and a gradual easing of restrictions on political activity. Undoubtedly with the approval of the other surnames, the Lins proposed to the city government that citizens and officials should collectively plan and enact that year's festival. The mayor concurred, and the contemporary Jilong Ghost Festival was born through an agreement that echoed the manner in which local elites had attempted to end native-place disputes during the 1850s. It grew into a widely publicized four weeks of events, including the main ceremonies at the beginning, middle, and end of Ghost Month, as well as numerous more secular

22. Huang Wenrong, *Jilong Zhongyuan ji*, 47–50. The amounts listed were in new Taiwan dollars (NT), which had devalued significantly since the original rate established in 1949 of five NT to one U.S. dollar. By the summer of 1959 the exchange rate had mostly stabilized at about twenty-five NT to one U.S. dollar, so the ten million yuan would have amounted to roughly $400,000, a significant sum, especially before Taiwan's economy took off in the 1960s and 1970s. See Ho, *Economic Development of Taiwan*, 396, "Statistical Appendix," table A66.

public activities, including art exhibitions, talent shows, and public markets. The Water Lantern Parade and burning of the water lanterns have remained the main public events, but modern technology has had its impact. The parade is now a huge, carnival-like event complete with gaudy, brightly lit motorized floats, and afterward, surname group members drive the lanterns to a beach on the coast and push them, ablaze, into the water while a crowd watches from the shore.[23]

In making these changes, the Jilongese did not bow to state pressure but drew clear connections between the Ghost Festival and their local and ethnic identities. When they re-formed the festival in 1984, they decided to write its name using the original, pre-1885 characters for Jilong (雞籠 rather than 基隆) as a reminder of the festival's local and cultural—that is, nonnational—roots. Their choice of characters referenced Taiwan's long history of Chinese settlement without linking the annual event to a Chinese nation-state. In 2005 some participants evoked the historical experience of Japanese rule during the Water Lantern Parade, when a group of youths wearing Japanese-style festival attire (*happi*) carried a lantern that was designed to resemble a Japanese portable shrine (*mikoshi*).[24] This act may have come out of a youthful interest in Japan, but it evoked a much deeper history. In 2006, for the first time in more than forty years, the main ceremonies returned to the dates long used for the local observance, the twenty-fifth and twenty-sixth days of the seventh lunar month, rather than the days that the Nationalist government in 1952 had designated for all locations. All these developments upended the oppressive re-Sinicization policies of the early postwar era on Taiwan, and they challenged the direction of the state's cultural policies during the Chinese Cultural Renaissance of the 1960s and 1970s. At that time, partly to counterbalance the PRC's devastating Cultural Revolution, government policy reemphasized the Three People's Principles and a Confucian orthodoxy of the sort advocated in the New

23. This description of the post-1984 festival is a combination of accounts and pictures contained in Huang Wenrong, *Jilong Zhongyuan ji*, and Li, Lai, and Ye, *Gui fu shen gong*; two festival pamphlets published by the city government in 2005 that list all of the activities during Ghost Month; and my own observations of parts of the festival in 2004 and 2005.

24. For these points I draw from Li Fengmao, *Jilong qing zan Zhongyuan*, and my own observations of parts of the festival in 2004 and 2005.

Life Movement of the Nanjing Decade.[25] By highlighting the Taiwaneseness of the Jilong Ghost Festival, and using it to advertise their city, local residents advanced the Taiwanization of Jilong identity.

Taiwanese also drew on their pre-1955 experiences with, and dedication to, social welfare and social work in their contributions to the creation of Taiwan's welfare state. Scholarship on the evolution of postwar social welfare stresses that the state did not promote social welfare systems on a large scale until after the democratization process accelerated during the 1980s and 1990s. From the late 1950s through the 1970s, state-sponsored social welfare existed largely in the forms of limited insurance programs and aid to soldiers and civil servants, as the central government remained focused on accelerating economic development as its top domestic priority, and delegated welfare to the local level. Subsequently, the growth of social movements and the demands of electoral politics pushed the expansion of initiatives for teachers, farmers, and fishers, leading up to the full National Health Insurance system in 1995, as well as to greater support for a range of social services and forms of assistance. From the late 1980s, separate initiatives for the disabled, women, children, the elderly, and youths joined together in a somewhat coherent social welfare movement that pressured the state to provide assistance to these disadvantaged groups. Meanwhile, creating and supporting social welfare programs became important issues in the local and general elections of the 1990s, especially for the opposition DPP candidates.[26] As a result, in spite of the Asian financial crisis of 1997, Taiwan established a robust welfare state by the end of the twentieth century. The roots of these impressive developments have not been well explored as yet, but the debates over *minsheng* and the significance of the creation of social welfare programs in Jilong during the late 1940s and early 1950s, as well as the central role of non–Nationalist Party actors in more recent years, strongly suggests that Taiwanese drove the creation of Taiwan's welfare state.

25. Lin Guoxian, "Zhonghua wenhua."
26. See Aspalter, *Democratization and Welfare State*, especially chaps. 4–6; Chan Hou-sheng and Yang Ying, "The Development of Social Welfare in Taiwan," and Hsiao Hsin-huang, "Taiwan's Social Welfare Movement since the 1980s," both in Aspalter, *Understanding Modern Taiwan*, 149–67 and 169–204, respectively; and Wong, *Healthy Democracies*.

I have stressed the uses of the past as indicators of the ongoing importance of Taiwanese ethnic formation, but I have skirted an issue that demands to be addressed head on: the concurrent, and much more widely discussed, expression of Taiwanese national identity. As my references to 2-28, White Terror, and cross-strait relations should indicate, as numerous scholars have argued, and as Shawna Yang Ryan vividly depicts in her sweeping novel of postwar Taiwan, a strong Taiwanese national identity emerged in and beyond Taiwan after 1945.[27] The 1950s to the 1970s saw the growth of the anti–Nationalist Party, anti-Chinese Taiwan Independence movement, both within Taiwan and, even more prominently, around the globe.[28] I discussed at the outset of this book the wealth of scholarship on the significance of the political opening of the 1980s and 1990s for the formulation and expression of Taiwanese nationalism. All the efforts to prove the differences between Taiwan and China, as well as research into the genetic makeup of Taiwan's residents, reflected the expanding community of Taiwanese nationalists rather than the extension of the borders of the Taiwanese ethnic group.[29] Their imagined terrain certainly grew, as seen in Taiwan's religiosity and its welfare state, but the drive to display non-Chineseness became the greater purview of Taiwanese nationalism. As academics and activists conflated Taiwanese consciousness with nationalism, and studied ethnic identities principally in other contexts, Taiwanese ethnicity lost any autonomous significance. In short, Taiwanese ethnicity was captured by, and subsumed within, Taiwanese national identity.

So what, then, is the continued significance of Taiwanese ethnicity in a world in which national identities dominate the political contexts in which Taiwanese live? Its presence highlights that Taiwan is, indeed,

27. Ryan, *Green Island*.

28. Phillips, "Building a Taiwanese Republic," 44–69.

29. Cai Youming, "Jiyin kexue yu renting zhengzhi: yuanzhumin DNA, Taiwanren qiyuan yu shengwu duoyuan wenhua zhuyi de xingqi," in Hsiau and Wang, *Zuqun, minzu yu xiandai guojia*, 315–70. Some have used genetic data to argue for an ethnic distinction between Chinese and Taiwanese—see, for example, a recent article in the *Taipei Times*, Pan, "Taiwanese, Han Chinese Ethnically Distinct"—but such arguments are overly deterministic and ignore the constructed nature of ethnicity.

a multiethnic country that contains significant populations of indigenous, Taiwanese, Chinese, Hakka, Hoklo, and other citizens, and multiethnic noncitizens as well, and thus its comparators should be drawn
from among other places with similar ethnic compositions and distri-
butions of social, political, and economic power among those groups.
Similarly, the history of Taiwanese ethnic formation draws attention
to the nested, overlapping nature of identity in general and the identities available to the people of Taiwan in particular, which include family, surname, native place, indigenous community, subethnicity, and
many others. Understanding which identities are most significant and
powerful in which contexts depends on a full awareness of their multi-
plicity. Viewed another way, in light of the well-documented ambivalence that most Taiwanese of the early twenty-first century hold toward
the pursuit of formal juridical independence, nationalism may not hold
a hegemonic status among residents of the island.[30] Through long experience with the oppressive policies of nationalizing regimes, and the
repeated rejections by national communities, Taiwanese on the whole
identify most strongly with alternative forms of consciousness, and
protect the borders of those identities with more dedication than they
do those of the imagined nation-state. In short, ethnicity remains viable for many as an alternative to nationalism and the nation-state, and
thus to the dominant conception of the arc of modern world history.

Twenty-first-century visitors to Jilong might arrive by train and,
upon leaving the station, walk between the water and the historical core
of the Taiwanese settlement, then cross the canal to wander through
the neighborhood east of the harbor. Turning right at the building that
houses the city government, constructed in 1932, they would pass streets
that once ran through the heart of the Japanese community, much of
the physical evidence of which exists in various stages of collapse. A
bit further on they would find themselves in front of an architectural
hodge-podge that combines a Japanese torii shrine gate with a Chinese
temple gate and indigenous Taiwanese motifs. Taking the staircase up
through this structure for a broad view of the contemporary port city,

---

30. See especially Rigger, *Taiwan's Rising Rationalism*, and the surveys made by
the Election Study Center at Chengchi University since 1992; see Zhengzhi daxue
xuanju yanjiu zhongxin 政治大學選舉研究中心, http://esc.nccu.edu.tw/main.php.

they would pass a post-1945 structure built in a Chinese style but surrounded on three sides by a bulky stone enclosure that more closely
resembles the walls protecting the imperial palace in Tokyo than those
around the Forbidden City in Beijing: the remnants of the Shinto Jilong
Shrine now contain an ROC Shrine to the National Martyrs. Further
uphill is the Ghost Festival altar, built by the city but rejected by festival
planners for more than a decade. This juxtaposition of sacred spaces
reveals the successive efforts of Japanese and Chinese nation-states and
settlers to inscribe their identities and visions of modernity on Taiwan
and its residents. However, the entire scene in its totality—the harbor
with its modern port facilities, the city and its contents laid out mostly
on the flat areas amid the hills—reveals how islander-Taiwanese used
those colonizing projects to create their ethnicity. In containing multiple pasts, it reveals the place that residents and regimes built through
collective efforts and a shared urban consciousness, and the process of
Taiwanese ethnic formation in resistance against, and dialogue with,
Japanese and Chinese nationalisms. Both the city and the ethnicity
endure, embracing and displaying elements from each phase of their
construction as they continue to move forward through time.

Glossary

The following are Chinese and Japanese terms that appear in the text, with transliterations, characters, and translations. The list includes concepts, positions, events, and some place names. Proper names of individuals and institutions, with their characters, appear in the index.

banshanren 半山人 "half-mountain people"

benshengren 本省人 "insiders"/Taiwanese

bentuhua 本土化 localization/indigenization

Bon matsuri 盆祭り/*o-bon* お盆 Bon Festival

bunka seikatsu 文化生活 cultural life

daihyōsha (Jp.)/*daibiaozhe* (Ch.) 代表者 representative

diguo shili 敵國勢力 Japanese influence

dōjō fukuro 同情袋 sympathy bags

Dōjō shūkan 同情週間 Sympathy Week

Gijū (Jp.)/Yizhong (Ch.) 義重 district of Jilong

guangfu 光復 retrocession

Haku'ai (Jp.)/Bo'ai (Ch.) 博愛 district of Jilong

hogo kaado 保護カード assistance cards

hōmen iin 方面委員 local welfare commissioners

hontōjin 本島人 islanders

hu'er 胡兒 China's historic enemies

huifu 恢復 recovery

Irifune (Jp.)/Ruchuan (Ch.) 入船 district of Jilong

jichi teki kannen 自治的觀念 self-reliance

jokyū 女給 café waitress

juancun 眷村 dependents' villages

kaishan fufan 開山撫番 "open the mountains, pacify the savages"

kanrijin (Jp.)/*guanliren* (Ch.) 管理人 manager

kazoku seido 家族制度 Japanese family system

Kōdō Bukkyō 皇道佛教 Imperial Way of Buddhism

kokugo katei 國語家庭 national-language household

kokumin seishin 國民精神 national citizenship

kokumin teki jikaku 國民的自覺 national consciousness

kokutai kannen 國體觀念 emperor-centered vision of the nation

laorongmin 老榮民 retired Nationalist soldiers

liuyong Riqiao 留用日僑 kept-on Japanese

lunzhi zhupu 輪值主普 master of the festival

luzhu 爐主 master of incense

minzoku yūgō (Jp.)/*minzu ronghe* (Ch.) 民族融合 ethnic fusion

moni xuanju 模擬選舉 mock election

naichi enchō 內地延長 national extension

naichijin 內地人 Japanese

naiTai yūgō 內台融合 Japanese-Taiwanese fusion

neidihua 內地化 Sinicization

neiTai yijia 內台一家 "one Chinese-Taiwanese family"

pinjin zhuyi 聘金主義 bride price-ism

podo (Jp.)/*pudu* (Ch.) 普度 or 普渡 universal salvation ceremony

pushi 普施 universal salvation ceremony

quyu weiyuan 區域委員 district commissioners

raojing 遶境 deity-welcoming festival procession

ryōsai kenbo 良妻賢母 good wife, wise mother

seikatsu kaizen 生活改善 life reform

shakai fukushi 社會福祉 social welfare

shakai jigyō 社會事業 social work

shakai kyōiku 社會教育 social education

shakai kyōka 社會教化 social civilization

shakai kyūsai 社會救濟 social welfare

shehui fuli 社會福利 social welfare

shehui fuwu 社會服務 social assistance

shehui zuzhi 社會組織 social organization

shengfan 生番 "raw" aborigine

shin chitsujo 新秩序 new order

shizenteki jōtai 自然的狀態 uncivilized

shōkon 招魂 Japanese ceremony for the dead

Shōwa no shūkyō dai kaikaku 昭和の宗教大改革 Shōwa religious revolution

shufan 熟番 "cooked" aborigine

shugoshin 守護神 protective deity

sidazhu 四大主 Four Great Pillars

Taiwan meishin 台灣迷信 Taiwanese superstitions

Taiwan shinshi 台灣紳士 Taiwan gentry

Takasago (Jp.)/Gaosha (Ch.) 高砂 district of Jilong

tuzhuhua 土著化 localization/ indigenization

waishengren 外省人 "outsiders"/ mainland Chinese

wenhua jiangyan 文化講演 culture lectures

wumie 侮蔑 defiled

xiesi 邪祀 evil rituals

yinci 淫祠 unorthodox temples

yingshen ji 迎神祭 deity-welcoming festivals

youying gongmiao 有應公廟 wish-granting temples

yulan penhui 盂蘭盆會, or *yulanhui* 盂蘭會 universal salvation ceremony

zhaijiao 齋教 vegetarian teaching/ lay Buddhism

zhaitang 齋堂 vegetarian hall

Zhongyuan ji 中元祭, Zhongyuan jie 中元節, or Zhongyuan pudu 中元 普度 or 普渡 Ghost Festival

zhuputan 主普壇 primary salvation altar

zongqinhui 宗親會 clan association

Bibliography

Archives and Libraries

Guoli Taiwan daxue tushuguan (National Taiwan University Library) 國立
臺灣大學圖書館. Taipei.

Guoli Taiwan tushuguan (National Taiwan Library) 國立臺灣圖書館.
Taipei.

Guoshiguan (Academia Historica) 國史館. Taipei.

Guoshiguan shuwei dang'an (Digitized Archives of Academia Historica)
國史館數位檔案. Taipei. http://ahdas.drnh.gov.tw.

Guoshiguan Taiwan wenxianguan (Taiwan Historica) 國史館臺灣文獻館.
Nantou.

Kerr, George. George Kerr Collection. Hoover Institution Archives, Stanford, CA.

Kokka toshokan (National Diet Library) 国家図書館, Tokyo.

Kokuritsu kōbun shokan Ajia rekishi shiryō sentā (Japan Center for Asian
Historical Records, National Archives of Japan) 国立公文書館アジア歴
史資料センター. www.jacar.go.jp/.

Nihon kokuritsu kōbun shokan (National Archives of Japan) 日本国立公文
書館. Tokyo.

Taiwan sheng xingzheng zhangguan gongshu dang'an (Documentary
Archives of the Taiwan Province Civil Administration) 臺灣省行政長
官公署檔案. http://ds2.th.gov.tw/.

Taiwan sōtokufu. Taiwan sōtokufu kōbun ruisan (Documentary Records
of the Taiwan Government-General) 臺灣總督府公文類纂. Accessible at
http://sotokufu.sinica.edu.tw/ or http://tais.ith.sinica.edu.tw/sinicafrs
Front/index.jsp.

Zhongyang yanjiuyuan Taishisuo dang'anguan (Archives of the Institute
of Taiwan History, Academia Sinica) 中央研究院台史所檔案館. Taipei.

Publications

Addams, Jane. *Twenty Years at Hull House, with Autobiographical Notes.* New York: Macmillan, 1910.

Allen, Joseph Roe. *Taipei: City of Displacements.* Seattle: University of Washington Press, 2012.

Ambaras, David R. "Social Knowledge, Cultural Capital, and the New Middle Class in Japan, 1895–1912." *Journal of Japanese Studies* 24, no. 1 (Winter 1998): 1–33.

Anderson, Benedict R. O'G. *Imagined Communities: Reflections on the Origin and Spread of Nationalism.* Rev. ed. London: Verso, 2006.

Andrade, Tonio. *How Taiwan Became Chinese: Dutch, Spanish, and Han Colonization in the Seventeenth Century.* New York: Columbia University Press, 2010.

Arikura Zenji. "Dairen shi no shakai jigyō" (Social work in Dairen) 大連の社會事業. *Shakai kenkyū* (Sept. 1926): 45–48.

Aspalter, Christian. *Democratization and Welfare State Development in Taiwan.* Aldershot, UK: Ashgate, 2002.

———, ed. *Understanding Modern Taiwan: Essays in Economics, Politics, and Social Policy.* Aldershot, UK: Ashgate, 2001.

Barclay, George W. *Colonial Development and Population in Taiwan.* Princeton, NJ: Princeton University Press, 1954.

Barclay, Paul D. "Cultural Brokerage and Interethnic Marriage in Colonial Taiwan: Japanese Subalterns and Their Aborigine Wives, 1895–1930." *Journal of Asian Studies* 64, no. 2 (May 2005).

———. "An Historian among the Anthropologists: The Inō Kanori Revival and the Legacy of Japanese Colonial Ethnography in Taiwan." *Japanese Studies* 21, no. 2 (2001): 117–36.

Barth, Fredrik. *Ethnic Groups and Boundaries: The Social Organization of Culture Difference.* Little, Brown Series in Anthropology. Boston: Little, Brown, 1969.

Bell, Catherine M. "Introduction." In *Medieval and Early Modern Ritual: Formalized Behavior in Europe, China, and Japan,* edited by Joëlle Rollo-Koster. Cultures, Beliefs, and Traditions 13. Leiden: Brill, 2002.

———. *Ritual Theory, Ritual Practice.* New York: Oxford University Press, 2009.

Bernstein, Gail Lee. *Recreating Japanese Women, 1600–1945.* Berkeley: University of California Press, 1991.

Bhabha, Homi K. *The Location of Culture.* London: Routledge, 1994.

Bol, Peter K. *Neo-Confucianism in History*. Harvard East Asian Monographs 307. Cambridge, MA: Harvard University Press, 2008.

Borao Mateo, José Eugenio. *The Spanish Experience in Taiwan, 1626–1642: The Baroque Ending of a Renaissance Endeavor*. Digitally printed version. Hong Kong: Hong Kong University Press, 2010.

Botsman, Daniel V. *Punishment and Power in the Making of Modern Japan*. Princeton, NJ: Princeton University Press, 2007.

Brook, Timothy. *Collaboration: Japanese Agents and Local Elites in Wartime China*. Cambridge, MA: Harvard University Press, 2005.

———. "Hesitating before the Judgment of History." *Journal of Asian Studies* 71, no. 1 (Feb. 2012): 103–14.

Brown, Melissa J. *Is Taiwan Chinese? The Impact of Culture, Power, and Migration on Changing Identities*. Berkeley Series in Interdisciplinary Studies of China 2. Berkeley: University of California Press, 2004.

Burton, Antoinette M. *After the Imperial Turn: Thinking with and through the Nation*. Durham, NC: Duke University Press, 2003.

Butler, Judith. *Excitable Speech: A Politics of the Performative*. New York: Routledge, 1997.

Cai Jintang. *Nihon teikoku shugi shita Taiwan no shūkyō seisaku* (Religious policies in Taiwan under Japanese imperialism) 日本帝国主義下台湾の宗教政策. Tokyo: Dōseisha, 1994.

Cai Longbao. *Tuidong shidai de julun: Ri zhi zhongqi de Taiwan guoyou tielu (1910–1936)* (Period of promotion: Taiwan's national railroads in the middle period of Japanese control, 1910–1936) 推動時代的巨輪: 日治中期的臺灣國有鐵路1910–1936. Taiwan shufang. Taipei: Taiwan guji, 2004.

Cao Mingzong and Chen Yaling. *Taiwan de yinshi wenhua: Jilong miaokou wenhua* (Taiwan's food culture: Jilong's Temple Market culture) 臺灣的飲食文化: 基隆廟口文化. Jilong: Jilong shili wenhua zhongxin, 1997.

Cao, Yonghe, and Leonard Blussé, eds. *Around and about Formosa: Essays in Honor of Professor Ts'ao Yung-Ho*. Taipei: Ts'ao Yung-ho Foundation for Culture and Education, 2003.

Carroll, John M. *Edge of Empires: Chinese Elites and British Colonials in Hong Kong*. Cambridge, MA: Harvard University Press, 2005.

Chang, Charles Chi-hsiang, and Hung-mao Tien, eds. *Taiwan's Electoral Politics and Democratic Transition: Riding the Third Wave*. Taiwan in the Modern World. Armonk, NY: M. E. Sharpe, 1996.

Chang, Lung-chih. "From Island Frontier to Imperial Colony: Qing and Japanese Sovereignty Debates and Territorial Projects in Taiwan, 1874–1906." Harvard University, Department of History, 2003.

Chatterjee, Partha. *The Nation and Its Fragments: Colonial and Postcolonial Histories*. Princeton Studies in Culture/Power/History. Princeton, NJ: Princeton University Press, 1993.

Chen, Cheng-siang. *The Port City of Keelung*. Keelung: Keelung Municipal Government, 1958.

Chen, Chung-min, Ying-chang Chuang, and Shu-min Huang, eds. *Ethnicity in Taiwan: Social, Historical, and Cultural Perspectives*. Taipei: Institute of Ethnology, Academia Sinica, 1994.

Chen Fangming, ed. *Taiwan zhanhou shi ziliao xuan: Ererba shijian zhuanji* (Historical materials on postwar Taiwan: The 2-28 Incident collection) 台灣戰後史資料選: 二二八事件專輯. Taipei: Ererba heping cujinhui, 1991.

Chen, Janet Y. *Guilty of Indigence: The Urban Poor in China, 1900–1953*. Princeton, NJ: Princeton University Press, 2012.

Chen Jingkuan. *Cong shengcheng dao Taizhong shi: yige chengshi de xingqi yu fazhan (1895–1945)* (From provincial capital to Taizhong City: The rise and development of a city, 1895–1945) 從省城到臺中市: 一個城市的興起與發展 (1895–1945). Yanjiu zhuankan 1. Taipei: Guoli Taiwan lishi bowuguan, 2012.

Chen Kongli. "Qingdai Taiwan shehui fazhan de moshi wenti: ping 'tuzhuhua' he 'neidihua' de zhenglun" (Various problems of Qing dynasty Taiwan's social development: A critique of the "indigenization" and "Sinicization" debate) 清代台灣社會發展的模式問題: 評「土著化」和「內地化」的爭論. *Dangdai* 30 (Oct. 1988): 61–75.

Chen Peigui. *Danshui tingzhi: shiliu juan* (Danshui Prefecture gazetteer: 16) 淡水廳志: 十六卷. Taiwan wenxian congkan 172. Taipei: Taiwan yinhang jingji yanjiushi, 1963.

Chen Qi'nan. *Chuantong zhidu yu shehui yishi de jiegou: lishi yu renleixue de tansuo* (Traditional systems and the structure of social consciousness: The deep search of history and anthropology) 傳統制度與社會意識的結構: 歷史與人類學的探索. Yun chen daxue congshu 1. Taipei: Yun chen wenhua shiye gufen youxian gongsi, 1998.

Chen Qingsong. "Ri zhi shiqi de wenshi guibao: Shiban Zhuangzuo" (Cultural treasures of the period of Japanese rule: Ishizaka Sōsaku) 日治時期的文史瑰寶: 石坂莊作. *Taiwan wenxian* 53, no. 2 (June 2002), 235–44.

Chen Rousen, Ye Wanqi, and Li Yirong, eds. *Chongsu Taiwan Pingpuzu tuxiang: Riben shidai Pingpuzu ziliao huibian* (Reconstructing an image of Taiwan's plains aborigines: Collected materials on plains aborigines from the Japanese era) 重塑台灣平埔族圖像: 日本時代平埔族資料彙編. Taiwan tuzhu yicong 1. Taipei: Yuanmin wenhua, 1999.

Chen Tsu-yu. "Hunyin yu jiazu shili: Ri zhi shiqi Jilong Yan jia de hunyin celüe" (Marriage and family power: The Jilong Yan family's marital strategy during the era of Japanese control) 婚姻與家族勢力: 日治時期基隆顏家的婚姻策略. In *Wusheng zhi sheng (II): jindai Zhongguo de funü yu wenhua (1600–1950)*, edited by You Jianming, Luo Jiurong, and Lü Miaofen, 173–202. Taipei: Zhongyang yanjiuyuan jindaishi yanjiusuo, 2003.

———. "Ri zhi shiqi Yan jia de chanye yu hunyin wanglu" (The production and marriage networks of the Yan family during the era of Japanese control) 日治時期顏家的產業與婚姻網路. *Taiwan wenxian* 62, no. 4 (Dec. 2011): 1–54.

———. *Taiwan kuangye shi shang de diyi jiazu: Jilong Yan jia yanjiu* (The first family in the history of Taiwan Coal Enterprises: Research on the Yan family of Jilong) 臺灣礦業史上的第一家族: 基隆顏家研究. Jilong wenxin congkan 112. Jilong: Jilong shili wenhua zhongxin, 1999.

Chen Xingtang, Qi Rugao, and Ma Zhendu, eds. *Taiwan "Er-erba" shijian dang'an shiliao* (Archival materials on Taiwan's 2-28 Incident) 台灣「二·二八」事件檔案史料. Taipei: Renjian chubanshe, 1992.

Chen Xinzhi. "'Tuzhuhua' yu 'neidihua' lunzheng de yige cemian: ping Chen Kongli 'Qingdai Taiwan shehui fazhan de moshi wenti'" (One side of the debate over "indigenization" and "Sinicization": A critique of Chen Kongli's "Various problems of Qing dynasty Taiwan's social development") 「土著化」與「內地化」論爭的一個側面—評陳孔立《清代台灣社會發展的模式問題》. *Shi yi* 21 (1990): 119–50.

Chen Yanru. "Zhongyuan pudu yu zhengshang zhi jian: Ri ju shiqi Jilong difang lingxiu de fazhan" (Government, commerce and the Ghost Festival: The development of local elites in Jilong under Japanese rule) 中元普度與政商之間: 日據時期基隆地方領袖的發展. Taiwan shifan daxue lishi yanjiusuo, 1998.

Cheng Chun-pin. "Jindai Jilong de shehui bianqian: yi lai Tai wairen de guancha wei zhongxin (1624–1877 nian)" (Modern Jilong society's transformation: Based on the views of foreigners who came to Taiwan [1624–1877]) 近代基隆的社會變遷—以來臺外人的觀察為中心 (一六二四〜一八七七年). *Taipei wenxian* 19 (Mar. 2002): 47–103.

Cheng, Robert L. "Language Unification in Taiwan: Present and Future." In *The Other Taiwan: 1945 to the Present*, edited by Murray A. Rubinstein, 357–91. Taiwan in the Modern World. Armonk, NY: M. E. Sharpe, 1994.

Ching, Leo T. S. *Becoming "Japanese": Colonial Taiwan and the Politics of Identity Formation*. Berkeley: University of California Press, 2001.

Chipman, Elana. "The De-Territorialization of Ritual Spheres in Contemporary Taiwan." *Asian Anthropology* 8, no. 1 (2009): 31–64.

Chou Wan-yao. *Hai hang xi de niandai: Riben zhimin tongzhi moqi Taiwan shi lunji* (The Maritime Age: Collected essays on Taiwan's history in the final stage of Japanese colonial rule) 海行兮的年代: 日本殖民統治末期臺灣史論集. Yun chen congkan 93. Taipei: Yun chen, 2003.

Chow, Kai-wing, Kevin Michael Doak, and Poshek Fu, eds. *Constructing Nationhood in Modern East Asia*. Ann Arbor: University of Michigan Press, 2001.

Chow, Tse-tsung. *The May Fourth Movement: Intellectual Revolution in Modern China*. Harvard East Asian Monographs 6. Cambridge, MA: Harvard University Press, 1960.

Christy, Alan S. "Making of Imperial Subjects in Okinawa." In *Formations of Colonial Modernity in East Asia*, edited by Tani E. Barlow, 141–70. Durham, NC: Duke University Press, 1997.

Clart, Philip, and Charles Brewer Jones, eds. *Religion in Modern Taiwan: Tradition and Innovation in a Changing Society*. Honolulu: University of Hawai'i Press, 2003.

Cohen, Paul A. *History in Three Keys: The Boxers as Event, Experience, and Myth*. New York: Columbia University Press, 1997.

Cohn, Bernard S. *Colonialism and Its Forms of Knowledge: The British in India*. Princeton Studies in Culture/Power/History. Princeton, NJ: Princeton University Press, 1996.

Conklin, Alice L. *A Mission to Civilize: The Republican Idea of Empire in France and West Africa, 1895–1930*. Stanford, CA: Stanford University Press, 1997.

Cooper, Frederick. *Africa in the World: Capitalism, Empire, Nation-State*. Cambridge, MA: Harvard University Press, 2015.

Cooper, Nicola. *France in Indochina: Colonial Encounters*. Oxford: Berg, 2001.

Corcuff, Stéphane. *Memories of the Future: National Identity Issues and the Search for a New Taiwan*. Taiwan in the Modern World. Armonk, NY: M. E. Sharpe, 2002.

———. "Taiwan's 'New Mainlanders,' New Taiwanese?" In *The Politics of Modern Taiwan*, edited by Dafydd Fell, 1:320–51. Critical Issues in Modern Politics. London: Routledge, 2008.

Craig, Albert M. *Chōshū in the Meiji Restoration*. Harvard Historical Monographs 47. Cambridge, MA: Harvard University Press, 1961.

Dai Baocun. *Jindai Taiwan haiyun fazhan: rongke chuan dao Changrong jubo* (The development of modern Taiwan's shipping: From junk ships to Evergreen liners) 近代台灣海運發展: 戎克船到長榮巨舶. Dianzang Taiwan 1. Taipei: Yushanshe, 2000.

Davidson, James Wheeler. *The Island of Formosa: Historical View from 1430 to 1900: History, People, Resources, and Commercial Prospects: Tea, Camphor, Sugar, Gold, Coal, Sulphur, Economical Plants, and Other Productions.* New York: Paragon Book Gallery, 1961.

Dawley, Evan N. "Changing Minds: American Missionaries, Chinese Intellectuals, and Cultural Internationalism 1919–1921." *Journal of American East Asian Relations* 12, no. 1/2 (2003): 1–31.

———. "Closing a Colony: The Meanings of Japanese Deportation from Taiwan after World War II." In *Japanese Taiwan: Colonial Rule and Its Contested Legacy,* edited by Andrew D. Morris, 115–32. London: Bloomsbury Academic, 2015.

———. "The Question of Identity in Recent Scholarship on the History of Taiwan." *China Quarterly* no. 198 (June 2009): 442–52.

———. "Women on the Move: Shifting Patterns in Migration and the Colonization of Taiwan." In *The Decade of the Great War: Japan and the Wider World in the 1910s,* edited by Toshihiro Minohara, Tze-ki Hon, and Evan Dawley, 281–300. Leiden: Brill, 2014.

De Bary, Wm. Theodore, and Richard John Lufrano, eds. *Sources of Chinese Tradition.* Vol. 2. 2nd ed. Introduction to Asian Civilization. New York: Columbia University Press, 1999.

DeGlopper, Donald R. *Lukang: Commerce and Community in a Chinese City.* SUNY Series in Chinese Local Studies. Albany: State University of New York Press, 1995.

de Groot, J. J. M. *Sectarianism and Religious Persecution in China.* Shannon, IE: Irish University Press, 1973.

Dikötter, Frank, ed. *The Construction of Racial Identities in China and Japan: Historical and Contemporary Perspectives.* Honolulu: University of Hawai'i Press, 1997.

———. *Crime, Punishment, and the Prison in Modern China.* New York: Columbia University Press, 2002.

Dirks, Nicholas B. *Castes of Mind: Colonialism and the Making of Modern India.* Princeton, NJ: Princeton University Press, 2001.

Doak, Kevin Michael. *A History of Nationalism in Modern Japan: Placing the People.* Handbuch der Orientalistik (Handbook of Oriental Studies), Section Five, Japan 13. Leiden: Brill, 2007.

Dodd, John. *Journal of a Blockaded Resident in North Formosa: During the Franco-Chinese War, 1884–5.* Taipei: Ch'eng Wen Publishing, 1972.

Dong, Madeleine Yue. *Republican Beijing: The City and Its Histories.* Asia: Local Studies/Global Themes 8. Berkeley: University of California Press, 2003.

Dower, John W. *Embracing Defeat: Japan in the Wake of World War II*. New York: W. W. Norton, 1999.

Duara, Prasenjit. *Culture, Power, and the State: Rural North China, 1900–1942*. Stanford, CA: Stanford University Press, 1988.

———. "Of Authenticity and Woman: Personal Narratives of Middle-class Women in Modern China." In *Becoming Chinese: Passages to Modernity and Beyond*, edited by Wen-hsin Yeh, 342–64. Studies on China 23. Berkeley: University of California Press, 2000.

———. *Rescuing History from the Nation: Questioning Narratives of Modern China*. Chicago: University of Chicago Press, 2007.

———. "Transnationalism and the Predicament of Sovereignty: China, 1900–1945." *American Historical Review* 102, no. 4 (October 1997): 1030–51.

DuBois, Thomas David, ed. *Casting Faiths: Imperialism and the Transformation of Religion in East and Southeast Asia*. Basingstoke, UK: Palgrave Macmillan, 2009.

———. "Introduction: The Transformation of Religion in East and Southeast Asia—Paradigmatic Change in Regional Perspective." In *Casting Faiths: Imperialism and the Transformation of Religion in East and Southeast Asia*, edited by Thomas David DuBois, 1–19. Basingstoke, UK: Palgrave Macmillan, 2009.

Elkins, Caroline, and Susan Pedersen, eds. *Settler Colonialism in the Twentieth Century: Projects, Practices, Legacies*. New York: Routledge, 2005.

Elliott, Mark C. *The Manchu Way: The Eight Banners and Ethnic Identity in Late Imperial China*. Stanford, CA: Stanford University Press, 2001.

Endō Masataka. *Kindai Nihon no shokuminchi tōchi ni okeru kokuseki to koseki: Manshū, Chōsen, Taiwan* (Nationality and family registry under modern Japanese colonial control: Manchuria, Korea, Taiwan) 近代日本の植民地統治における国籍と戸籍: 満洲・朝鮮・台湾. Tokyo: Akashi shoten, 2010.

Eskildsen, Robert. "Of Civilization and Savages: The Mimetic Imperialism of Japan's 1874 Expedition to Taiwan." *American Historical Review* 107, no. 2 (Apr. 2002): 388–418.

Everington, Keoni. "WWII Japanese Pilot Is a God in Taiwan." *Taiwan News*, Feb. 18, 2017. www.taiwannews.com.tw/en/news/3098140. Accessed May 17, 2017.

Fawaz, Leila Tarazi, C. A. Bayly, and Robert Ilbert, eds. *Modernity and Culture: From the Mediterranean to the Indian Ocean*. New York: Columbia University Press, 2002.

Fell, Dafydd, ed. *The Politics of Modern Taiwan*. Vol. 1. Critical Issues in Modern Politics. London: Routledge, 2008.

Fischer-Tiné, Harald, and Michael Mann, eds. *Colonialism as Civilizing Mission: Cultural Ideology in British India*. Anthem South Asian Studies. London: Anthem Press, 2004.

Fix, Douglas. "Reading the Numbers: Ethnicity, Violence, and Wartime Mobilization in Colonial Taiwan." In *Taiwan under Japanese Colonial Rule, 1895–1945: History, Culture, Memory*, edited by Liao Ping-hui and David Der-wei Wang, 327–57. New York: Columbia University Press, 2006.

Foucault, Michel. *Discipline and Punish: The Birth of the Prison*. New York: Vintage Books, 1979.

Fujitani, Takashi. *Race for Empire: Koreans as Japanese and Japanese as Americans during World War II*. Asia Pacific Modern 7. Berkeley: University of California Press, 2011.

———. *Splendid Monarchy Power and Pageantry in Modern Japan*. Twentieth-Century Japan 6. Berkeley: University of California Press, 1998.

Fushiki Yonejirō. *Gureito Kiirun* (Great Kiirun) グレート基隆. Zhongguo fangzhi congshu Taiwan diqu 215. Taipei: Chengwen chubanshe, 1985.

Garnot, Eugène Germain. *L'expédition française de Formose 1884–1885: Avec 30 grav. et 1 atlas de 10 ct. en couleurs*. Paris: Delagrave, 1894.

Garon, Sheldon M. *Molding Japanese Minds: The State in Everyday Life*. Princeton, NJ: Princeton University Press, 1997.

———. *The State and Labor in Modern Japan*. Berkeley: University of California Press, 1987.

Geertz, Clifford. *The Interpretation of Cultures: Selected Essays*. New York: Basic Books, 1973.

Gellner, Ernest. *Nations and Nationalism*. New Perspectives on the Past. Ithaca, NY: Cornell University Press, 1983.

Gladney, Dru C. *Muslim Chinese: Ethnic Nationalism in the People's Republic*. Harvard East Asian Monographs 149. Cambridge, MA: Council on East Asian Studies, Harvard University, 1991.

Gluck, Carol. *Japan's Modern Myths: Ideology in the Late Meiji Period*. Studies of the East Asian Institute, Columbia University. Princeton, NJ: Princeton University Press, 1985.

Gold, Thomas B. "Colonial Origins of Taiwanese Capitalism." In *Contending Approaches to the Political Economy of Taiwan*, edited by Edwin A. Winckler and Susan Greenhalgh, 101–17. Studies of the East Asian Institute, Columbia University. Armonk, NY: M. E. Sharpe, 1988.

———. *State and Society in the Taiwan Miracle*. Armonk, NY: M. E. Sharpe, 1986.

Goodman, Bryna. *Native Place, City, and Nation: Regional Networks and Identities in Shanghai, 1853–1937.* Berkeley: University of California Press, 1995.

Gordon, Andrew. *The Evolution of Labor Relations in Japan: Heavy Industry, 1853–1955.* Harvard East Asian Monographs Subseries on the History of Japanese Business and Industry 117. Cambridge, MA: Council on East Asian Studies, Harvard University, 1985.

———. *Labor and Imperial Democracy in Prewar Japan.* Berkeley: University of California Press, 1991.

Goscha, Christopher E. "'The Modern Barbarian': Nguyen Van Vinh and the Complexity of Colonial Modernity in Vietnam." *European Journal of East Asian Studies* 3, no. 1 (2004): 135–69.

Greene, J. Megan. *The Origins of the Developmental State in Taiwan: Science Policy and the Quest for Modernization.* Cambridge, MA: Harvard University Press, 2008.

Greenfeld, Liah. *Nationalism: Five Roads to Modernity.* Cambridge, MA: Harvard University Press, 1992.

Hamashita, Takeshi. "Tribute and Treaties: Maritime Asia and Treaty Port Networks in the Era of Negotiation, 1800–1900." In *The Resurgence of East Asia: 500, 150 and 50 Year Perspectives,* edited by Giovanni Arrighi, Mark Selden, and Takeshi Hamashita, 17–50. Asia's Transformations. London: Routledge, 2003.

Hanes, Jeffrey E. *The City as Subject: Seki Hajime and the Reinvention of Modern Osaka.* Twentieth-Century Japan: The Emergence of a World Power 13. Berkeley: University of California Press, 2002.

Hara machi shi hensan iinkai. *Hara machi shi* (Hara gazetteer) 原町誌. Azumachō, JP: Hara machi shi hensan iinkai, 1960.

Hardacre, Helen. *Shintō and the State, 1868–1988.* Princeton, NJ: Princeton University Press, 1989.

Harrell, Stevan, and Junjie Huang, eds. *Cultural Change in Postwar Taiwan.* Boulder, CO: Westview Press, 1994.

Harrison, Henrietta. *China. Inventing the Nation.* London: Arnold; New York: Oxford University Press, 2001.

———. *The Making of the Republican Citizen: Political Ceremonies and Symbols in China, 1911–1929.* Studies on Contemporary China. Oxford: Oxford University Press, 1999.

He Peifu and Lin Wenrui, eds. *Taiwan diqu xiancun beijie tuzhi: Yilan xian, Jilong shi pian* (Records of extant stone inscriptions in Taiwan: Yilan County and Jilong City) 臺灣地區現存碑碣圖誌: 宜蘭縣・基隆市篇. Taipei: Guoli zhongyang tushuguan Taiwan fenguan, 1999.

Henriot, Christian. *Shanghai, 1927–1937: Municipal Power, Locality, and Modernization*. Translated by Noel Castelino. Berkeley: University of California Press, 1993.

Henry, Todd A. *Assimilating Seoul: Japanese Rule and the Politics of Public Space in Colonial Korea, 1910–1945*. Asia Pacific Modern 12. Berkeley: University of California Press, 2014.

Heylen, Ann. *Japanese Models, Chinese Culture and the Dilemma of Taiwanese Language Reform*. Studia Formosiana 7. Wiesbaden: Harrassowitz, 2012.

Hiyama Yukio. "Riben zhi Tai shiqi dui Tai renshi de xingcheng: yi Taiwan zongdufu shiliao bianzuan weiyuanhui 'Taiwan shiliao' de bianzuan luoji wei lie" (Forms of knowledge of Taiwan during the period of Japanese control: The compilation logic of the Taiwan Government-General's Historical Materials' Compilation Committee's "Taiwan Historical Materials" as an example) 日本治臺時期對臺認識的形成—以臺灣總督府史料編纂委員會「台灣史料」的編纂邏輯為例. In *Di si jie Taiwan zongdufu dang'an xueshu yantaohui lunwenji*, translated by Hong Xinyin, 355–89. Nantou: Guoshiguan Taiwan wenxianguan, 2006.

Ho, Sam P. S. *Economic Development of Taiwan, 1860–1970*. Publication of the Economic Growth Center, Yale University. New Haven, CT: Yale University Press, 1978.

Hostetler, Laura. *Qing Colonial Enterprise: Ethnography and Cartography in Early Modern China*. Chicago: University of Chicago Press, 2001.

Howell, David L. *Geographies of Identity in Nineteenth-Century Japan*. Berkeley: University of California Press, 2005.

Hsiau, A-chin. *Contemporary Taiwanese Cultural Nationalism*. Routledge Studies in the Modern History of Asia 7. London: Routledge, 2000.

Hsiau A-chin and Wang Honglun, eds. *Zuqun, minzu yu xiandai guojia: jingyan yu lilun de fansi* (Ethnicity, nation, and the modern state: Rethinking theory and experience in Taiwan and China) 族群, 民族與現代國家: 經驗與理論的反思. Zhongyang yanjiuyuan shehuixue yanjiusuo zhuanshu 11. Taipei: Zhongyang yanjiuyuan shehuixue yanjiusuo, 2016.

Huang Chün-chieh, ed. *Gaoxiong lishi yu wenhua lunji* (Collected essays on Gaoxiong's history and culture) 高雄歷史與文化論集. Vol. 1. Gaoxiong: Chen Zhonghe weng cishan jijinhui, 1994.

Huang, Shu-Mei. "Rediscovering the Japanese Houses in Taiwan: A Contest between Postcolonial Inhabitants and the Creative City Regime." In *Politics and Aesthetics of Creativity: City, Culture, and Space in East Asia*, edited by Lu Pan, Hung Wah Wong, and Karin Ling-fung Chau, 119–51. Los Angeles: Bridge21, 2015.

Huang Wenrong, ed. *Jilong Zhongyuan ji* (Jilong's Ghost Festival) 基隆中
元祭. Jilong: Jilong shi zhengfu minzhengju, 1989.

Huang Yingzhe. *"Qu Riben hua" "zai Zhongguo hua": zhanhou Taiwan
wenhua chongjian, 1945–1947* (Uprooting Japan, implanting China:
Cultural reconstruction in postwar Taiwan, 1945–1947) "去日本化" "在
中國化": 戰後台灣文化重建, 1945–1947. Maitian renwen 118. Taipei:
Maitian chuban, 2007.

Huang Zhaotang. *Taiwan zongdufu* (The Taiwan Government-General)
台灣總督府. Translated by Huang Yingzhe. Rev. 1st ed. Taiwan wenshi
congshu 113. Taipei: Qianwei chubanshe, 2004.

Hughes, Christopher. "Post-nationalist Taiwan." In *The Politics of Modern
Taiwan*, edited by Dafydd Fell, 215–33. Vol. 1. Critical Issues in Modern
Politics. London: Routledge, 2008.

Hutchinson, John, and Anthony D. Smith, eds. *Ethnicity*. Oxford Readers.
Oxford: Oxford University Press, 1996.

Hutchison, William R. *Errand to the World: American Protestant Thought
and Foreign Missions*. Chicago: University of Chicago Press, 1987.

Hymes, Robert P. *Way and Byway: Taoism, Local Religion, and Models of
Divinity in Sung and Modern China*. Berkeley: University of California
Press, 2002.

Imai Kōji. "Nihon tōji shita Taiwan ni okeru shakai jigyō no tenkai:
fukushi no kindaika o motarashita Nihon tōji kōhanki no shakai jigyō"
(Development of social enterprise in Taiwan under the rule of Japan: The
modernization of welfare as an example of social work in the latter half
of Japanese control) 日本統治下台湾に於ける社会事業の展開: 福祉の近
代化をもたらした日本統治後半期の社会事業. *Gendai Taiwan kenkyū* 25
(2003): 22–41.

Inspector General of Customs. *Decennial Reports of the Trade, Navigation,
Industries, Etc., of the Ports Open to Foreign Commerce in China and
Corea and on the Condition and Development of the Treaty Port Prov-
inces, 1882–91*. Vol. 6. Statistical Series: Imperial Maritime Customs.
Shanghai: Inspector General of Customs, 1893.

Irie Kyōfū. *Kiirun fūdo ki* (A record of local conditions in Kiirun) 基隆風
土記. Jilong: Irie Kyōfū, 1933.

Iriye, Akira. "Japan's Drive to Great-Power Status." In *The Cambridge History of Japan*. Vol. 5, *The Nineteenth Century*, edited by Marius B. Jansen.
Cambridge: Cambridge University Press, 1989.

Ishizaka Sōsaku, ed. *Kiirun hanjō saku shō* (A collection of policies concerning Kiirun's prosperity) 基隆繁昌策集. Jilong: Kiirun shōkōkai, 1918.

———. *Kiirun kō* (The port of Kiirun) 基隆港. Taipei: Taiwan nichinichi shinpōsha, 1917.

———. *Kiirun shinyō kumiai shi kō* (Records of the Kiirun Credit Union) 基隆信用組合誌稿. Jilong: Kiirun shinyō kumiai, 1926.

———. *Ora ga Kiirun kō* (Our Kiirun) おらが基隆港. Taipei: Taiwan nichinichi shinpōsha, 1932.

Jacobs, J. Bruce. *Democratizing Taiwan*. Leiden: Brill, 2012.

———. "Taiwanese and the Chinese Nationalists, 1937–1945: The Origins of Taiwan's 'Half-Mountain People' (Banshan Ren)." *Modern China* 16, no. 1 (Jan. 1990): 84–118.

Jian Shenghuang, ed. *Ererba shijian dang'an huibian*. Vol. 2: *Guojia anquanju dang'an* (Compilation of 2-28 Incident archives: Archives of the National Public Security Bureau) 二二八事件檔案彙編 - 國家安全局檔案. Taibei xian, Xindian shi: Guoshiguan, 2002.

———, ed. *Ererba shijian dang'an huibian*. Vol. 11: *Taibei xian zhengfu dang'an* (Compilation of 2-28 Incident archives: Taibei Prefecture Government Archives) 二二八事件檔案彙編 - 台北縣政府檔案. Taibei xian, Xindian shi: Guoshiguan, 2002.

Jian Wanhuo. *Jilong zhi* (Jilong gazetteer) 基隆誌. Jilong: Jilong tushu, 1931.

Jiang Canteng. "Riben diguo zai Tai zhimin tongzhi chuqi de zongjiao zhengce yu fazhihua de quanli" (The establishment of religious policy and legalization during the early period of imperial Japan's colonial rule in Taiwan) 日本帝國在臺殖民統治初期的宗教政策與法制化的確立. *Zhonghua Foxue xuebao* 14 (Sept. 2001): 91–134.

———. *Taiwan Fojiao bainian shi zhi yanjiu* (100 years of history of Taiwanese Buddhism, 1895–1995) 台灣佛教百年史之研究: 1895–1995. Taipei: Nantian shuju, 1996.

Jilong canyihui. *Taiwan sheng Jilong shi canyihui diyiju dishici dahuiyi shilu (1949 nian 2 yue)* (Record of the first session, tenth meeting of the Taiwan Province Jilong City Assembly [February 1949]) 台湾省基隆市参议会第一届第十次大会议事录(1949年2月). Guanzang minguo Taiwan dang'an huibian 284. Beijing: Jiuzhou chubanshe, 2007.

Jilong gangwuju, ed. *Jilong gang* (The port of Jilong) 基隆港. Jilong: Jilong gangwuju, 1947.

Jilong shi canyihui. *Taiwan sheng Jilong shi canyihui diyiju disici dahuiyi shilu (1947 nian 5 yue)* (Record of the first session, fourth meeting of the Taiwan Province Jilong City Assembly [May 1947]) 台湾省基隆市参议会第一届第四次大会议事录(1945 年5 月). Guanzang minguo Taiwan dang'an huibian 213. Beijing: Jiuzhou chubanshe, 2007.

Jilong shi wenxian weiyuanhui, ed. *Jilong shi zhi: gaishu pian* (Jilong city gazetteer: Overview) 基隆市志: 概述篇. Vol. 1. Jilong shi zhi. Jilong: Jilong shi wenxian weiyuanhui, 1954.

——, ed. *Jilong shi zhi: renwu pian* (Jilong city gazetteer: People) 基隆市志: 人物篇. Vol. 20. Jilong shi zhi. Jilong: Jilong shi wenxian weiyuanhui, 1959.

——, ed. *Jilong shi zhi: shangye pian* (Jilong city gazetteer: Commerce) 基隆市志: 商業篇. Vol. 5. Jilong shi zhi. Jilong: Jilong shi wenxian weiyuanhui, 1954.

——, ed. *Jilong shi zhi: shehui zuzhi pian* (Jilong city gazetteer: Social organizations) 基隆市志: 社會組織篇. Vol. 11. Jilong shi zhi. Jilong: Jilong shi wenxian weiyuanhui, 1957.

——, ed. *Jilong shi zhi: yange pian* (Jilong city gazetteer: History) 基隆市志: 沿革篇. Vol. 3. Jilong shi zhi. Jilong: Jilong shi wenxian weiyuanhui, 1954.

Jilong shi zhengfu. *Jilong diyi* (Jilong number one) 基隆第一. Jilong: Jilong shili wenhua zhongxin, 2004.

——, ed. *Jilong shi nianjian* (Jilong yearbook) 基隆市年鑑. Jilong: Jilong shi zhengfu, 1946.

——, ed. *Jilong shi zhi: renkou pian* (Jilong city gazetteer: Population) 基隆市志: 人口編. Jilong: Jilong shi zhengfu, 1988.

Jilong shi zhengfu minzhengju, ed. *Jilong shi zhi: hukou pian* (Jilong city gazetteer: Households) 基隆市志: 戶口篇. Jilong shi zhi. Jilong: Jilong shi zhengfu, 1989.

Johnson, David G., Andrew J. Nathan, and Evelyn Sakakida Rawski, eds. *Popular Culture in Late Imperial China.* Studies on China 4. Berkeley: University of California Press, 1985.

Johnson, Ian. *The Souls of China: The Return of Religion after Mao.* New York: Pantheon Books, 2017.

Jones, Charles Brewer. *Buddhism in Taiwan: Religion and the State, 1660–1990.* Honolulu: University of Hawai'i Press, 1999.

——. "Religion in Taiwan at the End of the Japanese Colonial Period." In *Religion in Modern Taiwan: Tradition and Innovation in a Changing Society,* edited by Philip Clart and Charles Brewer Jones, 10–35. Honolulu: University of Hawai'i Press, 2003.

Jordan, David K. "Changes in Postwar Taiwan and Their Impact on the Popular Practice of Religion." In *Cultural Change in Postwar Taiwan,* edited by Stevan Harrell and Huang Chün-chieh. Boulder, CO: Westview Press, 1994.

Judge, Joan. "Reforming the Feminine: Female Literacy and the Legacy of 1898." In *Rethinking the 1898 Reform Period: Political and Cultural*

Change in Late Qing China, edited by Rebecca Karl and Peter Gue Zarrow, 158–79. Cambridge, MA: Harvard University Asia Center, 2002.

Ka, Chih-ming. *Japanese Colonialism in Taiwan: Land Tenure, Development, and Dependency, 1895–1945*. Transitions: Asia and Asian America. Boulder, CO: Westview Press, 1995.

Karazawa Shinobu. *Mogi gikai haya kiroku* (Brief record of mock assemblies) 模擬議會速記錄. Jilong: Niitaka shinpōsha, 1931.

Karl, Rebecca E., and Peter Gue Zarrow, eds. *Rethinking the 1898 Reform Period: Political and Cultural Change in Late Qing China*. Harvard East Asian Monographs 214. Cambridge, MA: Harvard University Asia Center, 2002.

Katō Morimichi. *Kiirun shi* (Kiirun city) 基隆市. Jilong: Kiirun shi yakusho, 1929.

Katz, Paul R. "Local Elites and Sacred Sites in Hsin-Chuang: The Growth of Ti-Tsang An during the Japanese Occupation." In *Belief, Ritual, and Society: Papers from the Third Annual Conference on Sinology, Anthropology Section*, edited by Lin Mei-rong, 179–227. Nankang: Institute of Ethnology, 2003.

———. *Religion in China and Its Modern Fate*. Menahem Stern Jerusalem Lectures. Waltham, MA: Brandeis University Press, 2014.

———. *When Valleys Turned Blood Red: The Ta-Pa-Ni Incident in Colonial Taiwan*. Honolulu: University of Hawai'i Press, 2005.

Katz, Paul R., and Murray A. Rubinstein, eds. *Religion and the Formation of Taiwanese Identities*. New York: Palgrave Macmillan, 2003.

Kawada, Minoru. *The Origin of Ethnography in Japan: Yanagita Kunio and His Times*. Japanese Studies. London: Kegan Paul International, 1993.

Kawahara Isamu, ed. *Taiwan hikiage ryūyō kiroku* (Documents on repatriation and misappropriation in Taiwan) 台湾引揚流用記録. 8 vols. Tokyo: Kabushiki kaisha yumani shobō, 1997.

Ke Bingxian. *Jilong Dianji gong yange jianjie* (A brief history of the Jilong Dianji Temple) 基隆奠濟宮沿革簡介. Jilong: Jilong shi Dianji gong guanli weiyuanhui, 1988.

Kertzer, David I. *Ritual, Politics, and Power*. New Haven, CT: Yale University Press, 1988.

Ketelaar, James Edward. *Of Heretics and Martyrs in Meiji Japan: Buddhism and Its Persecution*. Princeton, NJ: Princeton University Press, 1990.

Kiirun chō. *Kiirun chō dai ichi dai san tōkei sho* (First and third statistical tables for Kiirun Prefecture) 基隆廳第一第三統計書. Jilong: Kiirun chō, 1908.

Kiirun dōfūkai. *Kiirun dōfū seinen dan gairan* (An overview of the Kiirun Customs Assimilation Youth Group) 基隆同風青年團概覽. Jilong: Kiirun dōfūkai, 1937.

Kiirun jinja, ed. *Kiirun jinja shi* (Kiirun Shrine gazette) 基隆神社誌. Taipei: Taiwan nichinichi shinpōsha, 1934.

Kiirun kōekisha, ed. *Zaidan hōjin Kiirun kōekisha Shōwa ninen jigyō hōkoku* (Kiirun Public Welfare Society Foundation report on operations for 1927) 財團法人基隆公益社昭和二年事業報告. Jilong: Kiirun kōekisha, 1927.

Kiirun shi kyōka rengōkai. *Kiirun shi shakai kyōiku kyōka shisetsu gaikyō* (General situation of social education and civilization institutions in Kiirun) 基隆市社會教育教化施設概況. Jilong: Kiirun shi kyōka rengōkai, 1936.

Kiirun shi yakusho. *Kiirun shi shakai kyōiku gaiyō* (Overview of social education in Kiirun) 基隆市社會教育概要. Jilong: Kiirun shi yakusho, 1935.

Kiirun shinyō kumiai. *Kiirun shinyō kumiai jigyō hōkoku sho* (Annual report of the Kiirun Credit Association) 基隆信用組合事業報告書. Jilong: Kiirun shinyō kumiai, various years.

Kindleberger, Charles Poor. *The World in Depression, 1929–1939.* History of the World Economy in the Twentieth Century 4. Berkeley: University of California Press, 1973.

Kinebuchi Yoshifusa. *Taiwan shakai jigyō shi* (A history of social work in Taiwan) 臺灣社會事業史. Taipei shi: Dokutomukai, 1940.

King, Anthony D. *Colonial Urban Development: Culture, Social Power, and Environment.* London: Routledge & Paul, 1976.

Kingsberg, Miriam. *Moral Nation: Modern Japan and Narcotics in Global History.* Asia: Local Studies/Global Themes 29. Berkeley: University of California Press, 2014.

Kirby, William C. "Engineering China: Birth of the Developmental State, 1928–1937." In *Becoming Chinese: Passages to Modernity and Beyond*, edited by Wen-hsin Yeh, 137–60. Berkeley: University of California Press, 2000.

———. *Germany and Republican China.* Stanford, CA: Stanford University Press, 1984.

———. "The Internationalization of China: Foreign Relations at Home and Abroad in the Republican Era." *China Quarterly* 150, special issue (1997): 433–58.

Kirby, William C., Man-houng Lin, James Chin Shih, and David A. Pietz, eds. *State and Economy in Republican China: A Handbook for Scholars.* Vol. 2. Harvard East Asian Monographs 193. Cambridge, MA: Harvard University Asia Center, 2001.

Kita Ryūji, and Kiirunshi kyōikukai, eds. *Kiirun shi* (History of Kiirun) 基隆史. Jilong: Kiirunshi kyōikukai, 1934.

Kiyochika. *Taiwan san kei no nai Kiirun no ame* (Three views of Taiwan: The rain of Kiirun) 台湾三景之内基隆之雨. Woodblock print, 1896. Kokuritsu kokkai toshokan dejitaru korekushun. http://dl.ndl.go.jp /info:ndljp/pid/1301915.

Knapp, Ronald G., ed. *China's Island Frontier: Studies in the Historical Geography of Taiwan*. Honolulu: University Press of Hawaiʻi, 1980.

Kramer, Paul A. "Empires, Exceptions, and Anglo-Saxons: Race and Rule between the British and U.S. Empires, 1880–1910." In *The American Colonial State in the Philippines: Global Perspectives*, edited by Julian Go and Anne L. Foster, 43–91. American Encounters/Global Interactions. Durham, NC: Duke University Press, 2003.

Kuhara Masao. *Kiirun kō to sono sangyō* (The port of Kiirun and its industries) 基隆港と其の產業. Keizai panfuretto: Taiwan keizai ōrai 44. Taipei: Taiwan keizai kenkyūkai, 1935.

———, ed. *Kiirun no uta* (The Kiirun song) 基隆の歌. Jilong: Kiirun shi yakusho, 1933.

———, ed. *Kiirun shi tei sha rakusei kinen tenrankai* (Commemoration exhibition for the completion of the Kiirun city government building) 基隆市廳舍落成紀念展覽會. Jilong: Kiirun shi yakusho, 1933.

Kuhn, Philip A. *Chinese among Others: Emigration in Modern Times*. State and Society in East Asia. Lanham, MD: Rowman & Littlefield Publishers, 2009.

———. *Rebellion and Its Enemies in Late Imperial China: Militarization and Social Structure, 1796–1864*. Harvard East Asian Monographs 49. Cambridge, MA: Harvard University Press, 1970.

Kushner, Barak. "Nationality and Nostalgia: The Manipulation of Memory in Japan, Taiwan, and China since 1990." *International History Review* 29, no. 4 (Dec. 2007): 793–820.

Lai, Tse-han, Ramon Hawley Myers, and Wou Wei. *A Tragic Beginning: The Taiwan Uprising of February 28, 1947*. Stanford, CA: Stanford University Press, 1991.

Lamley, Harry J. "The 1895 Taiwan Republic: A Significant Episode in Modern Chinese History." *Journal of Asian Studies* 27, no. 4 (August 1968): 739–62.

———. "The Taiwan Literati and Early Japanese Rule, 1895–1915: A Study of Their Reactions to the Japanese Occupation and Subsequent Responses to Colonial Rule and Modernization." PhD diss., University of Hawaiʻi, 1964.

Lan, Shi-Chi Mike. "The Ambivalence of National Imagination: Defining 'the Taiwanese' in China, 1931–1941." *The China Journal* 64 (2010): 179–97.

Le Gendre, Charles. *Notes of Travel in Formosa*. Edited by Douglas Fix and John Shufelt. Tainan, TW: National Museum of Taiwan History, 2013.

Lee, Leo Ou-fan. *Shanghai Modern: The Flowering of a New Urban Culture in China, 1930–1945*. Cambridge, MA: Harvard University Press, 1999.

Lees, Andrew. *Cities, Sin, and Social Reform in Imperial Germany*. Social History, Popular Culture, and Politics in Germany. Ann Arbor: University of Michigan Press, 2002.

Leong, Sow-Theng. *Migration and Ethnicity in Chinese History: Hakkas, Pengmin, and Their Neighbors*. Edited by Tim Wright. Introduction and maps by G. William Skinner. Stanford, CA: Stanford University Press, 1997.

Li Fengmao. *Jilong qing zan Zhongyuan: jimaonian Lin xing zhupu jinian zhuanji* (Jilong celebrates the Ghost Festival: Special commemorative collection of Lin surname group as Master of the Festival in 1999) 雞籠慶讚中元: 己卯年林姓主普紀念專輯. Jilong: Jilong Lin xing zongqinhui, 2000.

Li Fengmao, Lai Zhengyu, and Ye Tinghao. *Gui fu shen gong: Jilong shi yinmiao diaocha* (Mansions of ghosts, palaces of spirits: Survey of Jilong's unorthodox temples) 鬼府神宮: 基隆市陰廟調查. Jilong wenxin congkan 130. Jilong: Jilong shili wenhua zhongxin, 2000.

Li Jinyong and Zheng Junbin. *Jilong shi zhi renwu liezhuan pian* (Jilong city gazetteer: Personal biographies) 基隆市志人物列傳篇. Edited by Jilong shi zhengfu. Vol. 7. Jilong shi zhi. Jilong: Jilong shi zhengfu, 2001.

Li Shinn-cherng. "Qingdai Yilan de guan ju zuzhang ji qi gongneng shentao" (The function of government-appointed patriarch in Qing I-Lan) 清代宜蘭的官舉族長及其功能探討. *Taida lishi xuebao* 55 (June 2015): 67–124.

Li Shiwei. "Haibin fu sheng dao: zhanhou Taiwan minjian Rujiao yu huodong (1945–1970)" (The shore supports the sacred way: Taiwan's postwar popular Confucianism and activities [1945–1970]) 海濱扶聖道: 戰後臺灣民間儒教與活動 (1945–1970). *Minsu quyi* 172 (June 2011): 205–30.

Li Yinghui. *Huaqiao zhengce yu haiwai minzu zhuyi, 1912–1949* (Overseas Chinese policy and overseas nationalism, 1912–1949) 華僑政策與海外民族主義, 1912–1949. Minguo shixue congshu 4. Taibei xian, Xindian shi: Guoshiguan, 1997.

Liao, Ping-hui, and David Der-wei Wang, eds. *Taiwan under Japanese Colonial Rule, 1895–1945: History, Culture, Memory*. New York: Columbia University Press, 2006.

Lie, John. *Multiethnic Japan*. Cambridge, MA: Harvard University Press, 2001.

Lin Guoxian. "'Zhonghua wenhua fuxing yundong tuixing weiyuanhui' zhi yanjiu: 1966–1975" (Research on the "Chinese Culture Revitalization Movement Implementation Committee": 1966–1975) 中華文化復興運動推行委員會"之研究: 1966–1975. MA thesis, Guoli zhengzhi daxue, 2001.

Lin Man-houng. *Cha, tang, zhangnao ye yu Taiwan zhi shehui jingji bianqian* (The tea, sugar, and camphor industries and socio-economic change in Taiwan) 茶、糖、樟腦業與臺灣之社會經濟變遷 (1860–1895). Taipei: Lianjing, 1997.

———. "The Ryukyus and Taiwan in the East Asian Seas: A Longue Durée Perspective." *Asia-Pacific Journal* 4, no. 10 (October 2006). http://japan focus.org/-Lin-Man-houng/2258/article.html.

———. "Taiwanese Merchants, Overseas Chinese Merchants, and the Japanese Government in the Economic Relations between Taiwan and Japan, 1895–1945." *Journal of Asia-Pacific Studies* 4 (2002): 3–20.

Lin Qiushan. *Muqian laorongmin shenghuo zhaogu ji hunyin wenti yinying duice zhuan'an diaocha yanjiu baogao* (Special project research report on the contemporary life conditions and care for retired soldiers and the reasons and solutions for their marital problems) 目前老榮民生活照顧及婚姻問題因應對策專案調查研究報告. Taipei: Jianchayuan, 2005.

Lin Shengwei. "Zhengzhi suanshu zhanhou Taiwan de guojia tongzhi yu renkou guanli" (Political statistics, postwar Taiwan's national control, and population management) 政治算數戰後台灣的國家統治與人口管理. PhD diss., Guoli zhengzhi daxue, 2005.

Lin Shuguang. *Dagou suo tan* (Humble discussions of Dagou) 打狗瑣譚. Xiangtuxue congkan 6. Gaoxiong: Chun hui chubanshe, 1993.

Lin, Wei-Ping. *Materializing Magic Power: Chinese Popular Religion in Villages and Cities.* Harvard-Yenching Institute Monograph Series 97. Cambridge, MA: Harvard University Asia Center. Distributed by Harvard University Press, 2015.

Lin Weisheng. *Luohanjiao: Qingdai Taiwan shehui yu fenlei xiedou* (Luohanjiao: Society and factional conflict in Qing Taiwan) 羅漢腳: 清代臺灣社會與分類械鬥. Taiwan lishi daxi. Taipei: Zili wanbao she, 1993.

Lin Yuru. *Qingdai Taiwan gangkou de kongjian jiegou* (Spatial networks of harbors in Qing Taiwan) 清代臺灣港口的空間結構. Mingshan zang 6. Taipei: Zhi shufang chubanshe, 1996.

Lingquan si yange (History of the Lingquan Temple) 靈泉寺沿革, n.d.

Lipkin, Zwia. *Useless to the State: "Social Problems" and Social Engineering in Nationalist Nanjing, 1927–1937.* Harvard East Asian Monographs 259. Cambridge, MA: Harvard University Asia Center, 2006.

Liu, Lydia H. *Translingual Practice: Literature, National Culture, and Translated Modernity: China, 1900–1937.* Stanford, CA: Stanford University Press, 1995.

Liu, Michael Shiyung. *Prescribing Colonization: The Role of Medical Practices and Policies in Japan-Ruled Taiwan, 1895–1945.* Asia Past and Present: New Research from AAS 3. Ann Arbor, MI: Association for Asian Studies, 2009.

Liu Mingchuan. *Liu Zhuangsu gong zouyi* (Memorials of Liu Zhuangsu) 劉壯肅公奏議. Edited by Taiwan yinhang. Taiwan wenxian congkan 27. Taipei: Taiwan yinhang, 1958.

Liu Qingfan. *Qing'an gong zhi* (Gazetteer of the Qing'an Temple) 慶安宮志. Jilong: Jilong shi Qing'an gong guanli weiyuanhui, 2001.

Lo, Jiu-tung. "Trials of the Taiwanese as Hanjian or War Criminals and the Postwar Search for Taiwanese Identity." In *Constructing Nationhood in Modern East Asia*, edited by Kai-wing Chow, Kevin Michael Doak, and Poshek Fu, 279–315. Ann Arbor: University of Michigan Press, 2001.

Lo, Ming-cheng Miriam. *Doctors within Borders: Profession, Ethnicity, and Modernity in Colonial Taiwan.* Colonialisms 1. Berkeley: University of California Press, 2002.

Maeno Tsuruwaka. *Yonjū nenkan no Taiwan* (Forty years of Taiwan) 四十年間の臺灣. Taipei: Taiwan nichinichi shinpōsha, 1935.

Maier, Charles S. "Consigning the Twentieth Century to History: Alternative Narratives for the Modern Era." *American Historical Review* 105, no. 3 (June 2000): 807–31.

Mani, Lata. *Contentious Traditions: The Debate on Sati in Colonial India.* Berkeley: University of California Press, 1998.

Manthorpe, Jonathan. *Forbidden Nation: A History of Taiwan.* 1st Palgrave Macmillan paperback ed. New York: Palgrave Macmillan, 2009.

Martin, Terry. *The Affirmative Action Empire: Nations and Nationalism in the Soviet Union, 1923–1939.* Wilder House Series in Politics, History, and Culture. Ithaca, NY: Cornell University Press, 2001.

Marui Keijirō, ed. *Taiwan shūkyō chōsa hōkokusho dai ikkan* (A report on the survey of Taiwanese religion, volume 1) 臺灣宗教調查報告書第一卷. Taipei: Taiwan sōtokufu, 1919.

Masuda Fukutarō. *Minzoku shinkō o chūshin toshite* (Popular faith at the center) 民族信仰を中心として. Tokyo: Diamondo sha, 1942.

———. *Taiwan hontōjin no shūkyō* (Religion of Taiwan's islanders) 臺灣本島人の宗教. Tokyo: Meiji seidoku kinen gakkai, 1935.

Matsuda Kyōko. "Inō Kanori's 'History' of Taiwan: Colonial Ethnology, the Civilizing Mission and Struggles for Survival in East Asia." Translated by Paul D. Barclay. *History and Anthropology* 14, no. 2 (2003): 179–96.

Meiguo gang gong diaochatuan, ed. *Zhongguo zhongyao haigang gaiyao* (Overview of China's important ports) 中國重要海港概要. Yanjiu congkan. Taipei: Jiaotong yanjiusuo, 1958.

Meskill, Johanna Margarete Menzel. *A Chinese Pioneer Family: The Lins of Wu-Feng, Taiwan, 1729–1895.* Princeton, NJ: Princeton University Press, 1979.

Meyer, Mahlon. *Remembering China from Taiwan: Divided Families and Bittersweet Reunions after the Chinese Civil War.* Hong Kong: Hong Kong University Press, 2012.

Mickey, Georgia A. "'Safeguarding National Credibility': Founding the Bank of China in 1912." *Twentieth-Century China* 37, no. 2 (2012): 139–60.

Minohara, Toshihiro, Tze-Ki Hon, and Evan N. Dawley, eds. *The Decade of the Great War: Japan and the Wider World in the 1910s.* Leiden: Brill, 2014.

Mitchell, Timothy. *Colonising Egypt.* Cambridge Middle East Library. Cambridge: Cambridge University Press, 2007.

Mitsubashi Yasurō. *Wa ga Kiirun* (My Kiirun) 我が基隆. Jilong: Kiirun shi kyōikukai, 1937.

Mitter, Rana. *The Manchurian Myth: Nationalism, Resistance and Collaboration in Modern China.* Berkeley: University of California Press, 2000.

Miyake, Yoshiko. "Doubling Expectations: Motherhood and Women's Factory Work under State Management in Japan in the 1930s and 1940s." In *Recreating Japanese Women, 1600–1945*, edited by Gail Lee Bernstein, 267–95. Berkeley: University of California Press, 1991.

Moody, J. Carroll, and Gilbert Courtland Fite. *The Credit Union Movement: Origins and Development, 1850–1980.* 2nd ed. Dubuque, IA: Kendall/Hunt Publishing Co., 1984.

Morris, Andrew D. *Colonial Project, National Game: A History of Baseball in Taiwan.* Berkeley: University of California Press, 2011.

———, ed. *Japanese Taiwan: Colonial Rule and Its Contested Legacy.* SOAS Studies in Modern and Contemporary Japan. London: Bloomsbury Academic, 2015.

Morris-Suzuki, Tessa. "Invisible Immigrants: Undocumented Migration and Border Controls in Early Postwar Japan." *Asia-Pacific Journal* 4, no. 8 (Aug. 14, 2006). http://apjjf.org/-Tessa-Morris-Suzuki/2210/article.pdf.

———. *Re-Inventing Japan: Time, Space, and the Nation.* Japan in the Modern World. Armonk, NY: M. E. Sharpe, 1998.

Mullaney, Thomas S. *Coming to Terms with the Nation: Ethnic Classification in Modern China.* Asia: Local Studies/Global Themes 18. Berkeley: University of California Press, 2012.

Musgrove, Charles D. *China's Contested Capital: Architecture, Ritual, and Response in Nanjing*. Spatial Habitus. Honolulu: University of Hawai'i Press, 2013.

Mutsu, Munemitsu. *Kenkenroku: A Diplomatic Record of the Sino-Japanese War, 1894–95*. Translated by Gordon Mark Berger. Princeton Library of Asian Translations. Princeton, NJ: Princeton University Press, 1982.

Myers, Ramon Hawley, and Mark R. Peattie, eds. *The Japanese Colonial Empire, 1895–1945*. Princeton, NJ: Princeton University Press, 1984.

Nagahama Minoru, ed. *Gan Kokunen kun shoden* (A biographical sketch of Yan Guonian) 顏國年君小傳. Taipei: Taiwan nichinichi shinpōsha, 1937.

Nagaoka Masami, ed. *Shokuminchi shakai jigyō kankei shiryōshū: Taiwan hen 1: Taiwan shakai jigyō sōran* (Historical documents relating to colonial social work: Taiwan 1: Overview of social work in Taiwan) 植民地社会事業関係資料集: 台湾編 1: 台湾社会事業総覧. Senzen senchū ki Ajia kenkyū shiryō 2. Tokyo: Kin-gendai shiryō kankōkai, 2001.

———, ed. *Shokuminchi shakai jigyō kankei shiryōshū: Taiwan hen 5: Taiwan shakai jigyō sōran* (Historical documents relating to colonial social work: Taiwan 5: Overview of social work in Taiwan) 植民地社会事業関係資料集: 台湾編 5: 台湾社会事業総覧. Senzen senchū ki Ajia kenkyū shiryō 2. Tokyo: Kin-gendai shiryō kankōkai, 2001.

———, ed. *Shokuminchi shakai jigyō kankei shiryōshū: Taiwan hen 39–40: Taiwan shakai jigyō sōran: Chijō shakai jigyō* (Historical documents relating to colonial social work: Taiwan 39–40: Overview of social work in Taiwan: Local social work) 植民地社会事業関係資料集: 台湾編 39–40 台湾社会事業総覧: 地上社会事業. Senzen senchū ki Ajia kenkyū shiryō 2. Tokyo: Kin-gendai shiryō kankōkai, 2001.

———, ed. *Shokuminchi shakai jigyō kankei shiryōshū: Taiwan hen 45: Taiwan shakai jigyō sōran: Chijō shakai jigyō 7* (Historical documents relating to colonial social work: Taiwan 45: Overview of social work in Taiwan: Local social work 7) 植民地社会事業関係資料集. 台湾編 45台湾社会事業総覧: 地上社会事業7. Senzen senchū ki Ajia kenkyū shiryō 2. Tokyo: Kin-gendai shiryō kankōkai, 2001.

Najita, Tetsuo. *Ordinary Economies in Japan: A Historical Perspective, 1750–1950*. Twentieth-Century Japan 18. Berkeley: University of California Press, 2009.

Nakajima Shinichirō. *Kiirun shi annai* (General information on Kiirun city) 基隆市安内. Jilong: Kiirun shi yakusho, 1930.

Nakayama Kaoru and Katayama Kiyō. *Yakushin Takao no zenbō* (A full account of rapidly advancing Takao) 躍進高雄の全貌. Zhongguo fangzhi congshu Taiwan diqu 289. Taipei: Chengwen chubanshe, 1985.

Naquin, Susan. *Peking: Temples and City Life, 1400–1900.* Philip E. Lilienthal Book. Berkeley: University of California Press, 2000.

National Taiwan University Medical College, "NTUMC—Deans." http://www1.mc.ntu.edu.tw/EN/ntucm_deans.html. Accessed July 19, 2017.

Nedostup, Rebecca. *Superstitious Regimes: Religion and the Politics of Chinese Modernity.* Harvard East Asian Monographs 322. Cambridge, MA: Harvard University Asia Center, 2009.

Neizhengbu. "Tongji baobiao" (Statistical reports) 統計報表. *Quanguo zongjiao zixunwang.* https://religion.moi.gov.tw/Home/ContentDetail?cid=Report. Accessed Jan. 21, 2018.

Neizhengbu huzhengsi. "Renkou tongji ziliao" (Population statistics) 人口統計資料. *Neizhengbu huzhengsi quanqiuwang.* https://www.ris.gov.tw/346. Accessed Jan. 21, 2018.

Niitaka shinpōsha. *Taiwan shinshi meikan* (Directory of notables in Taiwan) 臺灣紳士名鑑. Taipei: Niitaka shinpōsha, 1937.

Nomura Yoshimasa. *Kimura Kutarō ō* (The venerable Kimura Kutarō) 木村久太郎翁. Tokyo: Gyōsei gakkai insatsusho, 1938.

Nora, Pierre, and Lawrence D. Kritzman, eds. *Realms of Memory: Rethinking the French Past.* Vol. 1: *European Perspectives.* New York: Columbia University Press, 1996.

O'Dwyer, Emer Sinéad. *Significant Soil: Settler Colonialism and Japan's Urban Empire in Manchuria.* Harvard East Asian Monographs 377. Cambridge, MA: Harvard University Asia Center, 2015.

Okamatsu Santarō. *Taiwan kyūkan seido chōsa ippan* (The first study of the system of Taiwan's old customs) 臺灣舊慣制度調查一斑. Tokyo: Rinji Taiwan tochi chōsakyoku, 1901.

Oldstone-Moore, Jennifer Lee. "The New Life Movement of Nationalist China: Confucianism, State Authority and Moral Formation." PhD diss., University of Chicago, 2000.

Ōmi Tokigorō, ed. *Kiirun kō annai* (General information on the port of Kiirun) 基隆港案內. Jilong: Kiirun kōekisha, 1930.

———, ed. *Kiirun kō annai* (General information on the port of Kiirun) 基隆港案內. Jilong: Kiirun kōwankai, 1933.

Ōzono Ichizō. *Taiwan jinbutsu shi* (Gazette of people in Taiwan) 臺灣人物誌. Taipei: Tanizawa shoten, 1916.

Pan, Jason. "Taiwanese, Han Chinese Ethnically Distinct: Expert." *Taipei Times.* http://www.taipeitimes.com/News/taiwan/archives/2017/10/30/2003681322. Accessed Jan. 18, 2018.

Pepper, Suzanne. *Civil War in China: The Political Struggle, 1945–1949.* Berkeley: University of California Press, 1978.

Perdue, Peter C. *China Marches West: The Qing Conquest of Central Eurasia.* Cambridge, MA: Belknap Press of Harvard University Press, 2005.

Perry, Matthew Calbraith, Lambert Lilly, and George Jones. *Narrative of the Expedition of an American Squadron to the China Seas and Japan: Performed in the Years 1852, 1853, and 1854, under the Command of Commodore M. C. Perry, United States Navy, by Order of the Government of the United States.* United States, 33rd Cong., 2d sess., Senate. Ex. Doc. 79. Washington: A.O.P. Nicholson, 1856.

Phillips, Steven E. *Between Assimilation and Independence: The Taiwanese Encounter Nationalist China, 1945–1950.* Stanford, CA: Stanford University Press, 2003.

———. "Building a Taiwanese Republic: The Independence Movement, 1945–Present." In *Dangerous Strait: The U.S.-Taiwan-China Crisis*, edited by Nancy Bernkopf Tucker, 44–69. New York: Columbia University Press, 2008.

Qu Haiyuan and Zhang Yinghua, eds. *Taiwan shehui yu wenhua bianqian* (Taiwan's social and cultural changes) 台灣社會與文化變遷. Zhongyang yanjiuyuan minzuxue yanjiusuo zhuankan yizhong 16. Taipei: Zhongyang yanjiuyuan minzuxue yanjiusuo, 1986.

Rafael, Vicente L. *Contracting Colonialism: Translation and Christian Conversion in Tagalog Society under Early Spanish Rule.* Ithaca, NY: Cornell University Press, 1988.

Rankin, Mary Backus. *Elite Activism and Political Transformation in China: Zhejiang Province, 1865–1911.* Stanford, CA: Stanford University Press, 1986.

Reid, Anthony, Kristine Alilunas-Rodgers, and Jennifer Wayne Cushman, eds. *Sojourners and Settlers: Histories of Southeast Asia and the Chinese: In Honour of Jennifer Cushman.* Southeast Asia Publications Series 28. St. Leonards, AU: Allen & Unwin, 1996.

Renwen shehui kexue yanjiu zhongxin. "Ri zhi shiqi hukou diaocha ziliao ku" (Database of population research from the era of Japanese control) 日治時期戶口調查資料庫, n.d. http://www.rchss.sinica.edu.tw/popu/index.php. Accessed Dec. 27, 2017.

Rigger, Shelley. *Taiwan's Rising Rationalism: Generations, Politics, and "Taiwanese Nationalism."* Policy Studies 26. Washington, DC: East-West Center Washington, 2006.

Rightmire, R. David. *Salvationist Samurai: Gunpei Yamamuro and the Rise of the Salvation Army in Japan*. Pietist and Wesleyan Studies 8. Lanham, MD: Scarecrow Press, 1997.

Rinji kyūkan chōsakai. *Taiwan kyūkan chōsa jigyō hōkoku* (Report on the survey of Taiwan's old customs) 臺灣舊慣調查事業報告. Taipei: Taiwan nichinichi shinpōsha, 1917.

Robinson, Michael Edson, and Gi-Wook Shin, eds. *Colonial Modernity in Korea*. Harvard East Asian Monographs, Harvard-Hallym Series on Korean Studies 184. Cambridge, MA: Harvard University Asia Center, 2000.

Rogaski, Ruth. *Hygienic Modernity: Meanings of Health and Disease in Treaty-Port China*. Asia: Local Studies/Global Themes. Berkeley: University of California Press, 2004.

Rollo-Koster, Joëlle, ed. *Medieval and Early Modern Ritual: Formalized Behavior in Europe, China, and Japan*. Cultures, Beliefs, and Traditions 13. Leiden: Brill, 2002.

Roshwald, Aviel. *The Endurance of Nationalism: Ancient Roots and Modern Dilemmas*. Cambridge: Cambridge University Press, 2006.

Rowe, William T. *Hankow: Commerce and Society in a Chinese City, 1796–1889*. Stanford, CA: Stanford University Press, 1984.

———. *Hankow: Conflict and Community in a Chinese City, 1796–1895*. Stanford, CA: Stanford University Press, 1989.

Royce, Anya Peterson. *Ethnic Identity: Strategies of Diversity*. 1st Midland Book ed. Bloomington: Indiana University Press, 1982.

Rubinstein, Murray A. "'Medium/Message' in Taiwan's Mazu-Cult Centers: Using 'Time, Space, and Word' to Foster Island-Wide Spiritual Consciousness and Local, Regional, and National Forms of Institutional Identity." In *Religion and the Formation of Taiwanese Identities*, edited by Paul R. Katz and Murray A. Rubinstein, 181–218. New York: Palgrave Macmillan, 2003.

———, ed. *The Other Taiwan: 1945 to the Present*. Taiwan in the Modern World. Armonk, NY: M. E. Sharpe, 1994.

———, ed. *Taiwan: A New History*. Exp. ed. Armonk, NY: M. E. Sharpe, 2007.

Ryan, Shawna Yang. *Green Island*. New York: Alfred A. Knopf, 2016.

Sahlins, Peter. *Boundaries: The Making of France and Spain in the Pyrenees*. Berkeley: University of California Press, 1991.

Said, Edward W. *Orientalism*. 1st Vintage Books ed. New York: Vintage Books, 1979.

Sand, Jordan. *House and Home in Modern Japan: Architecture, Domestic Space, and Bourgeois Culture, 1880–1930*. Harvard East Asian Monographs 223. Cambridge, MA: Harvard University Asia Center, 2003.

Sangren, Paul Steven. *History and Magical Power in a Chinese Community.* Stanford, CA: Stanford University Press, 1987.

Sato, Barbara Hamill. "An Alternate Informant: Middle-Class Women and Mass Magazines in 1920s Japan." In *Being Modern in Japan: Culture and Society from the 1910s to the 1930s,* edited by John Clark and Elise K. Tipton, 137–53. Honolulu: University of Hawai'i Press, 2000.

———. *The New Japanese Woman: Modernity, Media, and Women in Interwar Japan.* Asia-Pacific. Durham, NC: Duke University Press, 2003.

Schoppa, R. Keith. "Patterns and Dynamics of Elite Collaboration in Occupied Shaoxing County." In *Chinese Collaboration with Japan, 1932–1945: The Limits of Accommodation,* edited by David P. Barrett and Lawrence N. Shyu. Stanford, CA: Stanford University Press, 2001.

Seiwert, Hubert Michael, and Xisha Ma. *Popular Religious Movements and Heterodox Sects in Chinese History.* China Studies 3. Leiden: Brill, 2003.

Sheehan, Brett. *Trust in Troubled Times: Money, Banks, and State-Society Relations in Republican Tianjin.* Cambridge, MA: Harvard University Press, 2003.

Shepherd, John Robert. *Statecraft and Political Economy on the Taiwan Frontier, 1600–1800.* Stanford, CA: Stanford University Press, 1993.

Shi bao (Poetry bulletin) 詩報. Jilong: Shi baoshe, 1931–42.

Shikamata Mitsuo, ed. *Shisei yonjū shūnen kinen Taiwan hakurankai kyōsankai shi* (Gazette of the Support Committee for the Taiwan exhibition to commemorate forty years of governance) 始政四十周年記念臺灣博覽會協贊會誌. Taipei: Shisei yonjū shūnen kinen Taiwan hakurankai kyōsankai, 1939.

Shizuko, Koyama. "The 'Good Wife and Wise Mother' Ideology in Post-World War I Japan." Translated by Gabriel A. Sylvain. *U.S.-Japan Women's Journal, English Supplement,* no. 7 (1994): 31–52.

Silverberg, Miriam. "The Café Waitress Serving Modern Japan." In *Mirror of Modernity: Invented Traditions of Modern Japan,* edited by Stephen Vlastos, 208–25. Berkeley: University of California Press, 1998.

———. "The Modern Girl as Militant." In *Recreating Japanese Women, 1600–1945,* edited by Gail Lee Bernstein, 239–66. Berkeley: University of California Press, 1991.

Sima Xiaoqing. *Taiwan wuda jiazu* (The five great families of Taiwan) 臺灣五大家族. Taiwan bentu xilie 3. Taipei: Zili baoxi, 1987.

Skinner, G. William. "Introduction: Urban Social Structure in Ch'ing China." In *The City in Late Imperial China,* edited by G. William Skinner and Hugh D. R. Baker, 521–53. Stanford, CA: Stanford University Press, 1977.

Skinner, G. William, and Hugh D. R. Baker, eds. *The City in Late Imperial China.* Stanford, CA: Stanford University Press, 1977.

Smith, Anthony D. *The Ethnic Origins of Nations*. Oxford: Basil Blackwell, 1987.

———. *Ethnicity and Nationalism*. International Studies in Sociology and Social Anthropology 60. Leiden: Brill, 1992.

———. *The Nation in History: Historiographical Debates about Ethnicity and Nationalism*. Menahem Stern Jerusalem Lectures. Hanover, NH: University Press of New England, 2000.

Smith, Kerry Douglas. *A Time of Crisis: Japan, the Great Depression, and Rural Revitalization*. Harvard East Asian Monographs 191. Cambridge, MA: Harvard University Asia Center, 2001.

Smith, Thomas C. *Native Sources of Japanese Industrialization, 1750–1920*. Berkeley: University of California Press, 2009.

Song Jiatai, ed. *Taiwan dili* (Taiwan's geography) 臺灣地理. Taipei: Zhengzhong shuju, 1946.

Sorensen, André. *The Making of Urban Japan: Cities and Planning from Edo to the Twenty-First Century*. Nissan Institute/Routledge Japanese Studies Series. London: Routledge, 2002.

Speidel, William M. "The Administrative and Fiscal Reforms of Liu Ming-Ch'uan in Taiwan, 1884–1891: Foundation for Self-Strengthening." *Journal of Asian Studies* 35, no. 3 (May 1976): 441–59.

Stapleton, Kristin Eileen. *Civilizing Chengdu: Chinese Urban Reform, 1895–1937*. Harvard East Asian Monographs 186. Cambridge, MA: Harvard University Asia Center, 2000.

Strauss, Julia C. "The Evolution of Republican Government." *China Quarterly* 150, special issue (June 1997): 329–51.

Su Shuobin. *Kanbujian yu kandejian de Taipei: Qingmo zhi Ri zhi shiqi Taipei kongjian yu quanli moshi de zhuanbian* (Seen and unseen Taipei: Changes in the space and structures of power in late Qing and Japanese-ruled Taipei) 看不見與看得見的臺北: 清末至日治時期臺北空間與權力模式的轉變. Rev. 1st ed. Taiwan kongjian & dushi yanjiu 2. Taipei: Qun xue, 2010.

Sung, Kwang-Yu. "Religion and Society in Ch'ing and Japanese Colonial Taipei (1644–1945)." PhD diss., University of Pennsylvania, 1990.

Suzuki Mitsuo. "Bon ni kuru rei: Taiwan no chūgen ki o te gakari toshita hikaku minzokugakuteki shiron" (Midsummer Ghost Festival in East Asia: A comparison of Japan's *bon*, Taiwan's *poto*, and Korea's *manghon-il*) 盆にくる霊: 台湾の中元節を手がかりとした比較民俗学的試論. *Minzokugaku kenkyū* 37, no. 3 (1972): 167–85.

Suzuki Seiichirō. *Taiwan jiuguan xisu xinyang* (Taiwan's old customs, local traditions, and beliefs) 臺灣舊慣習俗信仰. Translated by Feng Zuomin and Gao Xianzhi. Taipei: Zhong wen tushu gongsi, 1978.

———. *Taiwan kyūkan kankon sōsai to nenjū gyōji* (Taiwan's old customs, important family ceremonies, and annual events) 臺灣舊慣冠婚葬祭と年中行事. Taipei: Taiwan nichinichi shinpōsha, 1934.

Szonyi, Michael. "The Illusion of Standardizing the Gods: The Cult of Five Emperors in Late Imperial China." *Journal of Asian Studies* 56, no. 1 (Feb. 1997): 113–35.

Taihoku chō, ed. *Taihoku chō shi 2* (Taihoku Prefecture gazetteer 2) 臺北廳誌 2. Tai yiban. Zhongguo fangzhi congshu Taiwan diqu 202.2. Taipei: Chengwen chubanshe, 1985.

Taihoku chō shomu ka. *Taihoku chō daisan tōkei sho* (Third statistical tables for Taihoku County) 臺北廳第三統計書. Taipei: Taiwan nichinichi shinpōsha, 1916.

Taihoku shū, ed. *Taihoku shū hōmen iin meibo: fu hōmen iin sho kitei* (Taihoku Prefecture local welfare commissioners directory: Supplement of regulations) 臺北州方面委員名簿: 附方面委員諸規程. Taipei: Taihoku shū, 1941.

Taihoku shū chiji kanbō bunsho ka. *Taihoku shū tōkei sho* (Taihoku Prefecture statistical tables) 臺北州統計書. Taipei: Taihoku shū chiji kanbō bunsho ka, 1926–39.

Taihoku shū rengō dōfūkai. *Dōfūkai gairan* (An overview of the Customs Assimilation Association) 同風會概覽. Taipei: Taihoku shū rengō dōfūkai, 1929.

———, ed. *Hontō ni okeru migoto zenkō jitsuwa ki* (A collection of true stories of benevolent acts and worthy deeds in Taiwan) 本島に於サる美事善行實話集. Taipei: Taiwan nichinichi shinpō sha, 1928.

Taihoku shū sōmu bu sōmu ka. *Taihoku shū tōkei sho* (Taihoku Prefecture statistical tables) 臺北州統計書. Taipei: Taihoku shū sōmu bu sōmu ka, 1940–43.

Taihoku shū yaku sho. *Taihoku shū yōran 3* (Overview of Taihoku Prefecture 3) 臺北市臺北州要覽3. Zhongguo fangzhi congshu Taiwan diqu 204.3. Taipei: Chengwen chubanshe, 1985.

Taiwan kyōkai, ed. *Taiwan hikiage shi: Shōwa nijūnen shūsen kiroku* (A history of Taiwan repatriation: A record of the end of the war in 1945) 台湾引揚史: 昭和二十年終戦記録. Tokyo: Taiwan kyōkai, 1982.

"Taiwan no danhatsu fu kaisokai" (Taiwan Queue-Cutting and Dress-Preservation Association) 台灣の短髮服改組會. *Journal of the Tokyo Anthropology Association* (Tokyo jinrui gakkai zasshi) 27, no. 4 (1911): 253–54.

Taiwan sangyō kumiai kyōkai Taihoku shi shūkai. *Taihoku shū shita sangyō kumiai yaku shokuinroku* (Taihoku Prefecture producers' unions member list) 臺北州下產業組合役職員錄. Taipei: Taiwan sangyō kumiai kyōkai Taihoku shi shūkai, 1933.

Taiwan shaji shūkyō kankōkai, ed. *Taihoku shū shita ni okeru shaji kyōkai yōran* (Survey of temples and churches in Taihoku Prefecture) 臺北州 下に於ける社寺教會要覽. Taipei: Taiwan shaji shūkyō kankōkai, 1933.

Taiwan sheng xingzheng zhangguan gongshu, ed. *Taiwan sheng tongji yaolan* (Summary of statistics for Taiwan Province) 台湾省統計要覽. Taipei: Taiwan sheng xingzheng zhangguan gongshu tongji shi, 1947.

———, ed. *Taiwan sheng wushiyi nian lai tongji tiyao* (Summary of fifty-one years of statistics for Taiwan Province) 臺灣省五十一年來統計 提要. Taipei: Taiwan sheng xingzheng zhangguan gongshu tongji shi, 1946.

———, ed. *Taiwan xingzheng zhangguan gongshu gongbao* (Gazette of the Taiwan provincial government) 臺灣省行政長官公署公報. Taiwan: Taiwan xingzheng zhangguan gongshu, 1947.

Taiwan sheng xingzheng zhangguan gongshu minzhengchu mishushi, ed. *Taiwan sheng canyihui diyiju diyici dahui Taiwan sheng xingzheng zhangguan gongshu shizheng baogao (1946 nian 5 yue)* (Taiwan Provincial Council first meeting of the first session, report of the Taiwan Province Civil Administration, May 1946) 台湾省参议会第一届第一次大会台湾省 行政长官公署施政报告 (1946年5月). Guanzang minguo Taiwan dang'an huibian 93. Beijing: Jiuzhou chubanshe, 2007.

Taiwan sheng xingzheng zhangguan gongshu minzhengchu weishengju. *Guanyu chengsong Jilong shi Taibei xian deng weisheng yuan fangyi gong-zuo riji deng biaoce daidian* (Daily account of epidemic control measures presented by the sanitation offices in Jilong City and Taibei County) 關於 呈送基隆市台北縣等衛生院防疫工作日記等表冊帶電. Guanzang minguo Taiwan dang'an huibian 192. Beijing: Jiuzhou chubanshe, 2007.

Taiwan shinminpōsha chōsa bu, ed. *Taiwan jinshi kan* (A record of eminent Taiwanese) 臺灣人士鑑. Taipei: Taiwan shinminpōsha chōsa bu, 1934.

Taiwan sōtokufu. *Taiwan lieshen zhuan* (Biographies of Taiwanese gentry) 臺灣列紳傳. Taipei: Taiwan nichinichi shinpōsha, 1915.

———, ed. *Taiwan shehui yundong shi: wenhua yundong* (A history of Taiwan's social movements: The cultural movement) 臺灣社會運動 史: 文化運動. Translated by Wang Shilang. Taiwan zongdufu jingcha yange zhi dierpian zhongjuan. Taibei xian Banqiao shi: Dao xiang, 1988.

Taiwan sōtokufu kanbō bunsho ka, ed. *Taiwan shashin jō* (Taiwan photo album) 臺灣寫真帖. Tokyo: Taiwan sōtokufu kanbō bunsho ka, 1908.

Taiwan sōtokufu kanbō rinji kokusei chōsa bu, ed. *Dai ikkai Taiwan koku-sei chōsa yōran hyō* (Report on the first survey of national conditions in

Taiwan) 第一回臺灣國政調查要覽表. Taipei: Taiwan sōtokufu kanbō rinji kokusei chōsa bu, 1922.

Taiwan sōtokufu kanbō tōkei ka. *Taiwan genjū kokō tōkei* (Taiwan current population statistics) 臺灣現住戶口統計. Taipei: various years, 1905–31.

———. *Taiwan jinkō dōtai tōkei* (Taiwan demographic statistics) 台灣人口動態統計. Various cities: various years.

Taiwan wenxian weiyuanhui, ed. *Chongxiu Taiwan sheng fangzhi, juan 3-1: zhumin zhi zongjiao pian dierce* (Revised Taiwan Province gazetteer, vol. 3-1: Residents' gazette, religion, part 2) 重修臺灣省通志, 卷3-1: 住民志宗教篇第二冊. Nantou: Taiwan wenxian weiyuanhui, 1992.

Taiwan zhengyi chubanshe, ed. *Taiwan Ererba shijian qinli ji* (Personal accounts of the Taiwan 2-28 Incident) 臺灣二二八事件親歷記. Taipei: Taiwan zhengyi chubanshe, 1947.

Takao shi yakusho. *Takao shi sei yōran* (Overview of Takao city conditions) 高雄市勢要覽. Vol. 1. Zhongguo fangzhi congshu Taiwan diqu 292. Taipei: Chengwen chubanshe, 1985.

Takekoshi, Yosaburo. *Japanese Rule in Formosa.* Translated by George Braithwaite. Taipei: SMC Publishing, 1996.

Tanaka, Stefan. *Japan's Orient: Rendering Pasts into History.* Berkeley: University of California Press, 1993.

Tang Yu. "Bei Tai renwu zhuan: fu bei zhuan ziliao" (Biographies of northern Taiwanese: Including monument and biographical materials) 北臺人物傳—附碑傳資料. *Taipei wenxian* 76 (June 1986): 115–94.

———. *Jilong Yan jia fazhan shi* (History of the development of the Jilong Yan family) 基隆顏家發展史. Nantou: Guoshiguan Taiwan wenxianguan, 2003.

———. *Luguo Jilong Yan shi jiasheng* (Annals of the Yan family of Jilong and the state of Lu) 魯國基隆顏氏家乘. Taipei: Jilong Yan shi jiasheng zuan xiu xiaozu, 1997.

———. "Pingjie 'Ererba zhounian zhi'" (Reviewing the anniversary of 2-28) 評介"二二八週年志." *Taiwan shiliao yanjiu* 3 (1994).

Tang Yu and Taiwan kuangyehui zhi xiuzhi weiyuanhui, eds. *Taiwan kuangyehui zhi* (Taiwan Mining Association journal) 臺灣鑛業會志. Taipei: Zhonghua minguo kuangye xiejinhui, 1991.

Taylor, Jay. *The Generalissimo's Son: Chiang Ching-Kuo and the Revolutions in China and Taiwan.* Cambridge, MA: Harvard University Press, 2000.

Taylor, Jeremy E. "History and the Built Environment in Taiwan's Southern Capital." PhD diss., Australian National University, 2002.

Teng, Emma. *Taiwan's Imagined Geography: Chinese Colonial Travel Writing and Pictures, 1683–1895.* Harvard East Asian Monographs 230. Cambridge, MA: Harvard University Press, 2006.

Thal, Sarah. *Rearranging the Landscape of the Gods: The Politics of a Pilgrimage Site in Japan, 1573–1912*. Studies of the Weatherhead East Asian Institute, Columbia University. Chicago: University of Chicago Press, 2005.

Thongchai, Winichakul. *Siam Mapped: A History of the Geo-Body of a Nation*. Honolulu: University of Hawai'i Press, 2009.

Tierney, Robert Thomas. *Tropics of Savagery: The Culture of Japanese Empire in Comparative Frame*. Asia Pacific Modern 5. Berkeley: University of California Press, 2010.

Tipton, Elise K. "The Café: Contested Space of Modernity in Interwar Japan." In *Being Modern in Japan: Culture and Society from the 1910s to the 1930s*, edited by Elise K. Tipton and John Clark, 119–36. Honolulu: University of Hawai'i Press, 2000.

Tipton, Elise K., and John Clark, eds. *Being Modern in Japan: Culture and Society from the 1910s to the 1930s*. Honolulu: University of Hawai'i Press, 2000.

Tokyo denpō tsūshinsha. *Senji taisei shita ni okeru jigyō kyū jinbutsu* (People and enterprises under the wartime system) 戦時体制下に於ける事業及人物. Tokyo: Ōzorasha, 1990.

Tomlinson, John. *Globalization and Culture*. Chicago: University of Chicago Press, 1999.

Tomoseikai. *Gan Unnen ō shoden* (A biographical sketch of venerable Yan Yunnian) 顏雲年翁小傳. Taipei: Taiwan nichinichi shinpōsha, 1924.

Townsend, Susan C. "The Great War and Urban Crisis: Conceptualizing the Industrial Metropolis in Japan and Britain in the 1910s." In *The Decade of the Great War: Japan and the Wider World in the 1910s*, edited by Toshihiro Minohara, Tze-ki Hon, and Evan Dawley, 301–22. Leiden: Brill, 2014.

Ts'ai, Hui-yu Caroline. *Taiwan in Japan's Empire-Building: An Institutional Approach to Colonial Engineering*. Academia Sinica on East Asia. New York: Routledge, 2009.

Tsubamoto Giichi. *Kiirun kō daikan* (An overview of the port of Kiirun) 基隆港大觀. Taipei: Nankoku shuppan kyōkai, 1922.

Tsurumi, E. Patricia. *Japanese Colonial Education in Taiwan, 1895–1945*. Harvard East Asian Monographs 88. Cambridge, MA: Harvard University Press, 1977.

Tucker, Nancy Bernkopf. *Dangerous Strait: The U.S.-Taiwan-China Crisis*. New York: Columbia University Press, 2005.

Tzeng, Shih-jung. *From Hōnto Jin to Bensheng Ren: The Origin and Development of Taiwanese National Consciousness*. Lanham, MD: University Press of America, 2009.

Uchida, Jun. *Brokers of Empire: Japanese Settler Colonialism in Korea, 1876–1945.* Harvard East Asian Monographs 337. Cambridge, MA: Harvard University Asia Center, 2011.

Ujigo Tsuyoshi. *Ishizaka Sōsaku to "Kiirun yagakkō": Nihon tōchi ki Taiwan ni okeru ichi shiritsu gakkō no ayumi* (Ishizaka Sōsaku and the Keelung Night School) 石坂荘作と「基隆夜学校」: 日本統治期台湾における一私立学校の歩み. Yachiyo, JP: Ujigo Tsuyoshi, 2005.

Ujihira Motomu, ed. *Taichū shi shi* (Taichū city history) 台中市史. Vol. 2. Zhongguo fangzhi congshu Taiwan diqu 247. Taipei: Chengwen chubanshe, 1985.

"U.S. and China Honor American WWII Hero in Yunnan Province." *U.S. Embassy & Consulates in China,* Apr. 6, 2015. https://china.usembassy-china.org.cn/u-s-china-honor-american-wwii-hero-yunnan-province/. Accessed Jan. 18, 2018.

Vlastos, Stephen. *Mirror of Modernity: Invented Traditions of Modern Japan.* Twentieth-Century Japan 9. Berkeley: University of California Press, 1998.

Wachman, Alan. "Competing Identities in Taiwan." In *The Other Taiwan: 1945 to the Present,* edited by Murray A. Rubinstein. Taiwan in the Modern World. Armonk, NY: M. E. Sharpe, 1994.

Wakabayashi Masahiro. *Taiwan kangRi yundong shi yanjiu* (Research on the history of Taiwan's anti-Japanese movement) 台灣抗日運動史研究. Translated by Taiwan shi Riwen shiliao dianji yanduhui. Taipei: Bochong zhe, 2007.

Wakeman, Frederic E. "*Hanjian* (Traitor)! Collaboration and Retribution in Wartime Shanghai." In *Becoming Chinese: Passages to Modernity and Beyond,* edited by Wen-hsin Yeh, 298–341. Studies on China 23. Berkeley: University of California Press, 2000.

———. "A Revisionist View of the Nanjing Decade: Confucian Fascism." *China Quarterly,* no. 150 (1997): 395–432.

Wakeman, Frederic E., and Wen-Hsin Yeh, eds. *Shanghai Sojourners.* China Research Monographs 40. Berkeley: Institute of East Asian Studies, University of California, 1992.

Walkowitz, Daniel J. *Working with Class: Social Workers and the Politics of Middle-Class Identity.* Chapel Hill: University of North Carolina Press, 1999.

Wallerstein, Immanuel Maurice. *The Capitalist World-Economy: Essays.* Studies in Modern Capitalism. Cambridge: Cambridge University Press, 1979.

Wang Fu-ch'ang. *Dangdai Taiwan shehui de zuqun xiangxiang* (Ethnic imagination in contemporary Taiwan) 當代臺灣社會的族群想像. Taipei: Qun xue, 2003.

———. "Guangfu hou Taiwan Hanren tonghun de yuanyin yu xingshi chutan" (Causes and patterns of ethnic intermarriage among the Hokkien, Hakka, and mainlanders in postwar Taiwan: A preliminary examination) 光復後台灣漢人族群通婚的原因與形式初探. *Zhongyang yanjiuyuan minzuxue yanjiusuo jikan* 76 (Spring 1993): 43–96.

Wang Guang. *Zhongguo gangkou lun* (On China's ports) 中國港口論. 2nd ed. Taibei xian: Haiyun chubanshe, 1957.

Wang, Gungwu. *The Chinese Overseas: From Earthbound China to the Quest for Autonomy.* Cambridge, MA: Harvard University Press, 2000.

Wang Jianchuan. *Taiwan de zhaijiao yu luantang* (Taiwan's vegetarian teaching and phoenix halls) 臺灣的齋教與鸞堂. Nantian Taiwan yanjiu 3. Taipei: Nantian shuju, 1996.

Wang Jianchuan and Li Shiwei. *Taiwan Mazu miao yuelan* (Reading Taiwan's Mazu temples) 台灣媽祖廟閱覽. Taiwan yuelan shi 8. Taibei xian Luzhou shi: Boyang wenhua, 2000.

Wang Shih-ch'ing. "Huangminhua yundong qian de Taiwan shehui shenghuo gaishan yundong: yi Haishan qu wei li, 1914–1937" (Taiwan society's everyday life reform movement before the Kōminka: The case of Haishan District, 1914–1937) 皇民化運動前的臺灣社會生活改善運動: 以海山區為例 (1914–1937). *Si yu yan* 29, no. 4 (Dec. 1991): 5–63.

———. "Ri ju chuqi Taiwan zhi jiangbihui yu jieyan yundong" (Jiangbihui in the early period of Japan's occupation of Taiwan and the anti-smoking movement) 日據初期臺灣之降筆會與戒煙運動. *Taiwan wenxian* 37, no. 4 (Dec. 1986): 111–51.

Wang, Tay-sheng. *Legal Reform in Taiwan under Japanese Colonial Rule, 1895–1945: The Reception of Western Law.* Asian Law Series 15. Seattle: University of Washington Press, 2000.

Watson, James L. "Standardizing the Gods: The Promotion of T'ien Hou ('Empress of Heaven') along the South China Coast, 960–1960." In *Popular Culture in Late Imperial China,* edited by David G. Johnson, Andrew J. Nathan, and Evelyn Sakakida Rawski, 292–324. Studies on China 4. Berkeley: University of California Press, 1985.

Watt, Lori. "Imperial Remnants: The Repatriates in Postwar Japan." In *Settler Colonialism in the Twentieth Century: Projects, Practices, Legacies,* edited by Carrie Elkins and Susan Pedersen, 243–56. New York: Routledge, 2005.

———. *When Empire Comes Home: Repatriation and Reintegration in Postwar Japan.* Harvard East Asian Monographs 317. Cambridge, MA: Harvard University Asia Center, 2009.

Weber, Eugen. *Peasants into Frenchmen: The Modernization of Rural France, 1870–1914*. Stanford, CA: Stanford University Press, 1976.

Weber, Max. *Economy and Society: An Outline of Interpretive Sociology*. Translated by Guenther Roth and Claus Wittich. Berkeley: University of California Press, 1978.

Weinbaum, Alys Eve, and Modern Girl around the World Research Group. *The Modern Girl around the World: Consumption, Modernity, and Globalization*. Next Wave. Durham, NC: Duke University Press, 2008.

Weller, Robert P. *Unities and Diversities in Chinese Religion*. Seattle: University of Washington Press, 1987.

Wen Guoliang, ed. *Taiwan zongdufu gongwen leizuan zongjiao shiliao lubian (Meiji 34 nian 6 yue zhi Meiji 35 nian 8 yue)* (Collected historical materials on religion from the records of the Taiwan Government-General [June 1902 to Aug. 1903]) 臺灣總督府公文類纂宗教史料彙編(明治三十四年六月至明治三十五年八月). Zongdufu dang'an zhuanti fanyi 5, zongjiao xilie 2. Nantou: Taiwan sheng wenxian weiyuanhui, 2000.

Wen Zhenhua. "Ri ju shidai Gaoxiong diqu renkou de liudong" (Population flows in the Gaoxiong area during the era of Japanese occupation) 日據時代高雄地區人口的流動. In *Gaoxiong lishi yu wenhua lunji*, edited by Huang Chün-chieh, vol. 1. Gaoxiong: Chen Zhonghe weng cishan jijinhui, 1994.

Weng Jiayin. *Gucheng, xindu, shenxianfu: Tainan fu cheng lishi tezhan* (The story began here: Entrancing Tainan, old and new) 古城‧新都‧神仙府: 臺南府城歷史特展. Tainan: Guoli Taiwan lishi bowuguan, 2011.

Wicentowski, Joseph Charles. "Policing Health in Modern Taiwan, 1895–1949." PhD diss., Harvard University, 2008.

Wills, John E., Jr. "Maritime Asia, 1500–1800: The Interactive Emergence of European Domination." *American Historical Review* 98, no. 1 (1993): 83–115.

Wolf, Arthur P. *Religion and Ritual in Chinese Society*. Studies in Chinese Society. Stanford, CA: Stanford University Press, 1974.

Wolf, Margery. *Women and the Family in Rural Taiwan*. Stanford, CA: Stanford University Press, 1972.

Wong, Joseph. *Healthy Democracies: Welfare Politics in Taiwan and South Korea*. Ithaca, NY: Cornell University Press, 2004.

Wu Huifang. "Diyuan chongtu de xueyuan huajie? Jilong Zhongyuan ji yu xingshi lunzhi zhupu zhi" (Local conflict and the dissolution of bloodline? The system of *zhupu* rotation by surname in Jilong's Ghost Festival) 地緣衝突的血緣化解?基隆中元祭與姓氏輪值主普制. *Guoli zhengzhi daxue lishi xuebao* 31 (May 2009): 51–95.

———. "Jilong Zhongyuan ji li de zhuputan" (The zhuputan in Jilong's Ghost Festival) 基隆中元祭裡的主普壇. *Donghua renwen xuebao* 15 (July 2009): 221–62.

————. *Jilong Zhongyuan ji: shishi, jiyi, yu chuanshuo* (Midsummer Ghost Festival in Keelung: Historical fact, memory and legend) 基隆中元祭: 史實、記憶與傳說. Taipei: Taiwan xuesheng shuju, 2013.

————. "Xu Zisang yu Ri zhi shiqi de Jilong Zhongyuan ji" (Xu Zisang and Jilong's Ghost Festival during the Japanese era) 許梓桑與日治時期的基隆中元祭. *Guoli zhengzhi daxue lishi xuebao* 37 (May 2012): 147–96.

Wu, Rwei-ren. "The Formosan Ideology: Oriental Colonialism and the Rise of Taiwanese Nationalism, 1895–1945." PhD diss., University of Chicago, 2003.

————. "Monument of the Vanishing? The Elegiac Metamorphosis of Taiwanese Nationalism in the Late Colonial Period (1937–1945)." Paper presented at the Association of Asian Studies conference, Mar. 22, 2013, San Diego.

————. "Redeeming the Pariah, Redeeming the Past: Some Taiwanese Reflections on the Murayama Statement." In *Japan and Reconciliation in Post-War Asia: The Murayama Statement and Its Implications*, edited by Kazuhiko Togo, 68–90. New York: Palgrave Macmillan, 2013.

————. "Zhong ceng tuzhuhua xia de lishi yishi: Ri zhi houqi Huang Deshi yu Shimada Kinji de wenxueshi lunshu zhi chubu bijiao fenxi" (Historical consciousnesses of multilayered indigenization: A preliminary comparative analysis of the literary history discourses of Huang Te-Shih and Shimada Kinji) 重層土著化下的歷史意識: 日治後期黃得時與島田謹二的文學史論述之初步比較分析. *Taiwan shi yanjiu* 16, no. 3 (Sept. 2009): 133–63.

Wu Wen-hsing. "Ri ju shiqi Gaoxiong diqu shehui lingdao jieceng zhi fensi" (An analysis of Gaoxiong's social elites during the era of Japanese occupation) 日據時期高雄地區社會領導階層之分析. In *Gaoxiong lishi yu wenhua lunji*, edited by Huang Chün-chieh, vol. 1. Gaoxiong: Chen Zhonghe weng cishan jijinhui, 1994.

————. "Ri ju shiqi Taiwan de fangzu duanfa yundong" (Anti-footbinding and queue-cutting movements in Taiwan during the era of Japanese occupation) 日據時期臺灣的放足短髮運動. In *Taiwan shehui yu wenhua bianqian*, edited by Qu Haiyuan and Zhang Yinghua. Taipei: Zhongyang yanjiuyuan minzu yanjiusuo, 1986.

————. *Ri zhi shiqi Taiwan de shehui lingdao jieceng* (Taiwan's social elites during the period of Japanese rule) 日治時期臺灣的社會領導階層. Taipei: Wu nan, 2008.

Xia, Yun. "Engendering Contempt for Collaborators: Anti-Hanjian Discourse Following the Sino-Japanese War of 1937–1945." *Journal of Women's History* 25, no. 1 (Spring 2013): 111–34.

Xu Xueji. "'Taiwan guangfu zhijingtuan' de renwu ji qi' yingxiang" (Mission and influence of "Taiwan Retrocession Tribute Group") "臺灣光復致敬團"的任務及其影響. *Taiwan shi yanjiu* 18, no. 2 (June 2011): 97–145.

Xu Ziwei and Pan Gongzhao. *Jinri de Taiwan* (Taiwan Today) 今日的台灣. Shanghai: Zhongguo kexue tushu yiqi gongsi, 1945.

Yan Chuangyin, ed. *(Kiirun keitetsu kabushiki kaisha) Sōgyō nijūnen shi* (Twenty-year history of the establishment of the Kiirun Light Rail Corporation) (基隆輕鉄株式会社)創業二十年史. Jilong: Kiirun keitetsu kabushiki kaisha, 1933.

Yang Fang. *Luodi shenggen: juancun renwu yu jingyan* (Putting down roots: The people and experiences of the dependents' villages) 落地生根: 眷村人物與經驗. Taipei: Yun chen wenhua, 1996.

Yang Lianfu and Chen Qian, eds. *Minjian sizang minguo shiqi ji zhanhou Taiwan ziliao lubian, chanye pian yi di shiqi ce* (Collection of privately held postwar republican period Taiwan materials, issue 1, vol. 17) 民間私藏民國時期暨戰後臺灣資料彙編. 產業篇一 第十七冊. Boyang jingdian daxi 17. Xinbei shi: Boyang wenhua chuban, 2012.

Yeh, Wen-hsin, ed. *Becoming Chinese: Passages to Modernity and Beyond.* Studies on China 23. Berkeley: University of California Press, 2000.

———. *Shanghai Splendor: Economic Sentiments and the Making of Modern China, 1843–1949.* Berkeley: University of California Press, 2007.

Yip, June Chun. *Envisioning Taiwan: Fiction, Cinema, and the Nation in the Cultural Imaginary.* Asia-Pacific: Culture, Politics, and Society. Durham, NC: Duke University Press, 2004.

Young, Louise. *Beyond the Metropolis: Second Cities and Modern Life in Interwar Japan.* Studies of the Weatherhead East Asian Institute, Columbia University. Berkeley: University of California Press, 2013.

———. *Japan's Total Empire: Manchuria and the Culture of Wartime Imperialism.* Twentieth-Century Japan 8. Berkeley: University of California Press, 1999.

Yu, Yonghe. *Small Sea Travel Diaries: Yu Yonghe's Records of Taiwan.* Translated by Macabe Keliher. Taipei: SMC Publishing, 2004.

Zanasi, Margherita. "Fostering the People's Livelihood: Chinese Political and Economic Thought between Empire and Nation." *Twentieth-Century China* 23, no. 1 (Nov. 2004): 6–38.

———. "Globalizing Hanjian: The Suzhou Trials and the Post–World War II Discourse on Collaboration." *American Historical Review* 113, no. 3 (June 2008): 731–51.

Zarrow, Peter Gue. *China in War and Revolution, 1895–1949*. Asia's Transformations. London: Routledge, 2005.

———. "The Reform Movement, the Monarchy, and Political Modernity."
In *Rethinking the 1898 Reform Period: Political and Cultural Change in
Late Qing China*, edited by Rebecca Karl and Peter Gue Zarrow, 17–47.
Cambridge, MA: Harvard University Asia Center, 2002.

Zeng Jianmin. *1945 poxiao shike de Taiwan: bayue shiwuri hou jidong de
yibaitian* (1945, Daybreak in Taiwan: The exciting hundred days after
August 15) 1945破曉時刻的台灣: 八月十五日後激動的一百天. Taipei:
Lianjing, 2005.

Zhang Maogui, ed. *Zuqun guanxi yu guojia rentong* (Ethnic relations and
national identity) 族羣關係與國家認同. Zhiku congshu 38. Taipei:
Yeqiang, 1993.

Zhang Shengtu and Li Tianchun, eds. *Lingquan si tong jie lu* (Collected
monastic records of the Lingquan Temple) 靈泉寺同戒錄. Jilong: Yuemei
Lingquan si, 1955.

Zhang Yanxian. "Ererba minzhong shiguan de jianli: Jilong Ererba shijian
de beiqing" (The establishment of the people's historical view of 2-28:
The sadness of Jilong's 2-28) 二二八民眾史觀的建立: 基隆二二八事件的
悲情. *Taiwan shiliao yanjiu* 3 (1994): 9–14.

———, ed. *Jilong yugang Ererba* (2-28 in Jilong, the rainy harbor) 基隆雨港
二二八. Taiwan bentu xilie 2:49. Taipei: Zili wanbaoshe, 1994.

Zhao, Gang. "Reinventing China: Imperial Qing Ideology and the Rise
of Modern Chinese National Identity in the Early Twentieth Century."
Modern China 32, no. 1 (Jan. 2006): 3–30.

Zhao, Suisheng. *A Nation-State by Construction: Dynamics of Modern
Chinese Nationalism*. Stanford, CA: Stanford University Press, 2004.

Zhao Xingyuan and Wang Shih-ch'ing. *Gaoxiong shi zhi* (Gaoxiong city
gazetteer) 高雄市志. Vol. 4. Zhongguo fangzhi congshu 79. Taipei:
Chengwen chubanshe, 1983.

Zhao Youzhi. *Ri ju shiqi Taiwan shanggonghui de fazhan (1895–1937)* (The
development of chambers of commerce during the Japanese occupation
[1895–1937]) 日據時期臺灣商工會的發展 (1895–1937). 1895 xilie. Taibei
xian Banqiao shi: Dao xiang chubanshe, 1998.

Zhou Zhongxuan and Chen Menglin. *Zhuluo xian zhi* (Zhuluo County
gazetteer) 諸羅縣志. Jiayi shi: Jiayi xian zhengfu, 1993.

Zhu Zhongxi and Chen Zhengxiang. *Jilong shi zhi* (Jilong city gazetteer)
基隆市志. Vol. 7. Zhongguo fangzhi congshu Taiwan diqu 67. Taipei:
Chengwen chubanshe, 1983.

———. *Taiwan sheng Jilong shi zhi* (Taiwan Province Jilong city gazetteer) 臺灣省基隆市志. Vol. 12. Zhongguo fangzhi congshu Taiwan diqu 67. Taipei: Chengwen chubanshe, 1983.

Zhuang Guozhi, Chen Zhengliang, and Zhou Zhencai, eds. *Yi jiazi de chen qian zhengyan: Ererba shijian Jilong diqu koushu lishi* (Sixty years of deep critical testimony: Jilong's oral histories of the 2-28 Incident) 一甲子的沈謐證言: 二二八事件基隆地區口述歷史. Jilong: Jilong shi Ererba guanhuai xiehui, 2005.

Index

Italic page numbers refer to figures, tables, or maps.

HARVARD EAST ASIAN MONOGRAPHS
(most recent titles)